PENGUIN BOOKS

SEXY ORIGINS AND INTIMATE THINGS

CHARLES PANATI, a former physicist and for six years a science editor for *Newsweek,* is the author of many non-fiction and fiction books, including three previous works about "origins": *Sacred Origins of Profound Things* (1996), *Extraordinary Origins of Everyday Things* (1987), and *The Browser's Book of Beginnings* (1984). He has made a career out of exploring the origins of things. Researching his own family, he learned that he is not a "Panati" by blood, but through his father's adoption. His obsession with getting to the roots of things gave him a second family: the Hudsons of Kilbaha, County Kerry, Ireland.

Sexy Origins AND Intimate Things

The Rites and Rituals of Straights, Gays, Bi's, Drags, Trans, Virgins, and Others

CHARLES PANATI

Penguin Books

PENGUIN BOOKS

Published by the Penguin Group
Penguin Putnam Inc., 375 Hudson Street,
New York, New York 10014, U.S.A.
Penguin Books Ltd, 27 Wrights Lane,
London W8 5TZ, England
Penguin Books Australia Ltd, Ringwood,
Victoria, Australia
Penguin Books Canada Ltd, 10 Alcorn Avenue,
Toronto, Ontario, Canada M4V 3B2
Penguin Books (N.Z.) Ltd, 182–190 Wairau Road,
Auckland 10, New Zealand

Penguin Books Ltd, Registered Offices:
Harmondsworth, Middlesex, England

First published in Penguin Books 1998

5 7 9 10 8 6

LIBRARY OF CONGRESS CATALOGING IN PUBLICATION DATA
Panati, Charles, 1943–
Sexy origins and intimate things: the rites and
rituals of straights, gays, bi's, drags, trans, virgins,
and others / Charles Panati.
p. cm.
Includes index.
ISBN 0 14 02.7144 9 (pbk.)
1. Sex—Miscellanea. 2. Sex—Terminology. 3. Sex customs.
I. Title.
HQ25.P35 1998
306.7—dc21 97-30701

Printed in the United States of America
Set in Adobe Garamond
Book design by Deborah Kerner

TO MY
FAVORITE PUSSIES,
Boogie,
Jeep,
and Troll

Contents

CONTENTS

CONTENTS

Too Much of a Good Thing Is Wonderful

INTRODUCTION

Sex in France is a comedy, in England a tragedy,
in America a melodrama, in Germany a philosophy,
in Italy an opera.

ANONYMOUS

Sex has been called many things, some nasty, some nice, few neutral: "Nature's cruel trick to perpetuate the species," "Poor man's polo," "The formula by which one and one makes three."

My own favorite: "Sex is something children never discuss in the presence of elders."

What people say about sex says a lot about them and their sex lives. **Bette Davis,** who experienced career and marriage conflicts, claimed, "The act of sex, as gratifying as it may be, is God's joke on humanity."

Her contemporary **Mae West,** supposedly all talk and little action, nonetheless made memorable talk: "Sex is emotion in motion." "Oooh, to err is human—but it feels divine."

West's colleague **W. C. Fields** observed, "Some things are better than sex, and some are worse, but there's nothing exactly like it."

Comedian **Groucho Marx** said, "Whoever called it necking was a poor judge of anatomy."

Mexican poet **Octavio Paz** used soaring penile imagery to define sex as "the spindle on which the earth turns."

Poet **James Dickey** summed up many people's sentiment that sex is always, somehow, illicit and dirty: "The true feeling of sex is that of a deep intimacy, but above all of a deep complicity."

A famous philosopher agreed: "Sex touches the heavens only when it simultaneously touches the gutter and the mud." He was talking about *great* sex.

Woody Allen, in *Everything You Always Wanted to Know About Sex But Were Afraid to Ask,* arrived at the same conclusion: "Sex is dirty only when it's done right." Allen found one benefit in bisexuality: "It immediately doubles your chances of a date on Saturday night."

Singer **Willie Nelson** complained—or boasted: "If I don't do it every day, I get a headache."

President **John F. Kennedy** is said to have uttered the same line—and had few headaches.

Elizabeth Taylor was asked after one of her many divorces if she'd ever remarry: "Never. Never! I think sex is dead anyway." That was before she met Richard Burton, who is considered to have been one of the best-hung men in recent history. Along with Onassis.

Film actress **Candice Bergen,** years before she became TV's Murphy Brown, admitted, "I may not be a great actress but I've become the greatest at screen orgasms. Ten seconds of heavy breathing, roll your head from side to side, simulate a slight asthma attack, and die a little."

For actor **John Barrymore,** sex was "the thing that takes the least amount of time and causes the most amount of trouble."

Saints and popes have spoken out on sex—for and against. "Lord, give me chastity and continency, but not yet!" **Augustine** begged of God, years before he gave up sex for sanctity.

"Virginity is natural," said celibate monk and scholar **Saint Jerome.** To battle sexual temptation, he fled to the desert but to no avail: "My face was pale and my frame chilled from fasting, yet my mind was burning with the cravings of desire, and the fires of lust flamed up from my flesh." He never considered that maybe it was *sex* that was natural.

Protestant reformer **Martin Luther** was not all that fond of the sex act itself. Of sexual reproduction he said, "Had God consulted me in the matter, I should have advised him to continue the generation of the species by fashioning them of clay."

Some people are glad when the sex urge fades with age. Greek playwright **Sophocles** was asked, "How is your sex life? Are you still able to satisfy a woman?" He replied, "Gladly I am rid of it, as though I had escaped from the clutches of a mad and savage master."

Lord Chesterfield found sex embarrassing and its practice and preoccupation, particularly among men, a waste of time. "The pleasure is momentary, the position ridiculous, and the expense damnable."

Shakespeare, on the other hand, lamented, "Is it not strange that desire should so many years outlive performance?" In a sonnet, the playwright summed up sex as "The expense of spirit in a waste of shame / Is lust in action."

Sex, of course, need have nothing to do with love. Masturbation was defended by **Woody Allen:** "Don't knock masturbation. It's sex with someone I love."

"You mustn't force sex to do the work of love, or love to do the work of sex," advised **Mary McCarthy.**

In the nineteenth century, sex was not discussed in polite society. Women weren't supposed to move their bodies during intercourse, as a Victorian etiquette manual makes clear: "Ladies, don't move."

In the 1930s, **Pope Pius XI** advised wives whose husbands used condoms to forcibly resist "as a virgin would a rapist." If the overheated husband began the act, she was not to move, as a show of disapproval, but was to endure the travail as "stiff as a corpse."

Times have changed. Wives are now allowed to move around a lot. Even get on top. Even bed down another woman. Humorist **Fran Lebowitz,** writing of the difference between a lady and a tramp, advises men, "If you happen upon a girl who doesn't put out, do not jump to the conclusion that you have found a lady. What you have probably found is a lesbian."

Liberace, who until the end denied he was gay, claimed he was asexual. Any suggestion otherwise was "an outrageous attempt to assassinate my character."

Openly gay pop singer **Boy George** claimed early in his career that he was "not really all that keen on sex" and didn't clarify which sex he preferred.

Our attitudes toward sex changed dramatically in the liberating 1960s. During that time former fifties TV personality **Bishop Fulton J. Sheen** lamented: "Sex has become one of the most discussed subjects of modern times. The Victorians pretended it did not exist; the moderns pretend that nothing else exists."

For some people sex is a religion. "The orgasm has replaced the Cross as the focus of longing and the image of fulfillment," wrote author **Malcolm Muggeridge.**

Sex and religion have always gone hand in hand, usually in a fierce arm-wrestle. They make great conversational bookends. My last book, *Sacred Origins of Profound Things*, was all about religion's rites and rituals. It seemed fitting to follow it up with what I hope is a *sexy* sequel. What are the origins of sex's own rites and rituals?

For instance:

• When did humans start engaging in face-to-face intercourse? (Most animals, and all other primates, do it from the rear.)

• When did the human female begin to desire sex year-round? (Other mammals have periods of "heat.")

• What culture recorded in art and prose the first "blow job," and how did that inaccurate term originate? The first act of cunnilingus? Of coitus interruptus? The use of condoms?

• When did stiletto heels, bras, lingerie and lace, whips and chains become hot items?

• Who was the first prostitute—and did she make a living at it?

• Who was her first client—and did he get VD?

• How have various cultures regarded monogamy, polygamy, the missionary position, the woman on top, oral sex, anal sex?

• Do female animals enjoy orgasm?

• Why lavender for gay men?

• What animals, including man, have the biggest penis in proportion to body size?

• Who were the best-hung men in history—and how can we know for sure?

• How many different kinds of penises are there? (Hint: The Webbed, the Calcium Bone, the Doubleheader, the Mushroom, the Hooked, the Perpetual, the Reattached.)

• Do females—human and animal—prefer males with bigger appendages? Which shapes do they prefer?

• When did humans abandon cult worship of the male member? (Or did we?)

• At what age does a man's penis stop growing?

• Which three popes were gay?

- Why is gonorrhea called "the clap" when it's nothing to applaud?
- Who used the first dildo? Who gave it to her—or him? Was it of stone or wood?
- Why were virgin brides considered "more pure" for marriage after they were deflowered by a stranger? How could a male achieve the enviable career of "stranger?"
- Was there pornography—and centerfolds—before *Playboy?*
- What happens if a male fetus inherits an extra X, or female, chromosome? If a female fetus gets a Y, or male, chromosome?
- What were the ancient to modern "cures" for homosexuality—and why did they never work?
- Who had the first vasectomy?
- What really happens when homophobic males watch gay porn videos?
- Why did it take centuries for people to realize that sperm alone could not make a baby? Before the discovery of the egg, what was a mother's contribution thought to be?
- Oedipus complex, castration anxiety, penis envy, sublimation—was Freud right or wrong, or just sex-obsessed? Did he have the hots for Jung?
- Did sex researchers Masters and Johnson, who became husband and wife and then divorced, get bored watching 7,500 climaxes by women and 2,500 ejaculations by men?
- How did "drag" come to mean cross-dressing?
- What is history's first love poem?
- How did a wife sign history's first love letter?
- How did Kinsey alter forever what we once considered sexually "normal" and "abnormal"?
- Why is "heterosexuality" a relatively new category of sexual orientation?
- Why were "heterosexuals" once thought to be more degenerate that "homosexuals"?
- Is a lesbian's orgasm really more intense? (Hint: A lesbian "quickie" takes hours.)
- Where do terms come from: *cunt, cock, dick, cherry, cum, blue balls, fuck, merkin, size queen, dildo, clit, hairpie, honeypot?*
- Who had the first sex change in history? Was he/she happy with the results?
- How is foreskin related to the word "perfume"?
- What constituted "indecent exposure" among Greek men who worked out in the nude?

- Why do men have nipples? Will they one day breast-feed?
- How do porcupines do it? (Carefully, you can bet.)

Dates for word origins and phrases are from the *Oxford English Dictionary* and/or *Merriam-Webster's Collegiate Dictionary*.

CHARLES PANATI
FIRE ISLAND,
NEW YORK

Sexy Origins

and

Intimate Things

CHAPTER 1

Is That a Gun in Your Pocket?

"COCK" TO "WANG"

If the world were a logical place,
men would ride side-saddle.

RITA MAE BROWN

"COCK"; GEOFFREY CHAUCER, ENGLAND, 1386 ◆

No woman likes to be called "a cunt," to be labeled by a coarse slang term for her sex organ. But few men would object to being called "a cock"—if anything, it's a compliment. A man may be a "proud cock." He may be "cocksure" of himself and strut with a "cocky" gait, perhaps while walking his "cocker" spaniel. He may regale you with "cock-and-bull" stories and, after downing several "cocktails," appear "cock-eyed." Depending on his sexual orientation, he might even be a "cocksucker" or a "cocktease." How did all of these "cockamamy" expressions arise?

The origin of the word "cock" is evident in the echoic explosive "cock-a-doodle-doo," the sunrise declaration of a rooster. "Cock" is from both the Old English and Old French *coc*, where it originated as the echoic name for a male chicken. Most languages use an echoic for a rooster and his call.

"Allcocks"—What's in a Name?

Many centuries ago, when villages were small and people were known only by their first names, a farmer who breed roosters, for mating purposes or for cockfights, might be called "Joe All Cocks." In time, this became "Joe Allcocks," then "Joe Alcox." Calling people by their professions is one way in which surnames originated.

To give two another examples: "Michael-at-the-well," who fetched water for the village, became Michael Atwater. Breadmaker "Thomas the Baker" developed into Thomas Baker.

The father of novelist Louisa May Alcott, author of *Little Women*, changed the family name from Alcox. Would *Little Women*, a young girl's tale, have become a children's classic if its author's name appeared across the jacket as Allcox, or Allcocks?

Shakespeare's "Cock"

No one knows when "cock," the rooster's name, was first applied to a man, let alone to his private member. According to the *Oxford English Dictionary*, the earliest written example of a man being referred to as a "cock" comes from a description by the poet Geoffrey Chaucer (1340–1400) of a village worker who aroused other workers at daybreak by knocking on their doors. He served the function of a rooster. Soon the term was being applied to any leader of a group of men; he might be called "cock of gamekeepers," or, if he patrolled the streets to protect a town, "cock of the walk." Thus by the close of the 1500s a man could flatteringly be called a "cock."

In 1618, in Nathaniel Field's comedy *Amends for Ladies*, the term was first used unambiguously for a penis—an erect one at that: "Oh man what art thou? When thy cock is up?" The allusion here—"cock is up"—also suggests a rooster's *arousing* morning call, which got people's attention and got them *up*.

Shakespeare made many puns on the word "cock," as in *The Taming of the Shrew*:

KATHERINA: *What is your crest? A coxcomb?*
PETRUCHIO: *A combless cock, so Kate will be my hen.*
KATHERINA: *No cock of mine. You crow too like a craven* [a cock that will not fight].

Shakespeare liked to pun on "cock." Stained-glass window (right) of woman wearing a phallic bonnet, from the church of Saint-Aisne, fourteenth century.

In the 1590s, "cock" also referred to a jester's cap adorned with a strip of red cloth. This is a straightforward reference to a rooster's red comb—a "cock's comb" or "coxcomb" (first used in 1573)—a crown of erectile tissue normally flaccid but engorged with blood and proudly erect when the rooster is ready for sex. All display, for the female's sake. By Shakespeare's day, "cock" also meant a fool, or a vain, conceited man.

WHY YOU "COCK" A GUN ◆

"*Cock*" has entered the language in various forms. Before the introduction of automatic weapons, a man used to "cock a gun"—an allusion to the metal firing mechanism, which was shaped like a rooster. How fitting that a metal rooster should perch upon something as long, cylindrical, hard, and phallic as the barrel of a shotgun, which when fired shoots off "bullets."

A man squinting down a gun's barrel, ready to fire at a target, metal rooster in his peripheral view, was said to be *cock-eyed*.

Cock-and-Bull Story

A cock-and-bull story is an improbable tale that your listener doesn't believe for a minute. The phrase alludes to the animal fables of French poet Jean de La Fontaine (1621–1695), in which roosters and male oxen engage in arch banter and outlandish adventures. *Merriam-Webster's Collegiate Dictionary* traces the phrase to 1795.

The expression to "cock a gun" arose because a gun's firing mechanism was once shaped like a rooster.

Cocker Spaniel

A cocker spaniel is any of a breed of small spaniels with a compact body, short legs, long, silky hair, and drooping eyes. The dogs were originally used to hunt woodcocks, European migratory game birds that lived in wooded areas and whose call resembles a rooster's. *Merriam-Webster* traces the common usage to 1840.

Cocksucker

A cocksucker is, literally speaking, one who sucks a cock, either a fellatrix (female) or fellator (male). Figuratively speaking, it is a low, contemptible person. The word is undoubtedly more recent in origin than the sex practice it represents. It first appeared in a dictionary, *Slang and Its Analogues*, by John S. Farmer and William E. Henley, in 1890. Interestingly, the authors define "cocksucker" only with the entry *a fellatrix*—the feminine form. It was standard practice in those days not to define a word so common that everyone knew its meanings.

Cocktail

The origin of one of the most common cock-based words remains something of a mystery. The drink, originally a mixture of liquor, fruit juice, and ice, was popular in New Orleans in the late eighteenth century.

It is not true, as is often stated, that the word is a combination of "cock" (penis) + "tail" (a "piece of ass"), suggesting that when a man and woman drink to excess his penis ends up in her tail. Colorful but false origin stories are hard to dispel.

One theory—among dozens—holds that the word derived from the British *cock's ale*, a potent, sweet, alcoholic drink fed to roosters before a cockfight to bolster their bravery and make for bloody combat. Drunken roosters can apparently behave as badly as drunken men.

A more serious contender is the French word *coquetier*, "eggcup." In the French-speaking section of New Orleans, the liquor and fruit juice drink was originally served in small, deep eggcups. *Merriam-Webster* traces the origin of "cocktail" to 1806.

PENILE TERMS OF ENDEARMENT ◆

An old joke goes: Why do men name their penises? So they can be on a first-name basis with the person who makes most of their decisions.

The origins of many popular names for the male member are self-evident, based straightforwardly on either form or function: *lollipop, creamstick, flute, pipe organ, pile driver, pump, sausage, banana, tool, dipstick, poker, ramrod.*

Since intercourse can be a frenzied and fierce invasion of, or assault upon, another's body, it is not surprising that many nicknames are graphically violent: *pistol, cannon, weapon, battering ram, bayonet, sword, lance, warrior, trigger, cutlass, semiautomatic.* Sex and violence have often been linked in one way or another.

Other common names have less obvious origins—and interesting stories behind them.

Dick

"Dick Nixon before he dicks you." That slogan from the Vietnam War era reflects how the word "dick" has come to stand for "penis."

In the seventeenth century, the most ruthless British executioner at London's Tyburn Prison was named Derrick (or Derick). Since a criminal quickly asphyxiated by hanging can spontaneously get an erection and even ejaculate (moderate strangulation is an aphrodisiac), Derrick's name was applied to the erect penis that spectators keenly watched for. If the onlookers were lucky, the condemned man died with a "derrick," which in time became "dick." This is the most popular explanation for the word.

"Derrick" also means a hoisting apparatus employing a tackle rigged at the end of a beam. The image of a criminal hanged by Derrick, dangling from the end of a beam, is thought to be the origin for the name of the construction equipment. Hangman Derrick was such a celebrity in his day, when entertainment for ordinary folk often consisted of watching public executions, that all hangman for a time were professionally called "derricks."

Dork

Dictionaries of slang are divided on the origin of this word, a favorite with kids, who freely apply it to one another. The most likely explanation is that "dork" derived from the name of the town of Dorking in Surrey, England. The town was famous for a breed of domestic fowl called dorkings, which have large, heavy bodies, short, featherless legs, five-toed feet, and plumage of varied hues, and crow like a rooster. Dorklings go cock-a-doodle-doo. Thus, both "cock" and "dork" come from a male chicken.

Pecker

The pecking action of a sharp-billed woodpecker gave the bird its name—it pecks at trees. The pecking motion of copulation accounts for calling the penis a "pecker," though only the disinterested lie there like a piece of wood.

Peter

The proper name Peter derives from the Greek *petros*, meaning "stone" or "rock," and is how the Apostle Simon was christened by Christ as Saint Peter: "Thou are Peter, and upon this rock I will build my church" (Matt. 16:18). Most linguists feel that it is the rock-hard nature of an erection that led to the christening of the penis with the name "peter."

Not all erections, of course, are "peters," or rocks. The adolescent penis is more efficient at retaining blood and thus can remain rock-hard for quite some time. With age, though, this efficiency declines, and a proud rock can inevitably become a limp sponge.

As a man ages, his erection gradually softens, while its angle with respect to the abdomen goes from nearly straight up at age fifteen to ninety degrees (or horizontal) by age fifty. The drooping continues as long as he can get it up, so to speak; and at some point, usually after age seventy, it becomes a linguistic misnomer to call a penis a "peter" at all.

Calling a man a "prick" derives from the fact that the penis "punctures" the vagina.

The name Paul means "small," so, in a way, a man's erection over time goes from peter to paul. The old adage, "The angle of the dangle is proportional to the heat of the meat," would also be accurate if the word "heat" were replaced with "age."

Prick

The verb "prick" is from the Middle English noun *prike*, meaning a "small hole" or "dot" made by a sharp object. The idea that the penis (a pointed object) "punctures" the vagina (a hole)—and perhaps "pierces" the hymen—accounts for this slang reference.

An old joke goes: What's the difference between a penis and a prick? A penis is what a man uses to make babies. A prick is the rest of him.

Putz

In German, *Putz* is "plasterwork" and as a verb refers to plastering a ceiling. It is possible that plaster dildos, once used in rituals to deflower virgins, account for the penis being called a "putz." Defloration is discussed in another part of this book, but suffice it to say here that the superstitious fear of blood often lead to virgin brides being deflowered by dildos of wood, rock, marble, or plaster. With the hymen broken and blood spilled, a husband could then sexually, and "safely," claim his bride.

Yiddish-speaking Jews in Germany borrowed the word *Putz* and used it to mean both "penis" and "a foolish male." In *The Joys of Yiddish* (1968), Leo Rosten explains: "*Putz* is not to be used lightly, or when women or children are around. It is more offensive than *schmuck*, the latter may be used in a teasing and affectionate way, vulgar thought it is, but *putz* has a pejorative ambience."

It is amazing how many slang words mean both "penis" and "fool": putz, dork, prick, dick, weenie. Perhaps it's because a horny man thinks with his penis rather than his brain—the basis for many jokes:

Why don't women have penises? Women think with their brains.

What do you call a man who's just lost 90 percent of his brain? Newly divorced.

What is a man? A life-support system for a penis.

What do you call that useless flap of skin at the end of a penis? A man.

What did God say after creating man with a penis? "I can do better."

Shaft

The word is from the Latin *scapus*, meaning a "long, sharp stalk" used for piercing. Thus, to "give someone the shaft" is to skewer them—figuratively or literally.

Schlong

A flaccid penis slowly stretching into an erection looks something like a snake in motion. In fact, the biblical snake in the Garden at Eden is thought by many scholars to be an obvious metaphor for Adam's penis, which tempted Eve. And she took the bait. The German for "snake" is *Schlange*; the Yiddish is *schlong*.

The Yiddish language originated around the eleventh century with Jews from northern France who, driven into exile by the Crusades, moved throughout regions that are today Germany. They greatly modified their native Hebrew tongue by taking in countless local words. Consequently, Yiddish, regarded as a true Germanic language, contains the word "schlong," an altered version of the German *Schlange*.

Wang

Two explanations are given for this word, each dependent on its own spelling. "Wang" is thought to be a contraction of the verb "wangle," meaning "to wiggle." An expanding penis wiggles.

Linguists who spell it "whang" feel it comes from the echoic verb of that spelling, which means "to strike with a resounding blow" or to make a "whanning" ring. This explanation would have the penis being a weapon of violence that during intercourse delivers whacks or blows.

Weenie

The English verb "ween," from the Middle English *wenen*, originally meant "to desire." Through its Indo-European root, *wen*, it is related to the Latin *venus*, "love." Thus, a weenie has its own desires and seeks love from its ideal Venus. Some linguists say the penis was once called a "ween."

But "weeny" as an adjective means tiny [wee + (ti)ny], as the shrunken, retracted penis can be, especially when cold.

Furthermore, "weenie" is also the name of a frankfurter, from the German *Wienerwurst*, a small Viennese sausage. Which of these three derivations applies? Is "weenie" an expression of "desire"? A description of something small and shriveled? A reference to a tubular piece of meat?

Men do not like the diminutive sound of "weenie" or, worse, "wee-wee." As the joke goes: A husband, on his wedding night, pulls down his pants and proudly asks his new bride, "What do you think of *that?*"

"It's a wee-wee," she says.

He smiles and patiently explains, "No, honey, that's a *cock.*"

"No, honey," she answers, "I've seen lots of cocks and that's a wee-wee."

Wonk

The term is used in Australia as a pejorative for a male homosexual, the down-under equivalent of "fag." In America, "wonk" became associated with "penis" early in this century. It was first used in the 1950s to mean "nerd" —an unstylish, unattractive, socially inept person, slavishly driven by intellectual pursuits, especially, later on, in the field of computers.

The word "nerd" itself was coined by author Dr. Seuss (Theodor Geisel), for a creature in his children's book *If I Ran the Zoo* (1950).

Yoko Ono referred to John Lennon's penis as a "wonk," and once noted: "I wonder how men can get serious at all. They have this delicate long thing hanging outside their bodies which goes up and down by its own will. Humor is probably something the male of the species discovered through his own anatomy."

Penis means "tail." One of its many aggressive names is "ram."

PENIS, LATIN FOR "TAIL"—IT STOPS GROWING AT AGE SEVENTEEN ◆

*P*enis, the anatomically correct name for the male member, comes directly from the Latin *penis*, meaning "tail."

A recent poll of young American males found that more than half erroneously believe that their "boners," or erections, are caused by muscles tightening in the penis; an erection for them is a flexed muscle. Four percent think that a boner contains bone—a soft calcium bone that inflates and deflates. All report masturbating regularly—some three times a day—but only 28 percent seemed to know what they were holding in their hands.

While all men—and most women—know what a penis looks like, a surprising number of them are mystified by what's under the skin:

• Ancient Greek and Roman physicians knew. The inquisitive Greeks dissected penises regularly. The crueler Romans amputated many of their prisoners' erections after arousing the men with naked young women. The gush of blood convinced them that an inflated penis is the result of liquid under pressure, not an air-inflated bone.

There are no bones or muscles inside the penis. Two long cylinders of spongy erectile tissue, the *corpora cavernosa*, and blood vessels run down the penis. In response to sexual stimulation, the nervous system rushes extra blood into the spongy tissue, and the engorged cylinders expand, compressing the walls of the veins that normally carry blood away. An erection is caused by the pressure of trapped blood.

• The average erect penis holds eight times as much blood as a flaccid one. Hugely endowed men have reported getting light-headed and dizzy during erections. But as we'll see, there is a smaller range of sizes among erect penises than among flaccid ones. Erect, most men *are* created equal.

• A penis reaches full adult proportion by age seventeen—often a year or more earlier—with virtually no subsequent growth. Any added centimeters that appear in old age are due to the downward tug of gravity.

WELL-HUNG MEN OF THE TWENTIETH CENTURY ◆

*N*o list of well-hung men can really be authoritative, because research is nearly impossible to conduct. But from lovers' gossip and indiscretions, as well a particular man's own boasting, it is possible to assemble a list that is at least interesting to browse. Because our society dwells on celebrities, it is their endowments that largely make up the list. There is no way to know how many average Joes and Charlies were anything but average. I've augmented a list assembled by Leigh W. Rutledge in *The Gay Book of Lists* (1987).

Milton Berle, comedian
Berle's endowment is no secret in the entertainment industry. Shortly after the young Roddy McDowell arrived in Hollywood, he was favorably compared with Berle—and not for his comedic talent. When Berle and McDowell finally met, the older Berle allegedly challenged him to a show-and-measure in the men's room. Several friends accompanied them, placing bets. McDowell readily exposed all he had, but Berle supposedly showed only what he had to in order to win the wager.

Charlie Chaplin, filmmaker and actor
"The Eighth Wonder of the World" is how Chaplin himself referred to his member.

Gary Cooper, actor
Rumors have long surrounded the handsome Gary Cooper—that when it came to getting parts early in his career, he got a foot in the door by opening his fly. Actresses who performed love scenes with Cooper reported that they

A literal depiction of a woman being "goosed."

felt the overwhelming evidence even through heavy skirts. Leaving for Hollywood in the 1940s, Tallulah Bankhead candidly informed the press, "I'm going west to fuck that fantastic Gary Cooper."

Cooper developed considerable notoriety as one of Hollywood's most satisfying, and indefatigable, lovers.

Errol Flynn, actor

It's been said that *mature* well-endowed men like their secret to be known only to women, while *immature* men prefer that other men know. Immature men seek the approval of other men.

Errol Flynn is said to have belonged in this latter category. He thoroughly enjoyed showing his penis, even to strangers, delighting in their envious reactions. This is not to say that he did not expose himself to many women as well, but the motivation was different. Writer Truman Capote, who was personally well acquainted with Flynn's endowment, claimed that at a party the actor played the piano with his wang, beating out the tune "You Are My Sunshine." The song's title and lyrics—"My only sunshine / You make me happy, when skies are gray"—seem fitting.

Liam Neeson, actor

The handsome Welsh-born actor graced the cover of a leading men's magazine in 1995, and the interview inside addressed Hollywood rumors about his extraordinary size. Neeson did not deny them, and the interviewer, a woman, observed that his fingers were as thick and solid as most men's

---

WHAT WOMEN FIND SEXY IN MEN ◆ *Standards of sexual desirability change with the times. Before men in large numbers took to buffing their bodies in gyms, polls found that women were turned on to men for reasons other than brawn, general body bigness, and height. Those three attributes, according to a 1995 poll, now rank among the sexiest things that turn women on.*

When women are looking for a roll in the hay, and not a potential husband, here (by percentage) is what they're look for in terms of body:

Six-foot height or taller—88 percent
Imposing body massiveness—80 percent
Muscular, athletic build—76 percent
Broad shoulders—72 percent
Large penis—65 percent
Well-defined, muscular arms—64 percent
Small, tight rear end—60 percent
Full head of hair—55 percent
Sensual mouth—37 percent
Narrow hips—34 percent
Muscular legs—31 percent

Ranking 30 percent or less, in descending order of desirability: a slim build; a three-day beard; a strikingly bony nose; and clear, soft skin.

---

erections. The rumors were finally confirmed when Neeson shot full frontal nude scenes for *Rob Roy*. Not all the footage was released. But in the director's cut, Neeson himself is seen to be clearly uncut.

Aristotle Onassis, Greek shipping tycoon

Onassis had both billions *and* size. He often boasted of both his fortune and his good fortune. On numerous occasions he referred to his huge member as "the secret of my success," and it was not uncommon for press reporters to be pulled into a men's room and shown the secret itself. Maria Callas, his lover of many years, claimed that sex with Onassis made her "a different

*Priapus weighing his phallus, from
a fresco at Pompeii, first century.*

woman." In Terrence McNally's Broadway play *Master Class* (1995), the
Maria Callas character sighs that Onassis was hung "like a fucking bull—
and he let everybody know it."

Jason Priestley, actor

Jason Priestley's impressive endowment was supposedly well known to several
members of the cast of TV's *Beverly Hills 90210*. But according to Rutledge,
Priestly's secret became public knowledge when he worked on the 1993
movie *Calendar Girl*. The actor's member was so large that in a skinny-
dipping sequence it keep appearing on film no matter what camera angle the
director called for. Producers wanted a PG-13 rating for the film and knew
they wouldn't get it if Priestley's penis could be seen, so computer editors
had to touch up the footage frame by frame. The original film is supposedly
available on black market porn videos.

Grigori Rasputin, Siberian peasant and mystic

Reports that the mystic healer's penis was thirteen inches when fully erect
began to emerge when he was a lustful teenager and seducer of many women
in his native village. By 1905, Rasputin had settled in St. Petersburg. Though
he was "an unwashed peasant with a dirty beard and filthy hands" (according
to biographer Robert K. Massie), society ladies vied for invitations into his
bedroom, which he christened the "holy of holies." So famous was his celeb-

---

ADAM'S APPLE ◆ *Near the end of puberty, when a boy's penis is reaching its maximum size, something else is growing: his voice box, or larynx. It is visible from the outside as the Adam's apple, so named because Eve never had one—nor has any hormonally normal woman. On a slender neck, the Adam's apple can look painfully prominent.*

What is its origin?

Male sex hormones cause the vocal cords to increase in both thickness and length in the final stage of puberty. This causes a boy's voice to "break." The higher-pitched tones of childhood are gradually replaced by the deeper bass sounds of the adult male. It takes three to nine months for the larynx to grow to adult size. During this time, a boy's voice switches back and forth between piping childhood pitch and deeper adult tones. There are times in the process when only high squeaks are emitted as the growing chords adjust to their new size—and new home in the Adam's apple.

In time, a man develops thicker neck muscles, which make the Adam's apple appear less prominent.

---

rity as a lover and a healer—the kind of bogus cure known as "hysterical suppression of symptoms"—that the husbands of his conquests boasted that their wives had "belonged" to the incredible Rasputin.

Tales of his miraculous healing powers finally reached Czar Nicholas and Czarina Alexandra. The imperial couple's son, Alexei, was a hemophiliac, and Rasputin, through hypnosis and laying on of hands, supposedly brought the boy to full health. And he mesmerized the czarina herself. The lustful mystic became too powerful for the comfort of many noblemen, who, in 1916, had him assassinated, then sliced off his renowned member. Legend has it that the amputated organ was preserved in a wooden box by one of his lovers. She claimed it looked "like a blackened, overripe banana, about a foot long."

Arnold Schwarzenegger, actor and bodybuilder

In 1990, *Gentlemen's Quarterly* added Schwarzenegger to its list of the best-endowed men of the twentieth century. Other honorees include actors Matt

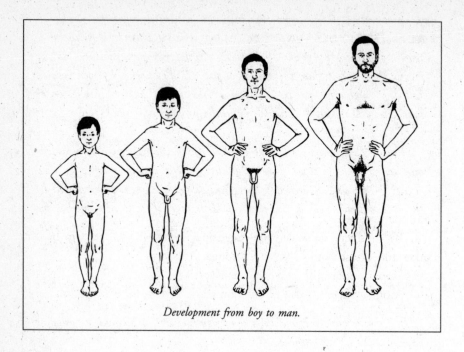

Development from boy to man.

Dillon, Robert Redford, Humphrey Bogart, Warren Beatty, and Marlon Brando, baseball great Babe Ruth, and President John F. Kennedy.

Frank Sinatra, singer

When it comes to superendowment, short, slender men often provide the greatest surprises. In one reliable study of 500 American men, the biggest penis belonged to the shortest, shyest, slightest-built man—wimps with whoppers.

Crooner Frank Sinatra apparently falls into the category of lightweight men hugely blessed, though only his several wives and many dozen lovers know for sure. Sinatra's second wife, the voluptuous actress Ava Gardner, was asked by the press why she married the "one-hundred-twenty-pound runt."

"Well," she smiled, "there may be only twenty pounds of Frank, but there are one hundred pounds of cock."

FROM BOY TO MAN •

A boy's genitals usually take about four years to develop to adult size—roughly from the age of around twelve to sixteen. By seventeen, just about everything is sized and in place:

1. At twelve, the testicles and scrotum begin to enlarge. The scrotal skin reddens and coarsens in texture.

2. At thirteen, sparse pubic hair starts to grow at the base of the penis.

3. The penis begins to enlarge in length and girth. The testes and scrotum continue to grow.

4. By fourteen, pubic hair has developed color. It continues to become darker and coarser and cover a wider area.

5. Upper lip, armpit, and body hair appear.

6. Around fifteen, sperm production reaches a level where nocturnal emissions, or wet dreams, begin.

7. The Adam's apple develops to accommodate thicker and longer vocal cords.

8. There is a sudden increase in muscularity and body strength. By seventeen, the penis and testicles have reach adult proportions.

"CONDOM"; EUROPE, SEVENTEENTH CENTURY •

T he origin of the word "condom" is unknown. It may come directly from the French town of Condom in Gascony; the stereotypical Gascon male of French popular literature is sexual, impetuous, and hotheaded, such as Edmond Rostand's character Cyrano de Bergerac. Or the name may derive from Dr. Condom, an English physician and earl of Condom who is said to have perfected the penile shaft casing in the mid-1600s to protect King Charles II from contracting venereal disease. *Merriam-Webster* traces the word back only to around 1706.

Ribs, Ticklers, and Sperm Caps

Penile sheaths have existed for many centuries. There is evidence that the Romans, and possibly the Egyptians, used oiled animal bladders and lengths of intestine as sheaths. The device's primary purpose was not to prevent pregnancy but venereal disease. When it comes to birth control, men have always preferred to let women take the lead.

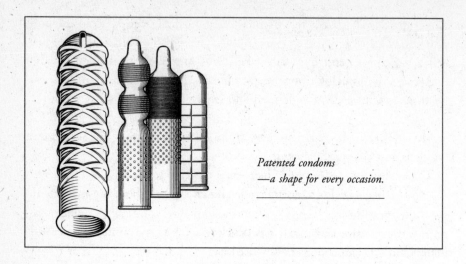

Patented condoms
—a shape for every occasion.

Gabriello Fallopio, the sixteenth-century Italian physician who first described the two slender tubes that carry ova from the ovaries to the uterus, is generally regarded as the "father of the condom," an anachronistic title since Dr. Condom would not make his contribution to the device for another hundred years.

In the mid-1500s, Fallopio, a professor of anatomy at the University of Padua, designed a medicated linen sheath that fit over the glans, or tip of the penis, and was secured by the foreskin. It represents the first clearly documented prophylactic for the male member.

His invention was tested on "over a thousand men, with complete success," as the doctor himself reported. The devices were euphemistically called "overcoats." Soon sheaths appeared for circumcised men. They were of a standard six-inch length and tied securely at the base with a pink ribbon, presumably an aesthetic touch for the woman's pleasure.

Penile sheaths in the sixteenth century were dullingly thick, made from animal gut, fish membranes, or oiled linen. Since they interfered with the pleasure of intercourse and only occasionally prevented disease—being improperly used and reused without being washed—they were unpopular with men and regarded with derision. A French marquis sarcastically summed up the situation when he called the cow-gut sheath he'd tried "armor against love, gossamer against infection."

Legend has it that the earl of Condom, the knighted physician to Charles II, improved the device's sensitivity by using stretched oiled intestine of sheep.

Condom's sheath caught the attention of noblemen, who adopted the prophylactics against venereal disease. Neither they nor the king were concerned about fathering bastards.

Sexually transmitted disease was feared far more than siring illegitimate children. *A Classical Dictionary of the Vulgar Tongue*, published in London in 1785, defines a condom as "the dried gut of a sheep, worn by men in the act of coition, to prevent venereal infection." The entry runs for several additional sentences, with no mention of contraception.

• *Rubber Condoms.* Sheaths made from vulcanized rubber appeared in the 1870s; the devices were soon known simply as "rubbers." A rubber condom was expensive and annoyingly thick. A man was instructed to wash it before and after intercourse. He reused it until the device cracked or tore.

• *Latex Condoms,* thinner, disposable, and sterile, were introduced in the 1930s. They allowed for such design niceties as ribs and tickle-fingers along the shaft (for the woman's pleasure) and a thimble sperm cap at the head to collect the ejaculate (for the man's convenience and the woman's protection). Today Japan is the leader in condom use; like cosmetics, they are sold door to door, by women.

• *Polyurethane Condoms* are the latest version. Thinner than latex, impervious to oil-based lubricants, the new condoms are ideal for men and women allergic to latex. Six years in the making, the new condom is a spin-off of Saran Wrap. Unfurled, the polyurethane sheath is clear and crinkly— more a Baggie than a rubber. Virtually frictionless, it requires less lubricant, and since it is only forty microns thick, its heat conductivity is excellent, offering natural "hot" and safe sex. Its only drawback is that it is less elastic than latex, which may pose problems for the Slim Jims of the world.

"MACHO"; AMERICA, 1920S •

*M*acho does not mean mucho," teased Zsa Zsa Gabor, implying that toughness in a man is indicative of nothing more.

"When I went to Buffalo in 1969," O. J. Simpson told *Sports Illustrated* (August 28, 1982), "I thought I had to show my macho, to go all out and play fierce."

G. Gordon Liddy, in a 1980 *Playboy* interview, complained of what feminists had done to the word:

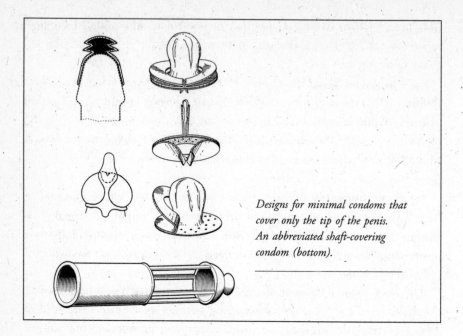

Designs for minimal condoms that cover only the tip of the penis. An abbreviated shaft-covering condom (bottom).

Macho was originally a perfectly respectable Spanish term for a manly man, a designation I'd feel perfectly comfortable with, but in recent years it's been expropriated as a code word by the women's liberation movement and twisted into a pejorative Archie Bunkerish caricature of the loutish, leering male who believes that the only natural position for women in this world is horizontal.

Liddy is not exactly accurate. In America, "macho" has always implied an aggressive, unnatural virility, verging on brutishness if not violence. Ernest Hemingway was often described as the quintessential macho man, someone who had a deep need to repeatedly prove his masculinity. Macho men like guns and blood sports—and obedient women. They are more than just "manly."

In Latin America, a macho male was one who often proclaimed his virility by fathering numerous children by different wives—and boasted of his accomplishments. Often he was a wife beater and took pride in being the aggressive boss of the family.

"Macho," Mexican Spanish for "male"—from the Latin *masculus*—entered American English as an adjective around 1928.

About two decades later, Americans started to use the noun "machismo," meaning at first "a strong, exaggerated sense of masculine pride," then later, in the feminist 1960s, "aggressive, violent masculinity."

Gay "macho" and Feminist "macha"

In the 1970s, the Village People, a gay disco group, recorded a string of platinum-selling singles specializing in faux macho themes: "In the Navy," "Y.M.C.A.," and "Macho Man." Costumed as a cowboy, construction worker, motorcyclist, American Indian, they gave the word a gay cultish spin, turning it into a parody of its original self.

In the 1980s, some female writers adopted the word for their gender: "The women exude an exhilarated pride that some might call female machismo" (*Town & Country*, June 1980); "another career-minded Hollywood powerhouse who might well be described as the modern macho woman" (*Elle*, August 1986).

There was even an attempt to coin a special term for "female machismo." One suggested word was *macha*, and its corollary *machisma*, with Spanish feminine -*a* endings: "This is a terrific *macha* book for women who want to get stronger, physically and psychologically" (Carol Troy, *New York Times Book Review*, May 7, 1981).

Another word for "female macho" that never really caught on was *facho*. "He's macho, she's facho"—sounds like a Punch and Judy routine.

The feminist move to coin "macha" and "facho" coincided with the arrival of militant feminist jokes and slogans such as: "The way to a man's heart is through his chest." "So many men, so little ammunition." "I don't have time to put on makeup. I need that time to clean my rifle." Macho, Mr. Liddy, has always gone hand in hand with guns and blood sports.

CHAPTER 2

Honeypots and Hairpies

"Cunt" to "Twat"

*The greatest discovery of the twentieth century
is that women like it too.*

GEORGE BURNS

"Cunt"; Proto-Language, Euro-Asia, 13,000 B.C.E. ◆

"Sticks and stones will break my bones, but names will never hurt me." So we say. But the most scurrilous, hurtful verbal stone a man can hurl at a women is "cunt"—the gender-opposite of "cock."

Women, when polled, report that "cunt" is the single most offensive word in the English language. "Bitch," "bimbo," "slut," and every other nasty slur of address can be shrugged off as reflections of the caller's own hang-ups, but "cunt" seems to be taken personally. Many mature women cup their hands over their ears when listening to a joke that contains this four-letter word.

Women virtually never use the C-word, either in mixed company or among themselves. The word has been taboo for at least six centuries and, until recently, was printed only in underground literature—and then at the risk of criminal prosecution. Prohibitions against it have been every bit as strong as those against "fuck," the subject of a later chapter.

Depiction of a woman as a "cunt" and a man as a "dickhead."

Sheilah Graham, in her memoir *A State of Heat* (1972), offered a psycho-analytic explanation for the taboo, which invokes penis envy and castration fears. A man has "something" between his legs, a woman has "nothing," said Graham, and the C-word plays up that major difference:

> *To call a man a cunt is to call him a woman: castrated, therefore not a man. To call a woman a cunt is to dismiss her absolutely: she is a zero, a nullity.*

Mr. and Mrs. Cuntless

Today, any family with the surname *Cuntless* would wisely change it, or risk subjecting their children to years of serious verbal abuse. But in thirteenth-century England, Cuntless (and Cuntles) was a proper last name, as was *Clawecunte* (claw cunt), *Wydecunte* (wide cunt), and *Gropecunte* (grope cunt). Today, "wide cunt" and "grope cunt" sound particularly offensive.

In medieval London, Gropecunte Lane was a red-light district in Oxford, which was later changed to Magpie Lane—a marginal improvement from a feminist viewpoint. It should be obvious by this point that "cunt" was not always a dirty word.

As an Anglo-Saxon surname, *Cunte* was first recorded in 1066, the year the Normans invaded England. The word then seems to have become either an acceptable, inoffensive prefix or suffix of other surnames: *Cunteshaw, Bellecunthe.* So common was the word that every town had its share of "cunts."

Chaucer uses the word several times, spelling it *queynte,* in *The Canterbury*

Tales. He believed that "cunt" derived from "quaint," which meant a many-layered, in-folded mystery.

An Italian medical text of the thirteenth century, *Lanfrank's Science of Cirurgie* [Surgery], renders the word in a valid anatomical usage: "In wymmen, the neck of the bladdre is short, and made fast to the cunte." It is easy to see how the fleshy folds of the vulva could be described as a "many-layered, in-folded mystery."

"Cunnilingus" = Vulva-Licker

From early on, the word we today recognize as "cunt" had explicit sexual connotation. The sexually liberated Romans wrote often, and approvingly, of *cunnilingus*—literally Latin for "vulva licker": *cunnus*, "vulva" + *lingere*, "to lick." Thus, for centuries, a word strikingly similar to "cunt" – *cunnus* – described the anatomical female region.

The word "cunt" was clearly taboo in Shakespeare's time. The playwright had great fun teasing with it in several of his works. When Hamlet asks Ophelia if he may lay his head in her lap, the prince reassures her that his motives are pure, that he's not thinking about "country [cunt-ree] matters."

In *Twelfth Night*, Shakespeare boldly spells out the word while referring to urination as well: Malvolio, attempting to decipher the handwriting on a letter, exclaims, "By my life, this is my lady's hand! These be her very C's, her U's, and ['n] her T's; and thus makes she her great P's."

If Shakespeare's dozens of wordplays on "cunt"—and on "fuck" and "prick"—were pointed out to high school students, it could prompt a renaissance of interest in the bard's works.

Ancient Origin: "Wife"

Many languages have equivalent C-word terms: *kunte*, German; *kunta*, Old Norse; *con*, French; *cunnus*, Latin; *qefent*, ancient Egyptian. Even the isolated Basque language has *kuna*. Over the ages not all of these words have been regarded as dirty.

Linguists believe that "cunt" is ubiquitous because about 15,000 years ago, when languages started to split off from a proto-language base, *kuni* seems to have been a term for "wife," "woman," and anything feminine. It is easy to imagine how a word like *kuni*, which represented such a fundamentally important group of female concepts, came to be associated with the visible female reproductive organ. No women today likes to be labeled by a body part. What man would like to be thought of as a "dick"? But, linguistically,

"Cunnilingus" means "vulva-licker."

it seems that all women were "cunts" at one time, and the usage was inoffensive.

"Cunt History" and "Clit Lit" ◆

*C*unt," for centuries unprintable and unspeakable in polite society, is now for some women a feminist salvo. Gloria Steinem has written:

> *The feminist spirit has reclaimed some words with defiance and humor. Witch, bitch, dyke and other formerly pejorative epithets have turned up in the brave names of feminist groups. A few women artists dubbed their new female imagery cunt art in celebration of the discovery that not all sexual symbols were phallic.*

Today, lesbian activists refer to the "lesbian past" and its prominent "dyke" achievers as "cunt history," just as, it should be pointed out, gay male activists speak proudly of their "queer history." Words, too, have come out of the closet.

Another example is "clit," which lesbians have adopted as one of their favorite political words. Lesbian fiction and nonfiction are called "clit lit." And a political separatist manifesto by the Collective Lesbian International Terrorists (CLIT) became infamous in the 1970s as the Clit Statement. The women, who threatened "lesbionage," called for "real dykes" to break their ties with straight women, who, having husbands and boyfriends, were hopelessly influenced by the "oppressive male regime."

CASANOVA: HISTORY'S GREATEST LOVER, ON "CUNT" ◆

Out of a hundred cunts, not one is quite like another; there is always some difference noticeable in them. In my belief, there is as much difference in the look of cunts as there is in noses. But sisters' cunts I think are generally somewhat alike.

A woman is like a book that, be it good or bad, must begin to please with its title page," said Giovanni Casanova, the notorious lover, who died in 1798, at age seventy-three, from toxic mercury treatments for his myriad venereal diseases.

Before the age of forty, Casanova was treated with mercury for no fewer than eleven bouts of syphilis and gonorrhea. In time, the toxic metal poisoned his kidneys, and his prostate became acutely inflamed. His last thirteen years were chaste, his only pleasure eating, of which a biographer noted, "Since he could no longer be a god in the gardens, he became a wolf at the table."

History's most notorious lover freely used the C-word in conversation and print. He loved to shock people with it. At eleven, he claimed, he had been a victim of sexual abuse, when the woman bathing him played with his penis, thus awakening his sexuality. Soon thereafter he lost his virginity, with two women at once. And when he entered the seminary of St. Cyprian to become a priest—he believed the priesthood would squelch his libido—he was expelled for sodomy *with* a priest.

Today, we'd say Casanova was a sex addict. His vivid autobiography, *Histoire de ma vie* ("The Story of My Life"), runs 4,545 pages and covers his sex life only up to the summer of 1774, when he was forty-nine. On his deathbed, after receiving the sacrament of extreme unction, he uttered his last words: "I have lived as a philosopher and die as a Christian."

Casanova wrote considerably about women's private parts, and he was obsessed with the word "cunt." And with the size of "pricks." One conclusion from his own sex research:

*Engraving for the posthumously
published* Memoirs *of Casanova.*

*I believe there never was a prick so big in any way that a cunt could
not take it without pain, and even pleasurably. Its tip might perhaps knock
at the portals of the womb too hard for some, but that is all. I have heard
women say that the harder those knocks were, the more pleasure it gave
them.*

*All the talk I have heard of pricks being so large that women could not,
or would not take them up them is sheer nonsense. Several women have
told me so. Some said they love to see and handle big ones. None said that
such stretches gave them more physical pleasure than those of moderate size.*

*The elasticity and receptivity of a cunt is in fact as wonderful as its
constrictive power. The small prick of a boy of thirteen it will tighten round
and exhaust, as well as one as big as the spoke of a cartwheel, and it will
give pleasure to both equally.*

CLITORIS—A MOST UNIQUE ORGAN ◆

The clitoris—Greek *kleitoris,* "a hill"—is the small, sensitive, erectile
organ at the upper end of the vulva. Hooded by skin, it looks tiny
to the naked eye. But, like an iceberg, most of the clitoris is hidden inside
the body. The external part is called the *glans* and is similar to the male's
glans, or head, of the penis.

Only in recent years has the full anatomy of the clitoris been adequately
studied.

The entire clitoris—what is exposed and what is hidden—consists of spongy erectile tissue, blood vessels, and nerves. Beneath the skin, the clitoris shaft separates into two legs—*crura*—which extend in a wishbone fashion for about three inches on either side of the vaginal opening. During sexual stimulation, the region fills with blood, and the glans, shaft, and legs swell and become firm. Since the clitoral legs run beneath the labia, any stimulation of the urethra, vagina, or anus indirectly stimulates the clitoris as well.

While the penis serves the functions of procreation and urination, the sole purpose of the clitoris is to give pleasure. In fact, it is the only organ in the human body whose sole function is to transmit sexual sensation.

But men don't have one. This has lead to the claim that men traditionally have been afraid of women's raw sexuality—that men secretly feel sexually inferior because women are better designed for eroticism and can have multiple orgasms in rapid succession. Whatever the reason, male writers and physicians have, historically, largely ignored or misrepresented the role of the clitoris.

CLITORAL ORGASM: HIPPOCRATES TO MASTERS AND JOHNSON ◆

*T*oday we know how women prefer to pleasure themselves. Of women who admit to masturbating, with fingers or vibrators, the breakdown in achieving orgasm is:

84 percent from clitoral and labial stimulation
20 percent from vaginal insertion
11 percent from mounting and rubbing objects
11 percent from breast stimulation
10 percent from squeezing thighs
5 percent from muscular contractions
2 percent from fantasy alone

As long as women have masturbated, they have known about the sensitivity of the clitoris. But how long have men known?

It's generally stated that Alfred Kinsey in the late 1940s and Masters and Johnson in the 1960s first informed millions of men about clitoral orgasms. Although these sex pioneers deserve considerable credit, the importance of

The importance of clitoral stimulation was known to ancient Greek and Roman physicians.

clitoral orgasm was known more than two thousand years ago. It had just gone underground during the Victorian Age, its existence ignored by husbands and denied by gynecologists.

Soranus of Ephesus, a Greek physician who practiced in Rome early in the second century, informed Roman men:

> *The vagina of a woman appears as follows: The visible external parts of this organ are called the 'wings,' constituting the so-called 'lips' of the vagina. They are thick and fleshy. Downward, they end at the thighs and are separated from each other by a slit. Toward the top, they reach up to what's called the clitoris, a most sensitive organ indeed.*
>
> *The clitoris, which stands right at the start of the two lips, consists of a fleshy little button, which resembles in function the male organ.*
>
> *Covered by skin, it is called the 'clitoris' because it is hidden away, just as a newlywed bride is hidden away from her groom by a veil.*

The "Father of Medicine" Had It Right

Hippocrates (460–370 B.C.E.) was equally well informed on the clitoris and its importance in orgasm. The most famous doctor of antiquity, who has given medicine its Hippocratic oath, also believed that women ejaculated, a topic that is controversial to this day:

During intercourse, once a woman is rubbed and her womb titillated, a lustful itch overwhelms her down by her clitoris, and pleasurable feelings and warmth expand out through the rest of her body [a blood flush].

A woman also has an ejaculation, furnished by her body, occurring at the same time inside her womanly parts, which have become wet, as well as on the outside . . . If a woman feels an orgasm coming on, she will ejaculate with him . . .

Her pleasure and warmth surge the moment the man's sperm descends into the womb, then it fades. Just as when wine is poured on a flame, it gives a spurt before it goes out for good.

Not only did most doctors of old believe that women had clitoral orgasms and ejaculated, many thought that conception occurred only if both the man and the woman ejaculated. They suspected that a man and woman "mixed fluids" to make a baby. (They were not that far off, in that it takes a sperm and an egg.) This lead physicians to emphasize the importance of sexual foreplay. Husbands were encouraged to lavish at least an hour of attention on the woman's body.

Avicenna (980–1037), the famed medieval Islamic philosopher and physician, thought two or three hours would be even better:

Husbands, take great time in playing with your healthy wife. You should caress her breasts and nipples and pubis, and enfold her in your arms without really performing the act of sex.

And when her desire is fully aroused, only then should you unite with the woman [enter her], rubbing all the while the area between the anus and the vulva—for this, gentlemen, is the seat of pleasure.

Keenly watch for the moment when the woman clings most tightly to you, when her eyes start to go red, when her breathing becomes more rapid, when she starts to stammer. This is the moment [of female orgasm and possible conception].

CLITORIS = SOURCE OF SIN ◆

One of the clearest explanations of the role of the clitoris was given by the renowned French surgeon Nicolas Venette (1633–1698). His sex manual for married couples, *Tableau de l'Amour Conjugal* (1687), was wildly popular, went into numerous editions, and was translated into Dutch, German, and English. Everyone then knew about clitoral orgasms:

One sees above the inner labia an organ about half-a-finger's-breadth tall, which the anatomist calls the "clitoris." I should call it the very passion and guide of Love. It is there that Nature has placed the throne of pleasures and sensuous joys.

It is there that Nature has endowed excessive sensitivity and, too, has established the zone of wantonness for women.

Thus, in the action of Love, the clitoris fills itself with life forces and stiffens like the penis of a man. It lacks neither a gland nor a foreskin, and if it had a little hole at the tip, one would say that it was exactly the same as the man's member.

At this point in Venette's manual, we get a hint as to why the clitoral orgasm went underground and why its existence was ignored and denied by husbands, physicians, and gynecologists. For Venette, the great sensitivity of the clitoris opened the door to the two great evils of masturbation and wifely adultery:

It is the clitoris that lewd women abuse. Sappho, the Lesbian, never would have gained her notorious reputation if she had had a smaller clitoris . . . So many prostitutes would not have taken to their trade . . .

I once saw an eight-year-old girl who had a clitoris half the length of a little finger. If this organ grows with age, as it appears it will, I am convinced it will become as thick and as long as the neck of a goose.

Thus the clitoris, being the seat of pleasure, became the source of sin. By denying the existence of the clitoral orgasm, Victorian men made their wives pure, nearly virginal, and faithful—or so they hoped.

Tender Button

By the time Gertrude Stein (1874–1946) published her abstractly erotic book *Tender Buttons* (1914), a married woman who experienced clitoral orgasm was considered neurotic and immature. Doctors taught that only a young girl masturbated with her clitoris; married women had only *vaginal* orgasms, if any at all.

The "tender button" of the title is the sensitive clitoris. At the time Stein was writing, acknowledgment of the clitoral orgasm by sexologists was a half-century in the future. Even Stein, who dropped out of medical school in her last term, garnered knowledge about the importance of the clitoris from her own lesbian affairs. Critic Edmund Wilson, reviewing *Tender Buttons*, explained that the book was deliberately hard to understand because Stein wrote in coded sentences ("The sister was not a mister") about the unmentionable sex between women.

FEMALE SEXUALITY AND "CUCKOLD" ◆

*I*t's been said that a husband likes to think of his wife as sexless in order to fend off worries about being cuckolded and thus having to raise another man's child. This belief is at the root of the word "cuckold."

Contrary to popular opinion, "cuckold" has nothing to do with the word "cock." It's from the Old French *cucu*, which is the echoic cry of the cuckoo bird. The female cuckoo has a habit of frequently changing mates—and, worse, of laying her eggs in another bird's nest. (Actually, the European cuckoo will lay her eggs in another bird's nest, but the American cuckoo, almost Puritanically faithful, hatches her own young. This was not known centuries ago when the word "cuckold" was coined.) Thus a husband who is "cuckolded" ends up with another man's child in his nest.

"BEAVER"; AMERICA, THE ROARING TWENTIES ◆

*W*hen Sharon Stone, in *Basic Instinct* (1992), uncrossed her legs and revealed to the movie audience a glimpse of bare crotch, reviewers observed she'd given cinema its first "beaver shot." Readers and moviegoers knew exactly what the expression meant. But the sexual connotation of "beaver" seems to have arisen only in this century.

One of its earliest recorded uses in reference to a woman's crotch appeared in a limerick published in 1927:

There was a young lady named Eva,
Who went to the ball as Godiva,
But a change in the lights
Showed a tear in her tights,
And a low fellow present yelled, "Beaver!"

The sexual connotation seems to have appeared from out of nowhere, although linguists suspect it came from one of two older nicknames for the female crotch: "beard" or "pelt."

The pelts of beavers were long used to make winter coats, and beaver skins were referred to as "beards." Add to this the fact that the female crotch's pubic hair has a long history of being referred to as a beard, and you have a plausible explanation for how the name of the animal, beaver, replaced its slang reference, beard.

Why might this have occurred in the 1920s?

The Roaring Twenties was a time of great linguistic innovation, with scores of buzzwords and expressions: *gams* for "legs," *bee's knees* for anything "wonderful," *giggle water* or *hooch* for "alcohol," *jazzbo* for a "ladies' man," *whoopee* for "fun," *upchuck* for "vomit." The Twenties also saw the heyday of *Greeks* (fraternities), of *hazing* of any freshman *Joe College*, and of the popularity on campus of raccoon coats, called "beavers." Perhaps some *jazzbo*, who'd drunk too much *hooch* and was *ossified*, glanced across the *speakeasy* and spotted a *flapper*, who parted her *gams*, and he shouted not "beard!" but *"beaver!"*

From the Twenties onward, a variety of "beaver" terms began appearing on college campuses across the country:

Beaver fever: to be horny
Beaver pose: a woman seated with her knees apart
Beaver shot: a glimpse of crotch
Beaver posse: a group of men in search of sex

Beaver Shooter

Yankee pitcher Jim Bouton, in his 1970 bestseller, *Ball Four*, irritated his teammates when he revealed that many practitioners of America's national pastime were full-time "beaver shooters":

"A beaver shooter is, at bottom, a Peeping Tom. I've seen guys chin themselves on transoms, drill holes in doors, even shove a mirror under a door all for a shot of beaver."

"PUSSY"; IRELAND, MIDDLE AGES ◆

A man who let's himself be bossed by a woman is "pussy whipped." Feminists must ban together to build, said Germaine Greer, "pussy power." Gossip between females is "pussy talk." A lesbian refers affectionately to her lover as "puss."

This last instance harks back to the previous century when the word "pussy" could still be used as a nonsexual endearment: " 'What do you think, pussy?' said her father to Eva" in Harriet Beecher Stowe's *Uncle Tom's Cabin* (1852). No father today would likely refer to his daughter as pussy.

How did "pussy" come to be slang for a women's crotch?

One explanation is that a young girl used to be affectionately called a "pussycat" because both a child and a kitten are cuddly and sweet. But, then, where did the name "pussycat" come from?

Actually, the inverse of the above argument is true: a girl was called a pussy before a kitten was. Here's how it happened:

Origin: "Mouth"

Our word "puss," meaning "face," is from the Irish Gaelic *pus*, which was slang for "mouth." It is easy to see how a word for mouth could come to represent an entire face.

It is equally clear, linguistically, that a woman's vaginal opening was long called "a mouth"—it's one of the oldest references to a "vagina."

And, too, a woman herself was called a "cat." By gossiping she was being "catty"—allusions perhaps to cats' hissing, purring, and meowing.

During the Middle Ages, both "puss" and "pussy" became female endearments: "puss" was an affectionate term for a mature woman; "pussy," the diminutive, applied to a young girl.

During these centuries, the English called a feline a "cat," from the Latin *cattus* for the animal. The French-speaking Normans who conquered England in 1066 brought with them their own words for a feline: *chat*, "cat," and *chaton*, the diminutive, "kitten." The animals were christened with the human female endearments of "puss," for cat, and "pussy" for kitten. That is, women were "pussies" before cats were.

Wuss

Today, one of the most hurtful slurs one young boy can sling at another is "pussy," meaning, in a sexist sense, that he is soft, weak, indecisive, womanlike.

A slur with a similar meaning, that seems to have originated in the late 1970s, is "wuss." Linguists believe it is a two-punch hybrid combining "w(imp) + (p)uss."

The expression "pussy" derives from the Gaelic slang pus, *meaning both "mouth" and "vagina."*

"PIECE OF ASS"; LATE ANGLO-SAXON ◆

*A*n early Middle English expression for any sexually desirable part of a woman and, originally, of a man was *piece of ass* or *piece of tail.* The reference to men died out; the reference to women stuck, and in time a woman's crotch was itself called a "piece."

"Piece" suggests food—as in "a piece of pie"—and it is not surprising that over the centuries men have concocted dozens of tasty food references for the female genitals: *hairpie, honeypot, sugar donut, muffin, cream jug, yeast biscuit, fig, clam, yum-yum cake, butter boat, jellyroll, cookie jar, milk jug, sugar scoop, jam pot.* Feminist Germaine Greer defined sexual intercourse as "the squirting of jam into a doughnut."

Pudendum
The word is from the Latin *pudendus*, "shameful." The Latin word was gender-neutral, but over time "pudendum" came to mean a female's external genitals. The plural, "pudenda," refers to the genitals of either sex.

Poontang
The word is a Creole pronunciation for the French for "whore," *putain.*

"SNATCH"; ENGLAND, PRE-SIXTEENTH CENTURY ◆

Today the word "snatch" is slang for the external female genitals. But centuries ago, it referred to quick, bang-bang sexual intercourse, involving only the basics; a "quickie," we'd say.

Even in Shakespeare's time the word could have this connotation: "Why, then, it seems some certain snatch or so / would serve your turns" wrote the bard in *Titus Andronicus*, implying that the character could use a "good lay." Gradually the word came to refer more to female genitals than to the act of coitus.

Slit

The word is slang for the female genitals, with obvious anatomical allusion. No one knows how ancient the slang expression is, but it was already common in 1648 when Robert Herrick published *Hesperides*:

> Scobble for Whoredome whips his wife, and cryes,
> He'll slit her nose, but blubb'ring, she replyes,
> Good Sir, make no more cuts in th'outward skin,
> One slit's enough to let Adultry in.

"TWAT"; OLD NORSE ◆

Old Norse *thveit*, meaning "slit," or "cut," is the most likely source for the word "twat." Like the Anglo-Saxon "slit," the Norse "twat" derived simply from the physical appearance of the female genitals.

Robert Browning was well acquainted with "slit" but thought "twat" meant "hat." He liked the poetic ring of the word—its double t's—and without researching its meaning used the word in "Pippa Passes," producing an unintentionally comic line: "The owls and bats, / Cowls and twats, / Monks and nuns, / In a cloister's moods."

How did Browning make this mistake? He'd read "Vanity of Vanities," written two centuries earlier, but had not realized that its author was being deliberately bitchy when he'd written:

> They talk't of his having a Cardinalls Hat,
> They'd send him as soon an Old Nuns Twat.

"Vulva"; Ancient Rome ◆

*T*he word "vulva"—describing the external female genitals, including the labia majora, labia minora, clitoris, and the entrance to the vaginal canal—is from the Latin *volva,* meaning a "wrapper," or "covering." Since Roman times, men have described all of a woman's privates that can be readily seem, or easily found, as a wrapper, perhaps a gift wrapper.

In erotic literature today, emphasis is placed on the clitoris, the primary organ for arousal. But that association was not always known—by men, that is; women who masturbated recognized it. Freud claimed that a young girl masturbating massaged her clitoris. He believed that the sign of physical and emotional maturity in a married woman was a shifting of arousal from the clitoris to her vaginal canal—which places, of course, great significance on the role of the penis.

The Perfumed Garden

Before the importance of the clitoris was medically understood, erotic literature gave considerable attention to the vaginal "lips"—Indo-European root *leb,* "to hang loosely." In oral sex, a man's lips kiss a woman's "lips."

Sheik Umar ibn Muhammad al-Nafzawi, author of *The Perfumed Garden,* written in the sixteenth century, was obsessed with vaginal lips of all shapes and colors. His book forms part of a long tradition of Muslim treatises that combined sex education, philosophy, and science. Like the *Kama Sutra,* its Sanskrit counterpart, *Garden* is much more than a sex manual and achieves far greater poetic height. For its pure, free, nonobsessional, guilt-free eroticism, it's been compared with the biblical "Song of Solomon."

The Perfumed Garden was discovered by a French army officer in Algeria in the mid-nineteenth century and championed in France by Guy de Maupassant. It was sensuously translated by the great Victorian erotophile and bisexual Sir Richard Burton. Through personal research, the sheik had cataloged thirty-four different types of vulvas. In his own words:

• *Crested One.* It is the name of a vulva furnished with a red comb, like that of a cock, which rises and reddens at the moment of enjoyment.

• *Swelling One.* So called because when a torpid member comes near it, and rubs its head against it a few times, it at once swells and stands upright. At the moment of crisis, it opens and shuts convulsively, like the vulva of a mare.

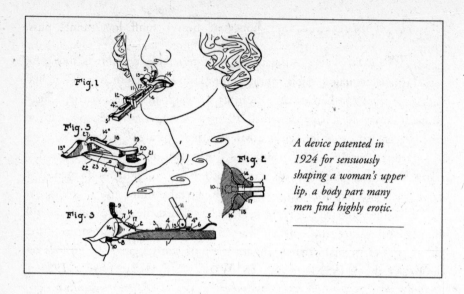

A device patented in 1924 for sensuously shaping a woman's upper lip, a body part many men find highly erotic.

• **Jumbo One.** This name applies to the vagina of women who are plump and fat. When such a woman crosses her thighs, one over the other, the vulva stands out like the head of a calf. If she lays back and lays it bare, it resembles corn planted between her thighs. And if she walks, it is apparent under her clothes by its wavy movement at each step.

• **Endless One.** This vulva extends from the pubis to the anus. It lengthens when a woman is lying down or standing up, and contracts when she is sitting. It looks like a splendid cucumber lying between the thighs.

• **Silent One.** This is the name of the vulva that makes no noise. The member may enter it a hundred times a day, but it will not say a word, it will be content to look on without a murmur.

• **Humpbacked One.** This vulva has the mount of Venus prominent and hard, standing like the hump on the back of a camel, and reaching down between the thighs like the head of a calf.

NICE AND NASTY TERMS FOR "VULVA" •

*W*hich words for female genitals do women themselves regard as nice or nasty? While no individual woman might agree with the entire list, here is a general breakdown, culled from several studies.

• **Nice Words:** Vagina, twat, honeypot, beaver, muff, love tunnel, puss, cunny, foxhole, fanny, love box, cooze, fur-burger, love nest, rosebud, baby factory, bush, fur pie, fuzzy-muzzy, garden of delight, hairy Mary, Holiday Inn, honeydew, home, jelly roll, kitty, lily puss, love cleft, playpen, pocket, poo-poo, poontang, poozle, put, snackbar, tee-tee, treasure box, vag, vertical smile, warmest place, wazoo.

• **Nasty Words:** Cunt, slit, snatch, crack, box, fish, stinkhole, bayonet wound, breaded clam, beaver trap, big cave, cheese factory, clit, empty tunnel, fish box, flabby lips, fuckhole, man trap, stink well, pee hole, rat hole, yeast bag, slash, snapper, stink pot, tuna, yeast mill.

WHAT MEN FIND SEXY IN WOMEN ◆ *According to a 1995 study, what people find sexy about others' bodies has changed radically over the last few decades. In the past, few women would have said that they liked a man with a large penis; now 65 percent do. Few men in the past would have openly stated that the shape of a woman's vulva was a major factor in her sexiness. Now many do.*

When a man is looking not necessarily for a wife but just good sex, here's what he's got in mind:

Sensuous, erotic mouth—83 percent
Full, firm breasts—80 percent
Long, shapely legs—77 percent
Slim, fatless figure—73 percent
Shaved pubis—67 percent
Rounded hips—64 percent
Shapely thighs—62 percent
Arched vulva—54 percent

Traits rated below 50 percent, in descending order: long, full hair; trim upper arms; small, firm breasts with large nipples.

CHAPTER 3

A Hard Man Is Good to Find

RACE TO RITUAL

*Anyone who knows Dan Quayle knows that
he would rather play golf than have sex any day.*

MARILYN QUAYLE

THE EVOLVING PENIS; AFRICA, 2 MILLION YEARS AGO ◆

Among all primates, human males have the largest penises; some measure eight to ten inches erect, and a few are bigger. With respect to body size, gorillas and orangutans have the smallest penises, a mere inch or two at most. A large, hirsute male body does not guarantee that its owner has a huge endowment.

Man, *Homo*, descended from apes: from *Homo habilis* ("handy man," or "toolmaker"), to *Homo erectus* ("upright man"—*erectus* suggests bipedalism not arousal), to *Homo sapiens* ("wise man"), to modern *Homo ludens* ("leisure-time man"). All evidence suggests that over the last 2 million years not only cranial capacity has been getting bigger. Without generating much scientific attention, the penis seems to have been evolving on its own—going, so to speak, *up* the size scale of evolution. The brain and penis have gotten bigger, and it's by no means certain that the process of enlargement has stopped.

Myths about penis size, like "big feet, big meat," are ancient. A 7,000-year-old rock drawing emphasizes one man's size.

Many myths surround the size—both length and girth—of a man's "most prized possession":

Big feet, big meat.
Tiny fingers, tickle fuck.
Big nose, big hose.
Full lips (on him), fill lips (in her)
All meat (big penis), no potatoes (small testes)
Hairy back, bad in the sack.

The last is an allusion to the belief that male sex hormones that might have contributed to a large penis were used up during puberty and thereafter to produce a hirsute body. By this reckoning (which no study has validated), the hairier the man, the smaller his endowment.

Height is also no guarantee that a man will be hung. One study of five hundred men found that the largest penis—a flaccid but firm five and a half inches—actually belonged to the shortest man in the group; he was under five-feet-five.

Any man who checks out his competition in the locker room discovers that all kinds of penile contradictions exist. A 250-pound football redneck can sport an adolescent-size member. A lanky, skin-and-bones drip can carry around a beer-can-thick dick. An obese Joe, with every part of his body burgeoning, can have a skinny prick.

Also, in some men, a small, flaccid penis can expand to a surprisingly large erection. On the other hand, some firm flaccid penises, impressive at rest, do not get appreciably bigger when engorged with blood. No study yet has correlated penile dimension with feet, hands, nose, height, earlobes, hairiness, or lips.

LIKE FATHER, LIKE SON •

*I*f you want to know the size of a man's erection before sleeping with him, the surest advice is, sleep with his father. Or ask his mother about the father. For what is in a man's jeans is first and foremost in his genes.

Penile size, as with many male physical characteristics, is largely a matter of heredity. A boy (XY) inherits his Y chromosome—the sex-determining one—from his father; he gets an X chromosome from his mother. Many body characteristics are "multifactorial," depending on mom, dad, the fetus's inuterine health, and the infant's proper nutrition early in life. Penis size has a lot to do with dad's size. If dad is hung, there's a good probability his sons will be too; and vice versa.

How Much Is Enough?

Worldwide studies show that the average man, regardless of race, rates his own penis as smaller than desirable. It's never big enough. African men feel this way, Asian men, Europeans, Hispanics, Eskimos, and Icelanders. American men rate *highest* on the scale of penile dissatisfaction—perhaps because American culture is saturated with the sexual imagery of big buffed bodies, and the general belief that "bigger is better" in everything. The average man, worldwide, realizes that his penis is perfectly functional but wishes it could be larger.

Within the last decade, several surveys on size have been conducted among gay men. Since a gay relationship involves *two* penises, it is only natural that there should be more comparison between "yours" and "mine." A gay man generally sees many more erections than his straight counterpart. With the added emphasis on competition, and a gay pornography industry based largely, if not exclusively, on superhung models, gay men rate higher than straight men in penis-size dissatisfaction.

One U.S. study on body image found that virtually all male respondents, except those few with truly extraordinary endowments, expressed doubts about their sexual performance based on penis size. In our modern culture,

Depiction of a man's large penis as a "feather in his cap," from Michelangelo's Scherzo, *c. 1512.*

women who get breast implants are often criticized for not being satisfied with their God-given body shape. But if surgical penile enlargement were as simple a matter as breast enhancement, studies suggest that men would probably outnumber women as candidates.

PENILE SIZE AND RACE ✦

*A*sians have tiny penises. Eskimos have fat ones. Irishmen have skinny ones. Italians sport sausage-size members. Blacks are blessed with colossal endowments. So goes conventional wisdom.

Most people when polled—men and women, in the United States and overseas—state that size is associated with race. Even though most people have not gone to bed with men from many different cultures, the suspicion is widespread and international.

The truth is, variation within races is enormous and no single study has come up with consistently satisfying answers.

Why do myths about size and race exist?

• Asians *are* shorter in stature than Europeans. Maybe this has lead to the erroneous conclusion that they have smaller penises.

• In America, blacks have historically been seen by some whites as a sexual threat—and temptation—to white women. Maybe this has led to the assumption that black men are sexually more potent and better hung.

• Italian men have been cast as the world's great lovers. Maybe this has led to the belief that they have thick penises that provide great pleasure. (A vagina is stimulated more by penile girth, which puts outward pressure on nerve endings, than by length, which is a much less significant dimension.)

• Irishmen traditionally have been pictured as having lean, tight, wiry frames with little flab. Maybe this has led to the belief that their penises are skinny and tightly circumcised—no spare skin.

• Eskimos, due to their cold climate, *are* round and fat. Maybe this has led to the belief that their penises are also round and fat.

We Americans seem to look at a man and, from his physical stature and country of origin, conclude what his erect penis must be like.

Kinsey researchers have reported that the largest flaccid penis they found among white men measured six and a half inches, while the largest soft penis among blacks was six and a quarter inches.

The average length for whites was four inches; for blacks four and a half inches. The average girth was one and a quarter inches for whites, one and three-quarters inches for blacks. As mentioned, there is less variation in size among erections.

THE ILLUSION OF BEING HUNG ◆

*M*ight there be some objective reason to back the apparently universal belief that black men have longer and thicker penises than white men?

During his extensive travels, bisexual explorer Sir Richard Burton collected measurements from men of Africa, India, Arabia, Europe, and South America. His conclusion:

> *Debauched women prefer negroes on the account of the size of their parts. I measured one man in Somali-land who, when quiescent, numbered nearly six inches. This is a characteristic of the negro race, and of African animals; e.g., the horse.*

Nineteenth-century French writer Louis Jacolliot dedicated three decades to surveying male members, especially the genitals of "semi-civilized" peoples from Africa to South America. He found the biggest penis—"a monstrous organ 11¾ inches long by 2.6 inches in diameter"—on a nineteen-year-old Mali boy. "This was a terrific machine . . . but this unfortunate young man

---

◆ HUNG LIKE A HUMPBACK WHALE ◆

Animal	Erect length
Humpback whale	*10 ft.*
Elephant	*6 ft.*
Bull	*3 ft.*
Stallion	*2½ ft.*
Walrus	*2 ft.*
Rhinoceros	*2 ft.*
Pig	*18 in.*
Elephant seal	*13¾ in.*
Tiger	*11 in.*
Man	*6 in.*
Sea lion	*5¾ in.*
Chimpanzee	*3 in.*
Gorilla	*2 in.*
Orangutan	*1½ in.*
Cat	*1 in.*
Mosquito	*$\frac{1}{100}$ in.*

---

could not find a Negress large enough to receive him with pleasure, and he was an object of terror to all the feminine sex."

Jacolliot's statistics on third world genitalia make up several volumes at the Kinsey Institute library. His primary conclusion:

> *In no branch of the human race are the male organs more developed than in the African Negro. I am speaking of the penis and not of the testicles, which are often smaller than those of the majority of Europeans . . . With the exception of the Arab, who runs him very close in this respect, the Negro of Senegal possesses the largest genital organ of all the races of mankind.*
>
> *The Negro is a real "man-stallion," and nothing can give a better idea (both as to colour and size) of the organ of the Negro, when erect, than*

Erotic mosaic of a black slave, emphasizing the belief that race and penis size are related, late first century.

the tool of a little African donkey. The absence of hairs on the pubes— which the Negroes remove—makes the resemblance more complete.

To repeat the question: might there be *some* objective reason to back the belief that black men have longer and thicker penises?

Whose Sponge Is Denser?

The solution may have something to do with the density of spongy penile tissue. By way of analogy, a dense kitchen sponge has lots of fibers and few holes; even when dry it does not shrink all that much. On the other hand, a sponge of less density has more airholes; as it dries, it shrivels. When wet —when both sponges are saturated fully with water—they may be about the same size.

Penises are really sponges—blood sponges. It has been suggested, but not proved, that blacks on the average have denser penile tissue than whites. Therefore, the flaccid penis of a black man may appear fuller and firmer. White men, with less dense erectile tissue, can watch their penises shrivel into their pubic hair, disappearing almost entirely from view.

If the observation on density is correct, then black penises *appear* larger when flaccid but expand less than white penises. White penises, on the other hand, start off small and shrunken but expand to comparable size. This would also account for the fact that there is less variation in size among erections by race—six inches, on average.

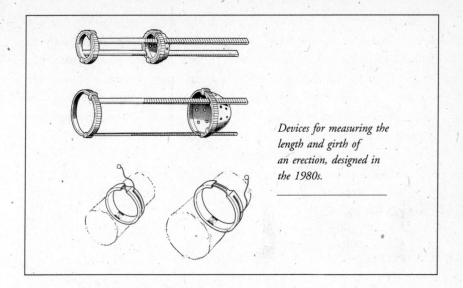

Devices for measuring the length and girth of an erection, designed in the 1980s.

Burton and Jacolliot came to these conclusions. From their extensive investigations, they argued that a large flaccid penis usually does not get much larger when engorged with blood:

> *The size of the Negro part, imposing as it is quiescent, does not increase proportionally during erection, as in the European male. Nonetheless, in my time, no man would take his womenfolk to Zanzibar on account of the huge temptation there, and thereby offend them.* Richard Burton.
> *The penis of the Negro, even when in complete erection, is still soft . . . . When pressed by the hands it feels like a thick India-rubber tube full of liquid. When flabby, the Negro's penis still retains a size and consistency that are greater than that of the European, whose organ shrivels up and becomes limp.* (Louis Jacolliot)

Always Semierect

The Bushmen of Africa's Kalahari region have what appear to Western eyes to be semierect penises all the time. The Bushmen's members are always slightly extended and moderately firm. Physical examination by touch has revealed that the inner penis cylinder is superdense in spongy erectile tissue. But—and here is the significant observation—when that tissue fills with blood, the solid erection is only slightly fuller and longer than the "flaccid" penis. Bushmen have dense sponges. It may be a misnomer to call a Bushman's penis "flaccid," since it never really shrinks to bantam size.

Interestingly, there are also white men, though fewer in number, whose penises appear to be perpetually semierect, always plump and slightly extended away from the thigh, and never flaccid. In locker rooms, these men are often embarrassed because other men assume they're aroused and sporting erections. Two of my friends have this problem—or fortunate condition. Even when taking cold showers, their penises never dwindle to wrinkled stubs. Both men are heterosexuals and feel uncomfortable with the attention their "semierect" penises get at the gym. "Gay guys think I'm a cocktease," one confessed to me, "but there's nothing I can do about it. I'm not trying to get their attention. My dick always looks semihard. It was *really* embarrassing in high school."

EVOLUTIONARY ORIGIN?—IN COLD WEATHER THE PENIS SHRIVELS ◆

*W*hy might black men have denser erectile tissue than whites? Might there be some ancient, evolutionary reason?

To put it another way—using the Bushmen as a modern-day example—why might the penises of black men in Africa not shrivel and retract close to the body?

The African climate is warm year-round, so the free-swinging penis runs no risk from windchill or frostbite. Farther north, where winters are frigid, men's flaccid penises shrink and protectively hide in the warmth of the pubic bush. They come out only when they see something that really interests them. A shrunken penis, warmed by its proximity to the crotch and shielded in dense hair, is a safe penis—one that will go on to reproduce itself. As the human race moved out of Africa and into cooler climates, perhaps penises that *could* retract—because they had less dense erectile tissue—had an adaptive advantage.

No man likes to undress in front of others in an ice-cold locker room. I have seen men, when the locker room is chilly, undress and immediately tug on their penises to lengthen them, before heading off to the showers.

As every man should know—and all women should be forewarned—six activities or conditions can make the average relaxed male penis shrink by as much as two inches:

- Standing or working in cold weather.
- Taking a cold shower.

*A man's penis shrinks a bit immediately after viewing or participating
in a sport's victory, a result of his satisfaction.*

- Extreme body exhaustion or mental fatigue.
- Intense nonsexual excitement: a pay raise, for example, or when a favorite team scores a touchdown or makes a basket. In stadiums across the country, every penis shrinks a little when the team its owner is rooting for scores. The intense nonsexual excitement causes his penis to retreat to a superrelaxed state. He's satisfied.
- Sex that was satisfactory—women are well aware of this.
- Sex that was disappointing.

"PENIS ENVY"; SIGMUND FREUD, 1925 ✦

*M*en *do* envy larger penises. But do women experience it, as Freud claimed in his most phallocentric idea?

One of the key concepts in Freud's theory of female sexuality is every little girl's sudden recognition—and horror—that she does not have a penis like her brothers or male playmates. For her, this traumatic truth is the first realization that she is different—and not in a positive sense.

The consequences are numerous, negative, and lifelong, if Freud is to be believed. A little girl becomes envious. Jealousy sets in. She blames her mother for having had her castrated—the only explanation for her lack.

THE ACCOMMODATING VAGINA ◆ *Most men when questioned say they want an erect penis eight to ten inches long, rather than the average six inches. But the average vagina is between three to five inches in length. In its normal "collapsed" state, it is wide enough to accommodate two to three fingers.*

During sexual arousal, helped immensely by foreplay, the inner two-thirds of the canal increases in length an additional two inches—and widens to a full two inches. This is known as the ballooning effect. *It protects a woman from the painful pounding of a long erection. Well-endowed men have an obligation to engage in adequate foreplay.*

While the inner two-thirds is elongating, the outer one-third—the first two inches—is narrowing, swelling up and getting tighter. This is due to vasoconstriction from blood engorging the tissues. The net result is that there is a gripping effect *around the penis, so girth may be less of a problem than most men think.*

The average penis and the average vagina make a perfect match, mainly because the vagina is remarkably accommodating. A man seeking a "tight" vagina along the entire tract is looking either for a virgin or a woman who is not aroused and thus not ready for penetration.

The vagina makes allowances for variations in penile size only to a point. Repeated childbirth—at least two births—stretches the vaginal muscles, and the canal loses tone and elasticity. (Certain exercises can help a woman regain some tightness.) A penis of average size can easily feel lost in the superrelaxed atmosphere of a stretched vagina. This is a common concern of wives in their late thirties and forties who've had several children, and a common complaint of husbands. Sex therapists deal with this private his-and-her problem all the time.

A woman's sexual pleasure depends less on penile length than on girth, because the inner two-thirds of the vagina has fewer nerves than the outer two inches, which are rich in nerve endings. For a woman, maximum arousal comes from stimulation of the first third of the vagina.

(Freud, of course, had a penis, as did his male followers who popularized the concept.) The girl develops a deep sense of inferiority. Eventually, to reacquire the missing penis, she symbolically "takes her father as a love-object," since *his* penis has never been cut off. Always on the lookout for her own lost member, she replaces her father in time with other men—who all have intact penises. Eventually, resigned to the loss of her own penis, she seeks to be fulfilled by having a child—as if the fetus, in exiting from her vagina, provides at least a temporary image of a penis.

This scenario has not pleased many people. Here is another spin on penis envy:

"BREAST ENVY"; 1980S ♦

That female sexuality and personality are based pivotally on a "deficiency"—penis envy—was first attacked in the 1930s by German-born psychoanalyst Karen Horney.

Thirty years later, the idea of penis envy was being trounced. Feminists like Betty Friedan allowed that Freud was a true genius but dreamed up the concept to account for the numerous frustrations—and consequent hysteria and neuroses—that Victorian women experienced in their sexually repressed times. With no outlets for their creative talents or sexual appetites, women acted screwy—men didn't—so Freud assumed it was because women didn't have penises and men did. Only a man would come to that conclusion.

Feminists today still hotly debate the concept. Some argue that penis envy refers not to a real anatomical organ but to society's general favoring of males above females. Women are envious of how society treats men. They don't want penises—just equality.

Others argue that unsuccessful men, who perform poorly in sports, fail out of college, and lose one job after another—when women are excelling in these areas today—are victims of "breast envy." The men have never gotten over the fact that their mothers had breasts and they didn't. They're jealous and feel inferior. They continually seek out relationships with large-breasted women as symbolic substitutes for what they themselves will never have. Some men secretly contemplate getting breast implants.

Feminists espousing this view at least have a sense of humor.

HELP IN GETTING IT UP: RODS, PUMPS, MEGS, AND INJECTIONS; 1980S TO PRESENT ◆

*W*e live in the golden age of penis science. Researchers who might have once built suspension bridges now specialize in penile-erection engineering or go into the related field of prosthetic penile plumbing, a subspeciality of hydrodynamics.

To date, these scientists are almost exclusively men, and their goal is make erections possible for other men by using ingenious mechanical aids. Due to traumatic penile injury, disease, or psychological impediments some thirty million American men are thought to need help in getting it up and keeping it hard. Help beyond what a mate or lover can provide. Help that can come only from a penile engineer. Unfortunately, only about five million of these men each year muster the courage—and overcome their embarrassment—to get to a doctor's office.

Rod Implant—the Long and Hard of It

In various forms, this implant aid has been available since the 1970s. It comes in two basic types: semirigid and flexible.

The semirigid implant rod gives a man a permanent erection, something familiar to many adolescents. During the day he must place his erection against the abdomen and hold it there with tight jockey shorts or the band of a jockstrap. If it breaks free, it is potentially a source of embarrassment.

Penile rods are about three to four inches long and are usually inserted in pairs down the sides of the penis. Sometimes the rods are thick enough that a penis has a normal erection girth.

The newer silicon flexirod resembles a small breadstick and has a firm wire running down its center. Bent into one position, up or down, it will stay that way indefinitely, like a child's plastic figurine whose arms and legs can be twisted into various configurations.

When a woman undergoes an operation to become a transsexual man, her new penis, fashioned out of folds of her own fat, tissue, and skin, is often implanted with a semirigid or flexible rod.

Inflatable Pump—the Ballooning Member

The pump is a state-of-the-art improvement over the silicon rod implant, a wonder of hydrodynamics miniaturization. The pump system comprises three parts that must be surgically inserted. In one version, a small squeeze pump

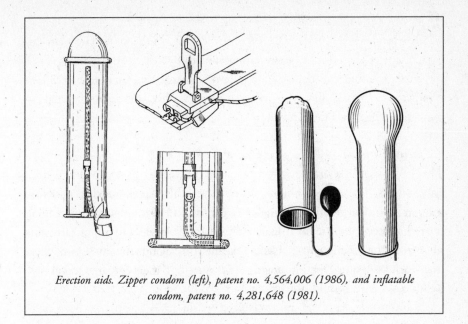

Erection aids. Zipper condom (left), patent no. 4,564,006 (1986), and inflatable condom, patent no. 4,281,648 (1981).

chamber is implanted inside the man's scrotum. It's connected by silicon tubes to a reservoir, containing sterile water, implanted in the lower abdomen, just above the junction where the penis connects to the torso. The scrotal pump is also connected by silicon tubes to two hollow rods running down the length of the penis.

When the man wants an erection, he manually squeezes his scrotum, maybe ten to fifteen times. This causes the scrotal pump to force water from the reservoir into the inflatable rods running along the penis. The penis slowly rises—and will stay up until the man squeezes an "off" valve in his scrotum (or in his abdomen) that drains the water out of the rods and back into the reservoir. Such inflatable prostheses have also been used in female-to-male transsexual surgery, given the newly created man his first—and fully functional—penis.

MEG—Male Electronic Genital Stimulator

The signal to get an erection comes from the pudendal nerves in the lower spine. Some cases of impotence result from malfunction of these pudendal nerves—"pudendal," from the Latin *pudendus,* "shameful."

The Male Electronic Genital Stimulator, or MEG, is a small, self-contained device that is battery operated. Before intercourse, the man inserts the device into his anus. With external controls, he turns on the current, which stimulates the pudendal nerves and creates an erection. The man can raise or lower the current, maintaining control over his performance. When the current is shut off, the erection subsides. Medically, the device is termed noninvasive. But the man who has to insert it into his anus before lovemaking may challenged that definition.

Vacuum Pump—Pump Up the Volume

This is a Plexiglas cylinder that a man places over his flaccid penis. With a hand pump, he creates a vacuum in the tube. This allows blood to flow into the penis, which gradually becomes engorged and erect. The cylinder is removed and an entrapment ring is clamped at the base of the shaft. The ring maintains the erection by keeping the blood from flowing back out of the penis. Since trapped penile blood is potentially dangerous, and eventually painful, the ring should not be left in place for more than thirty minutes.

As the story goes, the pump was invented in 1974 by an auto parts salesman who, at age seventy-two, found he was suddenly impotent. He built his own pump and tested it on himself. Then, door-to-door salesman that he was, he took the device on the road, demonstrating it to urologists—and any impotent man who would watch. What they watched was a grainy film of the inventor pumping up his erection and tying it off.

Needle Dick—One- to Six-Hour Hard-ons

More recently, doctors have developed a class of drugs that, when injected directly into the penile shaft, can induce an erection lasting up to an hour. One such drug, called a vasodilator, is alprostadil. It chemically causes dilation of the penile arteries. The shaft fills with blood, the penis becomes erect, and pressure inside the penis prevents most of the blood from draining off. Until, that is, the vasodilator wears off.

The technique was developed in the 1980s by British physiologist Giles Brindley, who served as his own guinea pig. Writing in a medical journal, he explained, "My penis has received forty-one intracavernosal injections for experimental purposes between August 1982 and March 1983 [i.e., about one experimental erection a week], and it is still capable of full erection [on its own]."

The quantity of drug injected is crucial. In the early days of experimentation, some subjects got full erections that lasted for six hours or more and became quite painful. A new class of vasodilators holds great promise for

Erotic dance around "The Tree of Life," 1832.

many impotent men. The one drawback is that a man must stick a needle into his penis every time he wants an erection. For some men, this might be enough to kill the desire entirely.

PENILE ENLARGEMENT: TWO INCHES IN LENGTH, ONE INCH IN GIRTH; 1990S ◆

At several U.S. clinics, a man can have about two inches added to the length of his penis and two more inches added to its girth—all for about six thousand dollars. The operation takes less than an hour, is performed under local anesthesia, and is gaining in popularity, although it has yet to be approved by the American Urological Association.

One pioneer of surgical enlargement is Dr. Melvyn Rosenstein, a Culver City, California, board-certified urologist. An avid promoter of the technique, Rosenstein has built a practice on the belief that thousands of men dream of being larger. "A young man's first wish is to be an instant billionaire," says Rosenstein. "The second wish is that the ten most beautiful women in the world find him irresistible. We all know what the third wish is."

The surgery is fairly simple. Rosenstein claims to perform about six operations a day and has done as many as fourteen in a workday. To understand how penile lengthening is achieved, you have to realize that the penis—and especially the erection—is held tightly to the lower abdomen by "suspensory ligaments," something like the cables that hold up a suspension bridge. When the ligaments are surgically cut, the penis falls forward, away from the abdominal wall (the pubic bone), effectively *appearing* longer—as much as two inches longer. What was once "hidden penis" in the abdomen is now hanging free.

This alters the look of an erection. With the penile cables snipped, a hard-on is never again as horizontal as it once was; the suspension bridge now dangles in the wind. An erection is still firm and now longer, if downwardly inclined.

During the operation, an inch or two of girth can be added to the penis. Fatty tissue is siphoned from other parts of the body, often the thigh or buttocks, and injected with a syringe under the skin of the penis. In its flaccid state, the fattened penis is soft, fleshy, and may feel a little lumpy. In its erect state, the fattened penis feels strangely mushy and pulpy for something dubbed a hard-on, or boner. Fat injections may have to be regularly updated.

More and more surgeons are performing the simple operation. Many are advertising, some with copy that preys on a man's personal sense of inadequacy:

- He's the nicest guy I ever dated, but he's just too small.
- Even after two hours of racquetball, he wouldn't take a shower.
- Why be average? Be a niner.

Rosenstein hopes that one day penis enlargement will be "as common as breast implants."

There is one drawback to the lengthening surgery. The added inches gained when the penis falls forward, away from the abdomen, are covered by pubic hair. Thus, a man must shave the upper end of his penis every few days or suffer pubic hair shadow and stubble.

JEWISH FORESKIN RITUAL; GENESIS 17:10–14, C. 1400 B.C.E. ◆

A five-minute operation, done within days of an infant's birth and without his consent, marks a male for life.

For doctors, circumcision is a highly profitable operation; it is America's most common surgical procedure. For parents, to circumcise or not is a vexing question, since medical evidence suggests that removal of the foreskin

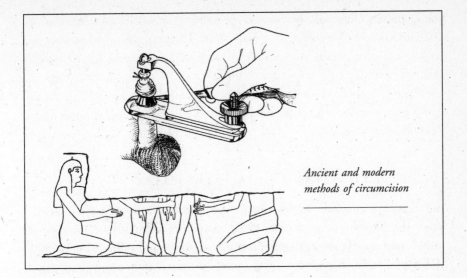

*Ancient and modern
methods of circumcision*

of the penis has negligible health benefits so long as a man practices good hygiene.

The word "circumcise" comes from the late ecclesiastic Latin *circumcidere*, "to cut around." Though the word is rooted in the Church Latin that developed during the early centuries of Christianity, the practice was of Semitic origin, prescribed in Hebrew Scripture, when God says to Abraham:

> *This is my covenant, which you shall keep between me and you, and with your seed after you: Every boy among you shall be circumcised . . . It shall be a token of the covenant between you and me . . . He who is eight days old shall be circumcised . . . And the uncircumcised child whose flesh of his foreskin is not circumcised, his soul shall be cut off from his people, for he has broken my covenant.* (Genesis 17:10–14)

Jewish infants have been routinely circumcised for three millennia. To this day Jews refer to the circumcision initiation of a newborn into Judaism on the eighth day after his birth as *b'rith*, meaning "pact."

The absence of a foreskin became the indelible "signature" on a spiritual contract, imprinted into the genitals of every male. Circumcision also became a sign of the Lord's divine protection over the Jewish people. Among the ancient Israelites, circumcision initially had nothing to do with health considerations.

Some people believe that God instituted circumcision. Others, including many modern biblical scholars, especially feminist ones, disagree. They claim that circumcision was the idea of male Israelite priests, an effort to start an exclusive all-male club—the Jewish priesthood—that could receive no female, since initiation was sacrifice of the foreskin. "Once women were priestesses in the Near East," writes one feminist scholar. "To get rid to them, a Levite clan of male priests dreamed up the rite of circumcision. Soon, there were no more priestesses."

CHRIST'S FORESKIN CURES INFERTILITY ◆

*H*erodotus, the fifth-century B.C.E. Greek historian, wrote that circumcision could prevent penile infections and supplant the need for regular washing. This was the first medical advice on the subject. By the time of Christ's birth, the practice was being advocated both for religious and hygienic reasons.

Being a Jew, Christ was circumcised on the eighth day after his birth, which the early Christian church would elevate to the Feast of the Circumcision, later dated January first.

For centuries, dried rings of skin alleged to be Christ's "holy prepuce"—Latin *praeputium*, "foreskin"—were venerated as sacred relics by dozens of churches throughout Europe. Many churches claimed to have the original; others claimed to have "relics by association," human foreskins that had once touched Christ's skin. Pastors used these relics to bestow fertility on barren parishioners, as well as to lessen the pain of childbirth, since Christ's mother, it is said, never experienced labor. The best-known relic of Christ's prepuce, at the Chartreuse abbey church, is said to be responsible for thousands of pregnancies.

MANLINESS MYTHS AND CIRCUMCISION; GREECE, FIFTH CENTURY B.C.E. ◆

*M*yths began to surround the Jewish religious ritual of circumcision. In the first century, Philo of Alexandria, a Hellenistic Jewish philosopher, taught that circumcision facilitated conception: "By the penis being circumcised, the seed proceeded in its path more easily, neither being scattered, nor flowing on its passage into what may be called the bags of the prepuce."

Philo asserted that people who enforced the practice, mainly Jews at the

Following Jewish law, Christ was circumcised eight days after his birth. His alleged foreskin was thought to have miraculous healing powers, especially in overcoming infertility.

time, would be the most prolific on earth, destined to be the most populous and influential race. This was an appealing promise for any man who wanted to rise up in station. Philo promised, in effect, that circumcised men would eventually rule the world. Philo himself was circumcised.

The Embarrassment of Jews at the Gym

Not all Jews in Philo's time were proud of their penile signature. When Hellenistic Jews living in Greek lands shared the gymnasia with their uncircumcised Greek friends, exercising in the nude, unavoidably revealing their mark of distinction, they often became the butt of ridicule, flouted for being "demanned." Still worse was the charge that Jewish men seemed to have constant semierections, the result of overly tight circumcisions.

Many Jews living in Greece underwent the unpleasantness of reconstruction therapy to restore genital foreskin. The procedure was known as "stretching." The residue of foreskin was forcibly pulled up over the glans penis and tightly tied. The mildly painful treatment was continued until a Jew had sufficient surplus skin to conceal the "seal of Abraham." From a religious standpoint, such a man was no longer a Jew. His soul, according to Genesis, was "cut off" from his people, since he'd broken his covenant with God.

WHY CHRISTIAN MALES ARE CIRCUMCISED; AMERICA, 1890S •

*I*n the decades following Christ's death, Gentile men wishing to convert to the new faith of Christianity balked at the thought of having their foreskins removed. Prior to the advent of antiseptics and anesthesia, the surgery performed on adults was both dangerous and painful—and intimidating.

Saint Paul realized that this ritual requirement was preventing many grown men from becoming Christians. The evangelist allowed male converts to forego the surgical cut for what Paul termed a "circumcision of the heart" —a fervent desire to become a Christian. Paul maintained contact with the major Christian churches of the day, and in his Epistle to the Romans (2: 28–29) he allowed circumcision "of the heart, in the Spirit, and not in the letter."

In 60 C.E., about two years after Paul wrote the epistle, the apostolic council ruled that Gentile proselytes could retain their foreskins.

In time, the sacrament of baptism became the covenant—or pact—for Christians that circumcision was for Jews.

For the next eighteen hundred years, Christian males were *never* circumcised—not in Europe (where the practice is still uncommon) or in the United States.

Why, then, are virtually all American Christian males circumcised?

Constant Horniness—or Satan's Curse?

Most American parents don't realize that prior to 1900 Christian infants were never circumcised. It simply wasn't done. Routine circumcision was adopted gradually, as a result of two factors: the Victorian era's strictures against masturbation and the medical community's belief that this odious form of "self-pollution" could be restrained by removal of a boy's foreskin. Nineteenth-century doctors convinced Christian parents—and priests and preachers—that a tight, gripping foreskin put a male in a state of continual arousal. The issue of cleanliness initially played no role in the matter.

The man who popularized the practice among non-Jews was the British surgeon and pathologist Sir Jonathan Hutchinson (1828–1913). A pioneer in the study of congenital syphilis, Hutchinson was an authority on eye and skin diseases, especially leprosy. Outside his specialty, he maintained that masturbation was a detriment to spiritual and mental health. Almost two

The condition of "continual horniness" depicted as "Satan's curse."

decades before he was knighted in 1908, he published "On Circumcision as Preventative of Masturbation," the first position paper for routine modern infant circumcision.

Thus the fundamental reason behind the practice was not so much medical as religious after all—not as a covenant with God but to prevent a boy or grown man from giving his soul to Satan. Only later did doctors affix to the procedure a health rationale.

After Hutchinson's paper was printed in America, parents begged physicians to circumcise their infant sons. There are many accounts of *adult* males willingly submitting to the surgery in the hope of breaking themselves of the habit of masturbation. British psychologist and pioneer sexologist Havelock Ellis (1859–1939) thought the idea of routine circumcision was utter nonsense, arguing, "Ninety-nine percent of young men and women masturbate occasionally, and the hundredth conceals the truth."

By the 1920s, a standard American medical text claimed that a foreskin leads to "nocturnal incontinence [wet dreams], hysteria [hyperactivity], epilepsy, and feeble-mindedness."

The year the film *Gone With the Wind* was released, 1939, the standard text on pediatrics, *Holt's Diseases of Infancy and Childhood,* stated that masturbation was "medically harmful" and advocated the remedy of "circumcision in boys."

How Hospital Births Made Circumcision Routine in America ◆

*T*he practice of routine male circumcision went hand in hand with another twentieth-century phenomenon: hospitalization for childbirth.

In 1900, less than 5 percent of American women delivered in hospitals; by 1920 the figure stood at 40 percent, and a decade later it was up to 75 percent. For the first time in history, most infants were not being born at home.

With the new mother recovering from delivery at one end of a hospital, and the father isolated in the waiting room, parents often had little say about—and even less awareness of—what was being done to their newborn son. The infant was given to the mother already circumcised, and she assumed that was standard procedure, surgery performed in the best interest of her baby. Few questions were asked in an era when doctors were revered without reserve.

It is no coincidence that the circumcision of male infants became widespread during the period when nearly all U.S. births took place in hospitals. Whether the fact that doctors charged for the surgery influenced their belief in its benefits is always open to debate and may never be thoroughly discredited.

Today, circumcision is an elective procedure. A recent study concluded that uncircumcised infants and adults males run a slightly higher risk of urinary tract infections if the area under the foreskin is not cleaned regularly. An open wound from a serious infection can become a site for entry of a more harmful bug, like the AIDS virus. A 1988 report suggested that the spread of AIDS among heterosexuals in Africa might be due to skin lesions beneath foreskins, the result of careless hygiene. However, proper hygiene seems to place cut and uncut males in the same risk categories for all kinds of infections and sexually transmitted diseases.

Male Genital Rituals; Worldwide ◆

*T*oday, the whole world knows about the horror of ritual female circumcision—cutting away the clitoris and most of the external genitals. The clitoridectomy, as it's called, is performed on young girls in Africa, India, and Egypt in the belief that it lessens a wife's sexual arousal and

> **PEELING THE PEARL** ◆ *If removal of the foreskin was thought to be the remedy for the sin of male masturbation, what did doctors advise —just decades ago—to prevent females from "self-pollution"?*
>
> *Believe it or not, the same medical text, Holt in its 1940 edition, advised surgeons to perform electrical female circumcision: "Cauterization of the clitoris, and blistering of the vulva and prepuce for recalcitrant female masturbators."*
>
> *This butchery was performed on institutionalized women—schizophrenics, depressives, criminals—who were caught stimulating their clitorises. The women had no say in the matter, and their families were told the procedure was done for the inmates' own sake. This is what textbooks were teaching American pediatricians on the eve of World War II.*

diminishes her desire for extramarital affairs. Since it makes intercourse so painful, it also discourages virgins from having sex before marriage.

In Egypt, about 80 percent of young girls are circumcised before puberty—usually by a village woman, in unsterile conditions, and without anesthesia. The medical complications from the surgery—shock, hemorrhage, infection, tetanus, blood poisoning—are a nightmare.

"Islam says circumcision for men is a tradition of the Prophet," says Egyptian cleric Sheik Taha Gad. "Men are obligated to emulate the Prophet and be circumcised. For women it is a virtue."

Less well known are the rituals of male genital mutilation. These are seldom discussed in the media, perhaps because journalists have traditionally been males, and men can be squeamish when it comes to any kind of penile surgery. Some rituals are ancient; others are still performed. Many leave the penis in unusual shapes. Some involve the testes.

Dumbo Dick

Polynesians slit the foreskin lengthwise at puberty. This is a form of partial circumcision that leaves a large fleshy flap of skin around the glans, or head. Flaccid, a penis at its tip looks like a fan; erect, it resembles Dumbo the elephant—all ears.

Nut Case

Most of the civilized world knows that a man's sperm count is a factor in achieving conception. The average ejaculate contains about 500 million sperm, most of which die before they even get near the egg. Only a few have a chance to implant themselves into the egg. Only one makes it. Since more sperm means better odds, two balls are better than one.

Except among some African peoples. In parts of equatorial Africa, a father who wishes to have a large family has one of his testes removed. This is done in the belief that he will be more potent, because the removed testicle is burned as an offering to the god of fertility.

Strength in Sperm

In ancient Greece, the most talented discus throwers, runners, and wrestlers would stretch the foreskin over the top of the glans penis and tightly tie it off. This prevented the athlete from having intercourse or masturbating, since even a slight erection was excruciatingly painful. Athletes believed then—and some believe today—that retaining sperm increases physical prowess.

Prick Piercing

In imperial Rome, musicians and actors often pierced their foreskin to have golden rings, coins, and other charms inserted. Men boasted of the number of rings in their foreskin, which were supposed to enhance a woman's pleasure during intercourse. For centuries the practice all but vanished—until recently. Penis piercing—and vagina piercing—have returned as a sexual trend among teenagers. They, too, report that it enhances the pleasure of intercourse.

Silver Bells

The Peguans of south Myanmar have for centuries surgically implanted tiny metal bells *under* their foreskins—turning dongs into dingdongs. The advantages are twofold: the tinkle of bells is a festive turn-on for women, who also like the hard feel of the bells during intercourse. Bells also give the man's penis extra girth.

Whistle Cock

In several African societies, only the chief and his eldest son, and sometimes the eldest sons of prominent tribal members, were permitted to father children. To make certain that no lesser males impregnated women, men had a traverse surgical cut made across the urethra at the juncture where the penis connects with the scrotum. A man could still get an erection and ejaculate, but his semen—like his urine—never shot out from the tip of his penis but dribbled from the incision. Europeans who first saw a penis with a hole whittled at its base dubbed it a "whistle cock."

Long Dong Silver—Eighteen Inches and Growing

Porn star Long Dong Silver claimed to have an eighteen-inch member. Many men in one part of the world actually do.

As noted, a boy's penis starts to grow at puberty and reaches adult size by age seventeen, except for boys of the Karamojong people of northeastern Uganda. Starting at puberty, the boys, who go around naked, have weights tied to the ends of their penis. When a boy gets accustomed to the pain of a light weight, it's replaced by a heavier one.

The weights are circular disks, sculpted from stone. They have a hole at the center, through which they're tied to the end of the penis. The combination of penis and disk resembles a clock's pendulum—and swings as freely. It is common for a teenage boy to eventually carry around a twenty-pound weight or more.

By the age of seventeen, his penis can easily measure eighteen inches. As impressive as that sounds, there's a catch. What the boy gains in length, he looses in girth, since the spongy erectile tissue that lines the shaft of the penis does not multiply, but only stretches. Stretched penises can get annoyingly long: men accidentally sit on them; most men take to tying their ropelike members into knots. And double knots. For Karamojong women, long, skinny penises are a turn-on.

THE LINK BETWEEN BURNED FORESKIN AND PERFUME; PRE-JUDAISM ◆

*I*n several parts of the world men are still burning foreskins as tokens of good luck. The practice is ancient and predates circumcision by many centuries.

Early peoples believed that nothing good in life was free; a god or goddess had to be paid for the gift of a plentiful harvest or bountiful offspring. A man's sexual prowess was viewed as a gift from the god of fertility. To maintain his virility, a man sacrificed a small part of his instrument of propagation—the smallest part possible. Among many clans, a bit of the

*Incense, used to mask the stench of burning sacrificial flesh,
evolved into perfume.*

excess skin at the top of the penis (not a full circumcision) seemed a fair payment. Cut off with a sharpened stone, the bit of foreskin became a burned offering.

To reduce the stench of burning flesh, incense like frankincense and myrrh were tossed into the flames, producing "perfume." The origin of this appealing word, which represents the multibillion-dollar fragrance industry, is from Latin, *per + fumus,* meaning "through smoke." Perfume originated to mask the scent of burned offerings. Large quantities of "perfume" were doused on the burning innards and carcasses that were also offered to various gods.

Egyptian writings and drawings from 3000 B.C.E. attest to the custom of offering a foreskin—with perfume. In most ancient rites, boys were circumcised not at birth but when they reached sexual maturity and were about to marry. The Arabic term for "bridegroom," *chatan,* supposedly derived from an ancient expression for "a husband is cut [circumcised]." Burned foreskin was the fee a husband "paid" up front (so to speak) for the guarantee of fatherhood.

Foreskins as Dowry

Perhaps the worst case of male genital mutilation occurred around the eleventh century B.C.E., when two hundred men were slaughtered for their foreskins. The gruesome tale comes from Book 1 of Samuel. Samuel, last of the Hebrew judges, was the nation's leader before Saul, the first king, was anointed. Times were bad. Religious worship was at a low, the economy in shambles, and the Philistine army threatened to destroy the nation of Israel. Saul, who was to commit suicide rather than be captured by the Philistines, assigned David a formidable task:

> *And Saul said, Thus shall you say to David, The king desires no dowry, but a hundred foreskins of the Philistines, to be avenged for the king's enemies . . . Wherefore David arose and went, he and his men, and slew two hundred Philistine men, and brought their foreskins, and gave them in full tale to the king, that he might be the king's son-in-law.* (1 Samuel 18:25–27)

MEN PREFER YOUNGER WOMEN ♦ *Worldwide, in every culture studied, most men prefer women who are younger than themselves. While an individual man may prefer an older woman, that is not the majority's choice.*

The age gap between men and the women they prefer varies from one culture to another. Scandinavian men like their women two years younger. American men prefer to marry women who are younger by one and a half to two and a half years. In Greece, the age gap is five years.

In Nigeria and Zambia, the age gap is seven years. The men of Yemen like their women to be a full ten years younger. In polygamous societies, like the Tiwi of northern Australia, the preferred age gap is twenty or even thirty years. A girl is considered ready to marry and bear children after her first period.

Interestingly, the age gap in all cultures widens as men age. Most men as they grow older find relatively younger and younger women sexually attractive. They may not find these women conversationally interesting—in fact, they may have nothing at all in common with them—yet they are sexually turned on by a woman's youth. The average American man in his fifties, for instance, prefers his ideal sexual partner to be at least ten to twenty years younger.

Whatever men's theoretical preference might be, in most cultures it is only high-status males, with position and money, who have easy access to much younger females.

Researchers have found this male preference for younger women throughout history. Like it or loathe it, it seems to be part of a man's genetic sexual programming. Younger women are, on average, healthier and sturdier, and they can bear more children and live longer to rear them.

Perhaps none of this should come as a surprise. Throughout the animal kingdom, most males prefer younger females. There are exceptions—especially among animals that breed only a few offspring at a time, like chimpanzees and gorillas. In these cases, a male may choose a slightly older female, because she has already demonstrated that she is fertile and can care for her offspring.

Apparently, at a fundamental level, the continuance of the species is programmed into all creatures' sexual selections. And youth is viewed as a major asset.

CHAPTER 4

Polishing the Pearl

DILDOS TO VIBRATORS

*I like to wake up each morning
feeling a new man.*

JEAN HARLOW

"CHERRY"—LOSS OF VIRGINITY; PRE-SECOND CENTURY C.E. ◆

When a girl looses her "cherry," she's no longer a virgin. For many centuries, a virgin's crotch was called a "cherry pie." A bride-to-be was "cherry ripe"; on the wedding night, the groom "popped her cherry." How did the name of a fruit come to symbolize the rupturing of the hymen?

Two word origins:

Cherry: from the Latin *ceresia,* a name derived by the ancients from the city of Cerasus, on the Black Sea, renowned for its cherry trees, which bore sweet, dark red fruit.

Hymen: Greek patron of marriage; with a lowercase *h,* a wedding song or poem; from the Greek *hymen,* meaning "a membrane," and, through the Indo-European root *syumen,* related to the word "seam."

The loss of a young woman's virginity has long been described as "popping her cherry," a reference to the similarity between blood and cherry juice.

As a fruit, the cherry is dark, blood red, with a firm outer skin that, when ruptured, exposes soft, juicy layers that, in turn, surround a pit. Cherry juice stains like blood, and the two bear a striking resemblance. A virgin deflowered on white sheets left the same stain as that left on a cloth used to squeeze out the juice of cherries. This is one theory on how the ancients came to associate the fruit with the hymen.

"Cherry Tree Carol"

Another explanation involves a tree quite different from the one in the Garden of Eden.

The "Cherry Tree Carol" is a fifteenth-century ballad that recounts how Jesus, still in the womb, performed his first miracle. As Mary and Joseph strolled through a cherry orchard, Mary asked her husband to reach up and pick a cherry, but Joseph refused. At that moment, Mary felt a kick in her womb, and the branch of one tree bent down and offered all of its fruit.

The only problem with relating this story to the loss of virginity is that Mary, in Roman Catholic theology, remained a lifelong virgin; her hymen was never broken. The appeal of the story for many Christians has more to do with its parallel to the fruit of the tree at Eden. The apple symbolizes disobedience and the entry of evil into the world; the cherry in the carol symbolizes obedience and redemption, through Christ, from evil.

VIRGINITY AS A PREREQUISITE TO MARRIAGE; ANTIQUITY TO TWENTIETH CENTURY ◆

Virgin: from the Latin *virgo*, "maiden"; akin to *virga*, meaning a new, young twig, or a slender, shapeless branch.

Virginity sounds like a straightforward concept: you are a virgin, or you aren't. The branch has been snapped, or it hasn't. But in different parts of the world, the concept has different meanings:

• In some cultures, an unmarried woman remains a virgin even if she is a prostitute. Only through marriage does she forfeit her virginity. She supports herself for years as a prostitute, but on the day of her wedding she is treated as a virgin, dressed in white, and presented to her husband as pure. It is he who steals her virginity.

• In other parts of the world, a married woman without children is a virgin: virginity is lost only when her first child passes through the vaginal canal. Virginity is destroyed not by intercourse but by becoming a mother. Thus, every non-mother, regardless of her sexual activity, is a virgin.

• Among some peoples who superstitiously fear the "blood of the first night"—blood has a long history of negative connotations—a man will marry a woman only after her hymen has been ruptured through intercourse with a stranger whose job it is to deflower virgins. The work is considered arduous, and the man is regarded as brave because he repeatedly accepts the danger of contact with blood.

A woman deflowered by a surrogate—we'll look at the concept in more detail—offers her husband an even purer form of virginity than she had before, as sex with her no longer presents a risk.

It is interesting that in the age of AIDS, all the old fears of blood take on new meaning.

If these definitions of virginity sound amusing or absurd to us, our own restricted use of the word might draw a wry smile, or disapproving frown, from people in other cultures. A woman in Western society technically remains a virgin until she has vaginal intercourse; oral or anal encounters, with any number of men, do not "deflower" her. Many engaged couples will refrain from vaginal intercourse in order to marry while the woman is a virgin, while allowing themselves other sexual experiences together.

By all measures, the virgin is an endangered species. In one poll, 56 percent of American high school girls admitted to being sexually active, and the figure was substantially higher for boys. In the 1970s, bumper stickers and lapel buttons displayed phrases like "Virginity Is Curable," and today couples typically live together before exchanging vows. Though many people are faithful to their vows of monogamy in marriage, they are less and less likely to be virgins when they are wed. One must wonder if the centuries-old concept of marriage-bed virginity as an ideal is not nearing its end.

DEFLOWERING A VIRGIN; ANTIQUITY TO THE AGE OF CHIVALRY ◆

A recent dictionary of slang lists over thirty expressions for deflowering a virgin: *cop a cherry, pluck the bean, trim the buff, crack the pitcher, ruin the rug, punch a hole, pop the puss, dock at harbor, crack a teacup, split a sheet, ransack, ruin, rummage, violate.*

The chief nonslang term is "defloration," or "deflowering"—the act of stealing a woman's prized "flower." It has been the picturesque term since the days of chivalry, when knights spoke of sex through "flowery" euphemisms.

In *The Second Sex* (1953), Simone de Beauvoir traced the origin of the term to a popular legend of a knight who

> *pushed his way with difficulty through thorny bushes to pick a rose of hitherto unbreathed fragrance. He not only found it, but broke the stem, and it was then that he made it his own. The image is so clear that in popular language to "take her flower" from a woman means to destroy her virginity; and this expression, of course, has given origin to the word "defloration."*

Merriam-Webster dates "defloration" to the fifteenth century and "deflower" to the fourteenth. Both words are from the Latin *deflorare* (*de* + *flor* [flower]), meaning "to remove the bloom."

We'll examine the origins of sacred defloration rituals, done by strangers, to virgins, with dildos of wood, stone, and marble. First, let's examine the dildo itself.

Satan encourages a young virgin to fish for a dildo, while demons look on, c. 1835.

DILDOS; ANTIQUITY TO MODERN TIMES ◆

A dildo is any object designed for—or recruited for—insertion into the vagina (or anus). Dildos don't vibrate, unless that's the intention of the user.

Today dildos are made of either vinyl or silicone rubber. Realistic dildos are flesh-colored, burgeoning with veins, buttressed at the base with balls, and constitute a large part of the sex-toy market. Some dildos are cast from the erections of popular and well-hung porn stars. Some are hollow vinyl shafts that attach to the body with an elastic strap and are really prosthetic penises, intended to aid a man who's only semierect or to give extra girth to a Slim Jim.

The latest, available in most sex paraphernalia shops, is the "Jelly Boy" dildo. It is "soft, pliable and full of air bubbles beneath the dildo's surface, giving it a festive carbonated appearance," write Cathy Winks and Anne Semans, in *The Good Vibrations Guide to Sex*, a manual for the "terminally hip and sexually jaded." The jelly formula includes aromatic petrochemicals that make the dildo smell like a cross between a beach ball and suntan lotion. "They are available in pink, orange and—just like the soft drinks of the '90s—in 'crystal' clear jelly. The flexible nature of jelly dildos makes them popular for packing." A travel dildo. The most popular model is the "crystal" clear.

Note of caution: Before insertion, all dildos, for purposes of hygiene, should be dressed in a condom.

"Dildo"—Word Origin

The word "dildo" is from the Latin *dilatare*, meaning "to open wide," to dilate, to expand. It is the basis for the Italian verb *dilettare*, "to give pleasure," which in turn gives us the term for a person who loves a field of knowledge in a superficial way: a "dilettante."

"Dildo" is also related to the Italian noun *diletto*, meaning "delight," which can also be used as the endearment "beloved." The word is chock-full of pleasurable and loving meanings. *Merriam-Webster* traces the spelling "dildo" to around 1598.

The practice of using dildos predates the word. Well-preserved artifacts have been found in most primitive cultures. Images of dildos were painted on ancient Greek pottery and Egyptian frescoes, chiseled into East Indian stone friezes, and carved into Chinese ivory artifacts. They provide humor in many classical plays, east and west. In a Greek play from the third century. B.C.E., one woman complains to another that she's tired of her friends' borrowing her beautiful new "scarlet leather-covered dildo" before she's had a chance to pleasure herself with it.

During the Hellenistic age, the Mediterranean seaport of Miletus—home of Thales, the first recorded philosopher of Western civilization—was renowned as the center of dildo manufacturing and export. The ancients were much less squeamish than we moderns when it came to having sex with a disembodied phallus. They loved sex toys, and many public rites and rituals are based on the bold, unembarrassed use of dildos.

THE BIGGEST DILDO PURCHASERS ◆

*T*he notion of a dildo as a substitute penis intimidates many heterosexual men, making them feel that their own organ is inadequate. Other straight men find dildos a sensible substitute for times when their wives are horny and they are not.

Lesbian couples are, perhaps understandably, big consumers of dildos. "During sexual arousal, the vagina balloons," says one lesbian who uses dildos. "It's only natural to want to full it up with something."

Gay male couples, with two real penises between them, are thought to be the biggest purchasers of dildos. Perhaps this has something to do with the unique way a gay man regards a penis. While a straight man loves his penis from an early age for the pleasure it gives him, the organ is never his primary object of desire. Quite the contrary, the vagina is—or some other female

Demons tempt a wife to be unfaithful to her husband by using a dildo, c. 1835.

body part. But for a gay man, a penis is both his own pleasuring device and, more often than not, his primary sex object. The penis serves a dual function for a gay man. Gay couples often own many different models and colors of dildos—something for every occasion.

Those who sell sex paraphernalia report a gender difference among people who purchase dildos. Lesbians and gay men are far more candid and comfortable when it comes to buying and talking about dildos. Straight women rank next in lack of embarrassment in making a dildo selection and purchase. Most squeamish of all are straight men, whose machismo seems wounded by the thought of having to buy a disembodied phallus. "The way they look at the models," says one employee of the Pleasure Chest, a chain of sex-toy stores, "you can tell they want to buy one, for whatever reason; maybe the guy's impotent. But they just don't have the balls to bring it over to the counter. I imagine it's almost like an admission: mine's not working. Or mine's inadequate for her needs."

Dual Dildo

Dual dildos have a penis at each end. This way the orifices of both lovers can be simultaneously accommodated. The dual dildo seems tailor-made to embody the cliché of "burning the candle at both ends"—make that "burying the candle at both ends."

The variety of modern types, colors, and textures would undoubtedly have pleased the ancients, who dreamed up the idea of penile substitutes. For dildos, in one form or another, in one size or another, have been around for centuries. In terms of rites and rituals, dildos are the invention of men, who used them on women for a number of practical, superstitious, religious, and pleasurable reasons.

DEFLOWERING BRIDES WITH SACRED DILDOS; GREECE, 600 B.C.E., TO NINETEENTH CENTURY ◆

typical bride arrives at the altar today already deflowered—by her husband-to-be or a past boyfriend, as the result of a one-night stand, or perhaps through her own use of a dildo. But in many cultures of the past, a young girl about to marry was deflowered for her husband-to-be in order to save him from the "unpleasant" task. Nicolas Venette, in looking back over past practices, found it sensible:

> I would not be surprised if the Phoenicians did, as reported, have their daughters deflowered by man servants before marriage. Nor would I be shocked if the Armenians deflowered their daughters at the temple of the goddess Anaitis to make the genitals more suitable and pleasing for the marriage bed.
>
> For it is impossible to predict all the toil and pain a man would suffer in this first foray. Far from igniting the passion of his wife, one often sparks such pain and anger that this can be quite a common reason for divorce. How much sweeter to embrace a woman accustomed to the pleasures of love than to caress one who has never known a man.
>
> It is the same as when we call a locksmith to make the springs move in a brand-new lock to avoid the annoyance we would face the first day of use. Thus those ancient races had valid reasons for establishing deflowering laws.

Stone Dildos, Hard Knocks

In ancient Greece, deflowering a young girl of marrying age, and who belonged to the aristocratic class, was commonplace and rich with symbolism. She ceremonially had her hymen pierced by the stone penis of the Greek god Priapus, the embodiment of fertility. The deflowered virgin was then fit for marriage and guaranteed many children, since her first "lover" was Priapus himself.

The son of Dionysus, god of fertility and wine, and Aphrodite, goddess of love, Priapus has lent his name to the medical condition known as priapism: a painful erection that will not subside because blood cannot drain from the penis.

In an era when phallus worship was commonplace, when statues and effigies sported erect members, it is not surprising to find numerous ceremonies in which virgins and childless women employed dildos for sacred reasons.

Today, no tourist to the Greek isle of Delos can miss the rows of gigantic erect stone penises and accompanying testes at the entrance to what was once a sacred temple of phallus worship. Though many stone penises have their tips broken off, and several testes have been crushed, others are fully intact and up to four feet long. The entire concept of phallus worship was begun by men—and inflicted on women. Women were forced by husbands, priests, physicians, and soothsayers to worship the male member. Anthropologists have found no instances of phallus worship in alleged matriarchal societies.

Wooden Dildos—and Splinters

In ancient Rome, the well-sanded wooden penis of the fertility god Liber was used to ceremoniously deflower brides-to-be. On March 17, his feast day, a six-foot-high wooden phallus—Greek *phallos*, "penis,"—was mounted on a wagon and drawn through the streets as part of the Liberalia celebration. Crowds followed the phallus, chanting to it, and a virgin, selected by high priests, crowned the effigy with a wreath.

Saint Augustine witnessed one such procession of "this disgraceful effigy." But he could not dissuade the Romans from a form of worship that he viewed as depraved and immoral, and which they viewed as sacred and essential for survival. Augustine was against phallus worship. He'd abandoned his own sexually licentious life in his early thirties; he'd previously bought prostitutes, cohabited with women out of wedlock, and fathered an illegitimate son. The saint expressed a curious attitude toward the defloration of virgins with dildos:

> During the wedding ceremony the new bride would be invited to sit on the post of Priapus . . . The modesty of the new bride is disgraced by this act, but her fertility is not stolen away, nor is even her virginity.

A deflowered virgin might also enhance her fertility before marriage by eating certain breads called *coliphia* and *siligonum* and shaped in the form of female and male genitals.

Varieties of the "bone of love," sold by a demon.

In ancient Greece and Rome, wooden dildos often came in leather sheaths. The leather could be sun-bleached to a light color or dyed ebony black. The ancients of the classical world, who owned many black slaves, clearly believed that black men were better endowed than white men. Their biggest dildos were colored black.

German "Bone of Love" Eclair—High-Calorie Conception

In Germany, during the Middle Ages, there existed equivalent fertility foods for brides-to-be and also for barren wives. In an age when a doctor could do nothing for an infertile couple, it is not surprising to find many superstitious customs in existence.

• The *mandelchen*—"almond sweet"—was an oblong cookie made of almond paste and crushed almonds, topped with two blanched nuts to represent testes.

• The *liebesknochen*—"bone of love"—was a thick, vanilla cream–filled éclair of unmistakable symbolism.

• The *vielliebchen*—"much love"—was an elongated pastry shell filled with such sweet confections as creams, candies, or chocolates and surrounded at one end by two walnuts, representing testes.

These were not ribald novelties but earnest folk remedies for infertility.

Elephant Tusk Dildos—the Ivory Coast

Artificial defloration continued into the nineteenth century among certain African peoples, especially in Uganda. A king would be insulted if he were offered a virgin bride whose hymen was still intact.

The first step toward marriage was fraught superstitiously with peril, since hymenal blood was viewed as an evil discharge. The task of rupturing the membrane with a phallic artifact—or the real flesh-and-blood thing—was relegated to the tribe's most pious man or, at the other extreme, to a total stranger who was paid for his services. That the deflowering agent was either religious or disinterested (in a social sense, that is) made him supposedly invulnerable to contamination and demonic possession. It was up to the agent to decide, case by case, whether to deflower with a dildo or his own member. One must wonder: was attractiveness a factor in his decision?

The artificial phalluses were made of metal, stone, or ivory and frequently decorated with the image of a tribal fertility god. This kind of defloration, as mentioned, did not rob a girl of her prized virginity but made her even purer in the eyes of her husband.

Banana Dildos—the Forbidden Fruit

Arab and Polynesian women used firm, unripened bananas as dildos. *The Arabian Nights* includes an ode to the phallus-shaped fruit:

> *O bananas, of soft and smooth skins, which dilate the eyes of young girls . . . you alone among fruits are endowed with a pitying heart, O consolers of widows and divorced women.*

Hebrew Scripture does not specify the fruit at Eden, plentiful on the tree of knowledge of good and evil, forbidden to Adam and Eve. Hebrew scholars believed the fruit was a pomegranate, a favorite of King Solomon and the prophets. In the seventh century, the prophet Muhammed argued that the fruit was a banana (really an herb), which was the basis of a thriving export trade on the Arabian Peninsula during his time.

The forbidden fruit in the Genesis myth can also been seen as a metaphor for sex, the one activity off-limits to the first, innocent, naked humans. They ate of the fruit—got to "know" each other in the biblical sense—and were no longer innocent; thereafter they covered their genitals. "Pomegranate"—from the Latin *pomum granatum*—means "an apple full of seeds." Bananas have been used as dildos in every culture where they grow. Thus, two of the suggested forbidden fruits have strong sexual overtones. The favorite Christian choice of fruit, the apple, has no such explicit sexual overtones; Christianity kept coitus out of the Garden, just as it kept it out of the conception of Jesus Christ.

BISHOP'S DILDO—FATHER KNOWS BEST ◆

*I*n southern France, phallus worship by betrothed Christian girls and barren wives took place at the shrine of Saint Pothin, the first bishop of Lyons, at Embrun. He was revered as a miracle worker by locals.

Fourteen centuries later, in 1585, when Protestants captured Embrun and destroyed the local church, they discovered several statues of the genitally tumescent saint. Priapus had been reincarnated, in a sense, as the Bishop Pothin. The tips of the penises were stained red, which generated a debate within the church as to whether the color was from an artist's brush or virgins' blood. And who had done the deflowering? Some authorities say the bishop himself.

The official church explanation holds that the worshiping women—brides-to-be and infertile wives—would pour red wine over the erect organ, thus staining it, and then drink the potency potion.

A famous German bishop, Burchard of Worms, wrote a penitential in 1012, making specific reference to the large number of Christian women who were thought to have used substitutes for their husbands' members. The practice apparently was not all that uncommon:

> *Have you done what certain women are accustomed to do, that is, to make some sort of device or implement in the shape of the male member, of a size to match your sinful desire?*
>
> *Have you fastened it to the area of your genitals, or those of another, with some form of fastenings, to fornicate with other women? Or has another done this to you?*
>
> *If you have done this, you shall do penance for five years on legitimate holy days.*

Burchard imposed a penance on women who masturbate with dildos. "Have you fornicated with yourself with the male device? If you have done this, you shall do penance for one year on legitimate holy days."

The bishop also castigated women for oral sex:

> Have you swallowed your husband's semen in the hope that because of your diabolical deed he might burn all the more with love and desire for you? If you have done this, you should do penance for seven years on legitimate holy days.

Doggy Style

Burchard of Worms was clearly sexist. While women received penances that ran for years, men—for equally pleasurable sins—got off with a slap on the wrist. For instance:

> Have you had sex with your wife or with another women from behind, like dogs do it [Latin, retro canino]? If you have done this, you shall do penance for ten days on bread and water.

Their only sin with a truly long penance—seven years of eating only bread and water on certain holy days—was for having sex with a nun. (The nun's penance was not stated.)

Today you can't buy liquor in some states on Sunday; in medieval Germany a husband couldn't have sex with his wife on the Lord's day. As Burchard chides, "Have you had sex with your wife on a Sunday? You shall do penance for four days on bread and water."

Antidildo Laws

Several states have antidildo laws, which come under the general proscription against selling any kind of "obscene device." The Texas penal code defines it as "any object designed and marketed as useful primarily for the stimulation of human genital organs."

Thus sex shops routinely label dildos as "condom practicing devices," as if sex educators were the state's only purchasers of dildos—as if the thousands of dildos sold were all being used in classrooms. Sometimes dildos are euphemistically labeled as novelty gag items—"gag" carries its own sexual overtones. Battery-operated vibrators are often pictured on the front of the box as tension-release aids to massage the neck and back.

Some states have stretched their antidildo laws to allow people to buy sex toys for "medical purposes," without a doctor's prescription. Others allow an adult to own one dildo, or two, or three, but no more than six—six suggests the "user" is actually a blackmarket *seller* of dildos. But, then, several states still have antisodomy laws on the books that prescribe the only way a husband and wife may legally make love to each other.

BEN WA BALLS; JAPAN, 2,500 YEARS AGO •

*I*n ancient Japan, wives, and especially geishas, would insert small, marble-size, ivory spheres into their vaginas to enhance sensation during masturbation or intercourse. The balls gave a sense of fullness, especially if the woman were a much used geisha or mother of many children. Supposedly it also gave the man copulating with her extra sensation. The imagery of a woman owning a dildo, and two *ben wa* balls, seems overly ripe for Freudian interpretation.

Modern-day *ben wa* balls come in two forms. One version has gold-plated or silver-plated ball bearings, measuring about three-quarters of an inch in diameter; the "duotone" version has two ball bearings encased in plastic spheres about one and a half inches in diameter, joined by a nylon cord. "Some women enjoy *ben wa* balls for their fantasy value or use them to tune into subtle sensations in the vagina," explain the authors of *The Good Vibrations Guide to Sex*.

> We have heard from women bus drivers and motorcycle riders who say they enjoy wearing ben wa *balls on the road, as their vehicle's vibration sets the balls in motion. Some women find that* ben wa *balls provide stimulation during intercourse . . . You should not use* ben wa *balls anally, as they could easily slip into your colon and out of your reach.*

Larger versions of *ben wa* balls—five plastic or rubber balls strung together on a nylon cord—are called anal beads and are used by some women, and by a larger number of mostly gay man, for rectal stimulation. The entire string of five balls is never fully inserted; at least one ball is left exposed for easy removal.

THE PERFECT FACE ◆ *When it comes to faces, both men and women look for features they regard as sexy. Women seem easier to please; at least they list fewer criteria that turn them on. A woman, for instance, may find a man sexy despite a pockmarked complexion. Men, in contrast, generally claim that for a woman to be sexy she must have clear facial skin.*

Women don't generally care about the size of a man's ears, but men do not like women to have big ears. Women may admire a man for his long eyelashes, but men actually look for long lashes in the women they attempt to pick up.

The nose is another trait in which men and women differ. Many women find irregular male noses—large, bony, or pug—a turn-on. Men, however, tend to like women to have slender, triangular-shaped noses.

Perhaps much of what a man finds attractive in a woman's face has been influenced by advertising and by women themselves—by the Christie Brinkleys and Cindy Crawfords who fill the media, and by the way women use makeup to achieve a certain "look."

According to a popular beauty-score system, the perfect female and male faces would have these traits:

MALE	FEMALE
Square face	*Oval face*
Bushy eyebrows	*Fine eyebrows*
Roman nose	*Small, straight nose*
Large eyes	*Large blue eyes*
Narrow lips	*Full lips*
Tan skin tone	*Rosy skin tone*
	Clear complexion
	Long lashes
	Flat ears
	Earlobes not too small

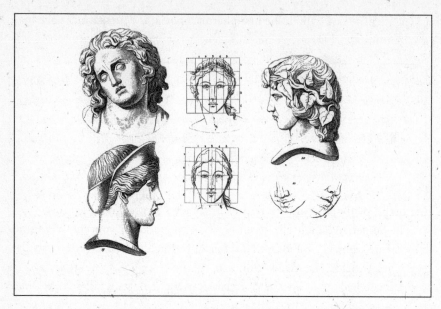

Men and women look for different features in the "perfect" face.

RIGHT OF THE FIRST NIGHT; SUMER, 3000 B.C.E., TO NINETEENTH CENTURY ◆

A young man and woman in love decide to marry. On their wedding night, the groom allows his new bride to have sex with his master, for that first night only.

This male privilege went by several names: *jus primae noctis* to the Romans of antiquity; *droit du seigneur* for the French in feudal Europe; and "the master's obligation," the euphemism used by the Southern white plantation owner who explained that it was his duty to sleep with a young black bride on her wedding night. Though the right of the first night may seem today like a transparent scrim for lust—as, indeed, it later was—its roots predate the Romans and hark back to religious superstitions of the Sumerians. At one time, an earthly king was revered as a god.

The Sumerian people inhabited the fertile valley between the Tigris and Euphrates rivers about five thousand years ago. Civilization's first true innovators, they gave us cuneiform writing; the concepts of grammar school and high school, along with teachers, principals, and a head disciplinarian called "man with a whip"; the first pharmacopoeia; the first farmer's almanac; the first bicameral congress; and history's first literary epic, *Gilgamesh*. In this five-cycle tale about the Mesopotamian King Gilgamesh, half-human and half-divine, who searches for immortality, we find mention of the right of the first night.

It was already a controversial practice.

The epic refers to the annoyance of the people of Uruk that their king clings stubbornly to the ancient custom that he sleep with every new bride in the realm. Husbands in Uruk express silent outrage but submit to the king's divine right. It is in the expression "divine right" that historians find the origin of the custom, which was not always scorned.

The Sumerian people also gave the Western world the concept of kingship and divine right. In 3000 B.C.E., religion was at the hub of Sumerian life, and priests wielded supreme authority. As the chief god's avatar on earth, a priest embodied divine power over harvests and human fertility; for a bride to spend the first night of her married life in the arms of the earthly incarnation of the fertility god guaranteed her and her husband many children.

But when invaders began regularly to attack Sumer, priests could offer no defense, and the position of king was created, a man to oversee armies and wars. In time, kings usurped much of the authority of priests, including earthly divinity and the accompanying right of the first night. In short: priests became celibate, kings promiscuous, and by the time of the Gilgamesh epic, bridegrooms wanted to deflower their own brides.

Kings, though, don't give paybacks, certainly not to commoners, and the custom of the right of the first night was transferred from the Sumerians to the Babylonians, who adapted *Gilgamesh* to their own prose style.

RITUAL RAPE, ROMAN STYLE ♦

*I*f Mesopotamian kings had a good thing going for them, ancient Roman chieftains had it even better. They argued, disingenuously, that *jus primae noctis* was in no way an abuse of their despotic power, nor was it pleasurable. To deflower virgin after virgin, night after night, was an exhausting task that they were willing to perform to ensure communal fertility. With further effrontery, to prove they did not enjoy the mandatory sex, they charged every new bridegroom a fee for deflowering his bride. The wife was raped, and the groom paid the rapist. A man who could not afford the price was forbidden to marry.

Right of the first night: A bridegroom pays to have his virgin bride deflowered by a feudal lord.

As the population of Rome expanded, not even a priapic ruler could personally fulfill *jus primae noctis*, and the use of artificial phalluses arose. Prior to consummating marriage with her husband, a bride ceremoniously straddled a stone statue of the fertility god, lowering herself onto his effigy.

This was not a private ritual but part of the public wedding ceremony, so that all the guests could witness the bloodied evidence of virginity, as well as the girl's avowal to be fruitful. Using the real penis of a king or the stone member of a statue, the right of the first night was also practiced by the Chinese, Kurds, and Muslims.

Priestly Privilege

The practice continued in Europe, on and off, until feudal times, when it became an egregious case of sexual abuse. The feudal nobleman—who was lord only by title, possessing no traditional divine right—instituted the practice on his estate with little pretense that he was fructifying the race or ensuring a good harvest. He called *droit du seigneur* a duty but reserved the right to waive this "lordly privilege" in some cases—perhaps with brides who were unattractive to him—leaving the task to her husband. The rejected brides-to-be may well have been relieved, while any bride invited into the master's bed could not decline.

Voltaire (1694–1778) was outraged by the practice. What goaded him most was the common knowledge that "some abbots and bishops enjoyed this privilege in their capacity as temporal lords; and it is not very long since that these prelates compounded their prerogative for acknowledgments in money, to which they have just as much right as to the virginity of the girls." Writing in 1769, he expressed his belief—and hope—that the right of the first night would never be used again by civilized peoples. He did not know what was going on in the New World.

BLACK BRIDES IN THE SOUTH ◆

*E*ven less pretense surrounded the right of the first night in the American South. Plantation lords owned slaves as property. The comely black daughter of a slave family could end up in the master's bed on the first night, second night, or any night—or day—he fancied her. As coercion without the cloak of tradition or ritual, the plantation practice does not really qualify as a true example of the right of the first night, a practice that really ended centuries ago when a high priest no longer could claim divinity and direct descent from a fertility god. Since then, everything else under the guise of "the right of the first night" has been rape.

VIBRATORS: STEAM-POWERED TO BATTERY-OPERATED ◆

A testimonial from a woman who loves her vibrator:

I love waking up in the morning with a jolting orgasm from my beloved vibrator. Better than a cup of coffee!

Some pregnant women claim that vibrators assist them through the travail of labor. In *Susie Bright's Sexual Reality* (1992), the author described how a properly placed vibrator eased her pain:

I have a photograph of me, dilated to six centimeters, with a blissful look on my face and my vibrator nestled against my pubic bone. I had no thought of climaxing, but the pleasure of the sweet rhythm on my clit was like sweet icing on the deep, thick contractions of my womb.

A 1994 study found that 16 percent of American women between the ages of eighteen and fifty-nine found the idea of using a vibrator or dildo at least "somewhat appealing." Four percent reported using such sex toys during the previous year. Four percent of this age group, in a female population of 135 million, amounts to several million women.

Some people are uneasy about the idea of using a vibrator: "Will I become addicted to my vibrator? Will it be better than by boyfriend? Will I stop wanting sex from my husband?" To allay the fears of many women—and men, *The New Joy of Sex* states:

> *Vibrators are no substitute for a penis. Some women prefer them to a finger for masturbation, or put one in the vagina while working manually on the clitoris. But vibrators are no substitute for the penis.*

Unlike dildos and *ben wa* balls, which are ancient, the vibrator is a relatively modern sex toy. Straight men are not all that fond of them, perhaps because the device does something the penis cannot—vibrate.

The history of vibrators dates back to the discovery of steam power.

PRESSURE COOKER—HOT, SAVORY MEAT; 1600S ◆

*S*team power has been used for centuries. The physical laws of steam were posited by the brilliant Irish physicist and chemist Robert Boyle (1627–1691). In 1682, a thirty-five-year-old French inventor, Denis Papin, demonstrated the first steam pressure cooker to Boyle and other members of London's Royal Society. The cooker rumbled and rattled like crazy, and Papin fed his distinguished guests history's first steam-cooked meal. The famed architect Christopher Wren wrote that thanks to the power of steam "the oldest and hardest Cow-Beef may now be made as tender and savoury as young and choice meat."

Crazy Masturbators Point the Way

After Papin's demonstration, inventors started to put steam to many ingenious new uses. Most were medical inventions, including a steam-powered body massager that allowed doctors to massage patients without themselves becoming exhausted. Steam pressure, moving from one small chamber to another, caused the device's arm to vibrate (none too rhythmically).

The possibility of an explosion led an American physician in 1860 to improve the steam massager, making it smaller and somewhat safer.

Smaller is the operative word here. When the arm of the steam massager got to be around the dimensions of a penis, someone—history has not recorded who—realized that the device could also be put in the vagina or up the anus. We know this because of references in the medical literature to the "horrible abuse" of steam massagers by patients in mental institutions, who were masturbating with them. Thus the first humans to pleasure themselves with vibrators were certifiably insane. Nonetheless, they started a trend.

Cure for Female Hysteria

By 1870, small steam-powered massage devices—little pressure cookers— were being advertised in medical catalogs as "ideal for the treatment of female disorders." Frigidity, for instance. (A *steam* vibrator seems metaphorically ideal for that *icy* condition.) Or for infertility. Who knows how many gynecologists and their female patients got off on this kind of therapy?

In many parts of Europe, massage therapy was by now standard treatment for female "hysteria," a catchall syndrome characterized by a set of vague "nervous" symptoms, which might include weepiness, exhaustion, and frequent fainting. Doctors had discovered that a hysterical female could be cured—or calmed—by the gentle massaging of her vulva. The object of the treatment was to induce "hysterical paroxysm," the doctor's euphemism for orgasm. A woman wanting sex with her doctor had only to feign hysteria. A doctor wanting sex with his patient had only to diagnose hysteria. The husband was out of the loop.

In 1907, inventor Clarence Richwood of Boston applied for a patent for his "liquid-actuated vibrator." He wrote that his water-powered vibrator, which featured a rounded blunt head (like the penis's glans), would allow personal massage in the privacy of one's bathroom or bedroom. For a time, faucet-powered vibrators were a female fad.

No one knows how small and safe these steam and water vibrators might have become if electric power had not been harnessed late in the nineteenth century.

ELECTRIC VIBRATORS FOR "HEALTH, VIGOR, BEAUTY" ◆

*I*n 1911, Los Angeles inventor John Keough applied for a patent for his "vibratory dilator." The blunt-shaped cylinder, with a metal and hard rubber body, plugged into a wall socket, making it one of the early electric vibrators.

Keough's "medical" vibrator was intended to stimulate the vaginas of frigid wives and to gently dilate the canals of "tight" women. The probe could be rewired to deliver a mild electric shock to the walls of the vagina. Such devices were popular in the practice of so-called "electric medicine."

The use of batteries made it possible to design a wide variety of portable, personal medical vibrators. At the time, no one dared suggest that these new handheld, tension-releasing devices were to be nestled between the legs. They were for the neck, shoulders, back, limbs—not for vaginal or anal insertion.

Unambiguous documentation does not exist, but from the start battery-powered vibrators were probably used for sexual pleasure. A lot can be read into the wording of an advertisement. A battery-operated vibrator ad from the 1930s assures the lady of the house that the handheld unit will give her "health, vigor, beauty—and bring a blush to her cheeks."

Another ad suggests that older women "with fading beauty" use a vibrator to restore the "delicious, thrilling, sensations of youth—it makes you fairly tingle with the joy of living." It seems clear that some women were deliberately buying a masturbation aid—a phallus substitute. And it was all made possible by the invention of the portable flashlight—the *Eveready* flashlight.

HOW THE FLASHLIGHT BECAME A VIBRATOR ◆

*B*oth flashlights and vibrators are battery operated. Both are long, hard, and cylindrical. Both are used in dark places. Both are kept in a drawer by the bed.

The battery-operated flashlight was invented in the early years of the twentieth century by Russian immigrant Akiva Horowitz. He'd arrived in New York in the 1892 and Americanized his name to Conrad Hubert. He landed a job with Joshua Lionel Cowen, who would soon create Lionel trains. When he hired Conrad Hubert, Cowen had just perfected the "electric flowerpot," a battery housed in a tube with a lightbulb at one end. It looked suspiciously like a flashlight—which had not been invented yet. The tube rose up through the center of a flowerpot and illuminated a plant—an "electric flowerpot."

Flowers and Sex

Conrad Hubert believed in the commercial potential of the electric flowerpot and convinced his boss to sell him the patent. When the novelty item didn't move off store shelves, Hubert found himself with an overstock. To salvage a portion of his investment, he separated the lights from the flowerpots,

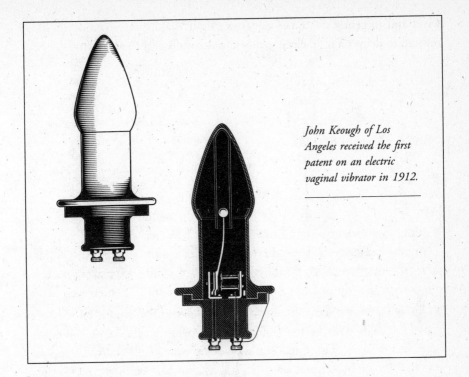

*John Keough of Los
Angeles received the first
patent on an electric
vaginal vibrator in 1912.*

lengthened the cylinders, and received his own U.S. patent for what he called a "portable electric light," the first flashlight.

The long, thick light with a head could be turned on with the flick of a switch and aimed in any direction. Hubert suggested that the ideal place to keep a flashlight was on the night table—ever ready, in case of emergency.

His new invention sold well, and he started the American Ever Ready Company. When he died in 1928, a very wealthy man, he left six million dollars to his favorite charities.

It was only one small step from the portable, battery-operated flashlight to the personal vibrator. It required only the insertion of a small oscillating motor. Just as Conrad Hubert had ingeniously turned the failed electric flowerpot into the flashlight, several other inventors quickly turned the flashlight into a "health vibrator" and applied for patents.

Many "medical" models came on the market in the 1930s and 1940s. They were pitched to women, which indicates that manufacturers knew they were selling masturbation aids. One ad promised, "The rhythms of life will tingle throughout your body." Another encouraged, "Glow from head to toe—health massage in the privacy of your own home."

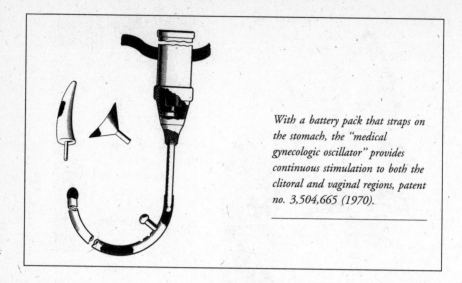

With a battery pack that straps on the stomach, the "medical gynecologic oscillator" provides continuous stimulation to both the clitoral and vaginal regions, patent no. 3,504,665 (1970).

Through underground sex films, husbands eventually caught on to what women could do with personal vibrating massagers. In the 1940s, vibrators began to appear in stag films. Actresses demonstrated the many ingenuous uses for a "home health massager." In smoky film parlors, men could see for themselves how the handy flashlight had been turned into a portable sex toy.

Phalliclike vibrators are still sold in department stores and drugstores, not as sex toys but as massagers. There is even a vibrator called the Ever-Ready.

In *American Sex Machines* (1996), Hoag Levins tells of a 1966 patent application for a product that represents the birth of the modern age of vibrating sex toys. Inventor Jon Tavel of Encino, California, presented the U.S. Patent Office with drawings of a cordless, one-piece, moisture-proof, battery-powered, variable-speed, torpedo-shaped, vibrating, plastic dildo. It was, writes Levins, "the culmination of ages of artificial phallus design. The Tavel concept became one of the best-selling and most popular sexual stimulators of all time."

THE G SPOT: DR. ERNST GRÄFENBERG; 1950 ♦

*T*he G spot is described as an area one to one and a half inches across and located about two finger joints deep beyond the vaginal entrance. The region's sensitivity to stimulation was first noted in 1950 by German physician Ernst Gräfenberg:

Nun advises maiden,
"Go find your G spot."

An erotic zone always could be demonstrated on the anterior wall of the vagina along the course of the urethra . . . Occasionally the production of fluids [due to its stimulation] is so profuse that a large towel has to be spread under the woman . . .

This convulsive expulsion of fluids occurs always at the acme of the orgasm and simultaneously with it . . . expelled not from the vulva but out of the urethra in gushes . . . it had no urinary character . . . no lubricating significance.

In an unstimulated state, the G spot is about the size of a dime and is difficult to detect—one reason why it tends to be bypassed. When stimulated, it swells to about the size of a half-dollar and feels quite prominent through the vaginal wall, assuming a rubbery or spongelike quality that feels firmer and more textured than the surrounding area. It is easiest to detect just before or during orgasm.

American researchers Beverley Whipple and John D. Perry dubbed the region the G spot in Gräfenberg's honor. In 1982, with colleague Alice Kahn Ladas, they created a publishing sensation with _The G Spot and Other Recent Discoveries About Human Sexuality._

Does the G spot really exist? Many women swear it does. Others have yet to find their own G spots—but not for lack of trying. Others claim to have located their G spot but find stimulation of it unpleasant.

Many women report that either the rear-entry or the woman-on-top position of intercourse provides the most direct stimulation of the G spot during partner sex. Some say they've always preferred these positions without realizing they were responding to G spot stimulation.

From current data, it is impossible to say what percentage of women have a G spot, what percentage experience a gush of fluid at the time of orgasm, and how frequently this occurs and under what conditions of stimulation. Some women report it's easier to reach their G spot from a squatting position. Another alternative is to purchase a specially designed G spot dildo or vibrator.

CHAPTER 5

The Dirty Deed

"Fuck" to "Screw"

SEX: The most fun you can have without laughing.

WOODY ALLEN

"Fuck"; England, Pre-Eleventh Century ◆

*N*o other word in the English language gets more colloquial usage than the notorious and taboo F-word. The word and its variations could fill a small dictionary. Before considering the ancient origin of the F-word, let's appreciate its many colorful and imaginative applications:

Absofuckinglutely, absolutely.
Ass-fuck, anal intercourse.
Bearfuck, a chaotic military undertaking.
Buddy-fuck, betrayal of a male friend.
Bumfuck, an unfortunate deal.
Butt-fuck, anal copulation.
Celebrity-fucker, a hanger-on among stars.
Dry fuck, lovers reaching orgasm with their clothes on.
Dumbfuck, a stupid person.

Dutch fuck, lighting one cigarette from another.

Eye-fuck, to gaze lecherously.

Fanfuckingtastic, wonderful, fantastic.

Fiddlefuck, to dillydally.

Fingerfuck, digital vaginal or rectal stimulation.

Fist fuck, insertion of a hand into the vagina or rectum.

Flying fuck, go to hell.

French fuck, rubbing the penis between a woman's breasts.

Fuck a duck, go to hell.

Fuckass, a contemptible or stupid person.

Fuck off, get lost.

Fucked by the fickle finger of fate, victimized by bad luck.

Fucked up, a hopeless situation, or stoned.

Fuck me, I'll be damned.

Fuck you, I don't give a damn about you.

Fuckable, sexually desirable.

Fuckaholic, a sexually promiscuous person.

Fuckaround, contemptuous treatment.

Fuckathon, an orgy.

Fucked over, taken advantage of.

Fuckee, the passive partner in sex.

Fucker, the active partner in sex, or an asshole.

Fucking-A, on target; absolutely accurate.

Fuckface, an ugly or despicable person.

Fuckhead, a stupid person.

Fuckhole, any hole a penis thinks it can fit into.

Fuck up, a bungler or social misfit.

Get fucked, go to hell.

Head fuck, same as "mind fuck".

Mind fuck, to play emotional games.

Motherfucker, a bastard; abbreviated as "mofo."

Rat fuck, a despised or hated person.

Starfucker, same as "celebrity fucker."

Tit-fuck, same as "French fuck."

That is about half of the word's recorded uses.

Why is "fuck" the richest slang in the language?

Sexual intercourse is and has been the single act that keeps our species in

*Literal depiction of
a "flying fuck."*

existence. Unlike single-celled organisms that reproduce through fission (individual cell division) and fusion (the merging of two cells)—forms of asexual reproduction—we propagate by *sexual* reproduction. We also have the gift of language. Thus it is not surprising that a short, graphic, four-letter expression of the act most central to our existence gained the greatest usage in our slang vocabulary.

Linguistic Origin—"To Beat Against"

"Fuck" as a word for copulation is at least a thousand years old and one of the few words that has always been taboo. It may date back to the sixth century, when the Saxons, ancient Germanic peoples, conquered and settled parts of England. Their short, expressive words—"shit," "piss," "sweat," perhaps "fuck"—were viewed by the French-speaking Normans, who conquered England in 1066, as vulgar elements of an inferior language. Within a short time, the Normans had replaced the "offensive" Saxon words, which were Standard English to the Saxons, with their own "polite" variations: "excrement," "urine," "perspiration," and "fornication." We have inherited many examples of "polite" (Norman) and "impolite" (Saxon) words. Examples include: dine/eat, deceased/dead, desire/want.

The Saxons may have said "fuck" as *foken*, which was an Old English word meaning "to beat against," an allusion to the male body beating against the female's during intercourse. But *foken* also meant to beat *anything* violently. Indeed, we still use "fuck" in this nonsexual way: "I'll fuck you over"

"Punishment of sodomy," detail of Michelangelo's Last Judgment *from the Sistine Chapel, 1536–1541. Copy of Witkowski.*

meaning "I'll do serious damage to you." And the expletive "fuck you!" is more an expression of violence than sexual intent. In imagery (the aggressive act of intercourse) and language (fuck = to beat against), sex and violence have always gone hand in hand.

"MOTHERFUCKER"; AMERICAN SOUTH, PRE-1900 ◆

One "fuck" word stands out from the others: "motherfucker." Or, in black dialect, "mofo" and, as a black euphemism, "moa-fugg." It is the most offensive of all the F-words.

Uttered by one man to another, the word's impact is strong enough to start a fight. "During my years in prison work," wrote a psychiatrist who'd had studied criminal behavior, "I had observed that one expletive, that referring to intercourse between son and mother, was at once the most dangerous and the most frequent on the lips of the psychopath. I had actually seen men killed for using it."

"Oedipus was a motherfucker," a popular saying, sums up the taboo's long associated with incest. The sin and crime of incest have troubled people in every culture since the dawn of written history some fifty-five hundred years ago. "Motherfucker" is the hot linguistic button one pushes to provoke a violent emotional outburst.

"Motherfucker" has been unprintable until recent times. Norman Mailer, in *The Naked and the Dead* (1948), could only write: "You know what the mother-fugger'll be like . . . We'll be lucky to get out of there with our

"Fuck" means "to beat against," a description of the act of intercourse.

goddamn heads ons." Two decades later, in *Why Are We in Vietnam?* Mailer could use the word in print: "How'd you get this motherfuck?" In 1973, Erica Jong dared to use the word in her bestseller *Fear of Flying*: "So I kept concentrating very hard, helping the pilot . . . fly the 250-passenger motherfucker."

The word is thought to have originated among Southern blacks sometime before the turn of the century. As early as the 1920s it began appearing in thinly disguised forms: *mother-fugge', mother-frigger, mother-plugger.*

"FORNICATE"—THE PROSTITUTE CONNECTION ◆

*T*he Normans obtained their word "fornicate" from early French via the Latin *fornix*, which was a small, vaulted chamber, popular in ancient Rome and rented for a night of pleasure. Roman prostitutes practiced their trade in such underground chambers, much the way a modern prostitute might rent a motel room.

Initially synonymous with "brothel," *fornix* became a verb, *fornicari*, meaning "to frequent a brothel." Finally it became the name of the activity conducted therein.

Since most European languages are related, it is not surprising that copulation—and the act of striking any kind of blow—was *fokken* in Middle

Dutch and *ficken* Old German. Men, who traditionally have both coined words and compiled dictionaries, apparently viewed sex with a woman as something akin to giving her a good beating. In their eyes, the heat and frenzy of passion, with its accompanying adrenaline rush, was not all that different from engaging in a brawl. In less civilized times, when there was less of a distinction between consensual sex and rape, maybe most sex was more like a fight and "to beat against" was lovemaking at its most literal.

FUG, FRIG, F—K, F**K •

*F*or centuries the word "fuck" was virtually unprintable. Even Shakespeare, who wrote in the common vernacular, avoided it, though he seems to have alluded to it in a bawdy section of *Henry V* with the expression *firk*.

Scholars of the F-word—some linguists have written their Ph.D. thesis on it—cannot find a clear written reference to "fuck" before 1475—undoubtedly because it was deemed so offensive. They have found many euphemisms for it, like "fug" and "frig". In the sixteenth century, the word began appearing in bawdy Scottish song lyrics, for the taboo against the word was apparently less severe in Scotland than in England.

To this day, most magazines will print the word only as "f—k" or "f**k". The *New Yorker*, in 1979, found all four letters so offensive it resorted to "****".

Why do we still find words like "fuck"—and "cock" and "cunt"—so offensive? Freud gave one explanation:

> *The off-color saying is like undressing the person of the opposite sex to whom it is directed . . . It obliges the attacked person to fancy that part of the body [cock, cunt], or that action [fuck], to which the word corresponds.*

"Penis" does not as readily conjure imagery of the organ as does "cock." "Cunt" conveys more of a picture than "vagina." "Fuck" makes the point better than "intercourse" or "coitus" or "lovemaking."

THE POWER OF DIRTY WORDS—PHONE SEX •

*T*here is a great emotional distance between the dirty word and the corresponding accepted word, between saying "Let's have coitus" and "Let's fuck." The latter is lusty, aggressive, and erotic and more truthfully reflects the expression of passion.

Dirty words have a great capacity for arousing emotions, for awakening passion. The appeal of erotic literature is based on its use of racy language. Many people masturbate to pornographic stories constructed largely of dirty words. The entire industry of phone sex and those costly 900 numbers is based on the power of dirty words alone to drive two strangers in cyberspace to climax. Together.

We know the first words ever spoken over a telephone: "Mr. Watson," called an excited Alexander Graham Bell to his assistant, on March 10, 1876, "come here. I want you." We'll never know the first dirty words spoken on the phone, but they could have been the same ones: "Come here. I want you."

Have you ever had sex with a foreigner who doesn't understand a word of your language? Psychologist Ariel C. Arango, in *Dirty Words: Psychoanalytic Insights* (1989), writes, "The significance of 'dirty' words in the art of love-making is shown by the fact that sexual pleasure decreases when one *fucks* with a foreign woman who speaks a different language." Dirty talk adds a dimension to passion. Obscene words are an aphrodisiac. Erotic literature is ancient, existing in all cultures.

Degradation as an Aphrodisiac

Freud argued that most people miss out on passion because of their fear of obscene words. This was particularly true during the Victorian era with its abhorrence of sexually explicit language. In "On the General Degradation of Erotic Life" (1912), Freud suggested that men, to overcome impotence, utter a string of passionate obscenities to their partners. Tell the woman what you want to do to her, and you'll be able to do it. This meant, Freud realized, a temporary "degradation" of the opposite sex, a small, naughty evil for a greater and pleasurable good:

> *Although it may seem unpleasant, and besides, paradoxical, it can be claimed that to be able to be truly free, and thus totally happy in erotic life, it is necessary to have lost respect for the woman.*

And the woman for the man, we'd add today.

Surveys show that three little words—*fuck, cock, cunt,* the act and the organs engaged in it—are the most taboo and, hence, erotic in the English language. The forbidden word is graphic, a turn-on—the reason it's forbidden.

Jane Austen. The novelist did not realize that "screw" was slang for "fuck" and unintentionally used it to bawdy effect in a novel.

"Screw"; England, Late Sixteenth Century ◆

Screw," as an expression of copulation, was first used in England around Shakespeare's time and originated as a euphemism for the taboo "fuck." "Screw" seemed politer than "fuck." But why "screw" and not some other active and aggressive verb?

The word's sexual connotation has an interesting and old origin.

"Screw," as a mechanical device for fastening things together, is from the Middle English *screwe* and the Middle French *escroue*. In its early usage, the hole in which the screw was turned was also called "a screw." This is because the word "screw" itself evolved from the Latin *scrofa*, meaning "to sow" a seed in the ground, which was related to *scrobis*, a Latin word for both "vulva" and "vagina." Hence, a "screw" was once any hole that received a seed or a shaft. As a latter-day euphemism for "fuck," "screw" was the perfect linguistic choice.

Jane Austen, never one to use vulgarisms, was unaware that "screw" was already popular euphemistic slang for "fuck." In *Emma* (1816), she wrote about a proper, old-fashioned mistress of a boarding school: "Miss Goddard was the mistress of a school—not of a seminary or an establishment or anything which professed, in long sentences of refined nonsense, to combine liberal acquirements with elegant morality upon new principles and new systems, and where young ladies for enormous pay might be screwed out of health and into vanity."

Although "screw" arose as a polite alternative to "fuck," it, too, became offensive to many people. In 1976, presidential candidate Jimmy Carter drew much criticism for his use of the word in a *Playboy* interview: "Christ says, Don't consider yourself better than someone else because one guy screws a whole bunch of women while the other guy is loyal to his wife."

In commenting on the interview, the *New York Times* refused to print the offending word. It referred to it merely as "a vulgarism for sexual relations." Carter was taken by surprise with all the fuss, and so was the interviewer, Robert Scheer, who admitted, "I had no premonition that the words 'screw' and 'shack up' which he uttered would cause a furor. I just didn't know that they were still dirty words."

"HUMP"; ENGLAND AND GERMANY, 1600S ♦

"*Hump*," as a protruding lump—especially on one's back—is from the Low German *humpe*, "a thick piece of flesh or bone." The word is short for "humpbacked." How did the noun "hump" come to be the verb "to hump," an expression for intercourse?

As a sex act, "to hump" refers to the man's hunchedback posture over the women during coitus in the missionary position. "To hump" has always taken a feminine object: "He humped her"—seldom "she humped him." In Edward Albee's *Who's Afraid of Virginia Woolf?* (1962), the husband, George, suggests, with reference to his wife, Martha, a party game called hump the hostess.

In *Othello*, Shakespeare linguistically allows both sexes to hump and, through imagery, expresses the origin of the expression: "Your daughter and the Moor are now making the beast with two backs." A man can't screw without a humped back.

In today's sexually equal society, we find in fiction and nonfiction such expressions "she humped his leg." Women, now liberated, can "hump."

Still, "hump" is really a man's word. Why were men given larger brains than dogs?

So they wouldn't hump women's legs at cocktail parties.

"TO BALL"; AMERICA, 1950S ♦

"*To ball*," as an expression for intercourse, is an Americanism of relatively recent origin. Linguists believe it arose in the 1950s since the printed phrase has not been located in earlier writings. It's thought to derive from the use of the word meaning "to have fun," as in "I had a ball last night." This usage, in turn, originated from the noun "ball," a social gathering with dancing, in which everyone had a good time.

"Knock Up"; England, Sixteenth Century ◆

*J*ane Austen, in *Mansfield Park* (1814), wrote: "If Fanny could be more regular in her exercise, she would not be knocked up so soon." Austen did not mean that Fanny was about to become pregnant. "Knock up," a British colloquialism, also means "to tire out," "to become exhausted" or "fagged" (which has nothing to do with homosexuality). Austen was saying that if Fanny took regular exercise, probably long walks (we'd say "a cardiovascular workout"), she would not become fatigued so early in the day. She'd improve her stamina.

In America and, to a lesser extent, England, "knock up" means "to get a woman pregnant." That usage originated in England around the sixteenth century, when *knock* meant "to copulate" (the knocking of two bodies together), and a *knocker* was a "penis." A young women having sex without protection—getting "knocked" by a "knocker"—could, weeks later, discover that she'd been "knocked up."

The word "knock" itself is from the Middle English *knokken* and the Old English *cnocian*, where "rapping on a wooden door" is meant. It's an echoic word, originating from the sound of the action it describes. We still use it this way in the humor known as "knock, knock" jokes:

"Knock, knock."
"Who's there?"
"O. J. Simpson."
"O. J. Simpson who?"
"You qualify for the jury."

"Rape"—"To Steal a Bride"; England, Dark Ages ◆

*C*enturies ago, when there were no more women in a village who could be taken as wives, grooms would steal their brides from a neighboring town. A groom would "rape" his bride not by forcing sex upon her but by seizing her and carrying her away by force. This is evident in the definition of the Middle English word *rape*, which comes from the Latin *rapere*, "to

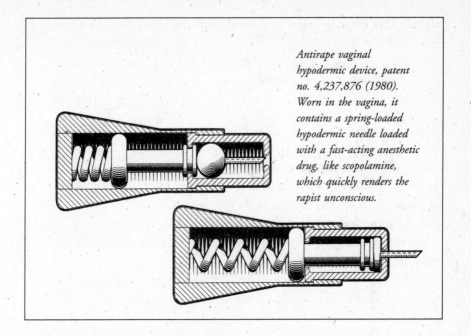

Antirape vaginal hypodermic device, patent no. 4,237,876 (1980). Worn in the vagina, it contains a spring-loaded hypodermic needle loaded with a fast-acting anesthetic drug, like scopolamine, which quickly renders the rapist unconscious.

seize". Likewise, when an army plundered a city, carrying off its women and treasures, the city was said to be "raped."

What the thieving men did sexually to the abducted women eventually came to be called "rape," and the earlier and broader usage became nearly obsolete. We still use the word in a nonsexual context to mean any outrageous assault or flagrant violation. "We are raping the environment of its natural resources."

Rape Oil to Canola Oil

For many years, the word "rape" was banned from print and polite discourse. A newspaper might report that a woman was forcibly "assaulted" or "molested" but never "raped." The word was felt to be every bit as coarse and violent as the act itself.

Today it is the only word we use to describe this violent sexual act—all euphemisms have been abandoned. Victims of rape are now encouraged to come forward and add a "face" to the crime.

We've become very sensitive about the word "rape." In fact, it has become so pejorative that companies that manufacture rape oil or rapeseed oil—from the rape plant (Latin *rapum*, "turnip"), which belongs to the mustard family—have changed its name to "canola" oil.

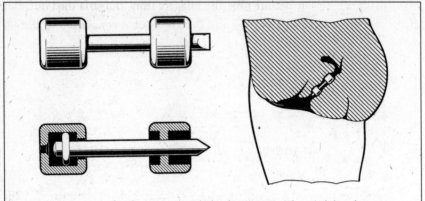

Antirape vaginal spike, patent no. 4,030,490 (1977). The possibility that any woman might be wearing the device acts as a deterrent. An attempted rape would not last long.

The preferred "canola" was first used in 1979. Canadian geneticists had improved the rape plant so that its seeds produced a vegetable oil high in monounsaturated fatty acids and low in erucic acid. No one wanted to call the new and improved low-acid product rape oil. The Canadian scientists opted for canola: "*Can*(ada) *o*(il) *l*(ow) *a*(cid)", c-a-n-o-l-a.

"To Bugger" versus "Cute Little Bugger"; England and France, Eleventh Century ◆

For about a thousand years, the verb "bugger" meant "to sodomize" —that is, to engage in nonprocreative oral, anal, or even vaginal sex. As a noun, the word "bugger" also stood for the man doing the buggering. "Bugger" derived from the Middle Latin *Bulgarus*, literally a Bulgarian, once considered to be any person from eastern Europe. An explanation is in order.

From the eleventh to the thirteenth centuries, "bugger" was applied to certain heretics from Bulgaria who settled in the south of France. These people believed that all human beings were inherently evil and that the human race should stop perpetuating itself—no more babies should be brought into the world. Thus, when these men had sex with their wives, they "buggered" them—that is, engaged in anal intercourse. Buggery was the Bulgarian's form of birth control. (The Greek's, too—so much so that it came to be called the Greek vice.)

Not surprisingly, in a short time the buggers from Bulgaria died out. But their name lived on as a term for any sodomite, or a contemptible person. Americans (but not the Brits) have softened the word and given it a nonsexual spin: "a cute little bugger" is "a rascal" or "a scamp."

"GETTING NOOKIE"; AMERICA, 1928 ◆

To "get nookie" is the same as to get "a piece of ass." The term is Scottish and arose from the old Scottish word *noke*, meaning "recess" or "crack." It is easy to see how it acquired its sexual overtones, especially since "crack" and "slit" are old expressions for "vagina." "Nookie" appeared in America in 1928, in the play *The Front Page* by Ben Hecht and Charles MacArthur.

"A GOOD LAY"; AMERICA, 1930S ◆

According to *The Dictionary of American Slang*, the sexual use of "lay"—which otherwise means "to put or set down"—first appeared in a short story by James T. Farrell: "Both agreed that the two girls looked like swells lays." Farrell might have coined the expression from a slightly older phrase, "to lay the log," meaning to put the penis in the vagina.

In *Wicked Words* (1989), Hugh Rawson gives an older and very convincing origin for the sexual use of "lay":

> Most likely, lay*'s sexual sense arose from the word's use as the past tense of* lie. *Since at least the twelfth century* lie with *and* lie by *have referred to sexual intercourse as well as to being in bed for the purposes of sleeping. The construction appears in the King James Bible (1611), e.g., "Come [said Lot's eldest daughter], let us make our father drink wine, and we will lie with him, that we may preserve the seed of our father . . . and the first-born went in and lay with her father."* (Genesis 19:32–33)

GRAFFITI ◆

The sex words found in this book often appear spraypainted on walls or scratched in wood by "graffiti artists"—1970s euphemisms for vandals and their crime.

During the Middle Ages, true graffiti artists worked in a visual arts form known as *sgraffito*, or *graffito*—from the Italian verb *graffiare*, "to scratch."

The technique, used in painting, pottery, and glass, consisted of putting down a primary surface (the "ground"), covering it with a second ("superficial") surface, and then scratching the upper layer so that the pattern or shape that emerged was of the ground color.

During the Middle Ages, especially in the illumination of sacred manuscripts, the ground layer was often of gold leaf. For wall murals, two layers of different-colored plaster were applied. In stained glass, the scratching was done on the top layer of colored glass, revealing clear glass beneath. The technique of sgraffito is still popular today.

Around 1850 the word *graffito* was adopted by archaeologists to characterize the rude writings and lewd drawings found on ancient remains. As the science of archaeology grew, "graffiti" came to describe any defacing scribbles, scrawls, erotic caricatures, etched elections results, fragments of poetry, limericks, and the like found on Egyptian, Greek, Etruscan, and Roman monuments. Archaeologists knew that these scribblings were unwanted in their own times, and that scribblers were considered a public nuisance, because of the many official warnings they found on public walls. For example, near Rome's Porta Portese, an inscription warned vandals not to scribble (*scariphare*) on public walls. Graffiti is an ancient headache.

To linguists, however, graffiti from a particular age is a gold mine of information. It is often closer to the spoken language of a period and place than the surviving written language. Graffiti says something about the times in which it was written.

While researching this book, I've collected contemporary men's room graffiti, which I'll record here. Each of the following is a wordplay on a well-known cliché. What this collection says about men in our age I'll leave to archaeologists of the future:

- The pen(is) mightier than the sword.
- If at first you don't succeed, suck and suck again.
- Chaste makes waste.
- Never jerkoff tomorrow if you can jerkoff today.
- An orgasm in the bush is worth two in the hand.
- A woman's place is on my face.
- Home is where the fart is.
- A pill a day keeps the stork away.
- Children should be seen and not had.
- Practice makes perverts.

One youth gives "the bird," finger language dating back at least
twenty-five hundred years.

- Better latent than never.
- Bare the rod and soil the child.
- Behind every great man there's an asshole.

FLIPPING THE BIRD; ANTIQUITY ◆

*I*t is a nasty sign, one of the oldest sex gestures around, and has gone by many names:

- ***The finger***, or "fuck you" sign, or "the bird" in America.
- ***The bird*** to the British.
- ***The daktylos***, finger, to the ancient Greeks.
- ***The digitus infamis***, notorious finger, to the Romans.
- ***The digitus destinare***, finger of fate, to the Christian theologian Tertullian.
- ***The insulting digit*** to monks in the Middle Ages.
- ***The forearm jerk***, or *vaffanculo*, to Renaissance Italians, who, for dramatic emphasis, extended the finger with a forceful forearm thrust.

The debauched Roman emperor Caligula liked to shock people who were offered his hand to kiss: he presented them with his extended middle finger. They had to kiss it. In effect, he was saying, Kiss my dick.

Many Roman gladiators offended by the emperor Nero's open homosexuality responded to his "thumbs down" gesture *(pollex infestus)* in the arena with their own *digitus lascivus*.

Why the *middle* finger?

The widely accepted explanation is that the longest human finger, fully extended, best resembles the erect penis and thus functions as a concise, to-the-point obscene gesture. Extension of the middle finger is at least 2,500 years old and possibly older. It appears in ancient Greek graffiti and plays. Aristophanes in *The Clouds* (423 B.C.E.) uses it as a literary device. He has Strepsiades, while taking with Socrates, deliberately confuse the obscene *daktylos* with the poetic dactyl:

SOCRATES: *Polite society will accept you if you can discriminate, say, between the anapest and common dactylic—sometimes vulgarly called "finger rhythm."*

STREPSIADES: *Finger rhythm. I know that.*

SOCRATES: *Define it then.*

STREPSIADES [Extending his middle finger in an obscene gesture]: *Why, it's tapping time with this finger. Of course, when I was a boy* [raising his phallus to the ready], *I used to make rhythm with this one.*

Is "the Finger" in the Bible?

Many scholars say it is. One of the earliest to point this out was John Bulwer, a British physician interested in sign language for the deaf. In his scholarly *Chirologia: or, The Natural Language of the Hand* (1644), he identified two passages that seem to curse the finger gesture:

If you remove the yoke from your midst, the pointing of the finger, and speaking wickedness, and if you give yourself to the hungry, and satisfy the desire of the afflicted, then your light will rise in darkness, and your gloom will become like midday. (Isaiah 58:9–10)

A worthless person, a wicked man, is the one who walks with a false mouth, with winks with his eyes, who signals with his feet, who points with his fingers. (Proverbs 6:12–13)

Several biblical scholars claim that "the finger" was known to the Israelites and considered a rude sign, and it is not surprising to find condemnation of the gesture in Hebrew Scripture. They argue that the fingers referred to in the above passages are not merely rude pointed index fingers, but obscene sexual gestures.

HOW ANIMALS DO IT ◆ *In the animal kingdom, sex can be wild and weird. For one thing, penises come in a mind-boggling number of sizes and guises. Some, like the human penis, are hydraulically operated pumps; others are fully retractable into the body. Some are ramrod straight, others have corkscrew twists. Some have barbs near the tip to prevent the female from changing her mind, and others have bones down the shaft and are true "boners." All are designed to do the same thing.*

Bedbug • *The penis of the bedbug is curved, sharply pointed, and, for his body size, very large—like a lance. He mounts her back, and because his penis cannot reach her vagina, he thrusts it through her back to deposit sperm into her body—a real prick.*

The sperm lies dormant until the bedbug sucks blood from her next human host. Once she's engorged with her belly distended with blood, the sperm awakens and swims to the ovaries. Promiscuity can be deadly for a female. If she mates with more than six males, she's likely to die from multiple stab wounds.

Spider • *The spider has no real penis to speak of, just a protrusion on his lower belly. He doesn't need a penis, since he hand-carries sperm to the female's web. By constricting muscles in his belly, he squeezes out sperm onto his web, scoops it up with a set of special hands or antennae, and delivers it to her web. He quickly departs, running for his life, since female spiders in heat are aggressive and will eat a male. If the experience is pleasurable for him, no one knows. But the faster he leaves, the happier she seems to be.*

Dog • *Dogs have rectractable penises, and both the males and female engage in foreplay. She nibbles at his neck and ears, and he licks her vulva, which greatly arouses her and sharply elevates her blood pressure. Her tail swings to one side, she glances over her shoulder, and her engorged vulva begins to rhythmically move up and down—like a human flexing his or her eyebrows.*

His penis is long and pointed. Once it is firmly in place, its tip fills with blood, swelling until it resembles a bulb. At the same time, the muscles of her vagina contract just behind the bulb, locking the animals together.

CONTINUED

This accounts for the familiar sight of two dogs, after sex, stuck together, facing in opposite directions, their rear ends touching, each glancing back at the other as if to ask, "What happened?"

What happened is that the bulb at the tip of his penis is still engorged with blood; and perhaps the muscles of her vagina are still contracted. A dowsing with cold water can cause the two to quickly deexcite and disengage.

Nature designed dogs to be locked together for some time because the male dog, unlike a human male, ejaculates very slowly. Breeders track the time by counting the pulsations at the base of the penis. If the male looks ecstatic, he apparently is. The semen is actively pushed into the uterus for as long as the animals remain in the lock of love.

Snake • The male has two penises, called hemipenes, one on each side of his body. The ends are soft and pointed, but the bases are a forest of stiff, backwardly aimed barbs. He uses only one penis at a time, depending on the direction in which he's aligned himself with the female. He can do it from the left or the right.

Flaccid hemipenes are light pink and resemble soft pockets in design. When erect, they turn inside out, flush to a deep purple, and form a grooved organ (not a tube) that allows semen to slide into the female. The barbs hold the male and female together, while they thrust and undulate—for as long as an entire day. Not only is mating protracted, the female's body can store sperm for several years. Some females in captivity have given birth five years after their last encounter.

Duck • The penis of the duck is a three-inch-long spiraling corkscrew, identical in design to a wine-bottle corkscrew. He quite literally screws his female. The penis is not a tube but a stiff spiraling rod with a deep groove down which sperm rushes into the female.

Male ducks can be veritable sex maniacs in the spring. Though some males and females "marry" and remain monogamous, other males remain bachelors and rape other males' "wives." Married females will go to great lengths to hide from marauding bachelors, concealing themselves for an entire day in high grass. Bands of three or four bachelors will seek out a hiding female and take turns raping her.

CONTINUED

If they can't find a female, the more aggressive males will mount the least aggressive male of the group. It is not uncommon for two bachelors to hold down a third while he's mounted by another male. Homosexuality is not at all uncommon among ducks—or geese, for that matter.

Porcupine • *There's a lot of truth in the old joke: How do porcupines make love? Very carefully.*

Mating is a strange and dangerous affair. With his pointed penis fully unsheathed and erect, he rears up on his hind legs and, from a distance of about six feet, begins to squirt her with urine—an amazing feat, since most male animals cannot urinate with an erection. She does not like the scent bath and growls, snarls, and snaps at him until he stops.

He often approaches her on only three paws, using one paw to hold his penis and gently stroke it. Before the male mounts the female from behind, she obligingly folds down the quills around her rear end. Otherwise mating would be impossible. When they make contact—and only if all of her rear-end quills are down—he thrusts his penis into her. This is the most dangerous time, since young, inexperienced females don't always lower all their quills fully or move their barbed tail out of the way.

A woman contemplates the expression "hung like a horse."

#

GENITALS TO BRAIN

Men are from Mars,
Women are from Venus

J O H N   G R A Y

SEX, PRE-1,000 MILLION YEARS AGO ♦

The origin of sex is ancient and decidedly unerotic. If sex is defined as the union of opposites—"maleness" and "femaleness"—in order to produce a new organism, its origin goes back almost to the beginning of life on earth, for one-celled organisms sometimes engage in sexual behavior.

Among the earliest forms of life, reproduction was accomplished by *fission:* a single cell spontaneously divided to produce two daughter cells. As long as food was plentiful and the cell population not too crowded, this process worked well and was the norm.

But the planet's environment changed. When temperatures became inhospitable, food scarce, and the population crowded, many single cells, in order survive, fused together—and the process created new organisms. It was as if some cosmic instinct told them that reducing their numbers by *fusion* increased the chances of survival for their "offspring," which in this case was a genetic combination of the parents themselves.

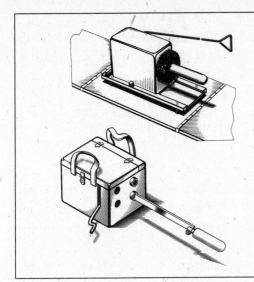

Two motorized "sex partners" for safe sex in the age of AIDS. Penile shaft with pubic hair base (top, 1988), which can accommodate a penile shaft (shown) or a rubber vagina attachment.

From external appearances these early "mothers" and "fathers" seemed indistinguishable. But they weren't entirely. A cell preferred a mate that was as different as possible from itself. In the paramecium, for example, two separate cell populations, or "families," if left alone, will reproduce by cell division or fission. But mix the two families, and each group somehow senses the presence of strangers and mates with *them* by fusion.

Attraction of Opposites

This principle, the attraction of opposites, is an ancient aspect of sex. Even the most primitive single-cell organisms sought mates that were different from themselves. The differences initially were extremely slight. A small cell sought out a larger one. A cell with limited food in its body preferred a mate possessing a nutritional bonanza. A cell lacking locomotion chose a mate with whiplike flagella. In fact, all kinds of sexual unions between one-cell organisms were, and still are, possible: a small, stationary, starving cell will still choose a large, motile one rich in nutrients. When it comes to the attraction of opposites, nothing has changed.

So sex as we know it today—a union of opposites—evolved out of a basic and vital quest for complementarity. Why? Because any organism producing a great variety among its offspring has offspring that have a better chance of survival in a hostile world.

As evolution advanced, cells increased in complexity, and differences between them became more pronounced. To size, motility, and food supply were added countless other survival attributes. This polarization of opposites resulted in "male" and "female" cells, culminating in the development of the sperm and egg, each the polar opposite of the other. Sperm was carried by the *male* of the species, eggs by the *female*. In order to produce an offspring, sperm and egg had to get together. Sex was born.

FACE-TO-FACE INTERCOURSE; 6 MILLION YEARS AGO •

*O*ur primate ancestors, chimpanzee-like creatures, mated from the rear, doggie style. Chimps, our nearest primate relatives, still do. Rear mounting is commonplace among almost all species, large and small, from elephants and horses, to cats and dogs, to parakeets and mice.

Rear mounting has disadvantages. It prevents eye contact between partners unless the female looks over her shoulder, as is the case with dogs. Rear mounting hampers intimacy. It prevents lip contact, or kissing. And in humans it actually discourages female orgasm, since the penis cannot produce direct friction with the clitoris.

When—*and why*—did our protohuman ancestors switch from rear mounting to face-to-face copulation?

Walk This Way—Bipedalism and Copulation

The answer has to do with the act of walking erect, or bipedalism, which evolved around 6 million years ago. From lumbering ape-like on feet and knuckles to walking erect was a gradual transformation. Almost certainly it did not happen so that the first humans could enjoy eye-to-eye contact and kissing while having sex; these niceties were secondary considerations.

There were three primary, and interconnected, advantages to bipedalism. (1) It freed the hands, allowing greater manual dexterity in building shelters and sculpting and using tools and weapons. (2) These things, in turn, necessitated an expanded development of the brain, which had many survival advantages. (3) And walking erect raised the eyes from the ground so they could better scam the horizon for predators and food.

Why did walking erect allow for face-to-face intercourse?

In order to walk erect all of the time, not just in brief spurts as chimps often do, the pelvic bone and its relation to the legs had to change. The pelvic bone narrowed, and the legs shifted forward to better support and balance the erect torso. Also, the point of entry of the spinal cord into the skull shifted. In primates, the opening for the spinal cord is toward the rear of the skull—as it is for all four-legged creatures—causing the head to hang. In modern humans, the opening is much farther forward, so that the head is balanced on the top of the spinal column.

Thus, to walk erect, the skeleton underwent major changes. Protohumans became upright, planar creatures, which, coincidentally, allowed for *full frontal body contact* and face-to-face intercourse. Two upright bodies, like two vertical planes, come together and touch at every point, top to bottom. By comparison, when two chimpanzees hug, their shoulders make contact, their heads pass beyond each other, and their hips remain far apart. For them, front-to-front sex is awkward if not impossible.

Frontal sex did more that enabled a man and a woman to be acutely aware of each other, to enjoy eye-to-eye, lip-to-lip contact. It joined sexual pleasure to a fundamental contact comfort: the warmth and pressure on the *front* of the body that is the infant's first source of security and love.

CONTINUOUS FEMALE SEX; 8 MILLION TO 4 MILLION YEARS AGO ◆

*T*he human female is capable of continual sexual arousal. She is physically capable of copulation every day of her adult life—even during pregnancy and shortly thereafter.

This is most unusual among members of the animal kingdom. No females of any other sexually reproducing species can do it so frequently. All other females have a period of heat, or estrus, during which they copulate. Sex at any other time is highly unusual—and unwelcome. In many species, females out of heat will attack or kill a horny male that tries to mount them.

"Heat"—Female Frenzy

We should pause for a moment and look at the word "estrus." Male zoologists choose this word to describe periodic female sexual receptivity. "Estrus" is from the Latin *oestrus,* meaning "frenzy," or "to rush violently about." A female in heat is in a sexual frenzy. Anyone who has owned a female cat and endured her high-pitched wails and agitation during periods of heat can appreciate the term.

But "estrus" means more. It is also Latin for "gadfly," meaning both a real fly (like the horsefly) that flits annoyingly about, biting its victims, and, figuratively, a person who seeks amusement in an idle, restless way. One

---

WHY MEN ARE BIGGER THAN WOMEN ◆ *Because the largest males probably brought back the greatest amounts of food and offered better shelter and protection from predators, they became the preferred mates for females. Thus, these bigger males fathered larger male offspring. Natural selection, then, favored the genes for large males. In time, this led to standard differences is size between males and females, in skeletons, musculature, height, and weight.*

In a sense, females' preferences for size created large males. And as we see below, males' preference for frequent sex probably created continous heat in females.

---

wonders if female zoologists would have chosen a different word for periodic female sexual receptively?

What is the origin of continuous estrus in human females?

According to a current theory, it harks back to the changes that occurred in the female when protohominids began walking erect. As mentioned, upright posture brought about a narrowing of the pelvic canal. This resulted in difficult and often fatal pregnancies. Natural selection favored those females with a proclivity for giving premature birth—to babies small enough to negotiate the narrowed cervical canal. These premature babies required more postnatal care than full-term ones and kept their mothers busier. Thus, these mothers became more dependent on males for food and protection.

Females with longer periods of heat had a greater advantage: they had something precious to offer males. By maintaining their "sex appeal" for longer periods of time, they acquired more food and protection than did their counterparts, who could offer males sex less frequently. Consequently, females who flaunted their sexiness were better fed, died less often of disease or predation, and produced more young, since they were more likely to become pregnant. In short, males preferred females who could give them more and more sex.

In time, succeeding generations of human females had disproportionately higher numbers of individuals who carried the gene for longer periods of heat. Female sexual "frenzy" went from days, to months, to years. This lead to the evolution of the gene for *continuous* female sexual receptivity, from puberty to menopause—and beyond.

There is an evolutionary reason why "Adam" is bigger than "Eve," why men in general are bigger than women.

FAMILY RESEMBLANCE—BABY RESEMBLES MOM OR DAD? ◆

*N*ot long after a baby is born the guessing game begins. Does the chubby, nearly bald tot look more like its mother or father? Most relatives equivocate or cite single features that favor one parent—"her" eyes, "his" nose. If you don't have a clue and want to guess, statistically, regardless of the tot's sex, the answer is always *dad*. Most babies early in life seem to resemble their fathers.

University of California psychologist Nicholas Christenfeld conducted an experiment that led to this theory. He showed college students photos of year-old infants. Each picture was accompanied by photos of the child's mother, father, and two total strangers. The students were able to pick out the baby's mother about 30 percent of the time. But they selected the baby's father 50 percent of the time—a rate significantly higher than might be expected by random guessing.

Why might a baby resemble dad more than mom?

The answer may be rooted in evolutionary biology, says Christenfeld. A mother, having carried the fetus, given birth, and taken over nurturing of the infant, can be certain the baby is hers—no matter what it looks like.

A father cannot be so sure. He may have been cuckolded. His wife bore the baby—but who fathered it? Another man?

To encourage paternal investment in a new baby, nature allows the baby to resemble the father, it seems. Dad feels more attached to the child and, by seeing his own features in it, feels confident—if only at an unconscious level—that he's the father. Now he will provide food for the baby, protect the mother, and, in time, pay college tuition. All because he "sees himself" in the tiny tot.

Of course, as the child grows up, it may resemble the father less and less. It may look more like the mother, or a grandparent, or an aunt or uncle. Or the mailman. But by this time the father has invested tremendous time and effort in rearing the child. "By the time the child is ten," says Christenfeld, "the guy has invested so much money, maybe he figures, 'What the heck, might as well pay for college!' "

IS SEX SAFE FOR A BAD HEART? ◆

*I*f you have had a heart attack, should you give up sex for the rest of your life?

An even longer-standing question in the medical profession is: if you have a weakened or diseased heart but have not yet had an attack, should you, as a precaution, never have sex again?

Opinions have varied over the centuries. Some argued that the physical exertion expended to reach orgasm was enough to trigger cardiac arrest in certain people. They pointed to many men, and fewer women, who had died while making love—perhaps not the worst way to go. Other doctors went further. They argued that even if a man assumes the passive bottom position in intercourse, with the woman straddling him and doing all the work, the adrenaline rush that *is* excitement itself is too much for a weakened heart to endure.

Clearer answers to these questions came in 1996.

In the largest study of its kind, doctors at Harvard Medical School followed the lives of hundreds of men and women who had survived heart attacks. They also studied healthy individuals. Their findings:

• The risk of a *healthy* person having a heart attack because of sexual activity is about one in a million.

• The risk to a person with heart disease is only *two* in a million. For these people, sex is still safer than driving a car.

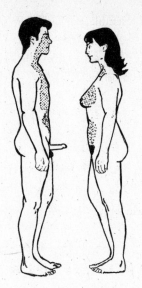

Sex flush during intercourse. Only 25 percent of men experience it, while 75 percent of women do. In both sexes the measles-like rash fades within five minutes after orgasm.

The First Two Hours After Sex

Sex is not without its hazards.

The first two hours after orgasm are the riskiest. If you are going to die from a heart attack from sex, this is when it will most likely occur—whether you have a weak heart, a strong heart, or have already had a heart attack. Make it through the first two postcoital hours, and you will live to have sex again.

Even this brief risk can be greatly reduced if heart patients regularly engage in moderately strenuous, or "conditioning," exercise—something as simple as vigorous half-hour walks several times a week. In fact, the study suggested that walking briskly uphill for thirty minutes every day virtually eliminates the risk of heart attack from sex, making intercourse as safe as any nonstrenuous activity for the heart.

MEN ARE FROM MARS, WOMEN FROM VENUS ◆

*M*en and women *are* different—the only dispute is how.

Psychologist John Gray says men are from Mars, women from Venus, and they must learn to communicate because they speak different languages.

Over the centuries, certain traits have been regarded as "masculine," others as "feminine." Conventional wisdom (CW) says women are more apologetic,

THE SAFEST SEX YOU CAN HAVE ♦ *If you've already had a heart attack, and are exercising daily, you can decrease your risk of death from sex even further by taking three special precautions.*

1. Have sex in a familiar surrounding—the same bed or room.

2. Plan it for the same time of day. The most risky time is within the first hour of wakening in the morning.

3. Most important of all, have sex with the same partner every time. A new partner can be deadly. While changing locales and times of day are risky, changing partners, as exciting as the prospect may be, can be just two much for a damaged heart.

men less apologetic. Men gossip less, women gossip more. Men are better at giving advice, women at taking advice. This kind of dichotomy is what prompted psychologist Deborah Tannen to write her 1990 bestseller about miscommunication between the sexes, *You Just Don't Understand.*

For better or worse, we have come to view each other through polarized thinking. The problem with dwelling on gender-different "truths" is that they can become self-fulfilling prophecies, a straitjacket, forcing men and women into certain roles in life.

"Mars and Venus," from Agostino Carracci's The Loves of the Gods, *c. 1602.*

That said, here are fifty-four gender traits taken from various sources and compiled by Cris Evatt in *He & She* (1992). They express a long tradition of stereotypical categorizing and popular opinion—mostly male opinion, it should be pointed out, since men have cataloged the bulk of the evidence.

How does your "maleness" or "femaleness" compare? Rate yourself. Score a perfect fifty-four points in the left-hand column and you're *all male*—and there's something seriously wrong with you. Score fifty-four in the right-hand column and you're all female—and equally troubled.

MALE	FEMALE
More self-focused	More other-focused
Need less intimacy	Need more intimacy
Fear engulfment	Fear abandonment
Identify with work	Identify with people
Need less approval	Need more approval
More independent	Less independent
More detached	More emotional
Worry less	Worry more
Express anger	Repress anger
Attention-getter	Attention-giver
Highly competitive	Less competitive
Less cooperative	More cooperative
More power-motivated	Less power-motivated
Respect very important	Respect less important
Obsessed with sports	Indifferent to sports
Talk more about things	Talk more about people
Talk more in public	Talk more in private
Take things literally	Look for hidden meanings
Less varied vocabulary	More varied vocabulary
Speak more directly	Speak more indirectly
Less responsive listener	More responsive listener
Quick decision maker	Slower decision maker
Gossip less	Gossip more
Give advice better	Take advice better
Focus more on solutions	Like to discuss problems
Less apologetic	More apologetic

Tell more jokes	Tell more stories
Less willing to seek help	Seek help readily
Boast about accomplishments	Seldom boast
Nag less	Nag more
Often intimidate others	Seldom intimidate others
Issue orders	Make suggestions
Important to be right	Not so important
Often seek conflict	Often avoid conflict
Like to be adored	Like to adore others
Fearful of commitment	Eager for commitment
Sexually jealous of mate	Emotionally jealous of mate
Accept others as they are	Hope to change others
Thrive on receiving	Thrive on giving
More polygamous	More monogamous
More sadistic	More masochistic
More sex-oriented	More love-oriented
Have fewer close friends	Have more close friends
Like group activities	Prefer intimate encounters
Worry less about others	Worry more about others
More sensitive to stress	Less sensitive to stress
Less trusting	More trusting
More aggressive	Less aggressive
Still in conversing	Animated in conversing
Less into dieting	More into dieting
Less health-concerned	More health-concerned
Take more physical risks	Take less physical risks
Less concerned about looks	More concerned about looks
Shop out of necessity	Shop for enjoyment

ORIGINS OF MALENESS AND FEMALENESS— SCIENTIFIC EVIDENCE; 1849 TO PRESENT ◆

From ancient times, people have always realized that the human body was sexed, male and female—the genitals are a dead giveaway, as are female breasts. But starting in the middle of the nineteenth century, scientists began to suspect that the human *brain* was also sexed, that many traits viewed as male or female have biological roots at a cranial level.

Today, we know that the human brain is every bit as sexed as the body. In terms of neural anatomy, men and women do have different circuitry, even if only a very small part of it has been mapped. All of the answers on the origins or maleness and femaleness—and, for that matter, "gayness"— won't be in for many years. But the evidence is growing, and some important questions can be partially answered—for now.

When Is the Brain's Sexual Circuitry Laid Down?

Largely in the fetal stage of development. And, too, in the early years of life, up to about age six, while the brain is still growing and forging neural connections.

Where in the Brain Is the Sexual Circuitry Laid Down?

Mainly in the hypothalamus, a structure at the base of the brainstem that is a primary center for sex drive and copulatory behavior. Also in the amygdala (above the ears), an area associated with aggression and violence. And, to a lesser extent, in the cerebral cortex, or "thinking center" of the brain.

Men and women apparently do think differently, not just because of social conditioning—which is undeniably important—but also because of brain differences. These neural differences, to some as yet undetermined degree, may be behind many of the Conventional Wisdom traits examined in the previous section. To paraphrase John Gray's metaphor: Men's *brains* are from Mars, women's *brains* are from Venus. And, it is not impossible that gay brains just might have their own point of developmental origin.

What Factors Influence the Masculinizing or Feminizing of the Fetal Brain?

In addition to the X and Y chromosomes inherited from mom and dad, other influencing hormones come from the mother's body *and* from various chemicals in the environment. This chemical soup floods the developing fetus in a hormonal bath—it *flavors* the baby—influencing the wiring of the brain.

These modern theories are based on scientific research that began in Germany in 1849. Much of the early work was done on animals. Scientists recently have begun to study the human brain's sexual circuitry. Here, in a nutshell, are the major highlights of sex and gender findings, a chronological history of the biological origins of maleness and femaleness:

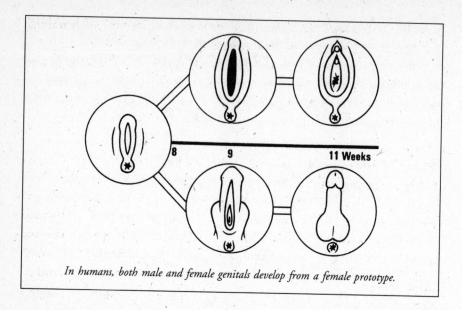

In humans, both male and female genitals develop from a female prototype.

Castrated Roosters, 1849

The first link between sex hormones and behavior was made in Germany by Arnold Berthold. He castrated six aggressive cockerels, and they stopped fighting with each other. They also lost interest in hens. He then transplanted testicles from one bird into the abdominal cavities of another, and again they fought. And again they mated with hens.

Berthold concluded that the transplanted testicles developed connections not with the nervous system but with the circulatory system. He suspected that the influence came from a blood-borne substance, which he later identified as a "hormone"—testosterone.

A Man with Ovaries and Uterus, 1865

An Italian anatomist autopsied a man who had never had visible testes. Doctors thought they had simply never descended, but the anatomist discovered, much to his horror, that the *man* had ovaries and a uterus. The "man," it would turn out, was genetically a woman whose external genitalia had been masculinized in the womb by an excess of male hormones secreted by the adrenal glands—a condition known as congenital adrenal hyperplasia, or CAH.

Today, CAH is the most common cause of masculinized genitals in newborn human females. The clitoris *becomes* a penis, and the vaginal lips seal shut to form a scrotal sack. The "male" genitalia are so convincingly real that CAH is undetectable except for a genetic test.

The defective gene that causes CAH is present at a strikingly high level among Yupik Eskimos. Among Caucasians, it occurs in one case out of seven thousand births. Untreated girls develop excess facile and body hair, their breasts do not mature, and they are infertile.

The Cow Who Thought She Was a Bull, 1916

Around 1915, Canadian-born researcher Frank Lillie observed that the free-martin cow—a female with XX chromosomes that, nonetheless, looks and acts like a bull and even mounts other cows—was always born with a male twin. These tough cows always had a bull brother. Lillie speculated—and research later proved—that a freemartin cow is "masculinized" in the womb by a flood of testosterone secreted by her male wombmate and twin brother. The freemartin cow, one might say, thinks like a bull trapped in a cow's body.

Today this masculinizing phenomenon is called the "twinning effect." It has been observed to varying degrees in all species studied, including, to some extent, humans. Three brothers in the womb can "supermasculinize" each other with their combined secretions of testosterone. Or, two brothers sharing a womb with a sister can masculinize the development of her brain, which might affect her adult behavior. A bath of testosterone is a potent thing. Additional human studies are underway.

Making Females With Penises, 1959

In a landmark experiment, William Young and Robert Goy at the University of Kansas injected pregnant guinea pigs with large amounts of testosterone. At birth, the genetically female animals in the litter had male genitalia *and* female ovaries. They were sexual hybrids.

When the females were ninety days old, the researchers removed their ovaries, then injected half of them with additional testosterone. The injected females began to act like males: they mounted other females and fought among males to dominate their groups. The researchers had changed not only the female animals' genitalia but had masculinized their brains.

In the early 1960s, Young and Goy concluded that hormones affect the brain in two ways: (1) In the womb, hormones imprint a code on the developing brain, as light stamps an image on film in a camera. The code may be "male" or "female," or some hybrid wiring. (2) After birth, and throughout life, other hormones activate the code, much as a chemical developer brings out a latent image on film. Behavior depends on both the prenatal code and the postnatal influences.

Testosterone, Nature's Weapon of Warfare, 1961 to 1971

Researchers at Rockefeller University, working with male and female rats, determined that a shot of testosterone during gestation affects *both sexes* in five fundamental ways. As adults, males and females display an increase in individualism, self-assurance, physical activity, aggression, and in a propensity toward violence. Later studies of violent institutionalized criminals revealed that they produce more testosterone than the average male.

Female Canaries Learn to Sing, 1967

At several laboratories, researchers injected the developing eggs of canaries with testosterone. They knew that among song birds *only the male* sings; he has a nodule on the front of his brain that is, literally, his song box. Female do not possess a true song nodule.

However, the female canaries treated in the egg with testosterone sang as adults and as beautifully as males. The researchers autopsied the "masculinized" females and discovered that their brains had grown true song box nodules.

It's known today that the extent of a masculinized female's song repertory is related to the amount of male hormone she receives during gestation.

Timing a Sex Change, 1968 to 1978

Several independent researchers discovered that just about any male animal, given the right dose of estrogen in the womb, can be turned into a female. And just about any female animal, given sufficient testosterone during gestation, can become a male. Researchers have done this with various birds and mammals.

The time during gestation when a developing fetus is injected with testosterone or estrogen is critical. If a female is given testosterone in the early stage of gestation, her genitalia will become more masculinized than her brain. If, on the other hand, she is given it days or weeks later, her brain will become more masculinized than her genitalia.

Virilizing Monkeys, 1981

Robert Goy, at Wisconsin's Regional Primate Research Center, altered the adult behavior of both male and female monkeys by giving them prenatal shots of testosterone. The "virilized" males engaged in more rough-and-tumble play and were exceptionally aggressive. The "virilized" females looked female in every way but behaved like males: they engaged in roughhouse play and mounted their peers—even their mothers, which is highly rare for rhesus monkeys.

Goy concluded: "It doesn't matter whether it's roughhousing, mounting peers, or attempting to dominate the group, it's all related to the *duration of* [hormone] *treatment* [in the womb]." The virilized females "behave like boys because of masculinizing hormones, not because of a male appearance that causes the other animals to treat them like boys."

Gays: Born or Bred? 1981

The first shot in this long-running debate came in a report from the Kinsey Institute that concluded that homosexuality has little to due with "overbearing mothers" and "distant fathers"—or any other influences in childhood. Homosexuality, said the researchers, appears to be as deep-rooted a sex drive as heterosexuality and as impervious to change; it may be determined before birth.

The Kinsey researchers concluded that a boy's relationship with his mother was "hardly worth mentioning" when it came to determining his sexual orientation. An unsatisfactory relationship with his father was only "slightly more important" in predicating sexual preference.

One childhood trait did set gays apart: "Youngsters failed to conform to generally accepted forms of behavior for their sexes":

• For boys, this involved a lack of interest in sports and an enjoyment of solitary activities like drawing, music, and reading.

• For girls, this involved the enjoyment of sports and outdoor play, as well as wearing boys' clothes. The girls were less interested in playing house, hopscotch, and jacks.

"This gender nonconformity occurs so early in childhood," said the researchers, "that it has to be biological." However, the Kinsey group was perplexed by the fact that "many heterosexuals also reported gender nonconformity in childhood."

Different Immune Responses in Women and Men, 1982

Immunologists reported that women have a double dose of immunity—twice as much as men.

Men are more susceptible to a variety of diseases, including central nervous system infections like polio, as well as staphylococcal infections, Legionnaires' disease, and certain forms of cancer. Researchers suggested that one reason why men experience lower resistance may be that they possess only one X chromosome, whereas women have two.

The X carries some of the genes that control immunity. With a pair of Xs, women have a backup. A double set of genes that regulate immunity may give women extra health insurance during pregnancy. A woman's immune system is slightly suppressed during this time to prevent an attack on the fetus, which is, in a sense, a foreign implant in her body. The additional gene may provide necessary protection during this immune-suppressed period.

But the female's extra immunity can also work against her. Women not only have superior antibody responses to viruses and microbes from outside the body, but they also form autoantibodies more readily against their own tissues. Because of this, autoimmune diseases such as rheumatoid arthritis, systemic lupus erythematosus (an inflammation of the connective tissue), and myasthenia gravis (a neuromuscular disorder) strike women more often than men.

Boys Raised as Girls, 1983

Scientists reported a dramatic study of babies apparently born and raised as girls, who suddenly began to produce testosterone at puberty. Subsequently the "girls" grew penises, body hair, and beards.

The "girls" had actually been ill-formed boys at birth and throughout their early lives, the result of a genetic flaw. Their testes remained hidden in their abdominal cavities. At puberty, when they began to produce large bursts of testosterone, the "girls" began to develop into normal-looking boys.

The most remarkable part of the study was that these children, though raised for thirteen years as girls, had no difficulty suddenly accepting the biological reality that they were boys. "Their brains were primed all along to work as male brains," said one researcher. "At puberty, the boys just started to behave as young men—as their brains told them to."

One prominent endocrinologist has commented on this dramatic study and the hormone evidence that has accumulated to date:

Sex hormones don't just appear and meander about the body at puberty. They know exactly where to go. The cells that are their targets have already been primed, in the womb, to respond to the hormones. This is true of the body, of the reproductive organs, the heart, lungs, and also true of the brain.

The tissues, neural circuitry and chemistry of the brain have already been stamped during fetal life by the sex hormones. And the foundations have already been laid for the range of behaviors that will characterize the organism as male or female in adult life.

The Boy Who Lost His Penis, 1983

Sex researcher John Money at Johns Hopkins Medical Center related another interesting case. A baby boy who was undergoing minor penile surgery accidently had his penis cut off. At the advice of doctors, the distraught parents opted to transform their son into their daughter, with a combination of hormone therapy and surgery. The unsuspecting son, who looked genitally like a girl, was raised as a girl, dressed as a girl, and had no trouble living with his sex reassignment. Until puberty.

At puberty, "she" got distinct feelings of being male. In fact, she had a love of cars and wanted to "become a mechanic." Money concluded that in the womb the fetal brain had been masculinized and wired to be a male brain. Amputation of the penis, later sex reassignment surgery, and hormone therapy could not alter that *male map* laid down in the brain before birth.

Similar cases have led researchers to conclude that true transsexuals possess the brain of one sex trapped in the body of the opposite sex. Thus a transsexual has little or no trouble adapting to sex-reassignment surgery.

Gays Are from Venus and Mars, 1984

Researchers studying a group of homosexual men found that their hormone-response patterns were midway between those of heterosexual men and heterosexual women. The study looked at three groups, heterosexual women, heterosexual men, and homosexual men, examining hormonal responses to the drug Premarin, a potent form of estrogen that is used to treat women with menopausal symptoms and uterine bleeding.

• Normal women given the drug early in the menstrual cycle experienced a characteristic change in the level of luteinizing hormone, or LH. Initially, the LH level in the blood fell, then rose to about double the original baseline level.

• In heterosexual men, a different pattern was seen. An initial drop in LH occurred, followed by a gradual return to baseline.

• In homosexual men, an intermediate response pattern was observed. While the level of testosterone dropped in both straight and gay men after Premarin, and in both groups this level eventually returned to normal, the return took longer in gays.

As the researchers concluded, "Most of the homosexual men are processing the estrogen differently from heterosexual men."

The Sissy Boy Syndrome, 1986

After a fifteen-year study of effeminate boys, Richard Green concluded in The "Sissy Boy Syndrome" (1987) that "most young boys who persistently act like girls grow up to be homosexuals or bisexuals." Such boys, said Green, are athletically inept, prefer music to cars, have difficulty making friends with other boys, and prefer to play with girls. They almost always spurn rough-and-tumble play, and many of them follow their mothers around the house, mimicking their activities.

Women Are Brainier Than Men, 1986

Researchers discovered an anatomical difference between human male and female brains. In females, the nerve bundle connecting the right and left hemispheres—the corpus callosum—is thicker and richer in connections than in males. Females, it seems, are more bilateral in their thinking, benefiting more equally from the "intuitive" right hemisphere and the "analytical" left hemisphere.

Some have interpreted this to mean that women have an overall superior brain, while men have a more specialized brain that allows them to excel in scientific and technological tasks.

The Gay Brain, 1991

Salk Institute researcher Simon LeVay studied forty-one brains and found that part of the hypothalamus was smaller in gay men than in straight men —about only half the size. He also found that a tiny region of the hypothalamus, which is involved in sexual behaviors, was, in gay men, more like that found in women than in heterosexual men.

He looked at four different grouping of cells, technically referred to as the interstitial nuclei of the anterior hypothalamus, or INAH. Others had already reported that INAH 2 and 3 were larger in men than in women. He found that the INAH-3 areas of most of the women and the gay men were about the same size. In straight men, this region was on average twice as large—about the size of a grain of sand.

The LeVay study was the second to find a difference between the hypothalamuses of gay and straight men. In 1990, a Dutch team discovered that another group of neurons in the same tiny gland was larger in homosexuals than in straight men. Some scientists believe that this structure governs daily rhythms, not sexual behavior.

Many feminists and gay activists are concerned that genetic and biological differences could be misused to oppress women and gays. If women are proved to be genetically better at verbal than spatial skills, might engineering schools give male applicants preferential treatment? If scientists find a genetic basis for homosexuality, might pregnant women demand to be tested to see if they are carrying a gay infant? Might parents opt to have abortions to eliminate gay offspring? Might genetic engineering be used to "cure" the gay fetus?

Such eugenic concerns are real, especially as research into gender behavior and sexual orientation accelerates. "What ethical obligations would a scientist—or a parent—face when armed with power to modify a trait as

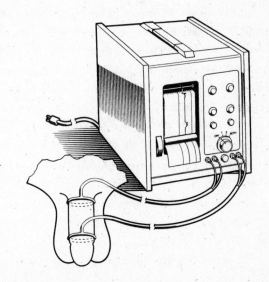

Electronic device to monitor the expansion of an erection.

LINE BETWEEN LOVE AND HATE ✦ *"Homophobic males, deep down in their psyches, are really latent, self-loathing homosexuals."*

This long-standing belief is supported by a recent study, the first of its kind. According to a 1996 article in the Journal of Abnormal Psychology, *homophobic men are more easily aroused by watching gay sex videos than nonhomophobic men.*

A research team at the University of Georgia recruited sixty-four young white men, all straight and with girlfriends. First they were shown a four-minute video depicting heterosexual sex, then one of the same duration depicting gay male sex. The men's responses were measured by a penile gauge that tracked changes in the organ's circumference; that is, measured their degree of erection.

The results: only one-third of the nonhomophobic men registered eventual arousal while watching the gay video, and the onset of their arousal was gradual. By contrast, 80 percent of the homophobic men showed penile expansion during the gay video, and the onset of their arousal was almost immediate.

Some degree of arousal from watching acts of penile stimulation is to be expected among most men. But by the end of the gay video, the homophobic men were on average more than twice as turned on as the nonhomophobic men.

The results of watching the heterosexual video were equally revealing. Nonhomophobic men were quickly turned on and became highly aroused. The homophobic men took longer to get an erection and reached an overall lower stage of arousal.

"Men who are upset by being around gay men probably have these tendencies themselves," the researchers concluded. Clinical psychologist Henry Adams, who headed the team said, "The thing you dislike most in yourself is the kind of thing you might jump on somebody else for."

disputed as homosexuality?" asks Chandler Burr in *A Separate Creation* (1996). "How will biological knowledge of sexual orientation increase our understanding of other controversial traits—from violence to intelligence to differences between men and women?"

We will just have to wait and see.

CHAPTER 7

This Thing Called Love

KISSING TO COURTING

Love, the quest; marriage, the conquest;
divorce, the inquest

HELEN ROWLAND

"LOVE"; PRE-TWELFTH CENTURY ◆

Our word "love" is from the Old English *lufu*, meaning "to be fond of," and is related to the Latin *libet*, "it pleases." When you love someone, you wish to please him or her.

Our English "love" is also related the Old English *leof*, meaning "dear." The person you love is dear to you.

The spelling l-o-v-e arose sometime before the twelfth century. Initially the word meant a strong affection for another person arising out of kinship or personal ties. The word was used most commonly to express the bond between a mother and child. Only later did "love" come to encompass affection based on sexual desire.

Love has been praised and cursed, called "the sweetest thing on earth" and "a sickness full of woes."

Shakespeare captured both views. Wickedly he teased in *Twelfth Night:*

Marrying for romantic love may always have been an ideal but became a reality for most couples only in modern times.

What is love? 'Tis not hereafter;
Present mirth hath present laughter;
*   What's to come is still unsure;*
*   In delay there lies no plenty;*
*   Then come kiss me, sweet and twenty!*
Youth's a stuff will not endure.

He took a nobler view in the sonnets when he penned:

Love's not Time's fool, though rosy lips and cheeks
Within his bending sickle's compass come;
Love alters not with his brief hours and weeks,
But bears it out even to the edge of doom.

Plato claimed that love was the appreciation of beauty, in objects, in youth—in girls *and* boys—and especially in abstract ideas and mathematical formulas.

Descartes argued that love was an emotion so deep and powerful that a person's very soul would attach itself to the lovable object or person.

Ortega y Gasset, in *On Love*, defined the emotion as "A centrifugal act of the soul in constant flux that goes towards the object and envelops it in warm corroboration, uniting us with it, and positively reaffirming its being."

THE CHEMISTRY OF LOVE ◆ *How do fools fall in love?*
Biochemically, we all fall in love in the same predictable way.

Scientists have just begun to unlock the chemistry of love. Genetics, psychological experiences, and even the sense of smell trigger an initial attraction to another person. The brain is then revved up by at least three natural body amphetamines, or "uppers": phenylethylamine, and the neurotransmitters dopamine and norepinephrine. They produce feelings of elation and euphoria. Love feels good.

During the early stages of love, large amounts of endorphins, morphine-like chemicals, flood the brain, leaving the lovers with a sense of security, peace, and calm. There is a chemical reason why you readily trust your lover and feel safe in his or her embrace. And why you feel so horrible when a love relationship ends: you're deprived of your daily hit of natural painkillers.

During these stages of "attraction" and "attachment," you are literally drugged *by your beloved. These chemically triggered states can last for two or three years, before they start to wane as the "love potions" peter out.*

Interestingly, divorce rates peak around the fourth year of marriage. The initial "highs" of love have lost their chemical underpinnings. If the relationship is not based on more substantial foundations, it can easily end. Marilyn Monroe's classic film The Seven Year Itch *should be retitled "The Four Year Itch."*

Early love, chemically based, is when you love the way the other person makes you feel. It is self-centered, feel-good love. Mature love, which comes later in a relationship, is love for whoever a person is. It is other-centered.

Even the intimacy of "cuddling" has a chemical base. Your brain's pituitary gland secretes oxytocin, a hormone that induces feelings of relaxation and satisfaction from whole-body contact; you can't get close enough to your lover. Your nerve endings are craving his or her soothing touch.

Cole Porter knew what he was talking about when he wrote "I get a kick out of you."

Dante, in the closing line of his great poetic work, painted love as *the* driving force in the cosmos: love "moves the sun and the other stars."

Tennyson took the optimist's view: " 'Tis better to have loved and lost / Than never to have loved at all."

Sir Walter Scott epitomized the viewpoint of history's great romantics, who believed that love had a transforming power over people's lives:

Love rules the court, the camp, the grove,
And men below, and saints above;
For love is heaven, and heaven is love.

Bisexual Oscar Wilde, jailed for his affair with Lord Alfred Douglas, wrote of love from his prison cell, taking a sour view:

Yet each man kills the thing he loves,
By each let this be heard,
Some do it with a bitter look,
Some with a flattering word.
The coward does it with a kiss,
The brave man with a sword!

Alfred Douglas got in his two cents: "I am the Love that dare not speak its name."

In 1970, Erich Segal, in *Love Story*, added a new, if sappy, epigram to history's long list: "Love means never having to say you're sorry."

The witty Dorothy Parker got in her shots at love:

By the time you swear you're his,
Shivering and sighing,
And he vows his passion is
Infinite, undying—
Lady, make a note of this:
One of you is lying.

Love is the entire message of Jesus Christ: *Love thy neighbor as thyself.*

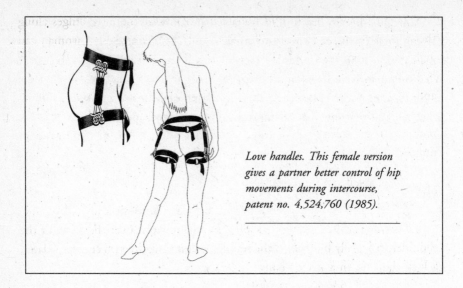

Love handles. This female version gives a partner better control of hip movements during intercourse, patent no. 4,524,760 (1985).

LOVE WORDS AND PHRASES ✦

*O*nce the word "love" appeared in English, sometime before the twelfth century, people began to couple it with other words to coin interesting expressions. The dates given below, taken from *Merriam-Webster* and the *OED*, represent the earliest recorded usage in the English language:

- **Love Affair**, 1591; a romantic attachment or episode between lovers.
- **Love Apple**, 1578, England; for the newly introduced fruit, the "tomato"—from the French for the fruit, *pomme d'amour*.
- **Love Beads**, 1968; a string of beads worn as a symbol of love and peace.
- **Love Bird**, 1595; any variety of small, multicolored parrots of the genus *Agapornis*, of Africa, that show great affection and monogamy toward their mates.
- **Love Bug**, 1966; a small black fly, *Plecia nearctica*, with a red thorax that swarms along highways in the Gulf states of America, so named because it is usually seen copulating; later the name of the Volkswagen Beetle.
- **Love Child**, 1805; an illegitimate child, formerly called a bastard.
- **Love Feast**, 1580; a gathering held to promote reconciliation and good feeling or show someone affectionate honor.
- **Love Grass**, 1702; any of a genus, *Eragrostis*, of grasses that resemble the bluegrasses but have flattened spikelets and deciduous lemmas.

• **Love Handles**, 1975; affectionate nickname for the fatty bulges along the sides at the waist (usually referred to only in men) which a woman can grab onto during sex.

• **Love In**, 1967; a gathering of people for the expression of mutual love, and/or sex.

• **Love-in-a-mist**, 1760; a European and African annual herb, *Nigella damascena*, of the buttercup family, which has whitish flowers enveloped in numerous finely dissected bracts.

• **Love Knot**, 1300s; a stylized knot, in rope of jewelry, used as an emblem of love.

• **Loveless**, 1300s; having no love in one's life; without a lover.

• **Lovelock**, 1592; a long lock of hair usually worn over the front of the shoulder, especially by men in the seventeenth and eighteenth centuries; later, a lock shorn from a lover's hair.

• **Lovelorn**, 1634; bereft of love or a lover.

• **Lovely**, 1200s; a adjective meaning "attractive" or "beautiful."

• **Lovelies**, 1652; two or more beautiful women, or objects of art.

• **Love-making**, 1400s; an expression of courtship, or a euphemism for copulation.

• **Love Seat**, 1902; a double chair, sofa, or settee for two persons; all the rage at the turn-of-the-century.

• **Love Score**, 1800s; a score of "zero" in tennis, an allusion to the fact that in the game of love both players are of equal affection; from a twelfth-century phrase, "to play for love."

• **Lovesick**, 1400s; languishing with love and yearning; the expression of a lover's longing, all the worse of unrequited.

• **Lovesome**, 1200s; winsome, affectionate, amorous.

• **Lovey-dovey**, 1886; expressing much love, or mushy sentimentality.

• **Loving Cup**, 1812; a large ornamental drinking vessel with two or more handles used in the ceremonial toasting of a victory; later a trophy.

THE GREEK INVENTION OF LOVE; SIXTH CENTURY B.C.E. ◆

*T*he emotion of love is, of course, ancient. It seems clear that other animals experience love for their young. But human societies have regarded love differently throughout history.

The ancient Egyptian equivalent for our word "love" meant "a long, long

FIRST LOVE POEM ◆ *The Sumerian people, who lived between the Tigris and Euphrates rivers in what is now southern Iraq, invented writing about 3500 B.C.E. Many of their clay tablets have survived. One tablet that archaeologists call "Istanbul number 2461" contains history's first recorded love poem.*

The author is unknown. The poem was undoubtedly recited by the chosen bride for Sumerian King Shu-Sin. In ardor and imagery the long Sumerian poem is reminiscent of the tenth-century B.C.E. biblical "Songs of Songs," a dialogue, attributed to Solomon, on the physical love between a young man and his bride.

Here, in part, is a recent translation of the older Sumerian poem:

Bridegroom, dear to my heart,
Goodly is your beauty, honeysweet . . .
You have captivated me,
Let me stand trembling before you,
Bridegroom, I would be taken by you to the bedchamber . . .

Bridegroom, let me caress you,
My precious caress is more savory than honey,
In the bedchamber, honey filled,
Let us enjoy your goodly beauty,
Lion, let me caress you . . .

History's first "love letter" was written with a stylus on another Sumerian clay tablet. The author expressed her affection for her husband and signed off with: "Your loving wife who has had a child."

desire." Egyptian poets and philosophers wrote about straight and gay love, and about "love at first sight." They wrote manuals on courtship and, just before the start of the Christian Era, gave us one of history's earliest femmes fatales: Cleopatra. Casting her sights on Mark Antony, she gave us one of history's first great love affairs.

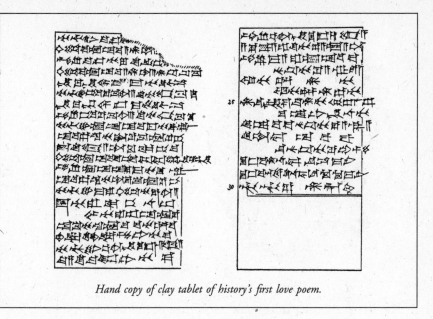

Hand copy of clay tablet of history's first love poem.

However, in terms of generating images and concepts of love that have endured, it was the Greeks who really invented love.

Greeks Words, Images, and Concepts

The ancient Greeks gave us *eros* for carnal love, and *agape* for selfless love.

Sappho wrote love poetry that has survived twenty-six centuries and is still true today.

Greek philosophers wrote voluminously about the distinctions between sexual and "Platonic" love. Plato himself viewed the love that would bear his name as an emotion that ascends from passion for an individual to contemplation of the universal and ideal. His concern was to construct an incorporeal metaphysics out of a sublimation of the desires of the flesh. Only later did people come to view "Platonic love" as a close relationship between two people in which sexual desire is nonexistent, or has been suppressed or sublimated.

The term *Platonic love* was first recorded in 1631.

The image of *Cupid* and his quiver of arrows is Greek. Some of history's greatest love affairs are between Greek men and women, gods and goddesses: *Odysseus and Penelope, Daphnis and Chloe, Eros and Psyche, Hero and Leander.*

Cupid and Psyche.

The Greeks, during their golden age, gave the Western world its concept of love. And, yet, for all these things we recognize today as images and symbols of love, in classical Greece it was something quite different from what it is today.

Greek Love Favored Men—Straight and Gay

Greek love was less of an ennobling and transforming goal of life than an amusing pastime—a distraction. "Its heartfelt expressions were poured forth not by young men and women who desired each other as mates," wrote Morton M. Hunt in *The Natural History of Love* (1959), "but by married men serenading courtesans, and by homosexuals (or lesbians) wooing others of their kind."

For all their writing about love, the Greeks recognized no equality between the sexes. Women were not allowed to be citizens. They were thought to be by nature irrational, hysterical, and obsessed with sex. Men typically married late in life, around age thirty—and they were not expected to be virgins. Women married in their teens and they were expected to be chaste. This meant that neither men nor women had equals of the opposite sex to fall in love with.

Diane Ackerman, in *A Natural History of Love* (1994), paints a typical Greek "love" scenario:

A cultured, educated, sexually experienced, politically active middle-aged husband would return home to his sheltered, illiterate sixteen-year-old wife. Teenage girls were not visible on the streets for men to idealize or fantasize about.

Beautiful teenage boys were, though, and they alone provided the erotic siren of youth. Friends often met at gymnasia, where they could watch the young men of Athens exercise naked (with the foreskin tied over the tip of the penis to protect it).

Since Athenian women were off-limits, it was common for men to have young male lovers or female courtesans, to whom they turned to for companionship, as well as sex, since respectable women were social exiles.

Married couples sometimes fell in love; but love had nothing to do with marriage, which was intended to produce children . . . The marriage formula went like this: "I give you this woman [my daughter] for the ploughing of legitimate children." Women were associated with agriculture, fields to be sown and reaped. Men stood for reason and culture; women for the wild forces of nature men were to tame.

This is not what *we* mean by love. And yet it is the Greeks who that gave us the notion of love. "It is therefore a paradox of no mean order," Morton M. Hunt wrote, "that modern love began with Greek love and owes so much to it, although the forms and ideals of Greek love are considered immoral and, to a large extent, illegal, in modern society."

CHRISTIAN LOVE—SUPPRESSION OF LUST, BEGETTING OF CHILDREN; FOURTH CENTURY C.E. ◆

*L*ove and marriage. They go together like . . . Well, that depends on the times.

Love to the Greeks and, later the Romans, involved a lot of lust and little marital affection.

Marital love to the early Christians, and to their descendants over many centuries, involved a suppression of lust and the birth of guilt. For the first time, guilt entered the institution of marriage and climbed into the marriage bed. A wife who secretly had desires and experienced sexual pleasure was made to feel guilty. A husband's desires—a given—were a curse he had to overcome if he expected eternal salvation. Marital love involved little affection and lots of penance. Its sole purpose was the begetting of children.

Lovemaking in marriage was sinless only if sensation, delight, and orgasm itself were restrained. Saint Jerome succinctly expressed the harsh new attitude around 390 C.E.:

> It is a disgrace to love another man's wife at all, or one's own too much. A wise man ought to love his wife with judgment, not with passion. Let a man govern his voluptuous impulses, and not rush headlong into intercourse . . . He who too ardently loves his own wife is an adulterer.

Never before had adultery been defined as too much love for one's own wife. In a way, that makes a mockery of the "sacrament" of matrimony.

Jerome went further. He said that every time a husband and wife had intercourse, even to beget children, they experienced a temporary separation from the Holy Spirit—for three days, in fact. Lovemaking had sullied them to that extent. In his penitential, Jerome warned priests not to serve the Eucharist, Christ's body and blood, to couples unless they "abstain from cohabitation [sex] for three nights" before approaching the altar. For a long time this was dogma.

Jerome himself was celibate. All of his teachings were predicated upon his one major assumption: "Virginity is natural, marriage came after the fall." Adam and Eve were virginal—"natural"—until they sinned, becoming "unnatural."

AUGUSTINE; SEXUAL LOVE, A BEAST TO BE TAMED ◆

Saint Augustine (354–430) was even more influential that Saint Jerome. The bishop of Hippo, a small north African seaport, Augustine became the first major theologian of Christianity. His views on love and marriage called the shots for the next fifteen hundred years. Augustine viewed sexual love as a wild beast to be tamed.

In his teens he had been monstrously wicked:

> And what was it I delighted in, but to love, and be beloved? But I kept not the measure of love . . . but out of the muddy concupiscence of the flesh, and the bubblings of youth, mists fumed up which beclouded and

overcast my heart . . . I was tossed about, and wasted, and dissipated, and I boiled over in my fornications.

When he was baptized into Christianity at age thirty-two, he gave up his sinning ways—his concubines, and his eighteen-year-old bastard son through an early dalliance. Guilt-ridden, he spent the rest of his life doing his best to make other men and women feel guilty about love and sex. He succeeded beyond his wildest imagination. Sexual love between married couples would not be liberated in America until the two great sexual revolutions of the twentieth century. We'll consider both shortly.

VALENTINE'S DAY—LOVE'S CELEBRATION; ROME, FIFTH CENTURY •

*W*e say "Happy Valentine's Day." But a more accurate phrase would be "Happy *Saint* Valentine's Day."

Valentine was a Christian bishop who was martyred in Rome, clubbed, then stoned to death, on February 24, 270. The day commemorating his memory was a holy day long before it was a holiday devoted to love.

Pagan Origins

Like many Christian holy days, Saint Valentine's Day began as an attempt by the church to usurp a popular pagan fertility rite. Rather than deny pagan converts to Christianity the rites and rituals they had long enjoyed, the church fathers simply restructured and renamed those events to make them distinctly Christian.

As early as the fourth century B.C.E., young Roman men engaged in an annual rite of passage to the god Lupercus. The names of virginal teenage girls were placed in a box and drawn at random by adolescent men. A lottery. Thus, a man was assigned a steady female companion for the duration of the following year, for their mutual entertainment and—more often than not—his sexual pleasure.

Determined to put an end to this practice, early church fathers sought a "lovers' " saint to replace the deity Lupercus. They found a perfect candidate in Valentine.

In Rome in 270 C.E., Valentine had enraged Emperor Claudius II, who had issued an edict forbidding marriage. Claudius felt that married men made poor soldiers because they were loath to leave their families for battle. The emperor needed soldiers, so Claudius, never one to fear unpopularity, abolished marriage.

Valentine, then bishop of Interamna, invited young lovers to come to him in secret, where he joined them in matrimony. Claudius learned of this "friend of lovers" and had the bishop brought to the palace. Impressed with his dignity and conviction, the emperor attempted to convert him to the Roman gods, to save him from otherwise certain execution. Valentine refused to renounce Christianity and then, perhaps imprudently, attempted to convert the insane emperor to Christianity. Days later he was martyred and, for good measure, beheaded, his skull mounted on a stake for all to see.

"From Your Valentine"—the Saints' Lottery

Legend has it that while Valentine was in prison awaiting execution, he fell in love with Asteria, the blind daughter of the jailer. Through his unswerving faith, he miraculously restored her sight. He signed a farewell message to her "From Your Valentine," a phrase that has survived its author's death.

From the church's standpoint, Valentine seemed to be the ideal candidate to usurp the popularity of Lupercus. So in 496, Pope Gelasius outlawed the mid-February pagan festival. But he was clever enough to retain the lottery, aware of Romans' love for games of chance. Now the box that once had held the names of nubile virgins received the names of female and male saints. Both young men and young women coming of age extracted slips of paper, and in the ensuing year they were expected to emulate the life of the saint whose name they had drawn. It was a different kind of game entirely, with different incentives. The spiritual overseer of the lottery was its patron saint, Valentine.

VALENTINE CARDS ◆

As Christianity spread, Saint Valentine's day became more popular —and secular—and lovers began to exchange Valentine greetings. The earliest "Valentine card" still in existence was sent in 1415 by Charles, duke of Orleans, to his wife while he was imprisoned in the Tower of London. Today the card is in the British Museum. Over the next century, Valentine cards became increasingly popular.

In the early seventeenth century, Saint Francis de Sales, bishop of Geneva, attempted to abolish the custom—and reinstate the lottery of saints' names. Rather than disappearing, the cards proliferated and became more colorful

Earliest extant Valentine's Day card, c. 1415, sent by Charles, duke of Orleans, to his wife while he was imprisoned in the Tower of London.

and decorative. Roman mythology's Cupid—son of Venus, Roman goddess of love—armed with arrows dipped in love potion, became the most popular Valentine image.

By the seventeenth century, handmade cards were oversize and elaborate. Men made their own heart-shaped valentine greetings. In 1797, a British publisher issued *The Young Man's Valentine Writer*, which contained scores of suggested sentimental verses for the young lover unable to express his own feelings.

"Obscene" Cards Through the Mail

In the eighteenth century, printers began producing a limited number of cards with verses and artists' sketches, called, for their impersonalness, "mechanical valentines." They were costly, but were they from the heart?

In the nineteenth century, as U.S. postal rates came within the reach of ordinary folk, there was a burst of "obscene" valentine postcards sent through the mail—obscene not by today's standards but by Victorian ones. In Chicago, for instance, authorities in the 1880s rejected some twenty-five thousand valentine postcards on the grounds that their sentiments of love, too ardently worded, were unfit to be carried through the mail. Postal workers claimed to have read each and every racy card.

The first American publisher of valentines was a printer and artist, Esther Howland. Her elaborate lace cards of the 1870s cost from five to ten dollars, with some selling for an exorbitant thirty-five dollars. Since that time the

---

XXX FOR KISSES ◆ *LOVERS who affectionately sign "XXX"s to valentine cards and letters are usually unaware that the custom goes back to the early Christian era, when a cross mark, or "X," conveyed the force of a sworn oath.*

The cross was, of course, a religious symbol. Not only did it refer to the cross of Calvary; as a cross mark it was the first letter (chi) of the Greek word for Christ, Christos.

In the days when few people could write, their signature cross, or "X," was legally binding. To emphasize their complete sincerity in an accord, they often kissed the mark, as a Bible was frequently kissed when an oath was sworn on it.

This practice of kissing the "X" led to its becoming a symbol of a kiss. During World War II, the British and American governments forbade their men in uniform from putting "XXX"s on their letters home, afraid that spies within the services might begin sending clandestine messages coded as kisses.

---

valentine card business has flourished. With the exception of Christmas, Americans exchange more cards on Valentine's Day than any other time of the year.

"KISS"; PRE-TWELFTH CENTURY ◆

Why do we kiss?

If you have ever watched a mother bird—or a father bird, for that matter—feed its young, then you know the evolutionary origin of kissing. Beaks, or bills, or lips were an ancient way for a parent to pass vital food to helpless, dependent offspring. In some human cultures, a parent will still chew food before passing it, lips to lips, to an infant. The osculating gesture was imbued with affection, and in time the touching of human lips came to symbolize love.

Technically a kiss is the anatomical juxtaposition of two orbicularis oris muscles in a state of contraction. When a newborn suckles at a breast, it is in effect kissing the mother's nipple.

Studies show that women enjoy kissing more than men and enjoy longer

*Kissing originated from
parents passing food lips-
to-lips to their young.*

kissing sessions. Women, far more often than men, report remembering their
first romantic kiss.

Our word "kiss" is from the Old English *cyssan*, which arose sometime
before the twelfth century.

"FRENCH KISS"; EARLY 1920S ◆

The term "French kiss" was first recorded in English in the early
1920s. The act involves open-mouth kissing with passionate tongue-
to-tongue contact.

The adjective "French" arose not because tongue kissing was a unique
passion of the French; it was common in many cultures, going by names like
tongue kissing, wet kissing, or soul kissing. But Americans and Britons had
long regarded the French as a sexually liberated (or perverse) people and
labeled many sex-related items "French":

- *French disease*, syphilis.
- *French love letter*, a condom.
- *French postcard*, any pornographic picture.
- *Frenching*, oral sex.
- *French woman*, a prostitute.
- *Sixty-nine*, simultaneous cunnilingus and/or fellatio, a visual description
of the figure the two partners form (69); believed to postdate the equivalent
French term for the sex act, *soixante-neuf*.

Because Americans and Britons thought the French rude, *to take French leave* meant to depart from a party without saying polite good-byes to the host or hostess. Not all "French" terms, however, have a derogatory slant: French toast (first recorded in English in 1871), French fries (1918), French horn (1682), French dressing (for salads; 1876), French pastry (1922), French cuff (1916)—the list is long and reflects the fascination that Americans have always had for things French.

Zoologist Desmond Morris gives a highly plausible and fascinating origin for the special kind of intimacy of "French kissing" in *Intimate Behaviour* (1971):

> In early human societies, before commercial baby-food was invented, mothers weaned their children by chewing up their food and then passing it into the infantile mouth by lip-to-lip contact—which naturally involved a considerable amount of tonguing and mutual mouth-pressure. This almost bird-like system of parental care seems strange and alien to us today, but our species probably practiced it for a million years or more, and adult erotic kissing today is almost certainly a Relic Gesture stemming from these origins.

> Whether it has been handed down to us from generation to generation . . . or whether we have an inborn predisposition toward it, we cannot say. But, whichever is the case, it looks rather as though, with the deep kissing and tonguing of modern lovers, we are back again at the infantile mouth-feeding stage of the far-distant past.

> If the young lovers exploring each other's mouths with their tongues feel the ancient comfort of parental mouth-feeding, this may help them increase their mutual trust and thereby their pair-bonding.

ROMANTIC KISS; EARLY EUROPEANS ♦

*W*hile lip kissing may have ancient evolutionary roots, not every culture engaged in romantic kissing or kissed in the same way. Working with evidence from both texts and art, authorities claim that romantic passionate lip kissing is a cultural trait chiefly of early European peoples. It was practiced by the Germanic Teutons, by the Greeks and Romans, and also by certain Semitic clans. These groups spread the practice. Romantic lip kissing came late to the Celts.

The ancient Chinese and Japanese kissed but only in private—kissing was not discussed or written about. When Europeans began to visit the Orient in the sixteenth century, the Chinese and Japanese were shocked, mortified, and hilariously entertained by Westerners' shameless exhibitionism of kissing in public. In the middle of the nineteenth century, when Chinese linguists began to translate Western novels into their own language, they had to invent a new written character to describe a romantic kiss.

Here are some of the many varieties of kisses:

Eskimo Kiss

This kind of kissing, in which noses are rubbed together, was prevalent among the peoples of Polynesia, parts of Asia, Africa, and the Arctic Eskimos.

Eskimos still "rub noses"—something of a misnomer since they actually place the mouth and nose against the cheek of the other person and *inhale*. They are smelling each other, itself an intimate act. In some Eskimo languages the word for kissing also means "smelling." Scent has its own erotic appeal and is the basis of the entire perfume industry.

Scholars have suggested that when blind Isaac asks Jacob to "kiss" him, before bestowing the blessing meant for Esau, his secret intention was to "smell" Jacob, to make quite certain who he really was. Only the deception of wearing Esau's clothes made the ruse work: "And he smelled the smell of his garments" (Genesis 27:27).

Cheek Kiss

North American Indian women engaged in this form of kissing in which a female softly presses her relaxed lips against a man's cheek, with no other motion, or sound. The only thing she's allowed to do is inhale the man's scent.

Hand Kiss

In parts of India and the Arabian Peninsula the custom arose of kissing hands. In certain cultures people kissed their own hands than pressed them against another's forehead. In other cultures two men greeted each other with a small peck on the back of the other person's hand. In Europe the kissing of a lady's hand became known as *Handkuss*.

During the Middle Ages, some rabbis in the East adopted the practice of wearing thick gloves in both winter and summer to discourage thoughts of lust. The gloves prevented the men from feeling a woman's soft lips on their hands during the customary hand kisses, which were given out of respect on the sabbath and certain holy days.

The hand kiss takes different forms in different cultures.

Lip-Sucking Kiss

The peoples of India developed a form of kissing, mentioned in the *Kama Sutra*, that involved sucking passionately on the other person's lips. In one form of the kiss, the man sucked on the woman's upper lip while she sucked on his lower lip. "I could just eat you," they're saying to each other. In fact, some female animals, primarily insects, eat their mates after sex.

Ceremonial Kiss

When Odysseus returned from his arduous journey, his male friends joyously kissed him on the head, hands, and shoulders. Centuries later, such male kissing was common among Christian bishops and priests: a bishop kissed a newly ordained priest; priests kissed the feet of popes. Roman Catholics kissed altars, statuary of saints, relics, the wounds of Christ on the cross, and dead relatives. The Jews kissed the Torah (but never dead relatives). During the Middle Ages, a new knight, after his indoctrination, was kissed by older knights—sometimes by the king himself.

Hand kissing, especially among men, is really a gesture of homage and deference. According to one Christian legend, the origin of kissing the pope's toe or foot is an offshoot of hand kissing. As the story goes, in the eighth century, a passionate woman not only kissed the pope's hand, but squeezed it tightly and sucked on his fingers. The horrified pontiff, once he'd reclaimed his wet digits, discontinued the custom of offering his hand and substituted his foot, which he thought would inspire less spontaneous ardor. Legend aside, the kissing of the feet of kings was an ancient pagan custom.

Butterfly Kiss

Several cultures developed the intimate lovers' gesture of lightly fluttering the eyelashes against the beloved's cheek. Going eyelash to eyelash is called the "double butterfly."

The butterfly kiss mimics the tactile antennae "kissing" of insects—the repeated light flutter of small hairs against hairs as a prelude to mating.

Through experimentation, two young people madly in love can make up any number of novel kisses.

COURTING AND WOOING ◆

*M*en have been "courting" women since the sixteenth century, when the word "court" came to mean "seeking one's affection." "Court" is thought to derive from the Latin *cohors*, meaning an enclosed garden, or a "court" yard. (Knights courted ladies in such picturesque settings.)

Men have been "wooing" women since the twelfth century, when the Middle English *woo* came to mean "to sue for the affection of"—usually in marriage.

In colonial America, courting was a formalized ritual. A man donned his best clothes, his *courting suit*, rode his specially groomed *courting horse* to his lady's house, and, through a hollow tube, which prevented eavesdropping, whispered "sweet nothings" into her ear.

Lexicographer Stuart Berg Flexner, in *I Hear America Talking* (1976), examines the ritual in detail. Here are some of the terms lovers have used over the years:

- *Billing and cooing* was a popular seventeenth-century expression for the coy, often nonsensical chat of young lovers.
- *To spoon*, originating in the 1850s, meant that a couple nestled their heads in each other's neck, spoon-fashion.
- *To go a sparking* was how a man boasted of his efforts to court a girl. The *Police Gazette* (1888) reported that in New York City there were up to "40 couples 'sparking' in Tompkins Square on Sunday evenings and it is a charming rendezvous for 'spooney' young men and women."
- *To spunk up a girl*, 1840s, meant to fondle her; to "feel her up" we'd say.

*Courting and wooing are all about "billing
and cooing," making "goo-goo eyes"
and eventually wedding plans.*

- **To lollygag**, 1860s, meant to caress and tongue-kiss a girl—"lolly" being English dialect for "tongue."
- **To mash**, 1860s, meant to flirt shamelessly with girl. A *masher* was a hard-core flirter. By the 1920s, "to mash" had been replaced by *to make a pass at*.
- **To be lovey-dovey**, 1870s, meant a couple was serious—heavily into billing and cooing.
- **To make goo-goo eyes**, 1890s, was to give amorous, flirtatious glances.
- **Flame**, 1700s, was a sweetheart.
- **Apple of his eye**, 1700s, was a special, beloved girl.
- **Steady**, 1870s, was a boy's fiancée.
- **Puppy love**, 1830s, was a youthful flirtation.
- **Love cracked**, 1830s, was to be so foolish in love that you were asking to have your heart broken.
- **Crush**, 1880s, was an infatuation.
- **Engagement** arose in the seventeenth century from the Old French *engager*, "to pledge."
- **Wedding** dates from the ninth century, derived from the Old English *weddung*. In Old English a *wed* was either a "pledge" or the act of "redeeming" it.

• **Marriage** is a thirteenth-century word, from the Latin *maritus*, meaning "husband."

• **Bride** and *bridegroom* are both Old English words: *bryd* was a girl just married, while *bryd* + *guma* (man) was a recently married man.

• **Bridal shower** is an American term of the 1890s.

• **Honeymoon** has been a popular expression since the sixteenth century. Initially it meant the first month of a couple's marriage (no trip was necessary). Perhaps because during that month the newlyweds drank *honey*-spiced wine. Some linguists say the word "moon" indicates that affections change like phases of the moon. Thus, "honeymoon" suggests that the first month of married life is sweet, but thereafter affections may wax or wane.

FLYING SOLO, OR SELF-LOVE ◆ *As the old joke goes: 97 percent of men admit they masturbate and the other 3 percent are liars.*

Self-love is commonplace. One study found that, by age eighteen, 80 percent of males and 60 percent of females masturbate. The most sexually active teenagers masturbate more frequently than those engaging less frequently in partner sex.

There is an interesting gender-based difference: male teenagers tend to masturbate less when they are involved in a sexual relationship, while female teenagers masturbate more frequently when they are involved in a sexual relationship. Why?

For a young man, a night's sexual encounter almost always ends in orgasm; he has no need to go home and masturbate. For a young woman, a sexual encounter may be too fast and incomplete for her to reach orgasm. The lovemaking has left her sexually tense and frustrated, so she goes home and engages in self-stimulation for physical release—and does not tell her boyfriend.

What are adult men's and women's most common masturbation fantasies?

Fantasy	Males (%)	Females (%)
Sex with a loved one	75	80
Sex with strangers	47	21
Multiple partners	33	18
Experimental activity	19	28

CONTINUED

Forced into sex	10	19
Raping a partner	13	3
Homosexual sex	7	11

Most men fly solo with a single technique. They encircle the shaft of the penis with the hand and move it up and down, stimulating the shaft and sometimes the glans of the penis, accelerating the activity as they approach orgasm.

Men call "jerking off" by many names: bashing the bishop, chocking the chipmunk, pounding the pud, jerkin' the gherkin, flogging the poodle, snapping the twig, spanking the monkey, whacking the wonk, beating your meat on the toilet seat, dating Rosie Palm and her five sisters, taking care of business. *Interestingly, rhyme predominates in euphemisms for this rhythmic activity.*

Women tend to polish the pearl *in a variety of ways, clitoral stimulation being the primary goal. Many women rub up and down on the clitoral shaft in a circular motion or pull on the vaginal lips, causing the skin that covers the glans to slide back and forth. Some rub or squeeze their thighs together or massage the entire mons pubis area. Others use a combination of techniques. Masters and Johnson found that most women tend to stimulate the entire mons pubis rather than restricting stimulation to the glans of the clitoris alone, because of its extreme sensitivity.*

The word "masturbate" is from the Latin masturbari, *"to disturb with the hand."*

MAKING WHOOPEE—THE FIRST SEXUAL REVOLUTION; LATE NINETEENTH CENTURY TO 1920S ◆

*F*or centuries, marriage was viewed a means of suppressing lust, and the only valid reason for having sex in marriage was to beget children. Love was not the central basis for many marriages—in most it was not. It was "abnormal" for a woman to admit to feeling sexual passion. The distinctions between "normal" and "abnormal" were strange by today's standards.

Starting in the nineteenth century, a group of distinguished doctors—

The "good old days" when a young woman remained a virgin until her wedding night and married the man her parents selected.

chiefly Havelock Ellis and Sigmund Freud—began to redefine "normal" and "abnormal" sexual behaviors. Each of these men had his own neuroses, hang-ups, and unconventional sexual attitudes.

English psychologist Ellis (1859–1939) married novelist Edith Lees, with a prenuptial agreement stipulating that they live together only half of each year. This allowed him to have mistresses—and he shared the details of these intimacies with his wife, a tortured woman.

Austrian psychiatrist Freud (1856–1939), as indicated in his numerous letters to Carl Jung, his disciple, was clearly bisexual and almost certainly in love with the younger, good-looking Jung. "Sometimes a cigar is just a cigar," Freud cautioned in reference to the overuse of phallic imagery. But Freud's cigars—from which he developed cancer of the mouth—may sometimes have been substitutes for Jung's penis.

It was not their intention, but these men, and other pioneer researchers in human sexuality, expanded the description for "normalcy." They liberated love in marriage, legitimized women's sexual urges, and coined words like *heterosexual, homosexual,* and *bisexual.* Unknowingly, they paved the way for history's *second* sexual revolution, which would begin with the birth control pill in the early 1960s and would, in the medical profession at least, redefine homosexuality as nonpathological.

The first sexual revolution introduced doctors to a string of new sex-related words, thanks largely to Freud: *libido, Oedipus complex, penis envy, castration anxiety, transference, defense mechanism, dream interpretation.*

Ordinary folk and lovers developed new terms of their own for the new century:

- *To pin*, 1900; to become engaged by pinning one's fraternity pin on a girl; *being pinned* became popular in the mid-1930s.
- *To date*, 1902; to make an appointment for a specific time for romantic involvement. In busy modern life, even love had to be scheduled.
- *Heavy dating*, 1923; a serious romantic involvement, with or without sex, that consumed much of one's time—and almost certainly lead to marriage.
- *Double date*, 1924; two couples jointly going out for a romantic evening. The automobile contributed greatly to the practice. Cars were expensive and young men doubled up for a night out on the town, often sharing the expense of fuel.
- *Blind date*, 1925; pot luck for him and for her. The car caused many young men to "fix up" their buddies with dates. The girlfriend of the boy who owned the car usually arranged for the blind date, introducing her boyfriend's buddy to one of her female friends.
- *Petting*, 1910; kissing, hugging, and general body touching with the hands, which might or might not lead to sex—an allusion to the affectionate stroking, or petting, of a animal pet. *Petting parties* became popular in the 1920s. One's favorite girl was a *pet*.
- *Necking*, 1910; Southern equivalent for the Northern "petting"; the term spread north after World War I. The couple were *neckers*. A *necker's knob* was a handheld knob on a car's steering wheel that allowed a boy to drive with one hand while fondling his girl with the other. He was called a *one-arm driver*.
- *Hickey*, 1920; a bruise on the neck made by passionate kissing and sucking, usually explained to parents as a result of having accidentally walked into a rope or suffered a similar mishap; from the popular expression of the day, "doo-hickey," any small gadget.
- *Sex appeal*, 1920s; popularized by publicists promoting movie stars.

The intellectual basis for the first sexual revolution was laid in Europe, but the ground troops that fought the battles resided in America. One major leader was Margaret Sanger, who believed that women could never really relax and enjoy sex unless they could overcome the fear of pregnancy.

"MARRIED LOVE" AND MARGARET SANGER, MOTHER OF PLANNED PARENTHOOD •

*M*argaret Sanger (1879–1966) was an Irish Catholic housewife, mother, and one of eleven children. As a visiting nurse, she worked among the poor in New York City; later she waged a historic fight for women's sexual freedom. It was based not on the ideas of Ellis or Freud, which did not concern her, but on the right of women to control their own bodies when it came to pregnancy. She'd seen too many unwanted pregnancies, too many fatal self-administered abortions.

She coined the term *birth control* in 1914. She also made *contraceptives* and *planned parenthood* common words in America. Her ideas, at first viewed as radical, are now part of every married couple's consciousness.

Sanger's argument was both simple and profound, and it changed the proverbial battle between the sexes forever. She argued that married love would remain uncivilized and brutish, and women held under the thumb of husbands, as long as couples could not have sex without the fear of unwanted pregnancies. Women could not enjoy sex until they could stop working about getting "knocked up"—*especially* by their husbands. Sanger's own mother had not *wanted* eleven children.

Champion of Condoms

Sanger championed the use of condoms and the dissemination of all kinds of birth control information. She published information on contraceptives in her own monthly magazine, *Woman Rebel*—an accurate if antagonistic title —which earned her nine counts of defiance against obscenity laws and resulted in her journal being barred from the U.S. mails. She believed that fewer children, spaced further apart, could help many families attain a better standard of living. Most women at that time did not understand the natural reproductive cycle of their own bodies.

In 1916, Sanger opened the world's first birth control clinic in Brooklyn. She was arrested and jailed; all her condoms were confiscated, but that didn't stop her. Nor did the fact that her church painted her as a modern-day Satan. A U.S. court of appeals eventually ruled that doctors could provide condoms to women for the "cure and prevention of disease" but not for contraception. The door had been left cleverly ajar.

By the late 1930s, the United States had more than three hundred birth-control clinics.

By the 1940s, over 80 percent of American couples regularly bought condoms. Maybe every husband didn't get his wife's full consent before having sex, but there were certainly fewer marriage-bed rapes—and unwanted pregnancies.

"A woman's body belongs to herself alone," wrote Sanger. Every woman must have the absolute right "to dispose of herself, to withhold herself, to procreate, or to suppress the germ of life." Today this seems so sensible.

In the late 1930s, Margaret Sanger backed research on an oral contraceptive; a pill. She died six years after the Pill debuted.

LOVERS' DREAM—THE PILL: THE SECOND SEXUAL REVOLUTION; 1960 ♦

*F*ree love. Wife swapping. *Playboy.* Group sex. *Penthouse.* Recreational sex. Edible panties. Strawberry-flavored lubricant. Nipple rings. Chippendale dancers. Masters and Johnson. Shere Hite. *Sex and the Single Girl. The Feminine Mystique. The Joy of Sex.*

None of these might have happened had it not been for the liberating power of the pill. No event in the long and ingenious history of contraception has had a more profound effect on sex attitudes in general—and birth control in particular—than the introduction of the oral contraceptive.

Pope John XXIII was informed in 1958 that the pill was about to debut. He predicted that it would socially and sexually change the world.

The pill originated with an unexpected discovery made in the jungles of Mexico in the 1930s. There, chemistry professor Russell Earl Marker, on leave from Pennsylvania State College, was experimenting with a group of plant steroids known as sapogenins, which produce a soaplike foam in water. He discovered a chemical process that transformed the sapogenin diosgenin into the human female sex hormone progesterone. The wild Mexican yam, *cabeza de negro*, proved to be a rich source of the hormone precursor.

At the time, progesterone was used to treat menstrual disorders and prevent miscarriages. But the drug was available only from European pharmaceutical companies, and methods of preparing it were laborious and costly. Still, Marker was unable to acquire financial backing from an American pharmaceutical company to pursue synthetic progesterone research.

He rented a lab in Mexico City, collected ten tons of yams, and at his own expense isolated pure diosgenin. Back in the United States, he synthesized more than two thousand grams of progesterone, which at the time was worth $160,000. The synthesis was far simpler than the traditional methods and would eventually bring down he price of sex steroids from eighty dollars to one dollar a gram.

Tests on a Catholic Island

In the early 1950s, Margaret Sanger visited chemist Gregory Pincus at the Worcester Foundation for Experimental Biology in Shrewsbury, Massachusetts. She convinced him of the need for a simple oral contraceptive and encouraged him to perfect the development of a pill. Pincus knew the idea was feasible. In 1958, he tested a yam-derived ovulation inhibitor, norethynodrel, on 1,308 volunteers in Puerto Rico.

The pope heard of the experiments on a Catholic island and was deeply disturbed. The church protested the work, but the experiments continued. Searle Pharmaceuticals applied for FDA approval to market the pill.

In May 1960, American women were introduced to Enovid, history's first oral contraceptive. By late 1961, a half-million American women were on it.

Researchers now believe that oral contraception will remain the major form of birth control, replaced perhaps by an antipregnancy vaccine.

SEX AND THE SINGLE GIRL ◆

By 1962, one million American women were on the Pill. Few products in the country were hotter and selling faster.

One of the most discussed books that year was *Sex and the Single Girl*, by Helen Gurley Brown. In high-spirited, saucy prose, it advised single young working women, many of whom were on the Pill, to seek more than domesticity, not to rely on men, and to enjoy being "a bachelor girl"—who, like a bachelor boy, has sex.

By the end of 1963, the pill was being manufactured by the ton. Possibly the most talked about book that *year* was *The Feminine Mystique*, by housewife, mother, and magazine writer Betty Friedan. More than a bestseller, the book was a manifesto, a call to arms. Friedan had issued a battle cry: "We can no longer ignore that voice within women that says, 'I want something more than my husband and my children and my house.'"

That "something" was a career, respect, and equal opportunity in every aspect of life.

In 1966, the year of Margaret Sanger's death, American women were consuming 2,600 tons of birth control pills annually. One can only conclude that more women were having more sex—and enjoying it more—than at

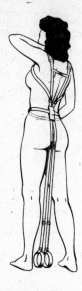

Sex harness with double stirrups to give the partner more control during intercourse, patent no. 4,343,299 (1982).

any time in history. The old belief, that women didn't really enjoy sex, had been turned on his head.

Feminist Gloria Steinem, cofounder of *Ms.* magazine, believes that men and women have a better chance of succeeding at love than their forebears; never have they had more options, more equality. In *Revolution from Within* (1992), she sums up all that love is, or can be, in our times:

> It's possible to raise children with a loved partner and then move on amicably to a new stage of life, to love someone and yet live apart, to forge new relationships at every phase of life, even at the very end—in short, to enjoy many different kinds of love, in a way that doesn't hurt but only enriches.

In a nutshell:

The first sexual revolution had sought to rid sexual pleasure of guilt. It had even tried to make sex outside of marriage as acceptable for a woman as it was—and often has been—for a man. On the first count it was modestly successful, on the second it failed dismally.

The second sexual revolution addressed not the issue of guilt but of civil rights—everybody's. It worked, and continues to work, to decriminalize oral and anal sex between consenting spouses, and between consenting unmarried adults. It worked to expand the rights of adults to read, write, publish, and watch material that was overtly erotic, even pornographic. It worked to give

WHAT WE LOOK FOR IN MATES ◆ *Sex is not everything. When it comes to what we look for in a life partner, "good sex" rates near the bottom of the list. It's not that we don't want a good sex life in marriage, but we've learned from years of dating and disappointing relationships that good sex alone can't hold two people together very long.*

Even love is not as important as friendship. A recent survey of "Sex and Singles" found out what we really deem important when seeking a mate for life:

Friendship—61 percent
Love—58 percent
Honesty—57 percent
Trust—56 percent
Sense of humor—55 percent
Faithfulness—47 percent
Respect—45 percent
Loyalty—39 percent
Understanding—37 percent
Kindness—36 percent
Good conversation—30 percent
Similar interests—29 percent
Physical attraction—29 percent
Good sex—29 percent
Financial security—12 percent

women as much say in sexual matters as men have always had, whether the rules of the game were explicit or tacit.

The second sexual revolution (inseparable from the women's liberation movement) has been so far-reaching and successful—liberating women, gays, lesbians, bisexuals, and transsexuals—that it's usually referred to as *the* sexual revolution, the *first* in Western civilization.

The next two chapters could not have been written and published without it.

We're Here, We're Queer

"FAG" TO "DYKE"

There's a lot of talk these days about homosexuals
coming out of the closet. I didn't know they'd been in the closet.
I do know they've always been in the gutter.

JERRY FALWELL, PREACHER

We are all in the gutter,
but some of us are looking at the stars.

OSCAR WILDE, PLAYWRIGHT

"GAY"; FRANCE, POST-THIRTEENTH CENTURY ◆

Across America there are at least one hundred thoroughfares named Gay Street, Gay Lane, or Gay Drive, which may or may not have gay people living on them. Many of them must, since one out of ten (or of six) people—estimates vary—is homosexual. For centuries a *gay fellow* was a guy with a cheerful disposition; a *gay time* was a happy occasion. "Don we now our *gay apparel*, fa-la-la" did not mean dressing up like the Village People. A *gay lifestyle* described a wealthy, jet-setting husband and wife.

"Gay" is not what is used to be. Residents of Gay Street in West Seneca, New York, petitioned the town in 1987 to change the name to Fawn Trail —as if that were less embarrassing.

When did "gay," meaning "happy" and "cheerful," acquire overtones first of perversion, then of pride?

*Troubadour sings of the virtues of
"courtly love."*

The Cult of Courtly Love

"Gay" goes way back in history.

To the Anglo-Saxons, *gai* meant "swift." A good Anglo-Saxon warrior was *gai* on his feet, fast and nimble, and *gai* in the expert way he wielded a sword.

To the Franks who spoke Old French, *gahi* meant "impetuous." Any passionate, impulsive Frank lover, male or female, was *gahi*.

These words are the source of our "gay," meaning variously "joyous" and "loving," "merry" and "happy," "bright" and "brilliant" as in "gay colors."

"Gay" took on sexual overtones in thirteenth-century France. The words *gai* and *gahi* had by then come to refer to the "cult of courtly love," a euphemism of the time for same-sex love.

Courtly love is a concept that's often misrepresented. It is history's strangest expression of the human emotion of love. The original *amour courtois* of the eleventh century had been heterosexual. Chivalrous troubadours serenaded chaste ladies extolling the virtues of "true love," which involved kissing, touching, fondling, and naked body contact—never intercourse. Copulation was scorned as "false love," a base animal instinct. Love ended when sex began. Penetration burst the bubble of affection.

By the twelfth century, horny troubadours were violating chaste maidens all over western Europe, and *l'amour courtois* had to be redefined. For most upper-class people, it now meant passion outside of marriage. As Marie, countess of Champagne, the high arbiter of courtly love, proclaimed in 1174:

We declare and hold as firmly established that love cannot exert its powers between two people who are married to each other. For lovers give each other everything freely, under no compulsion of necessity, but married people are in duty bound to give in to each other's desires.

Thus *l'amour courtois* went from chaste puppy love to an adulterously passionate affair. By the thirteenth century the perverse, extramarital nature of courtly love allowed the term to be applied to homosexual relationships. A man had *sex* with his wife but an affair of *courtly love* with another man.

A homosexual lover was a *gai* or *gaiol*, which in time became *gay*. Troubadour poetry of the period explicitly describes, and at times praises, homosexual *amour courtois*.

"Gay" on the Silver Screen—*Bringing Up Baby*, 1938. ◆

Once the word "gay" acquired sexual overtones in the thirteenth century, it was gradually assigned to various groups.

A prostitute was for a time a *gay woman*, her brothel a *gay house*. She led a *gay life*, and sex with her was *to gay it*.

Later, any social undesirable was called *gay*. In the homophobic British culture of Victorian times, the word came to describe both homosexuality and a male homosexual himself.

The first appearance of "gay" with a decidedly homosexual slant in a dictionary was in Noel Ersine's *Underworld and Prison Slang*, 1935: "Gaycat . . . a homosexual boy."

One of the first public uses in the United States—aside from pornographic fiction—was the 1938 Hollywood comedy *Bringing Up Baby*. Cary Grant, wearing a negligee, explains that he's "gone gay."

"Fag" and "Faggot"; 1914 ◆

There are many conflicting views on how these two pejorative terms came about. *Faggot* ranks with *nigger, spick, kike,* and *mick* as a particularly hurtful personal slur.

Today it is common for a derogatory or "hot" term to become a minority's battle cry. Feminist Germaine Greer challenged women to join forces as "clit power." Blacks use "nigger" as an insider's endearment among themselves.

Lesbian activists call their lovers "cunts," while in-your-face gays boast of themselves as "queers." Larry Kramer, author of the 1978 semiautobiographical novel *Faggots*—about "a 39-year-old faggot who must find true love by 40"—referred to himself as a faggot in interviews when the book was published.

But over the centuries the word has meant different things to different people.

Weaving Faggots—the Faggot Stitch

The oldest spelling is found in the Middle English *fagge*, a noun meaning "broken thread." The frayed end of a piece of cloth or rope was *fagge*. A seamstress weaving a decorative hemstitch was "fagotting." To this day, needlework drawn in crisscross or barlike stitches across an open seam is fagotting.

In time the word *fagge* also came to mean "remnant" or "the last and worst part of anything." Some linguists argue that it was this meaning that allowed the word to be used pejoratively for an individual; a social deviant was a "fag" or "faggot."

Burning Faggots—Kindling and Cigarettes

Fagot is also an old word in its own right. It is both Middle English and Old French for a bundle of sticks, twigs, or branches used as firewood—from the Vulgar Latin *facellum*, meaning "bundle," which in turn is related to the Greek for firewood, *phakelos*.

Some linguists believe that in the days when "sodomites" and "buggers" were burned at the stake, they came to be associated with the kindling that caused their death. It is from this usage of *fagot* that the British in the 1880s began calling a burning cigarette a "fag."

In the science of metallurgy, a "fagot" is a heap of iron or steel pieces to be worked into bars by hammering or rolling at welding temperature. At one time the metallurgist who did the hammering was a "fagot," a usage that now exists only as a joke.

Buggering Faggots—Boys Will Be Boys

As a verb, *fag* was also an old British word meaning "to make tired by hard work." A servant at the end of a long day might sigh, "I'm fagged." In fact, the word became a noun for "servant" in the 1780s, as well as for a boy hired to do tiring work. He was a fag.

World War I "yanks" with "fags," a British expression for cigarettes
dating to the 1880s.

In the English public school system, where a younger boy acted as a servant for older boys, performing menial chores, the junior was a "fag." Because these younger boys were often used sexually by older boys, some linguists feel that this is how "fag" got its homosexual meaning. The earliest recorded use of "faggot" to mean a male homosexual dates from 1914.

In his memoirs, nineteenth-century British author John Addington Symonds described his early years at public school, where "fagging" was common: "Every boy of good looks had a female name, and was recognized either as a public prostitute or some bigger fellow's 'bitch.' "

"FAG HAG"; AMERICA, 1920S ◆

A "fag hag" is a single woman who spends much of her free time socializing with gay men, seldom dating straight men. She has become a standard part of gay lore, films, novels, and real life. Typically, she prefers the sensibilities of gay men. But perhaps more important, she enjoys the freedom of being able to relax, play, and dress up or down as she likes, without worrying that men are sexually sizing her up and hitting on her.

In the days before gay liberation, when men could not dance together legally in public clubs, one fag hag dancing amid a dozen men legitimized

"Fag hag"—"fagot" was a Middle English word meaning "firewood."

the ensemble. The lavish attention such a woman gets, and from good-looking, sexually nonthreatening men, is another appeal of the fag hag role. In terms of marriage prospects, however, it's a dead end.

Considering the origin of "hag," the expression "fag hag" is not a complimentary phrase:

"Hag" is from the Middle English *hagge*, "a witch." That word in turn derived from the Old English *haga*, meaning "hedge rider"—that is, broomstick rider. For centuries, a hag was an ugly, evil, old woman who cast spells. Shakespeare, in *Richard III*, employed the term: "Have done they charm [curse], thou hateful, withered hag."

The term "fag hag" apparently arose in the 1920s among gay men, not because all single women who hang out with them are ugly—many are quite beautiful—but because the two words rhyme irresistibly. If anything, the term began as a compliment—though it no longer is perhaps because with the emergence of gay culture, the role of a fag hag has been drastically downsized.

"DINKS" = DOUBLE INCOME, NO KIDS; 1990S ◆

*A*ccording to the Simmons Market Research Bureau, gay men and women have incredible market muscle. Compared with straight men, gay men are 6.2 times more likely to buy 10 to 15 hardcover books each year. They are 6.9 times more likely to engage in regular exercise at a private gym or club. Gay men are 5.5 times more likely to travel to Europe, 3.2 times more likely to purchase a suit, ten times more likely to purchase CDs.

Gay men and gay women have their own special sensibilities. These come no doubt from factors as diverse as biology, rearing, environment, and socializing—among heterosexuals and among themselves. In terms of marketing, homosexuals are an important and growing part of the so-called "big spenders" category, and today the gay dollar is actively courted. In consumer marketing circles, gay couples are known as dinks: double income, no kids. Simmons Research estimates that gays represent a twenty-four-billion-dollar market.

DINKS tend to be more affluent and better educated. One survey found that about 60 percent of gay and lesbian couples have college degrees, compared with 20 percent for the general population.

In the early 1990s, a demographic study showed that gay men had an average household income of $51,325 and lesbians $45,927, compared with the national average of $36,520. The estimated twenty-five million homosexuals in America make up what manufacturers call a "dream market."

"Fairy," "Flit," "Fruit" ◆

Cupcake, cream puff, lulu, fruitcake, pansy, queer, gladiola, brown-noser, gazelle, swish, homo, cornholer, buttercup, quack-quack, nancy boy, flit, fruit, and *sissy* rate with "fairy" among the most hurtful slurs that can be slung at a boy. A bully knows that a "fruit" is easy pickings.

Cecil Beaton, English designer and photographer who was *not* straight, "was a true confessor, at least to his diary," reported the *New York Times* in 1986, six years after Beaton's death: "Every time he was called a 'fairy,' a 'lulu,' a 'pansy,' a 'gladiola,' or a 'queer,' he recorded the dreadful moment and squirmed a second time, on the diary page."

In nursery rhymes and fairy tales, a fairy is described by "feminine" adjectives—tiny, graceful, delicate. Fairies flit about, light as a cream puff. They live in fairyland. It's easy to see how "fairy" and its "feminine" adjectives came to be used on slightly built effeminate men. J. D. Salinger, in *The Catcher in the Rye* (1951), wrote, "Sometimes it was hard to believe the people he said were flits and lesbians."

Fate Is in the Hands of Fairies

The word "fairy," in reference to the beings of folklore, is from the Middle English *faerie*. This word, in turn, is from the Vulgar Latin *fata*, meaning "one of the Fates"—enchanted, magic creatures that controlled human destiny. *Fata* itself is related to the Latin *fatum*, "fate." A "fairy," then, directs one's fate—as in *Cinderella*, where the fairy godmother transforms the sad and sooty chambermaid into a poised and elegant princess. That is the work of a fairy.

As Hugh Rawson points out in *Wicked Words*, "fairy" first acquired homosexual overtones in turn-of-the-century America. The word first appeared in the article "Sex and Art," by Colin A. Scott, in the January 1896 issue of the *American Journal of Psychology*:

> *Coffee-clatches, where the members dress themselves with aprons, etc., and knit, gossip and crochet; balls where men adopt the ladies' evening dress are well known in Europe. "The Fairies" of New York are said to be a similar secret organization. The avocations which inverts follow are frequently feminine in their nature.*

Did such a secret, underground society once exist in New York? Rawson reports that it did; he found confirmation of an organization called the Circle Hermaphroditos, in *The Female-Impersonators* (1922), an autobiographical work by the pseudonymous Ralph Werther: "On one of my earliest visits to Paresis Hall [in New York City]—about January 1895—I seated myself at one of the tables. I had only recently learned that it was the androgyne [*andro*, man; *gyn*, woman] headquarters—or 'fairie' as it was called at the time."

During this period, *swish* became a name for effeminate homosexuals with a swinging walk. The word is probably of onomatopoetic origin, the sound of a flowing dress or gliding movement.

GAY SEX—REALITY VERSUS FICTION ◆

*S*traights are often confused about gays. Most of the confusion has to do with sex. What do lesbians and gay men *really* do in bed? What are their sexual preferences? Is there any difference in their levels of sexual arousal or gratification?

If lesbians have more intense and frequent orgasms, perhaps it's because "a lesbian quickie takes hours."

The questions arise because not much gay sex information exists in the public domain.

Do lesbians, for instance, experience better and more frequent orgasms than straight women do? The answer seem to be yes—but not for any biological reason. Lesbians typically spend more time arousing and making love to their partners. As the old joke goes, "A lesbian quickie take hours."

Lesbian Orgasms

In *Lesbian Origins* (1985), Susan Cavin surveys the scant evidence that exists on the subject. Past studies, which treated lesbianism as a perversion, often concluded that lesbians in a relationship almost always achieved orgasm. These studies may have been biased since female orgasm was often associated with women who possessed lust that bordered on perversion.

One small 1940s study, in George William Henry's *Sex Variants*, involved forty "long-term, active homosexual women" and concluded that 95 percent

regularly achieved orgasm during homosexual activity. This is a much higher proportion than has been found among women in any married group indulging in heterosexual intercourse or in individuals practicing solitary masturbation.

Even if that figure is high, the number is still amazing. It suggests that lesbians understand the importance of the clitoris as opposed to mere vaginal insertion—and the importance of patience.

In a much larger study, Shere Hite questioned almost two thousand women and found that most of them did not experience orgasm during heterosexual intercourse that involved solely penile penetration.

> It was found that only approximately 30% of the women in this study could orgasm regularly from intercourse—that is, could have an orgasm during intercourse without more direct manual clitoral stimulation being provided at the time of orgasm . . . For most women, orgasming during intercourse as a result of intercourse alone is the exceptional experience, not the usual one.

BLOW JOB VERSUS KISSING AND CUDDLING ◆

*T*he popular opinion, that gay men are fixated on oral and anal sex almost to the exclusion of everything else, is reinforced in books, films, and jokes. But the origin of this impression, and the only reason it still exists, is simply ignorance. In recent years, poll after poll conducted among gay men across the country has shown the belief to be false.

In 1996, *Genre* magazine surveyed more than a thousand gay men, asking them, "What is the most important sexual activity?"

A full third answered that *kissing* was the primary turn-on for them; for 24 percent it was *cuddling* and for 9 percent, *masturbation*. Only 24 percent reported that *oral sex* was the most gratifying sexual activity, and only 15 percent found *anal sex* the ultimate experience. Yet most straights think of gays in terms of buggering or of obsessing about "big dicks."

Does Size Matter?

The *Genre* survey asked gay men, "Does size matter?" The answers are not all that different from those of straight women when asked the same question.

Only 7 percent of gay men responded that size mattered to them; 16 percent said that size usually counted but could be outweighed by attributes such as a muscular body, a well-defined chest, or simply nice eyes. (A man's face turned out to be one of the most significant turn-ons.) Twenty-nine percent said that size mattered only sometimes—for one-night stands. A whopping 35 percent claimed that in most cases size was not an issue, and 13 percent said it *never* mattered to them.

All men, straight and gay, may want big dicks for themselves. But surveys of gay men—and straight women—repeatedly conclude that the size of a partner is not a critical issue, especially if the pair is engaged in a loving, long-term relationship.

THE IDEAL GAY GUY ✦

*W*hat gay men want in their ideal "marrying" man turns out to be no different from what straight women desire in husbands: normalcy, kindness, cleanliness, consideration.

In the *Genre* poll, the majority of gay men (52 percent) reported that their ultimate fantasy was "the boy-next-door type": sweet, clean-cut, polite, brown hair (only 30 percent sought blonds), well spoken, and well educated.

Three-quarters of gay men like their men "clean shaven," without beards or mustaches. Sixty-three percent say the "eyes" have it when it comes to favorite facial features. Forty percent go for well-developed chests. Thirty-one percent keep their eyes on the butt. And virtues like honesty, loyalty, fidelity, dependability, sympathy, and understanding rank high as attributes in the ideal gay guy.

Many such modern studies are helping to dispel the notion that gay men are into kinky, S&M, anonymous sex. A small percentage is, of course—as is a small percentage of heterosexuals. But the vast majority of gay men and women want in their partners the same virtues—and lack of vices—that straights seeks. Gays and straights are far more alike than they are different.

"BLOW JOB"; PRE-1960S ✦

*T*he term "blow job," for oral-genital sex performed on a male, is surprisingly new in terms of its widespread understanding and usage. It started to appear in slang dictionaries in the mid-1960s, around the time pop icon Andy Warhol released his film *Blow Job*, containing several explicit depictions of the act. The term had been used by college men and prostitutes, and was printed in underground pornography, but it was not yet commonplace.

To many Americans in the forties and fifties a "blow job" was a faster-than-the-speed-of-sound "jet airplane," which took off and gave everyone nearby a "blow job." *The Thesaurus of American Slang* (1953) records an example of this usage from an issue of the *San Francisco Examiner* in 1945: "A P-59 jet propelled Airacomet, affectionately called the 'blow job' by flyers, will make several flights in 1946."

Linguists think the sexual connotation of "blow job" evolved from "blowoff," an expression meaning to finish off, to climax, to end. "Blowoff" in this sense is related to "blow off steam," to put an end to an emotionally frustrating experience. When a prostitute gave a client a blow job she was helping him "blow off" the steam of sexual arousal. In the 1930s, street-walkers offered oral sex with the phrase, "I'll blow you off." It suggests "I'll cool you down," "I'll release your steam."

Some linguists think the term "blow job" evolved gradually from an eighteenth-century European name for a prostitute, *blower*. A popular name for penis at the time was "whorepipe," and it is easy to see how the woman who played the instrument came to be called a "blower." But was the act called a "blow job"? There's no indication of that.

Today the word is commonplace, uttered as often by women as men. In the following limerick, from Ray Allen Billington's *Limericks Historical and Hysterical* (1981), a widow has just had her cheating husband's body cremated and is about to dispose of his ashes:

> *A bitter new widow, quite tough,*
> *To her mate's ashes said in a huff,*
> *"You've diddled young girls,*
> *Never brought me no pearls,*
> *And wanted me to blow you—so puff!"*

"PANSY," "SISSY," "QUEEN" ◆

"Pansy" is from the French *pensée*, "a deep thought"—Latin *pensare*, "to ponder, weigh carefully"—and is the name of a small garden flower of the violet family, with flat, broad, velvety petals, in many bright colors. Early botanists thought that the flower's head resembled a human face in deep thought.

In Victorian England, dandies like Oscar Wilde often wore velvet suits and jackets, accessorized with brightly colored scarves. They resembled the showy flower. The name of "pansy" for a male homosexual arose during this period. Dandies jokingly referred to themselves as "pansies." For their critics the name became an easy visual slur.

The pseudonymous Earl Lind, in *Autobiography of an Androgyne* (1919), relates that homosexuals used the word in a campy fashion at Manhattan's Paresis Hall:

> *In a few minutes, three short, smooth-faced young men approached and introduced themselves as Roland Reeves, Manon Lescaut, and Prince Pansy—aliases—because few refined androgynes would be so rash as to betray their legal name in the Underworld.*

Members of the club also called themselves "sissies," a straightforward steal from "sisters." "Sissy" is an old expression homosexuals coined for themselves from the image of themselves not as a group of sportive brothers but gossipy sisters.

Members of the underground club also called themselves "queens"—a campy reference to a "drag queen's" haughty, regal bearing and her authoritative, bitchy manner. The word "queen" is from the Gothic *qens*, "woman," and the Old English *cwen*, "wife of a king."

"QUEER"; EARLY TWENTIETH CENTURY ◆

*A*nything that is "queer" is odd, different from the ordinary, strange; may evoke giddy feelings; is counterfeit, not genuine. Little wonder that homosexuals, in the minority and unable to reproduce, were long regarded as queer. Many minorities are perceived to be "odd" or "strange" yet are not labeled "queer." How did the homosexual minority come to acquire a monopoly of the moniker, which has eclipsed all other shadings of the word?

The word "queer" itself is relatively new, dating only from 1508. It seems to be a hybrid of the German *quer*, meaning "crosswise," or "not aligned with the majority," and the Middle High German *twer*, "crooked," having no scruples. Centuries ago, a counterfeiter was a "queer," a criminal released from prison was a *queer bird*, a city councilman out of order at a meeting was *queer as a duck*, and a bankrupt gentleman was *on Queer Street*.

It has also been suggested that "queer" originated from the Scottish dialect of a street beggar's cant: "Here, here, here . . ."—an incessant plea for handouts—which in local dialect sounded more like "Queer, queer, queer."

This origin is interesting with respect to modern activists' chant, "We're here! We're queer! Get used to it!"

A Male of Refined Sensibilities

"Queer" as a word referring to a homosexual male first appeared in print in America. It's found in a 1922 publication of the Children's Bureau of the U.S. Department of Labor, in a survey of personality traits associated with juvenile delinquency in particular and crime in general. The Labor Department then believed that a male of delicate facial features and "refined sensibilities"—a sense of color coordination, an eye for design, an instinct for tastefulness, love of opera—had the makings of a criminal, as well as perverse sexual tendencies. At the time criminal pathology and perversion were seen as going hand in hand.

The bureau quoted one study, *The Practical Value of Scientific Study of Juvenile Delinquents*:

> *A young man, easily ascertainable to be unusually fine in other characteristics, is probably 'queer' in sex tendency.*

With that personality profile defined, the homosexual became a "queer." And a criminal.

"DYKE"—"THE FUN OF IT" ◆

*F*ormerly an insult addressed to a masculine lesbian, "dyke" is another of those put-downs that has become a badge of pride.

As the word was used in lesbian circles, it was always accompanied by a prefix denoting some kind of distinctive style:

• A *bulldyke* (1920s) or *diesel dyke* (1940s) was physically large and intimidating.

• A *lipstick dyke* (1960s) wore make-up and frilly feminine attire—popularly called a "lipstick lesbian."

• A *leather dyke* (1970s) preferred S&M gear.

• A *root dyke* was a "butch," but her distinctive attire was an African or Asian costume expressing her ethnic "roots."

World War I ad with
unintentional overtones.

Harriett Gilbert, in *Fetishes, Florentine Girdles, and Other Explorations Into the Sexual Imagination* (1993), points out that for a lesbian to be called a "dyke" she has to have some personal, deliberate "mark of style":

> In Toronto one can find baseball dykes *(who belong to the Not-So-Amazon softball league)* . . . and Birkenstock dykes, *named after the footwear popular in feminist intellectual circles. In California, there are* SM dykes, granola dykes, *and* beach dykes. *And everywhere one can find everyone's darling,* baby dykes *(who are, needless to say, just over the age of consent). And everyone's nemesis,* bar dykes.

Why does "dyke" take a prefix?

Any woman can be a lesbian, but "being a dyke is a willful act," says Gilbert, "an act of defiance, of creativity, of humor. Lesbians may exist for nasty reactionary politicians and for well-meaning sociologists, but dykes exist only for one another, dressing up, showing off and creating new meanings just for fun." The fun is expressed in the prefix.

"BULLDYKE" FROM "DITCH-DIGGER" ◆

*T*he etymology of "dyke"/"dike" is obscure. In several languages "dike" means "ditch" or "watercourse": Old English, *dic;* Old Norse, *diki;* Dutch, *dijk;* German, *deich.*

"Diking" meant to "drain a ditch."

In fact, "bulldiking" is one of the earliest phrases in which the term "dike" has tough female overtones. It appeared in the American South in the nineteenth century, used by American blacks. Some linguists believe that strong black women who helped dig watercourses on Southern plantations were called "bulldikes."

Others, however, claim that "dike" is really a corruption of "dick," slang for "penis," and has nothing to do with ditchdigging. They argue that in the American South, black men who worked on plantations were called "bull dicks" by their white owners. Genteel Southern women were supposedly fascinated by "bull dicks." The pejorative phrase, or envious compliment, was picked up by black men and used to characterize any tough woman who acted like a man. In time, the expression was applied to any masculine lesbian who swaggered as if she had a dick and balls.

Complimentary names for a lesbian by decade:

- *Sapphist*, 1920s; a woman modeled after the poet Sappho.
- *New Woman*, 1930s; sign of an emerging lesbian pride, spearheaded by the aggressive roles played in Hollywood films by women like Bette Davis and Barbara Stanwyck.
- *Collar-and-Tie*, 1940s; a woman working in what was still a man's world. Also *Major*, a reference to lesbians who served in World War II.
- *Slacks*, 1950s; All women, straight and gay, were beginning to wear pants as leisurewear.
- *Lavender Menace*, early 1970s; allusion to feminist power.

"LESBIAN"—INHABITANT OF LESBOS ◆

*L*esbian—Greek *Lesbios*—is the straightforward name for the people of Lesbos, a small Greek island in the Aegean Sea, 630 square miles in size, off the coast of Asia Minor, home of the poet Sappho. Everybody on Lesbos—men, women, and children—was, by definition, a Lesbian.

Lesbian firsts:

- "Lesbian" was first used to denote a female homosexual in 1883. It appeared in the American medical journal *The Alienist and Neurologist*, in an analysis of Lucy Ann "Joseph" Lobdell, a woman who dressed like a man.
- "Lesbian" was first used in a major American newspaper in January 1892

Sappho's poetry focuses on the physical world of female experiences, from friendship to love.

when the *New York Times* ran this titillating headline: "Lesbian Love and Murder."

The story told of how nineteen-year-old Alice Mitchell, daughter of a wealthy Memphis merchant, jumped out of a riding carriage and slit the throat of her seventeen-year-old lover, Freda "Fred" Ward. Mitchell and Ward had exchanged "wedding" rings and made a compact to kill each other if anyone every separated them. Freda Ward's parents, southern planters, not only separated the lovers but forbade Ward ever to mention Alice Mitchell's name. When Ward returned the ring, Mitchell resolved to kill her.

SAPPHO'S POETRY ◆

*S*appho wrote erotic and sensual verse. Only fragments of her poems remain, some as brief as a few words. Sappho wrote in a new, personal mode, expressing individual feelings and impulses; earlier poetry had been of an epic nature, expressing the collective sentiments of a people or nation.

Sappho's vocabulary, like her dialect, is for the most part vernacular, not literary. Her phrasing is concise, direct, picturesque, and highly sensual. On the pleasure of watching young lovers, she wrote:

For while I gazed, in transport tossed,
My breath was gone, my voice was lost.

My bosom glowed: the subtle flame
Ran quick through all my vital frame;
O'er my dim eyes a darkness hung;
My ears with hollow murmurs rung.

In dewy damps my limbs were chilled;
My blood with gentle horrors thrilled;
My feeble pulse forgot to play—
I fainted, sunk and died away.

Is Sappho's poetry merely sensual, or is some of it about female-female love?

Certainly Sappho was preoccupied with the physical world of female experiences: "For whenever I catch sight of you," she writes of a lover confronted by the beloved, "then my voice deserts me / and my tongue is struck silent, a delicate fire / suddenly races underneath my skin." And Sappho celebrated a woman's "radiant, sparkling face," which she greatly preferred to the fierce expressions of men in warfare.

Anacreon, a younger contemporary of Sappho, bemoaned his unrequited love for a young girl "because she is from Lesbos and gapes after another woman." But scholars believe that the ancient Greek phrase "to play lesbian" meant to engage in promiscuous sexual behavior, either heterosexual or homosexual.

SAPPHO; C. 610–C. 580 B.C.E: WHAT IS KNOWN ABOUT HER ✦

Sappho—whose name is also spelled *Psappho*—is thought to have been married to Cercolas, a wealthy man from the island of Andros. She had at least one child, a daughter named Cleis. And she made her brother, Charaxus, the subject of many of her poems.

Evidence strongly suggests that her family belonged to the upper class of Lesbian society—that is, society on Lesbos. The tradition that she was banished and went to Sicily is likely to be true, but it cannot be confirmed from the fragments of her poetry.

In Sappho's day, it was the fashion on Lesbos for women from good families to assemble in social groups and compose and recite poetry. Sappho became the leading poet of one of these groups, attracting a large number of fans on Lesbos and from neighboring islands. Men loved the erotic nature of her poetry, while women seem to have loved its celebration of female friendship, intelligence, and beauty. Sappho expressed her feelings for women in terms ranging from gentle affection to passionate love. Was she a lesbian forced into marriage? Or a bisexual who chose to marry and have a child?

The claims of lesbianism came mainly after her death.

It is not known how her poems were published and circulated in her own lifetime. But in the era of Alexandrian scholarship, especially the third and second centuries B.C.E., the remains of her work were collected and republished in a standard edition of nine books of lyrical verse and one of elegiac. Greek male writers, reading this opus, concluded that Sappho was addicted to "lesbianism," that love of women was her primary sexual impulse.

Book Burnings—"A Lewd Nymphomaniac" ◆

Unfortunately for scholars, the Alexandrian edition did not survive the Middle Ages—or the Catholic church. On at least two occasions the church burned Sappho's books, and one pope, on studying her surviving verse, labeled the poet "a lewd nymphomaniac."

By the eighth century, Sappho was represented only by long quotations in other poets' and writers' works. Only one poem, twenty-eight lines long, was complete; the next longest was sixteen lines.

The little that remained of her works in Rome and Constantinople was burned in the eleventh century under another papal edict. But not all was lost to history.

In 1897, archaeologists working in Egypt unearthed coffins lined with scraps of papyrus scrolls that happened to be fragments of Sappho's poetry. Soon thereafter, more papyrus scraps of poetry were discovered bunched into balls in the abdominal cavities of mummified crocodiles, used to keep the eviscerated animals looking lifelike. Sappho lived—if in unlikely places.

What has been salvaged today represents about 5 percent of her work, several hundred lines of an estimated twelve thousand. No complete, unmutilated new poem has yet been found.

To prurient Victorians, Sappho's poetry was grossly pornographic. To modern feminists, Sappho is the first major writer on female concerns, female values, and female emotions. To lesbians, Sappho of Lesbos is something of a role model.

Paul II (1464–1471). His first biographer described him as a "gay" spendthrift, flawed by the vice of lust.

THREE GAY POPES ◆

There were many periods during the Middle Ages and into the Renaissance when the power of the papacy went unchallenged, when the office itself was a political appointment, and when the pope was more a politician than a holy man. The so-called Chair of Saint Peter was at times bought by wealthy men; at other times it remained in the hands of one powerful Italian family or another, passing from generation to generation. The rule of celibacy was often ignored. Several popes fathered illegitimate children. At least a half-dozen were acknowledged bisexuals. *At least* three were gay:

Pope Paul II, 1464–1471

Born in Venice on February 23, 1417, Pietro Barbo, who took the name Paul, belonged to a rich merchant family. He was supposed to go into the family business, but when his maternal uncle became Pope Eugene IV, young Pietro entered the priesthood, sensing that the papacy was within his reach.

In remarkably short time, he became a priest, then archdeacon of Bologna, then bishop of Cervia, on to the bigger job of bishop of Vicenza, and at age twenty-three received the title of cardinal deacon. It was a rapid rise. At forty-seven he was pope. Handsome and extraordinarily vain, he wished to be known as Pope Formosus—the Latin adjective *formosus* meaning "beautiful, handsome." After much persuasion, he settled for the humble name of Paul.

Paul loved theater—and theatrics. He delighted the public with extravagant sporting events and entertainments, and spent lavishly on clothes, jewels, and papal furnishing. He was famous for his promotion of spectacular carnivals, to which he forced Jews to contribute heavily. To his credit, he installed the first printing shop in Rome.

What we know of Paul's sex life comes in part from the papal biographer Bartolomeo Sacchi, who called himself Platina and wrote five years after Paul's death. Platina paints a portrait of a fun-loving, spendthrift pontiff, "prone to lust," who surrounded himself with handsome young men and shunned the close company of women. Paul loved to wear the glittering, gem-studded papal tiara as much as possible—in public and private. Because he could easily be reduced to tears by a slight from one of his favorite Italian boys, whom he awarded with gifts, his cardinals called him "Our Lady of Pity."

His official cause of death was listed as "a stroke," brought on by "eating a surfeit of melons." But Platina, who was never on good terms with the pontiff and had once been imprisoned by him, claimed that Paul had suffered a heart attack while being sodomized by his favorite boy.

Paul was succeeded by another gay pope.

Pope Sixtus IV, 1471–1484

Born at Celle, near Savona, of impoverished parents on July 21, 1414, Fransesco della Rovere, who took the name Sixtus, was educated by the Franciscans. He was a priest and skilled theologian at the time of Pope Paul II's sudden death.

According to the *Oxford Dictionary of Popes*, his election to the papacy was "assisted by lavish gifts to the duke of Milan, who strongly backed" Sixtus's candidacy. Once in office, he was ruthless and unscrupulous and "inaugurated a line of pontiffs who systematically secularized the papacy."

The spiritual business of the holy office took second place to Sixtus, whose main concern was the aggrandizement of his own family. Immediately after his election, he violated his papal oath by appointing his two handsome nephews, Pietro Riario and Giuliano della Rovere (later Pope Julius II), as cardinals. By all accounts, Pietro was the pope's lover; and the pontiff enriched his nephew on a scale unprecedented in the history of the papacy. Pietro was a "party animal," living a life of extravagant excess and debauchery, scandalously chronicled by writers of the time; he died at age twenty-eight.

Sixtus IV (1471–1484). He made his two handsome nephews cardinals, and there were rumors that he was lovers with both young men.

(Rumor had it that Giuliano was also a lover of the pontiff, which would make him, as Pope Julius II, at least a bisexual pope.)

In 1478, Sixtus was implicated in a messy conspiracy to murder Lorenzo and Giuliano de' Medici; Lorenzo escaped with a wound, but Giuliano de' Medici was killed.

"Most of the thirty-four cardinals he created were men of little worth," states the *Oxford Dictionary of Popes*. Six of them where his nephews. On the positive side, he transformed Rome from a medieval town into a Renaissance city, opening up new streets and widening and paving old ones. He drew to Rome the greatest painters and sculptors of the day, improved church music, and founded the Sistine choir—filling it with beautiful young boys, several of whom were his favorites. Sixtus is perhaps best remembered as the creator of the Sistine Chapel.

Pope Julius III, 1550–1555

Born at Rome on September 10, 1487, son of a well-known jurist, Giovanni Maria Ciocchi del Monte, who took the name Julius, studied law at Perugia and Siena. After taking holy orders, he became chamberlain to Pope Julius II, the young nephew—and possible lover—Pope Sixtus had promoted to cardinal.

Although he was an outstanding canonist, Julius was "a typical Renaissance pontiff," states the *Oxford Dictionary of Popes*, "generous to relatives, pleasure-loving, devoted to banquets, the theater, hunting."

*Julius III (1550–1555). He made
a beautiful young hustler a
cardinal, then secretary of state.*

Julius's careless homosexuality, especially as he got older, created a scandal for the papacy. In his sixties, he picked up a fifteen-year-old youth on the streets of Parma. The boy, ironically named Innocenzo, was stunningly beautiful, and the pope was so enraptured with his prize that he forced his brother to adopt Innocenzo. Julius audaciously named the unschooled youth to the rank of cardinal—perhaps the first hustler-cardinal. Later the pope appointed his young favorite to the secretariat of state, without executive functions. The pope lived his last few years with gout, dying at age sixty-seven.

CHAPTER 9

Out of the Closet

"HETERO" TO "HOMO"

I don't see so much of Alfred anymore
since he got so interested in sex.

MRS. ALFRED KINSEY

"HOMO" VERSUS THE GENUS *HOMO*; 1929 ◆

"Homo" is a prefix as well as a slur. Actually, "homo" is *two* prefixes. In Greek, *homo* means "same" and is the basis for "homosexual," a lover of the *same* sex. In Latin, *homo* means "man" and is the basis for "Homo sapiens," literally "sapient (or wise) man." Human beings belong to the genus *Homo*. All "homos" are sapiens, but it's been estimated that only about 10 percent of *Homos* are queer.

Milk that is "homogenized" has been made the same throughout; no fat globules separate out from the liquid. A "homophone" is a word that sounds the *same* as another word but is spelled differently and has a different meaning—*bore* and *boar*, for instance. But a "homunculus" is a "little man" or "male dwarf."

Some words take as their prefix the Greek *homo* ("the same"), while others take the Latin *homo* ("man"). It's what's up front that counts.

As an American street slur, "homo" has been dated to 1929. It's psychiatric use for male sexual perversion is several decades older.

Scholar John Boswell claims that at one time homosexuals were allowed to exchange "marriage" vows.

"HOMOSEXUAL"—KARL MARIA KERTBENY; MAY 1868 ◆

The term "homosexual" has been dated to 1868. It first appeared in the correspondence between two German sex reformers who wanted to change restrictive sex laws. The word was coined by writer Karl Maria Kertbeny in letters to Karl Heinrich Ulrichs.

Kertbeny introduced several new words; one survived, two fell into oblivion:

- *Monosexual,* a man or woman who primarily masturbates.
- *Heterogenit,* sex acts between humans and animals.
- *Homosexual,* erotic acts performed between members of the same sex.

"Heterosexual"

Kertbeny also coined the word "heterosexual," from the Greek *hetero,* meaning "other," "different."

For many years the term applied *not* to loving, procreative sex between a husband and wife but to "morbid sexual perversion" between a man and a woman seeking selfish pleasures without risk of pregnancy—using contraceptives, for instance.

Married couples who engaged in "different" (versus "normal") sex practices—fellatio, cunnilingus, anal sex, mutual masturbation—were "de-

Less than a hundred years ago, "heterosexuals" were defined as sick, fun-loving men and women who had sex solely for pleasure, thwarting conception.

praved heterosexuals" consumed by an "unfettered capacity for degeneracy." From the birth of Christianity to late nineteenth century, sex in the Western world was *not* divided into heterosexual and homosexual; such clear-cut categories simply did not exist. The sexual world was divided sharply down the lines of "normal" procreative sex versus "degenerate," nonprocreative sex. Heterosexuality as we know it today—*all* sex acts between a consenting man and woman—is a shockingly recent concept.

As recently as 1923, *Merriam-Webster's New International Dictionary* defined as a medical term

heterosexual: morbid sexual passion for one of the opposite sex.

A married couple who wanted sex but no kids was degenerate.

"Homosexuality"

Kertbeny first publicly used his new term *homosexuality* in the fall of 1869, in an anonymous leaflet arguing against adoption of the "unnatural fornication" law throughout a united Germany.

In 1909, the term entered *Merriam-Webster's New International Dictionary* as "morbid sexual passion for one of the same sex." Thus, at this point in history, both "homosexuals" *and* "heterosexuals" were perverts. How the latter group escaped the stigma, and how the former group is still trying, are discussed later.

Ulrichs, fellow sex reformer, had his own special words: A "true man" who loved women was a *Dionaer;* a man who loved other men was a *Uranier;* a woman who had a "masculine love drive" and thus loved other women was a *Urninde*.

A husband and wife attempting to have children were "Dioning," while "gays" having sex for pleasure were "Urning." Dioning and Urning, dating from the early 1860s in Germany, are the legitimate forebears of our words "heterosexual" and "homosexual."

"Pervert"

Not everyone liked the words coined by Ulrichs and Kertbeny. In 1897, Havelock Ellis wrote, " 'Homo-sexual' is a barbarously hybrid word and I claim no responsibility for it." Ellis was the first to use *"pervert"*—Latin *pervertere*, "to corrupt"—for a male homosexual in *Studies in the Psychology of Sex*: "A pervert whom I can trust told me that he had made advances to upwards of one hundred men."

"Out of the Closet"

Closet Republicans. Closet Conservatives Closet Doves. Closet Liberals. Politics is a house with many closets.

Homosexuals began to come *"out of the closet"* with the advent of the gay liberation movement, touched off by a confrontation with New York City police at the Stonewall Inn in Greenwich Village in the summer of 1969. Instead of backing down in the face of police harassment, the gay men and drag queens who frequented the bar fought back.

For many centuries the "closet" had been a place where skeletons and secrets are hidden: "There are stage-sins [on public display] and there are closet sins" is an early seventeenth-century example.

The phrase "out of the closet" drew national attention in the 1990s with the phenomenon of "outing," in which gay activists "outed" gay politicians and celebrities who were closeted about their sexuality.

HOW TO SPOT A MALE HOMOSEXUAL ◆

*I*t used to be easy. There was even a checklist—several in fact. La Forest Potter, in *Strange Loves: A Study in Sexual Abnormalities* (1933), offered doctors and parents what he claimed was a surefire inventory of traits:

- A brisk, mincing walk
- Pink, pointed, overdeveloped nipples, easily aroused
- Thick, luxuriant hair on the head, often long

- A smooth, flat, hairless chest
- Sloped shoulders and general bad posture
- Soft, delicate, flawless facial skin: "acne spots, so frequently present in normal men, are usually absent"
- Lack of willpower, perseverance, and goals in life
- Swinging motion of the hips—caused by a malformation of the pelvis; the Marilyn Monroe Walk
- Deposits of fatty tissue in the hips, breasts, and thighs
- Heart-shaped "feminine buttocks," with abnormally wide hips

One would think that this kind of checklist disappeared long ago, but it hasn't. In July 1975, Dr. Lawrence J. Hatterer published an article in *Harper's Bazaar* entitled "How to Spot Homosexuality in Children." Parents apparently are still looking for early warning signs. Hatterer argued that if homosexuality could be caught early enough, the child could be "converted" to a heterosexual. A parent was to watch for:

- Reluctance to engage in rough-and-tumble play
- Feminine hand and body movements
- Fear of aggressive peers
- Excessive passivity and submission to one's peers
- No close friends of the same sex
- Playing with dolls
- Dressing up like a girl

"No one sign is evidence," Hatterer cautioned parents. "You must consider the aggregate of signs, or the cumulative pattern of behavior. And even then, you must not immediately assume that your child will become homosexual." A parent spotting signs was advised to seek a professional opinion from an expert—such as Hatterer.

HOW TO SPOT A LESBIAN ◆

*I*n *Lesbian Lists* (1990), Dell Richards culled from turn-of-the-century medical journals signs for spotting a lesbian. The advice was given by physicians and, interestingly, the tips often correlate with the vogue of the day in unacceptable female behavior. With additional research, I've augmented the list to cover more than 150 years.

Not long ago, any woman who played a "man's" game was considered a lesbian.

- **1800s.** In the "Gay '90s"—that is, the 1890s—a sure sign of a lesbian was a woman who smoked in public. Earlier in that century, a woman who donned bloomers to go bicycling was a lesbian. But when cycling in pants and smoking in public became acceptable behaviors, physicians changed their checklist.

- **1900.** At the turn of the century, women who threw away their whalebone corsets for the freedom to breathe easily were labeled by men as lesbians. They had forsworn the fashionably tiny waist and hourglass figure—all unnaturally achieved—for a "manly" look.

- **1920s.** In the early 1920s, when many women had stopped wearing old-fashioned corsets, the new sign of lesbianism was close-cropped or bobbed hair. The boyishly built, carefree flapper, who always bobbed her hair, was assumed by many people to be bisexual.

- **1930s and 1940s.** When some women dared to wear slacks, they were called lesbians. Women who entered the workforce were suspected of homosexual tendencies; they'd abandoned home and hearth.

- **1950s and 1960s.** As more women started to work outside of the home, charges of lesbianism were leveled at women who didn't marry and want children. In the tumultuous late 1960s, women who burned their bras in protest demonstrations were called lesbians. Deviation from accepted behavior was synonymous with being a sexual deviate.

- **1970s.** When the women's movement emerged in the 1970s, all feminists were suspected of harboring lesbian tendencies. They wanted independence and equality—what men *had*—which translated into the suspicion that they wanted to *be* men.

According to the above definitions, a lesbian is any female who does not fit the male ideal of womanhood for a given decade. To this day, a man can expresses his disapproval about some feminine behavior or article of attire by stating that a lesbian would do that or wear that.

"Cures" for Gayness ◆

While Dr. Potter was spotting homosexuals with his handy checklist of swishy, effeminate traits, gay men could select from a variety of "cures" for their "perversion":

- *Testicular castration* diminished the sex drive and thus lessened the urge to commit the love that dare not speak its name.
- *Electroshock therapy* jolted the aberrant brain to its senses.
- *X-raying glands* "worked" because homosexuality resulted from a glandular imbalance.

If these remedies failed and the urge persisted, lobotomy was indicated. Only a few decades ago, it was a real option for gays and lesbians.

Lobotomy; 1930s to 1950s ◆

In 1935, American neurologists C. Jacobsen and J. Fulton reported that they'd made a violent chimpanzee docile by surgically removing part of the frontal lobe of the cerebral hemispheres. Five years later, Dr. Walter J. Freeman (1895–1972) began performing the surgery on violent patients and institutionalized homosexual men and women.

A surgical instrument, a "precision leucotome" (a blunt knife), was inserted into small holes made in the temples at the side of the person's skull. The blade was swept up and down to slice nerve fibers that ran between the frontal lobes and the limbic system, the brain's emotion center. Violent patients were calmed, homosexuals lost a good deal of their libido, and all patients lost large chunks of memory, speech, and emotion. They experienced such gross personality alterations that Freeman could boast that they'd become "different people." Indeed they had.

Lobotomy did not "cure" homosexuality. It merely made a gay man or lesbian into an emotionless, sexless automaton who often did not recognize his or her family. Maybe that's how the family wanted it.

Gay Zombies

The dapper, charismatic Dr. Freeman, in his eagerness to bring the succor of lobotomy to the largest number of sufferers of violence and perversion, simplified his procedure. In the new and improved surgery of the late 1940s, a homosexual was stunned by an electric shock to the head. A sharp metal icepick was quickly hammered up through the thin bone above the eye and then twisted from side to side to randomly dice the frontal lobes. Freeman apologized to homosexuals and their families for what he saw as the surgery's main unwanted side effect: black eyes for several weeks.

Dr. Freeman was a showman and toured the country, performing lobotomies in lecture halls and on closed-circuit television, often without sterile precautions. Violent women, female masturbators, and institutionalized lesbians came increasingly under his knife. He liked particularly to set women on the virtuous straight and narrow. He boasted to colleagues that each side of the brain could be "done in a couple of minutes," and "an enterprising neurologist [could] lobotomize ten to fifteen patients in a morning." One day in 1951, in Spencer, West Virginia, Dr. Freeman himself lobotomized twenty-five gays and criminals in a single day's work.

Critics of the surgery deplored the lobotomized patient's dullness and total disinterest in an emotional life. Freeman responded, "It does disturb me to see the number of zombies that these operations turn out." But, on the positive side, zombie homos were no longer a threat to young children. Pedophilia, thought Freeman, was a sickness soon to be wiped out.

Model Gay Citizens

"Lobotomized patients make good American citizens," wrote Freeman. "The operation has potential for controlling society's misfits—schizophrenics, homosexuals, and radicals." Political radicals, he meant.

By 1955, more than nineteen thousand Americans—gays, lesbians, chronic masturbators, and violent criminals—had been turned into docile, sexless zombies. They were good citizens, one must conclude, because there had never been a zombie revolution or even a small zombie protest.

Finally, a storm of public protests in the late 1950s put an end to the operation—on the eve of the decade that would teem with exactly the kinds of radicals Freeman wanted to lobotomize: Allen Ginsberg, William Burroughs, the Black Panthers, Malcolm X, Martin Luther King.

Soon a variety of psychopharmacological drugs were found to help in treating many psychiatric disorders. And, in the 1970s, psychiatrists concluded that homosexuality had never been a disorder in the first place—merely a misdiagnosis. The American Psychiatric Association removed homosexual orientation from their manual of mental disorders.

Some historians of this sad period of contemporary history argue that lobotomies were well intended, that the "cure" just happened to be worse than the "disease." But if there is no disease to "cure" in the first place . . .

But ideas die hard, and in the late 1970s, Dr. Fritz D. Roeder, following Freeman's lead, announced that he had "cured" several homosexuals through brain surgery. Roeder used an electrode to burn out a portion of the hypothalamus gland. The men were not zombies, reported Roeder, and most were "promptly transformed into the straight world." From straitjacket to straight world. Some doctors—and parents—are still looking for *the cure*.

CAUSES OF HOMOSEXUALITY; MEDIEVAL TO MODERN •

- Demonic possession: *The devil made me do it.*
- Planetary influences: *It's in the stars.*
- Dominant mother, milquetoast dad: *My parents are to blame.*
- Hormonal imbalance; too much estrogen, or too little testosterone: *It's my glands.*
- A hereditary trait: *I've got the gay gene.*
- Neurological wiring; a smaller hypothalamus in gay men than in straight men, from the 1991 study of "gay" brains by Simon LeVay: *It's biological determinism.*
- Prenatal chemical influences that flood the fetus and "masculinize" or "feminize" the developing brain: *Mom smoked, drank, did drugs during my pregnancy.*
- Being reared by a homosexual couple: *They were my role models.*
- A pleasurable same-sex encounter early in youth: *My born-again conversion.*
- Freudian "castration anxiety," which makes some men fearful of women:

"Bisexual" Greek men prized beauty in both young men and young women.

Women suffer penis envy; I'm not going to let one get her hands on my cock.

• Constructionism—the issue here is not sex but power; gays wish to construct a world that welcomes erotic diversity: *Lesbianism is a statement of my equality with men. I lick pussy like guys do. We're equals, get it?*

• A lifestyle choice, having nothing to do with genes, hormones, or sexual indoctrination, made out of a headstrong willfulness: *I wanna hurt mom and dad, be different, antagonize organized religion, be a despised minority.*

ORIGIN OF BISEXUALITY; 600 TO 200 B.C.E. ◆

The ancient Greeks were not concerned with the causes of the "homosexual" behavior that thrived in their population. A straight general or scholar, married and with children, might take a pubescent boy under his wing; the youth got an all-around education under his mentor. Such bisexual behavior was fully accepted by the man's wife and the boy's parents.

The truth—hard though it may be for us to grasp today—is that people in the past did not define themselves by their sexuality, as we have a strong tendency to do. There were no "homosexuals." No "heterosexuals," either. And no "bisexuals"—though this is the behavior many Greek men actively engaged in. People didn't think of themselves in these terms before the advent of psychology and sexology in the last century. Neither ordinary folk, nor physicians, nor philosophers, nor theologians got into discussions about "sexual orientation," "childhood bisexual inquisitiveness," or "adult erotic experimentation."

All Desire Springs from Beauty

The ancient Greeks, who gave us the foundations of government, philosophy, ethics, and love, viewed themselves as innately attracted to beauty—in a man or woman, a young boy or girl. A person's beauty justified attraction to that person. The person's sex was secondary.

French historian and philosopher Michel Foucault (1926–1984), in his groundbreaking *The History of Sexuality*, observed:

> *The Greeks did not see love for one's own sex and love of the other sex as opposites, as two exclusive choices, two radically different types of behavior. The dividing lines did not follow that kind of boundary.*

A happily married Greek man, with perhaps a mistress or two, could openly express his simultaneous desire for a handsome fifteen-year-old boy. There was no Dr. Kinsey to tally sexual trysts, but written works from the period make it clear that liaisons between men—especially between men and boys—were commonplace. They might involve something as innocent as intimate talk, or kissing, or embracing, or sleeping and cuddling without sex. Or they might involve sex to orgasm.

Aristotle disapproved of two grown men reaching orgasm together, but he felt that all sexual activity short of that was healthy. "Love and friendship," he wrote in the *Nicomachean Ethics*, "are found most and in their best form between men."

Foucault asks:

> *Were the Greeks bisexual? Yes, if you mean by that a Greek [free man] could, simultaneously or in turn, be enamored by a boy or a girl.*
>
> *But if we wish to turn our attention to the way in which they conceived of this dual practice, we need to take note of the fact that they did not recognize two kinds of "desire," two different or competing "drives," each claiming a share of men's hearts or appetites.*
>
> *We can talk about their "bisexuality," thinking of the free choice they allowed themselves between the two sexes, but for them this option was not referred to a dual, ambivalent, and "bisexual" structure of desire.*
>
> *To their way of thinking, what made it possible to desire a man or a*

woman was simply the appetite that nature had implanted in man's heart for "beautiful" human beings, whatever their sex.

LOVE IN THE MILITARY—"DO ASK, DO TELL" POLICY ◆

"Don't Ask. Don't Tell. Don't Pursue" is the military's policy for the 1990s. Love between homosexuals in the armed forces is unpunishable as long as it remains unknown, so the theory goes. Opponents of gays in the military argue that acknowledged homosexuality would undermine heterosexual morale. Straight men wouldn't shower with gays. Straight women wouldn't sit on the same toilet seats as lesbians.

A few decades earlier, when the military was about to racially integrate its ranks, opponents argued that white men wouldn't sit on the same toilet seats as blacks. Worse, white men would never bond with black men, a vital emotional tie if a soldier is to save his buddy in battle.

"Don't Ask, Don't Tell" would have impressed the Greeks as a militarily dangerous policy. Greek soldiers recruited young men with homosexual and bisexual desires, and favored their use in certain hazardous battle situations.

Gays as the Bravest Soldiers

In ancient Greece, the love between an older and younger man was thought to enhance both of them, especially in the army. Love in the military was encouraged, and men were often assigned to battalions based on their mutual affections. Affairs were conducted in the open.

Why?

Bravery was said to result from shared affections—loyalty and courage too. Two lovers would rather die together in battle than act cowardly in each other's sight. Also, straight soldiers had wives and children waiting for them at home; two gay lovers fighting side by side were their own family. For this reason, the famous Sacred Band of Thebes, a courageous corps of frontline shock troops, was composed entirely of paired homosexual lovers. Side by side they marched into bloody battle ready to die for one another if necessary.

Greek policy on "gays in the military" went further. Military promotions were often made not only on merit but on looks: beauty was its own reward. Xenophon, historian and Greek military leader, stated flatly, "Generals who do not choose handsome men for commanders of their troops are mad."

In *The Natural History of Love*, Morton M. Hunt observes:

Paired male lovers were considered the bravest of soldiers in the Greek military.

In Sparta, every trainee of good character had a mature lover who was a teacher to him and a model of manhood. It was deemed a military asset for them to fight near each other. Aristogeiton and Harmodius, a lover and his beloved, murdered Hipparchus, the tyrant of Athens, in 514 B.C.E., when he pestered young Harmodius sexually. Later Athenians took this to mean that homosexuality was a force for democracy.

History's Greatest Gay Funeral

Alexander the Great (356–323 B.C.E.), king of Macedonia and military conqueror, helped spread Greek culture from Asia Minor and Egypt to India. Regarded as one of history's greatest generals, Alexander was openly bisexual, and his love of men and boys is well documented. He staged one of history's most spectacular funerals for his lover, Hephaestion, who had fallen in battle. Alexander openly mourned his lover for many days, then planned his funeral.

Hephaestion's body was burned in Babylon atop a two-hundred-foot pyre, the most extraordinary ever assembled. It was built up in tiers of softwood, with huge flammable sculptures of ships, carved wooden bulls, centaurs, lions, and thousands of dried herbal wreaths. Preparations took half a year to complete. When the funeral was over, Alexander, still openly grieving, conceived a lasting memorial for his lover. He ordered that Mount Athos, in its entirety, be sculpted by hundreds of artists into a living likeness of Hephaestion. But the great conqueror himself died before the project had begun.

"EROS" = "EROTIC" ◆

*E*ros was the Greek god of *sexual* love. According to one tradition in Greek mythology, he was the son of the love goddess Aphrodite and the war god Ares. In classical art, he was depicted as a handsome, curly-haired youth, with a lean athletic body. He tamed wild beasts and broke Zeus' thunderbolts in two, and the love he symbolized was frankly sexual, giving rise to these terms:

- *erotic*, first recorded in English in 1651; anything intending to arouse sexual love and desire.
- *erotica*, 1854; literary or artistic works having a sexual theme.
- *eroticism*, 1881; insistent sexual impulse or desire.
- *eroticize*, 1914; to make erotic.

"Cupid" = "Desire"

In early classical times, Eros was viewed as something like the patron saint of homosexual love, specifically between older and younger men. Statues of Eros were common in gymnasiums, those academies for athletics where men and boys exercised naked. Eros was a man's idealized "gay" young lover.

As the concept of love became more romanticized, Eros got younger and younger, evolving into the image of a sweet child, sporting wings and equipped with a bow and quiver full of arrows. The Romans called this sentimental Eros by the names of *Amor* ("love") or *Cupido* ("carnal desire"). It was this Roman avatar of love that gave rise to the chubby cherub we know as Cupid. Ironically, the most common figure on heterosexual lovers' Valentine cards today originated as *the* primary symbol of homosexual desire.

FREUD'S "BISEXUALITY"; LATE NINETEENTH CENTURY ◆

*S*igmund Freud used the term "bisexuality" to refer primarily to a combination of "masculine" and "feminine" traits in the same person. While the Greeks had viewed "bisexual" desires as normal in adults, Freud viewed both same-sex and opposite-sex attraction as completely normal only in young children. A child could be bi, but an adult shouldn't be. A child's sexuality, said Freud, was still pliant and taking shape, so it was only natural

The image we know as Cupid evolved from the Greek character of Eros, an idealized "gay" young lover.

for a child to experience both same-gender and opposite-gender attraction—or confusion.

For Freud, adults who engaged in bisexual fantasies—or actual experiences—were not yet fully mature and, possibly, sick. By adulthood, a man or a woman was supposed to have worked out any bisexual confusion. A bisexual who functioned well in society was not necessarily sick but might just be a little immature, muddled in the head, lacking a solid sense of self.

Modern feminism and gay liberation have forced psychiatrists to rethink bisexuality. So, too, have polls that reveal that many people, heterosexual and homosexual, occasionally or frequently engage in bisexual fantasies. A straight woman might imagine herself in a sexual three-way with a man and another women; a straight man might picture himself in a three-way with a woman and a man.

Is this residual childhood sexual immaturity, as Freud would have it? Or is it simply the reality that both sexes, male and female, share virtually the same genetic makeup and thus can, when all taboos are lifted (as can happen in fantasy), relate sexually to another human being in whom they see desirable traits, like beauty?

Our view of bisexuality today is much closer to that of the Greeks than of Freud. The Greeks gave us bisexual love.

"BREEDERS" VERSUS "NON-BREEDERS"— FIRST SEXUAL CATEGORIES; BIBLICAL TIMES TO TWENTIETH CENTURY ✦

*S*traight. Gay. Lesbian. Bisexual. Transsexual. Transvestite. Heterosexual cross-dresser.

We have a talent for dividing people up by their bedroom preferences or attire—by their "sexuality," though we seldom question why it seems so normal.

Michel Foucault argued that all of our modern sexual categories have been "culturally constructed." They were brought into existence by our urge during this century to talk endlessly about sex. Foucault called this our obsessive "incitement to discourse." Sex talk was begun, said Foucault, by the professions of psychiatry, medicine, and law in an effort to differentiate "normal" practices and desires from "abnormal"—or criminal—ones. We have *talked* ourselves into sexual categories.

There's validity to this view, but talk about sexual categories began a long time ago, not in psychiatry or law but religion. Judaism and Christianity made the first attempts to define "normal" and "abnormal," in terms of virtue and vice. Religion gave us sex's first two categories, and they were not "hetero" and "homo" but "breeder" and "nonbreeder," two polarized sexual types.

Procreative versus Nonprocreative Sex

Breeders had sex with the intent to have children—*procreative sex*, religion termed it. Breeders were always married. Breeders *never* practiced birth control. (Jews were an exception. A married couple was required to have a minimum of two children—preferably two boys, but a boy and girl would suffice—and could then abandon procreative sex by using contraceptives. Roman Catholicism never got that liberal.)

Nonbreeders had sex with the intent to *thwart* conception at every copulation. They too might be married, but they sometimes, or always, sought sex for pleasure's sake alone. Maybe they reached climax through cunnilingus, fellatio, anal intercourse, or mutual masturbation. *Nonprocreative sex*. Maybe they already had all the children they could support. Homosexual relationships fell into the nonbreeder category, but they were of minor concern.

All sex, procreative and nonprocreative, was supposed to be confined to marriage. These two harsh categories, which existed for over two thousand years, would give way to broader, saner categories only in the century.

For centuries people were divided morally into two major categories:
breeders, who practiced procreative sex, and nonbreeders,
who engaged in sex with the use of contraceptives.

Let's examine the real origins of "heterosexuality" and "homosexuality." Much of the information that follows has only recently become known.

"HETEROSEXUAL" = "MORBID SEXUAL PASSION FOR ONE OF THE OPPOSITE SEX"; CHICAGO, 1892 ◆

*M*ost people don't realize that in the United States the earliest use of the word "heterosexual"—Greek *hetero*, "other," "different"— occurred only about a hundred years ago. The term had been bandied about in Europe since 1868.

In May 1892, "heterosexuality" was defined by Dr. James G. Kiernan as male-female "abnormal manifestations of the sexual appetite." To be a heterosexual was to be mentally ill—and spiritually bereft. Kiernan, in "Responsibility in Sexual Perversion," published in the *Chicago Medical Recorder*, included a lot of people under the umbrella category "heterosexual":

• Men and women who are "inclined to both sexes"—we'd say "bisexuals," and
• Men and women who engaged in all "abnormal methods of gratification"—that is, nonprocreative methods of sexual pleasure: cunnilingus,

fellatio, anal intercourse, and mutual masturbation. Such "heterosexuals" were guilty of the social and religious sin of "reproductive deviance."

The prefix *hetero* then did not mean attraction to the opposite, or "different," sex, but simultaneous interest in *two different* sexes, as well as sexual practices *different from* procreative coupling. Everything "different" was damned.

Dr. Kiernan's article also contained the earliest known publication of the word *homosexual* in the United States. For Kiernan, the "pure homosexual" was a person whose "general mental state is that of the opposite sex"—we'd say a transsexual: a man who feels trapped in a woman's body or vice verse. Kiernan thought that all gay men had a deep desire to be women, and all lesbians wanted to be men.

As late as the 1890s, sexuality was not yet organized on our modern-day "different-sex" versus "same-sex" foundation—as "straight" and "gay."

In *The Invention of Heterosexuality* (1995), Jonathan Ned Katz writes:

> The norm wasn't "heterosexual." It was reproductive. So any sex that wasn't procreative was perverted. This included non-reproductive intercourse between men and women. By this procreative standard, heterosexuals and homosexuals stood together in the pantheon of sexual perverts.

In 1893, German neuropsychiatrist Richard von Krafft-Ebing, best known today for his groundbreaking examination of the variety of sexual passions, had used *hetero-sexual* to mean "normal" attraction to the opposite sex. But Krafft-Ebing too emphasized that sexual normalcy was linked closely to reproductive intercourse. If a husband and wife were to be "normal heterosexuals," they had to engaged in sex *primarily* to have children.

Krafft-Ebing used the term *homo-sexual* to signify same-sex desire and, interestingly, defined it as pathological mainly because it was non-reproductive.

HETEROSEXUALITY BECOMES THE NORM; 1930S ◆

*B*y Dr. Kiernan's definitions, "heterosexuals" were sicker and more dangerous than "homosexuals." This was because "heterosexuals" loved both sexes, were hopelessly confused about their gender, and engaged in sex for pleasure and not to conceive children. "Heterosexuals" were de-

Pottery art of a man and a woman engaging, perhaps, in the vice of nonprocreative sex.

generates who, if their numbers were allowed to multiply, threatened the existence of society—the continuation of the species. Breeders who refused to breed were more dangerous than "homosexuals," who were merely sick but harmless.

As the words "heterosexual" and "homosexual" were first used in America, the more depraved group was "heterosexuals." They deliberately thwarted the primary intent of marriage.

As we saw earlier, in 1923 the *Merriam-Webster's New International Dictionary* defined "heterosexual" as "morbid sexual passion for one of the opposite sex." All that was "morbid," of course, was that a man and woman wanted pleasure without pregnancy.

Not until 1934, in Webster's hefty *Second Edition Unabridged*, do we find a definition of "heterosexual" that we'd accept as valid today:

> *heterosexual: manifestation of sexual passion for one of the opposite sex; normal sexuality.*

As Katz concludes, "Heterosexuality had finally attained the status of norm."

In other words, heterosexuals were now, in the 1930s, being allowed to engage in nonprocreative sex for the sheer fun of it, without being labeled sick and depraved for doing so.

How had this happened? How did one group, the breeding majority, escape the centuries-long taint of perversion to be allowed to engage in non-procreative sex for fun? (Of course, some religions, Roman Catholicism for one, still do not accept this liberated view.) And why was the other group, homosexuals, the nonbreeding minority, left in the dust of deviancy?

SEX OUTSIDE OF MARRIAGE; AMERICA, EARLY TWENTIETH CENTURY •

*I*n 1900, in Philadelphia, sex pioneer Havelock Ellis began to publish his multivolume *Studies in the Psychology of Sex*. Trained as a physician, Ellis lectured throughout America, telling people that it was normal to feel sexual passion *outside* of marriage. A loving wife could have sexual feelings for a man other than her husband and not be labeled "neurotic" or "perverted"—or a "female man," as such women were popularly disparaged.

Ellis defended what he called "normal sexual love" against the breeder/nonbreeder legacy of religion, mainly Christianity. The Christian attitude toward procreative sex alone, he preached, had "so poisoned the springs of feeling" that "all our words of sex" are "bespattered with filth." Normal, sexual adults, said Ellis, "have no simple, precise, natural word for the love of the sexes."

Ellis proposed "heterosexual."

• In 1915, in *Sexual Inversion*, Ellis removed "heterosexuality" from the long category of sexual deviations.
• In 1974, the American Psychiatric Association would do the same for the word "homosexuality."

Ellis was saying in essence that men and women who had sexual urges outside of marriage—and perhaps acted on them—should not feel ashamed or dirty. Also, a married couple who wanted to make love for years without bearing children should not feel they were degenerates. All such people should be proud—even a little defiant—of their nonprocreative sexual mentality. Procreation, Ellis argued, was no longer to be the basis of sexual normalcy. Though he didn't realize it, Ellis was paving the way for making homosexuality normal decades later.

Had Ellis made his statements at any earlier time in history, he'd have become merely a footnote to it. But he preached his new definition of "het-

For centuries, any woman with a passionate sex drive was considered abnormal, especially if she initiated sex.

erosexuality" just as the times were changing: during the sexual upheaval of the Roaring Twenties.

Interestingly, heterosexuality became normal during the first sexual revolution of this century, and homosexuality became normal during the second, kicked off in the 1960s. A mere one hundred years ago, Americans would not have understood what we mean when we speak of heterosexuals and homosexuals.

HETEROSEXUALS COME OUT OF THE CLOSET; AMERICA, 1920S ◆

*W*omen, not men, ushered in the new image of the free-loving, nonbreeding "heterosexual." Havelock Ellis and others had offered textbook definitions and philosophies, but the turning point in terms of behavior and popular attitude came in America in the 1920s.

The years between the election of President Warren G. Harding in 1920 and the catastrophic stock market crash of 1929 were a wild joyride of sexual experimentation. A time of sexually liberated flappers, bootleg gin, women smoking cigarettes *in public*, hot jazz, condoms, flivvers, and backseat sex. The automobile gave couples a bedroom away from home. *Parking* was more than maneuvering a car's tires into a tight space.

More than anyone, the flapper epitomized the emancipated "new woman." She was daringly outspoken, defiantly sexual, and let it be known that she practiced "birth control." The term itself had been newly coined. She had the right to vote like men, she drank and smoked like men—even *with* men—and she could choose her own sexual partner, for her own pleasure—even a woman. The liberated attitude of the freewheeling decade would not surface again until the sexual revolution of the 1960s.

Women Redefine Sexual Normalcy

By the time of the stock market crash, to be a "heterosexual" meant to have a strong, "normal" drive toward the opposite sex—no thoughts of procreation were necessary. The flapper had escaped the breeder/nonbreeder straitjacket of sex, and she had liberated other women. Men had always indulged their out-of-marriage passions for women, but now women could admit that they had sexual stirrings for men other than their husbands and boyfriends.

"By the end of the 1920s, heterosexuality had triumphed as the dominant, sanctified culture," writes Jonathan Ned Katz in *The Invention of Heterosexualtity*. "In the first quarter of the twentieth century the heterosexual came out, a public, self-affirming debut the homosexual would duplicate near the century's end."

"Hetero"—1933; "Homo"—1929 •

By the 1930s, American magazines and newspapers were using the new words "heterosexual" and "homosexual." The former had the meaning we'd recognize today, and the latter still represented an illness, but they were gaining public awareness and more frequent usage.

According to the *Oxford English Dictionary*, the first published appearance of the colloquial abbreviation "hetero" occurred in 1933 in a satirical English novel, *Ordinary Families*, by Eileen A. Robertson.

"Homo" had begun to appear four years earlier, in 1929, as street slang and in underground publications.

"Straight"; 1941 •

The earliest recorded usage of "straight" to refer to a heterosexual man or woman is in the glossary of *Sex Variants: A Study of Homosexual Patterns*, by George W. Henry; "straight" was now popular slang among homosexual men to mean:

. . . not homosexual. To go straight is to cease homosexual practices and to indulge—usually to reindulge—in heterosexuality.

"Straight" was coined (by gays) not to describe a practicing heterosexual (as we use it today) but to describe a homosexual who was abandoning same-sex behavior for "the straight path"—an allusion to the "straight and narrow" path of acceptable, relatively limited, and majority-approved behavior.

Thus, by the start of World War II, Americans had five new sex words: *hetero, homo, straight, heterosexuality,* and *homosexuality.*

"HOMOSEXUAL" IS NOT IN THE BIBLE ◆

To clear up a common misconception, the remarkably new word "homosexual" does not appear in Hebrew or Christian Scripture. It simply didn't exist back then.

As Yale historian John Boswell writes in *Christianity, Social Tolerance, and Homosexuality* (1979):

> *In spite of misleading English translations which may imply the contrary, the word "homosexual" does not occur in the Bible; no extant text or manuscript, Hebrew, Greek, Syriac, or Aramaic, contains such a word. There are of course ways to get around the lack of a specific word in a language, and an action may be condemned without being named, but it is doubtful in this particular case whether a concept of homosexual behavior as a class existed at all.*

The Bible does clearly state prohibitions against same-sex acts, but at the same time it states that a child who curses his mother or father shall be put to death; that a man who touches a menstruating women, even his wife, shall be exiled from his people; that a suspected adulteress is required to drink poison as a test of her guilt; that a leper's infection is a sign of his moral guilt.

These are all ideas that religion has grown beyond. All but one, that is.

ONE IN TEN MEN IS GAY—KINSEY SEX SURVEY; 1948 ◆

*T*he number-four book on the *New York Times* bestseller list in 1948 was sex researcher Alfred C. Kinsey's *Sexual Behavior in the Human Male*. Kinsey informed Americans that:

- 85 percent of all married heterosexual men have had premarital sex.
- 50 percent of married heterosexual men were at one time or another unfaithful to their wives.
- Semiskilled laborers were the most sexually active group of straight males, with professional men ranking second, day laborers third, and white-collar workers last.

Shocked readers had to ask themselves what constituted "normal" and "abnormal" sexual activity.

The biggest shock was Kinsey's estimate of the number of male homosexuals in the population: as many as ten out of a hundred men were gay. More unnerving still: "homosexual experience is much more common than previously thought," since in many males "there is often a mixture of both homo and hetero experience." Young men experiment sexually; they fool around with other men.

Kinsey was using the new words "hetero" and "homo" and scaring—or comforting—many people with them.

A CONTINUUM OF SEXUAL DESIRES ◆

*P*erhaps the most enlightening statement in Kinsey's study was his explanation of a "continuum" of human sexual desires and practices. The sex researcher used a rating scale of zero to six for the extremes of "hetero" and "homo" behavior. He cautioned that human beings are "not to be divided into sheep and goats," an allusion to the biblical metaphor of conformity and licentiousness:

> *Only the human mind invents categories and tries to force facts into separated pigeon-holes. The living world is a continuum.*

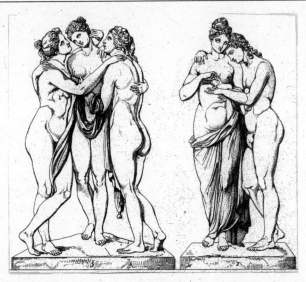

Alfred Kinsey described a "continuum" of human sexual desires and practices.

GAY AND LESBIAN FACTS ◆

51.6 percent of lesbians cohabit with a partner.

37.5 percent of gay men live with a partner.

56.2 percent of homosexual couples have annual incomes over $50,000.

26.3 percent of gays and lesbians have graduate degrees.

79.3 percent of homosexuals make purchases based on gay media advertising. Gays are one of the most loyal consumer groups.

2.4 percent of gay men are fathers with part-time custody of their children.

15.6 percent of lesbians own four or more cats or dogs.

81.1 percent of gay men have dined out more than five times in the past month.

13.1 percent of gay men are Republicans.

65.3 percent of lesbians go camping.

14.4 percent of gay men do cross-country skiing.

31.7 percent of gays live in suburban areas.

In 1985, in the *New York Review of Books*, Gore Vidal, long a pioneering sex reformer, recast Kinsey's findings in a modern light:

> *There is no such thing as a homosexual or a heterosexual person. There are only homo- and heterosexual acts. Most people are a mixture of impulses if not practices, and what anyone does with a willing partner is of no social or cosmic significance.*
>
> *So why all the fuss? In order for a ruling class to rule, there must be arbitrary prohibitions. Of all prohibitions, sexual taboo is the most useful because sex involves everyone . . . we have allowed our governors to divide the population into two teams. One team is good, godly, straight; the other is evil, sick, vicious.*

Today, a "gay culture" exists. There are gay films, gay magazines, gay bars, gay dance clubs, gay cruises and resorts, gay Club Med vacations, gay skiing weekends, gay day at Walt Disney World. Gay rights. Even gay marriages— which one day may be legally recognized. Neither the Greeks nor the Romans, who freely engaged in homosexual sex, would have understood the unique gay and lesbian culture that has sprung up in the last twenty-five years. As it exists today, it is the first gay culture in human history.

CHAPTER 10

Sale of Two Titties

"Boobs" to Bra

Brevity is the soul of lingerie.

DOROTHY PARKER

"TIT"; ENGLAND, PRE-TWELFTH CENTURY ♦

Our slang "tit" for the female breast is a common Old English word dating from before the twelfth century. To the Anglo-Saxons, *tit* meant not an entire breast but only the nipple, the raised protuberance on any mammalian gland or udder through which milk flows during suckling of the young.

The Anglo-Saxons called the entire pendulous mammary gland an *uder*, origin of our word "udder." A *tit* topped off an *uder*.

Linguists believe the word "tit" in its earliest usage meant "little," the reason why it was applied to only the nipple at the center of the areola. In this sense of smallness, "tit" appears in "titmouse", a family of tiny, plump birds, many gray and tufted, that live throughout much of the world.

The French who conquered England in the eleventh century found "tit" vulgar. They substituted their own anatomical word, *teat*—still a proper British term. When a female dog is pregnant, her *teats* swell.

AMERICAN "TITS"; THE ROARING TWENTIES ◆

*O*ver the centuries, "tit" came to have a variety of meanings. A young horse, or filly, was a "tit"—an allusion to the animal's smallness with respect to its mother.

A delicate morsel was a "tit bit," a tiny amount, which evolved into "tidbit." In this latter context, a delectable young woman was called a "tit" or "tit bit."

In America, the Roaring Twenties gave us many new "tit" expressions:

• **Tits**—street slang for female breasts: "He ran his *meat hooks* (hands) all over her *lily white* tits," or "She's all tits and *gams* (legs)."

• **Tits and ass**—a reference to the flaunting of a woman's sex appeal; later shortened to *T & A*.

• **Tit man**—fraternity slang for a "college Joe" obsessed with breasts.

• **Tough titty**—college slang for "that's too bad," or "hard luck"—an allusion to how "tough" or frustrating it was for a "Joe" or "Charlie" to get a feel of "titty."

It is ironic that "tits" came to be slang for breasts in the Roaring Twenties. The preeminent female icon of that era was the slender, boyish flapper who tried hard to appear "titless." Men, perhaps starved for the sight of breasts, began to use the word as a substitute for the real thing.

"BOOBS"; AMERICA, PRE-1945 ◆

A "boob" is a stupid person, a boor, a Philistine, a dullard or dolt. The word, which became popular in America around 1900, is a shortened version of the British slang "booby" meaning "a stupid mistake," "a blunder."

Two or more stupid mistakes were "boobies" or "boo-boos," the origin of our expression for a child's minor injury, a "boo-boo."

"Booby" itself derived from the Spanish *bobo*, "fool," and from the Latin *balbus*, "stammering." A stammerer, or stutterer, was considered a "fool" or "booby." The nonsexual connotations of "boob" appear in many common terms:

• A **booby prize** (first recorded in 1889) is an award for the poorest performance in a game or competition.

- A **booby hatch** (1840) is a raised framework with a sliding cover over a small confined hatch on a ship; or an insane asylum, another type of confinement.
- A **booby trap** (1850) is a pitfall or a trap for the unwary or unsuspecting.
- **Boob tube** (1966) is a disparaging nickname for a television.

How, then, did "boob" and "boobies" come to be slang for female breasts? Is it that men make utter fools, or boobs, of themselves over large breasts, stammering at the sight of them? Are such men "booby-trapped? Or do they take the "booby prize" for their stupid performance in the presence of a buxom woman? Some linguists have suggested that, pointing to the fact that one of the earliest uses of "boob" meant a stuttering fool. After all, when we say that television is "the boob tube," we imply that it's a conveyance for nonsense that makes fools, or boobs, of us all.

Others maintain that "boob" as slang for "breasts" originated from *bubbies*, the Elizabethan word for that part of the female anatomy. This theory holds that "bubbies" in time became "boobies."

Nasty or Nice?

In *Talking Dirty* (1993), Reinhold Aman reports the results of a survey comparing "boobs" with "tits." Which is the "nice" term, which is the "nasty" one?

Two-thirds of men polled thought "boobs" was the nicer term, one that women did not find offensive.

Women were almost equally divided on "boobs"; as for "tits," twice as many women found it nasty than nice.

The few lesbians polled thought "boobs" was a nice word; no lesbian viewed it as nasty. However, about two-thirds of lesbians considered "tits" nasty.

Gay men, four to one, thought "boobs" was nicer and politer.

Overall, "boobs" rated nicer than "tits."

MEN MAKE UP WORDS ◆

*M*any men are obsessed with female breasts. They are certainly introduced to them early in life. While female infants grow up to have their own breasts, men are always on the search for someone else's.

The best evidence of this obsession is found in the extraordinary number of slang terms for breasts that linguists have cataloged. Some derive straightforwardly from the shape and function of breasts. Others are strange sounds

Most women think "boobs" is a nicer word than "tits."

and meaningless expressions, sexy codes that have no dictionary definitions and lost origins.

A sampling:

Knockers, melons, globes, jugs, cantaloupes, tomatoes, peaches, dairy farms, hooters, bazooms, mazoomas, head-lights, groodies, love-pillows, nice set, handfuls, norks, sweet valley, warm valley, balloons, knobs, honkers, hangers, puppies, pretty lungs, porcelain spheres, cadabies, dzwonies, beaver tails, bells, boobulars, blossoms, mountains, nay-nays, vavooms, waawaas, bubbies, boulders, diddies, dugs, bellys, tetas or *tetitas* (Spanish, "titties"), *tsitskelakh* (Yiddish, "titties"), *cycuski* (Polish, "titties").*

"MAMMA" = MAMMARY GLAND ◆

*W*e've looked at slang expressions for "breast." There are also many legitimate, dictionary words:

• **Bosom** is from the Indo-European root *bhreus*, meaning "to swell" or "to sprout," coming to us through the Old English *bosm*. The term arose sometime before the twelfth century. By 1590, "bosom" could also mean a close, intimate friend, a "bosom buddy."

• **Bust** is from the Italian *busto*, a piece of sculpture of the head and torso

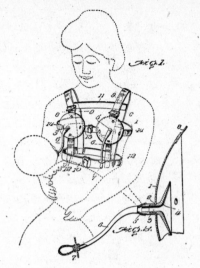

"Nursing attachment" with hoses to allow a mother to breast-feed an infant in public without exposing her breasts, patent no. 949,414 (1910).

down to and including the breast. The term first appeared in English in 1645.

• **Buxom** describes a woman who is vigorous, healthy, plump, and especially full-bosomed. The word is from the Middle English *buxsum*, "to bend"—an allusion to the drooping bend characteristic of heavy breasts. The term appeared in English sometime before the twelfth century.

• **Mammary**, as in mammary glands, is fittingly named from the Latin *mamma*, meaning "breast" or "udder." This is also the origin of our maternal endearment "mamma." "Mammary" first appeared in English in 1682, while its medical cousin, "mammary gland," appeared in 1831.

• **Breast** is from the Old English *breost*, which also evolved from an Indo-European root, *bhreus*, "to swell" or "to sprout." The allusion is clearly to the mammary glands on a pregnant mammal. The term first appeared in English sometime before the twelfth century.

"Breast" was a taboo word during the nineteenth, and much of the twentieth, century. The revulsion that most people felt is evident in *Peter Simple* (1834), by Frederick Marryat, in a dinner table scene, involving a breast of turkey:

Fate had placed me opposite a fine turkey. I asked my partner if I should have the pleasure of helping her to a piece of the breast. She looked at me

> **BREAST ANATOMY** ◆ *The best way to imagine the inside of a female breast is to picture the thinly encased segments in a cross section of an orange. The adult female breast, or mammary gland, consists of fifteen to twenty-five segments, or lobes, that are separated by fibrous tissue. Each lobe resembles a multibranched tree that is embedded in fat.*
>
> *About twenty-four hours after childbirth, milk produced in the alveoli of each lobe—the "leaves" of each "tree"—travels along small ducts into the main "trunk" or milk duct. This duct is enlarged to form a reservoir just below the areola, the dark ring visible around the nipple. A narrow continuation of the duct links this reservoir with the nipple's surface. Each of the breast's fifteen to twenty-five lobes has its own opening on the nipple's head. The basic anatomy of the breasts was known to Greek physicians.*

indignantly and said, "Curse your impudence, sir. I wonder where you learnt your manners. Sir, I take a lily turkey bosom, if you please."

NIPPLES—IN MEN AND WOMEN ◆

The nipple is the protuberance of the mammary gland upon which, in females, the lactiferous ducts open, and from which milk is drawn.

• The word "nipple" dates to the 1500s and is probably a diminutive of the English *nib*, the sharpened point of a quill pen. *Nib* itself is thought to derive from the earlier Old English *neb*, meaning "beak" and, later, "mouth."

• The word "milk," dating from before the twelfth century, is from the Old English *meolc* and is derived from the Indo-European root *melg*, meaning "to squeeze out," as an animal's udder is worked for its fluid. In a sense, a child asking for a glass of milk is asking that an udder be squeezed.

Witch's Milk

Many baby boys are born with tiny swollen breasts. A whitish fluid may ooze from their nipples. The viscous, sweetish secretion was called "witch's milk" and was highly prized for its paucity and alleged magical potency. A midwife

"Nipple" once meant "beak," a reference to the feeding of young offspring.

might "milk" a baby boy for the precious fluid, which, if drunk, was thought to cure infertility and a host of sex-related problems.

Why do some baby boys produce milk?

Human breasts are glands, and early in life they react to maternal hormones still in the baby's blood. For many days after birth, a male baby's breasts are under the influence of its mother's potent mix of hormones. Doctors do not recommend squeezing a male infant's swollen breasts, which only stimulates milk flow. In about a week's time both the milk and swelling will disappear.

WHY DO MEN HAVE NIPPLES? ✦

*T*his old conundrum is really no mystery at all.

Some men lactate; some men get breast cancer. Most men's nipples can become erect when stimulated, and many men get turned on by it. A percentage of gay men report that rough nipple play, coded TT ("tit torture") in personal ads, can lead to orgasm. "Tit clamps," which resemble small alligator-toothed clothespins, are a not uncommon sex toy among women and gay men. Some gay men into regular "tit torture" report that continual and vigorous nipple stimulation can lead to lactation.

There is a simple reason why men have nipples:

Eve Came First

During the first five weeks of fetal life, the reproductive organs are the same for both genders. They have the basic ingredients to be either male or female:

- A raised genital ridge on the embryo can develop into either a penis or clitoris.
- Raised folds of embryonic skin can develop into either a scrotum or vaginal lips.
- Certain tissues inside the embryo can develop into either testicles or ovaries.

Nature has efficiently designed both sexes from a *single template*. Sex modifications are made later on.

In truth, the basic template for a human being is *female*. *Male* sex modifications are made later on. If a baby boy has inherited programming for maleness from his father's Y chromosome, then during the fifth to eleventh week the embryo begins to produce testicle tissue, which soon produces its own testosterone. Thus, what might have become a clitoris elongates into a penis, and the folds that might have become vaginal lips seam shut to from the scrotum, which one day will house the testes. All adult men have *vestigial* blobs of tissue near their prostate glands that could have developed into . . . a uterus.

"Eve" comes first in the womb. It's "Adam" who springs from *her* "rib," so to speak.

All embryos are originally programmed to be female. It is only male hormones, once they start to flow, that suppress the female-making tissue from fashioning a baby girl. If something goes amiss and a boy-to-be's testes are malformed, or produce insufficient hormones, "he" will develop into an ersatz "she"—a sad problem we examined earlier.

Breast-Feeding Dads

Part of Eve's design is mammary glands with nipples. Some doctors have argued that male nipples are merely vestigial organs. But they're more.

In some mammals, male nipple development is completely suppressed by male hormones. In humans, however, males develop full-size nipples, which are rich in blood vessels and nerves. Adult males medically placed on estrogen therapy can have their dormant milk glands suddenly awakened. Male body-

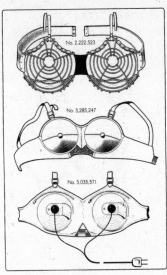

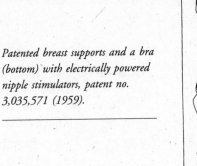

Patented breast supports and a bra (bottom) with electrically powered nipple stimulators, patent no. 3,035,571 (1959).

builders taking large doses of testosterone (which shut down the testes' own production of the hormone) sprout fleshy "bitch tits."

In former East Germany, imprisoned rapists once had their libidos suppressed by subdermal implants of round-the-clock trickling estrogen. Full-size female breasts and nipples, with lactation, were a common consequence of the treatment. Many of the rapists developed such alluring breasts, peaked nipples, and enlarged dark-brown areolas—as well as fleshy hips and buttocks—that they resembled women enough to be raped by other inmates.

Some researchers have suggested that measured estrogen shots given to new dads might one day allow them to share breast-feeding duties with mom. Mom might work during the day while dad breast-feeds, then dad would go off to work at night while mom takes over. Congress might have to modify the Family and Medical Leave Act.

OTTO TITZLING: INVENTOR OF THE BRA? ◆

*L*egend has it that a German engineer named Otto Titzling invented the bra around 1900. Such an appropriate name sounds too good to be true: a tit-sling is exactly what a bra is.

Several fashion encyclopedias repeat the claim, as well as many books on modern inventions. After a long search for Otto Titzling, I finally found the single source for all of the claims: a slender book, *Bust Up: The Uplifting Tale of Otto Titzling*, by British journalist Wallace Reyburn. Published in

Mechanical equivalent of the modern bra has independent cups as well as shoulder and back straps, patent no. 24,033 (1859).

England in 1971, the book appeared a year later in an American edition, published by Prentice-Hall.

Reyburn's workmanlike biography is rich in details, filled with photographs, diagrams of bra designs tried and rejected, and bra patent applications. Reyburn weaves in so much of the factual history of women's corsets and undergarments that it is difficult to pass judgment on the veracity of the details. Apparently, many people believed that Otto Titzling was a real man and accepted him as inventor of the bra.

In the end, though, the book contains too many obvious jokes for any information on Otto Titzling to be taken seriously.

But for all his sophomoric humor, Reyburn had the last laugh. His fictitious hero has been immortalized in fashion encyclopedias and books on modern inventions.

BREAST ENHANCEMENT; GREECE, 2000 B.C.E. ♦

*B*ody modification has been a turn-on for most peoples in most cultures. The Chinese bound the feet of female children. South American Indians stretched earlobes. Africans inserted plates into their lips and elongated their necks with stacks of metal rings. Other cultures have filed their teeth to sharp points, tattooed and scarred their flesh, and constricted their waists with punishing corsets. Today, many Americans turn to plastic

THOMAS CRAPPER AND THE FLUSH TOILET ◆ *Two years before* Bust Up *appeared, Wallace Reyburn published another amusing slim "biography,"* Flushed With Pride: The Story of Thomas Crapper. *It, too, is out of print but lives on as part of the lore of Latrinalia: that the flush toilet was the invention of Englishman Thomas Crapper. Here's the historical truth:*

The first flush toilet was invented in England in 1596, for the private use of Queen Elizabeth. The inventor was Sir John Harington, the queen's godson. He used the device, which he called "a privy in perfection," to regain the queen's favor, for she had banished him from court for circulating Italian pornography.

The next flush device of distinction appeared in 1775. It was patented by Alexander Cumming, a British mathematician and watchmaker. Cumming's toilet was an improvement over Harrington's in that it had a "stink trap," a neck of pipe constantly filled with water to separate the user from a reflux of cesspool fumes.

Born in 1837, Thomas Crapper apparently was a real person, a plumber by trade, and he made mechanical improvements on the toilet's flush mechanism, mainly having to do with valves. He started his own company in London, "T. Crapper, Chelsea," but he did not invent the toilet.

Nor could he have been embarrassed by his surname. "Crapper" as slang for toilet was first recorded in 1932. "Crap," meaning excrement, dates to 1897.

Linguistic evidence suggests that "crap," for "excrement," became "crapper," meaning "toilet," in America in the 1920s. Servicemen serving in England during World War I spotted "T. Crapper, Chelsea" on British WCs (water closets) and brought the term home as a pun. Only then did Thomas Crapper become the butt of jokes and get credit for the entire flush toilet.

Thomas Crapper and his workmen testing a new flush mechanism.

surgeons for breast implants and liposuction—all in the name of sex appeal.

Most cultures have enhanced the penis and breasts in one way or another, often in brazenly explicit ways. Among some New Guinea peoples, men wrap their penises in eighteen-inch-long sheaths, which are tied against the abdomen to give the appearance of a constant hard-on. But no body part has received as much modification—and all-around attention—as female breasts.

Throughout history, as the female bosom has gone in and out of favor as the focus of fashion, so too have the breasts themselves gone in and out of public view. Around 2000 B.C.E., Minoan women on the Greek isle of Crete wore "bra bands" that lifted their bare breasts entirely *out* of their garments, cantilevering the naked breasts over the abdomen. Women who had it couldn't help flaunt it. Bare breasts were the vogue for centuries. The Greek bra band was history's first bust enhancement of its kind.

THE BRA IS BORN; ROME, FIFTH CENTURY B.C.E. ◆

Roman women in the fifth and fourth centuries B.C.E. wore simple, sensuous, draped tunics, tied at the waist with cord. The Romans made no attempt to lift and enhance the breast to prominence or to recontour it by artificial means.

Exceptions were made for female athletes, for women who had physically demanding jobs (like lifting), or women with overdeveloped breasts. These women contained their "mammary glands" in a breast band of soft, beaten

Minoan goddess with corseted bodice and tight waistbelt, c. 1600 B.C.E.; a later costume.

leather, a *mamillare*, which tied in the back with leather straps. An ancient mosaic in Sicily shows two women athletes, perhaps jugglers, in outfits that look exactly like modern bikinis. This Roman garment, meant merely to contain a full bosom, is history's first brassiere.

Most women did not wear this kind of brassiere. In the male-oriented classical world, many Greek and Roman wives—and most virgins—strapped on a breast band to *minimize* their bust size. A decent women was not suppose to draw attention to her most obvious erotic zone. Men did not want the daily distraction, and husbands and fathers did not want other men staring at their wives and daughters. This kind of concealment is found in other cultures—notably Arab and Islamic—where men force women to cover their faces with veils, their hair with scarves, and their bodies with full-length tunics. For centuries, men have dictated female fashion.

BREAST SIZE AND INTELLIGENCE ◆

*D*ownsizing the bosom by use of a breast band reached new heights of popularity during the early years of Christianity. Several prominent church fathers recommended that women conceal their breasts as much as possible. Large breasts on a women were viewed as a sign of inferior intelligence.

Why? For one thing, prostitutes had large breasts—or at least attempted

Female athlete in bra and briefs, on a vase dating from the fifth century B.C.E.

to make them appear larger than they were. And large breasts were a turn-on for men, who condemned the object of their affection in an attempt to keep themselves virtuous. Body shape has always played a large part in how men viewed women—and still does.

Protestant reformer Martin Luther, in *Table Talk*, does not mention large breasts, but he focuses on other body features:

> *Men have broad shoulders and narrow hips, and accordingly they possess intelligence. Women have narrow shoulders and wide hips. Women ought to stay at home; the way they were created indicates this, for they have broad hips and a wide fundament to sit upon to keep house and bear and raise children.*

Men have dreamed up many disparaging terms for big breasts:

drooper, draggy udders, flabby melons, flapjacks, saggy tits, milk cans, waterbags, tired titties, stretched prunes, pig teats, dzwony (Polish, "big bells"), *Euters* (German, "udder"), *Hangers* (German, "hangers"), *cow tits, fried eggs, floppers, fat sacks.*

Men have also reserved certain terms, often related to inferior intelligence, for women with big breasts:

- **Bimbo**—from the Italian *bambino*, "baby"; an infant has no intelligence at all. Though the word predates the Roaring Twenties, it was popularized during that decade.
- **Broad**—believed to derive from "broad-beamed," meaning "wide" or "large." The term is an Americanism dating to the early twentieth century.
- **Doll**—a sixteenth-century term for an attractive but empty-headed woman. It has usually suggested that the women was well endowed.
- **Moll**—once the diminutive of "Mary"; by the sixteenth century it was synonymous with "whore"—and thus a woman who advertised her breasts. Daniel Defoe gave the name to the heroine of *Moll Flanders* (1722) because of her checkered past, which he states in the book's subtitle: "twelve year a whore, five times a wife (whereof once to her own brother), twelve year a Thief, eight year a Transported Felon."
- **Dame**—from the Latin *domina*, meaning "lady" or "mistress"; over time it became associated more with a mistress, a home wrecker, a wife's chief adversary. The word first appeared in the thirteenth century; in America, during Prohibition, it meant a sexy, stacked woman.
- **Cheesecake**—most likely from the adjective "cheesy," meaning "cheap" or "of inferior quality." It's also been suggested that calling a buxom center-fold "a piece of cheesecake" is an allusion to its delectability. Describing the pastry, the word dates to the fifteenth century. Describing a well-built woman, it seems to be of recent origin, perhaps the 1940s, when it arose to describe the female counterpart of a *beefcake*: a muscular male, scantily clad.
- **Cow**—a reference to a cow's milk-filled udders. Men have been calling large-breasted women "cows" for centuries.

MODERN BRA: MARY PHELPS JACOB; NEW YORK, 1913 ◆

*T*he first modern bra debuted socially in 1913. It was the nifty needlework of New York socialite Mary Phelps Jacob, who claimed she almost single-handedly was responsible for the demise of the centuries-old corset.

A gifted promoter, Ms. Jacob boasted that she was a descendant of a passenger on the *Mayflower* in her autobiography, *The Passionate Years* (1953):

I am also descended from Robert Fulton, inventor of the steamboat. I believe that my ardor for invention springs from his loins—I can't say that the brassiere will ever take as great a place in history as the steamboat, but I did invent it.

At the beginning of the twentieth century, fashionable women were still wearing a boxlike corset of whalebone and cordage that was uncomfortable and impeded movement. Her concern, though, was not comfort but appearance. In 1913, she purchased an expensive, sheer Paris evening gown for a society ball. The gossamer fabric too clearly revealed the contour of her corset, so with the assistance of her French maid, Marie, she devised a brief, backless bra from two white handkerchiefs, a strand of pink ribbon, and a piece of cord. It was a makeshift bra but, according to its inventor, the first of its kind.

Female friends who admired the lightweight, impromptu fashion found that a few days later they received one as a gift. This trend snowballed, and soon Mary Jacob was making dozens of bras—but not for money. It was a letter from a total stranger, containing a dollar bill and a request for "one of your contraptions," that prompted the socialite to submit sketches of her design to the U.S. Patent Office.

Warner Brothers Bras

In November 1914, a patent was awarded to Mary Jacob for the "backless brassiere." Aided by a group of friends, she produced several hundred handmade garments, but without proper marketing the business venture soon went flat. By chance, at a social gathering, Mary Jacob was introduced to a designer for the Warner Brothers Corset Company of Bridgeport, Connecticut. She mentioned her invention, and the astute man immediately foresaw the demise of the corset—and the loss of his livelihood.

Warner Brothers Corset moved quickly to offer the socialite fifteen hundred dollars for patent rights, and Mary Jacob accepted. The forfeiture turned out to be one of the biggest "boo-boos" in patent history, making Mary Jacob something of a "boob" herself. The bra patent has since been valued at more than fifteen million dollars.

But did Mary Phelps Jacob *really* invent the modern bra?

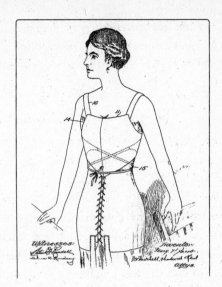

Mary Phelps Jacob was granted patent no. 1,115,674 for this garment in 1914.

BATTLE OF THE BRAS ◆

*M*any other claims have been made for the first modern bra. In 1989, *Life* magazine ran a cover story announcing that it had determined that the modern bra was in fact created by French corsetmaker Herminie Cadolle in 1889. The device was called a *soutien-gorge*, the French term still used today.

In *American Sex Machines: The Hidden History of Sex at the U.S. Patent Office* (1996), Hoag Levins presents irrefutable evidence that, prior to Jacob's design, *several* inventors had applied for modern "breast support" patents—some with independent cups, others with "backless" support. Mary Phelps Jacob's February 1914 patent application (no. 1,115,674) for her "brassiere" really described a modest lightweight "chest wrap," not what we would think of as a bra: it *diminished* the size of the bosom.

Some recent authors, notably Anne L. MacDonald in *Feminine Ingenuity: Women and Invention in America* (1992), have begun to redefine Jacob's role in history from inventor of the bra to inventor of the "backless bra." This is slightly more accurate. But a patent for a "backless strap system" bra was issued to a Dora Harrison of Lansing, Michigan, in 1907, seven years before Mary Jacob filed for her patent.

What can be said with certainty is that Mary Phelps Jacob was the first person to widely promote a backless, corset-replacing device that restrained

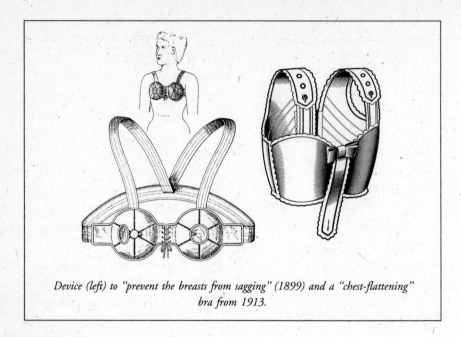

Device (left) to "prevent the breasts from sagging" (1899) and a "chest-flattening" bra from 1913.

only the breasts. A relentless self-promoter, she later married financier and poet Harry Crosby and changed her name to Caresse Crosby. A friend of artists Salvador Dalí and Max Ernst, Mrs. Crosby founded two publishing houses, which brought out the early works of such luminaries as William Faulkner and Ernest Hemingway.

Based on U.S. Patent Office records, Levins offers this concise origin of the modern bra:

> *The first American device that was unmistakably recognizable as the "modern bra" was registered by Marie Tucek in 1893, several years before Jacob was born.*
>
> *Other devices, documented in the Patent Office files as early as 1859, can also make strong arguments to the claim of being the prototype of the modern bra. And still others, documented in period fashion illustrations, show that modern-bra-like constructions were incorporated as separate upper sections of corsets as early as 1844 and also qualify as a bra "prototype."*

HOW THE BREAST AGES ◆ Prepuberty. *During a woman's life, her breasts undergo great changes. Before puberty, the breast, like a boy's, is merely a nipple projecting from a pink area, the light-colored areola.*

Puberty. *Around age eleven, the areola bulges, pushing the nipple farther forward. Secretion of the hormones estrogen and progesterone stimulates internal breast changes. The milk ducts develop from the nipple inward, and fat accumulates around them so that by age sixteen or so, a girl's breats are prominent. A slim woman may have large breasts, and an obese woman might have small breasts; body shape and breast size vary enormously—as much as a man's body size and the size of his penis.*

Pregnancy. *Two early signs of pregnancy are breast tenderness and a swelling of the areolae, followed by a marbled appearance produced by prominent veins under the skin. In the first three months, changes in the blood supply and the growth of milk ducts and alveoli enlarge the breasts by 25 percent. Toward the end of pregnancy, they are about a third larger than normal. Breast-feeding triggers further developments, but the breasts resume their former shape once it ceases.*

Later life. *Around menopause, breasts become less firm and begin to droop. Fibrous tissue has lost its elasticity, and the milk ducts and alveoli shrink. As the internal shrinkage continues, the breasts appear deflated, lying almost flat against the abdomen.*

"BRASSIERE"; FRANCE, FOURTEENTH CENTURY ◆

*T*he word "brassiere" sounds and looks distinctly French—and it is. But the French never used the word to mean a breast halter; Americas introduced that meaning.

"Brassiere" originated in fourteenth-century France as the name of an "arm guard," or shield, worn by soldiers—*bras*, French for "arm," and related to our word "bracelet." Frankish soldiers, who spoke Old French, protected their sword arm from injury in battle with a metal "arm protector" called a *braciere*, the forerunner of "brassiere." Eventually "brassiere" came to mean any kind of upper-body harness with arm straps.

The word was applied to many objects. *Larousse's French Dictionary* defines

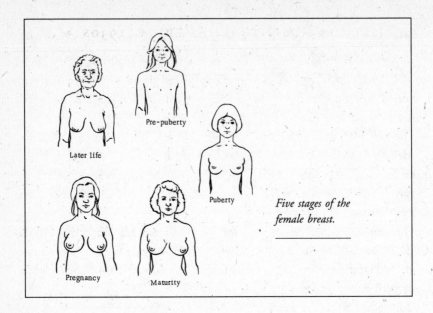

Pre-puberty

Later life

Puberty

Pregnancy

Maturity

Five stages of the female breast.

"brassiere" as "a harness, leading strings or the shoulder straps of a rucksack." The *Oxford English Dictionary* states that a "brassiere" came to mean "an infant's underbodice"—an undershirt.

When the French wanted to talk about a halter for the breasts, they used the term *soutien-gorge*, literally "bosom support."

During the first two decades of the twentieth century, "brassiere" was synonymous with "bodice," describing any bust-supporting garment that wrapped around the entire torso. By the 1920s, the term applied to cupped breast-support garments like those manufactured by the Warner Brothers Corset Company and Maidenform.

"BRA"; AMERICA, 1935 •

*M*ary Phelps Jacob was a Francophile, and after World War I she moved to Paris. She liked the sound of *brassière* and assigned it to her invention, while other manufacturers opted for *bandeaux*. For a time, the breast halter was called by both terms, but "brassiere" won out, and by 1935 it had been shortened to "bra."

CUP SIZE: IDA ROSENTHAL; AMERICA, 1930S •

*I*n the bra's early years, there were several innovations on Mary Phelps Jacob's design. In fact, the bra seems to be continually reinvented, with Victoria's Secret's *Miracle Bra* of the 1990s—with cleverly angled, underwire cups and removable pads—the latest, but not the last, improvement.

The first innovation came in the 1920s. Elastic fabric was introduced to bra design, as well as an easy metal fastener in the back. Elastic fabric would make it possible in the 1930s to manufacture the *strapless bra*, which cut sharply into a woman's flesh in order to stay in place. The discomfort was said to be worth the effect.

The woman chiefly responsible for *sized bras* was Ida Rosenthal (1886–1973), a Russian-Jewish immigrant who, in 1922, with the help of her husband, William, founded the Maidenform Company, a name once synonymous with bra.

During the flapper era of the 1920s, fashion forced women to adopt a flat-chested, boyish look. Any woman with a bosom who hoped to look chic had to bind her breasts before putting on a sacklike chemise. Ida Rosenthal had a full bosom, and her husband, it was said, had a fetish for large, shapely breasts; they both realized that prominent breasts would come back into fashion. So Ida, a seamstress and dress designer, bucked the trend of the day, encouraged by her business-minded, bust-minded husband.

Combining her own design experience and the standard paper-patterns for do-it-yourself dressmaking, Ida grouped American women into bust-size categories. This had never really been done before. She and her husband produced a line of sized bras intended to lift the female breast through every stage of its blossoming, from the hills of puberty to the mountains of maturity, and beyond.

The Alphabet Bra: A, B, C, D

Ida did not give her cup sizes catchy names. The alphabet bra, which came in four cup sizes—A, B, C, and D—was introduced in 1935 by Warner Brothers, the company that had bought out Mary Phelps Jacob's patent. Not all women fit comfortably into four cups, and a few years later Warner came out with the double-A and double-D sizes.

But Ida Rosenthal had led the way. Her belief that prominent breasts would one day return to fashion proved prescient. Following the depression, breasts became big business: *seamless bras* were introduced to be worn under sheer blouses, the *strapless bra* was for bare-shoulder gowns, the *whisper bra* weighed "barely a feather."

FALSIES AND "LEMON BOSOMS" ◆

*T*he first public advertisements for what would become known as "falsies" appeared in nineteenth-century Paris. The device, called the Bust Improver, consisted of wool pads inserted into a boned bodice. The cup-bra had not yet been invented, and small-breasted women who wished to appear larger had been stuffing the bodice of their corsets with paper, rags, or any cloth remnants at hand. Wool pads itched but were said to give a smooth, nonlumpy inflation that did not go flat with extended wear.

Later that century, French women could purchase the first rubber breast pads, called "lemon bosoms" because of their shape and size—but not color. They were black, the only color rubber came in at the time, and easily showed thorough sheer fabrics.

One inventor, Frederick Cox, designed inflatable rubber breast pads in the 1870s; they were blown up like balloons. Synthetic rubber was the "miracle" invention of the time, and it also appeared in items like condoms and garden hoses.

PROSTHETIC BOOBS ◆

*D*uring the Gay Nineties, the "breast pad harness" gained popularity with some flat-chested women. Precursors of the modern bra-cup structure, it featured individual, fully padded breasts—sometimes of rubber—connected to elastic shoulder and back straps. Quite simply, a woman strapped on a pair of prosthetic breasts.

Throughout these years, "brassieres" were usually extensions of corsets, not separate garments. The corset split into two parts, a waist cincher and a separate breast support, around 1908. Fashion historians have never been able to identify a single person—or patent—that launched this innovation. But the upper breast support, or "liberty bodice" as it was enticingly called, with its whalebone stays and full-torso wraparound fabric, was not what a modern woman would consider a bra. It was the liberty bodice that drove Mary Phelps Jacob to "invent" the modern bra.

In the 1930s, inventors began to experiment with plastic pouches filled with water or oil and, after World War II, with silicone gel. The goal was

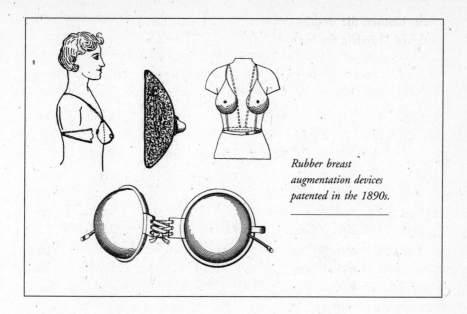

*Rubber breast
augmentation devices
patented in the 1890s.*

to come up with falsies that had the natural *feel* of real breasts through a
sweater or blouse. One of the earliest "silicon breast pads" was designed in
the late 1940s by Ella Burnhardt of New York. She filled vinyl pouches with
a "comfortable gel," Dow Corning's DC 220 silicone fluid, which Ella
thought mimicked the feel of living tissue.

Exploding Tits

During the 1950s, new, durable plastics allowed inventors to devise "air
inflation bladders," bras with built-in blowup falsies. A woman could strap
on a bra and, with a small, hidden hand pump, inflate her breasts at will
and to any reasonable size. She might do this at a party to draw the attention
of a particular man, who was not supposed to see the breasts expanding—
just the result.

Because the air bladders were not leakproof, an augmented bosom would
slowly deflate if left unattended. Air-falsies suffered one serious drawback:
fully inflated, they could explode on the era's poorly pressurized airliners. A
female passenger who was buxom on takeoff might disembark flat-chested.
One inventor, William Buckley, attempted to get around the problem. He
patented a bra with multicompartmental bladders to minimize overall
pressure.

> **BREASTS' SEXUAL RESPONSE** ◆ *Sexual stimulation, direct or in-direct, affects the breasts in several ways. The nipples become erect and enlarged, then intermittently soft and pliable. Increased blood supply causes their temporary enlargement by as much as 25 percent, especially in younger women who have not nursed children.*
>
> *In younger women the areolae often swell enough to engulf the base of the nipple. In women over fifty, the swelling is less marked and may occur in only one breast.*
>
> *In many younger women, a pink flush mottles the breasts just before orgasm. After orgasm, the flush vanishes and then the areola swelling, but nipple erection may persist for hours. This is especially true in older women or in those who have not reached a full release of sexual tension.*
>
> *As mentioned earlier, a small percentage of gay men report having reached orgasm solely through intense and prolonged nipple stimulation.*

THE BRA COMES OUT OF THE CLOSET; 1940S AND 1950S ◆

*T*he debut of the strapless bra at the close of the 1930s marked a turning point in the public's awareness of sexy, but until then unmentionable, women's undergarments. During World War II, the popularity of the curvaceous pinup girl, epitomized by the shapely Betty Grable (famous for her legs), turned the Rosenthals' Maidenform business into a forty-million-dollar industry.

Bras, once unspeakable undies, took on alluring names. The Lovable Bra was designed by Pagan, a deliberately suggestive name. A woman in the 1940s could buy the "Roman Folly" bra or the "Confidential" bra. The "Merry Widow" bra—really a "corselette"; half corset, half bra—was a product tie-in with Lana Turner's 1952 film *The Merry Widow*. The "Merry Widow" could squeeze any women into a knockout shape, building up her breasts and thinning her torso. After Lana Turner had worn the corselette for several hours during filming, she sighed, "I'm telling you, the Merry Widow was designed by a man. A woman would never do that to another woman."

The 1940s and 1950s are called the Great Bra Boom years. A single

Hollywood actress could launch a new bra craze. Lana Turner, in a sharp, cone-shaped bra—the hard cones achieved by tight circular stitching—became America's "Sweater Girl," launching an entirely new look for women. A tight sweater, which accentuated the pointed breasts, became American women's—and men's—favorite topwear.

JANE RUSSELL AND THE CANTILEVERED BRA; 1940S AND 1950S •

The buxom Jane Russell had a bra specially designed for her by her lover, America's wealthiest man, aviation pioneer Howard Hughes. The bra was designed to address a particular problem: Russell's bust bounced too much for the cameras and for the eyes of Hollywood censors. Legend has it that Hughes, using calipers to measure the depth and circumference of the actress's bust, calculated the points of maximum stress and designed a tight, comfortable, no-bounce bra on the suspension principle in little over an hour.

In 1947, Jane Russell introduced the Hughes *cantilevered bra* to American women in her film *The Outlaw*. A cantilevered bosom hung out over the abdomen like a well-supported balcony—with no bounce. Some people feel that it was the bra, rather than acting ability, launched her to the height of stardom.

The cone and cantilevered bras reached their peak (literally) in the late 1950s. Bra tips were so firm and pointed by then that they poked through a sweater's wool. The aim of the new bras was to create an exaggerated high, pointed bosom, an achievement in which nature was wholly replaced by artifice. The bras might be stiffened with stays or wires and built up with rubber padding.

Pearl Binder, a writer on the history of fashion, announced to European women that in America "the ideal shape aimed at by women is two spiked cones never before seen in Europe and related only to the female form in African sculpture." The Jane Russell look became so popular that thereafter the bra industry kept abreast of Hollywood's every trend.

PLAYTEX "CROSS YOUR HEART" BRA •

During the 1950s and 1960s, Ida Rosenthal kept Maidenform in the forefront of the bra business. When latex became a thin and comfortable fabric, due to advanced manufacturing and weaving techniques, Maidenform introduced one of the most popular bust supports of the century:

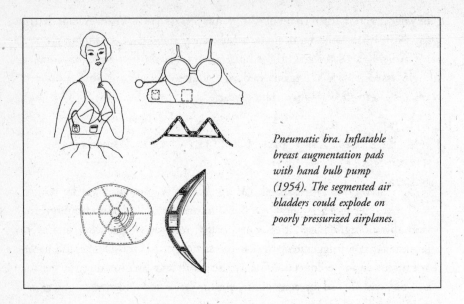

Pneumatic bra. Inflatable breast augmentation pads with hand bulb pump (1954). The segmented air bladders could explode on poorly pressurized airplanes.

the Playtex (as in "playful texture") "Cross Your Heart" bra, which "lifts and separates"—a phrase that became commonplace and a part of every stand-up comedian's routine. With its graphic ads appearing nationwide, high school boys scrawled such graffiti as, "You can't get to Heaven in a Playtex bra / 'Cause a Playtex bra won't stretch that far." Mild by today's standards but racy for its time.

During the late 1960s, when young women were burning their bras as a symbol of female liberation, Ida Rosenthal was asked if the action signaled the demise of the brassiere business. "We're a democracy," she answered. "A person has the right to be dressed or undressed." Then she added, "But after age thirty-five a woman hasn't got the figure to wear no support. Time's on my side."

CONE BUSTIER; JEAN-PAUL GAULTIER, 1984 •

*P*erhaps no bra of the century was more outlandish than the 1984 eight-inch cone bustier, by French designer Jean-Paul Gaultier, made famous by the decade's Material Girl, Madonna. A bustier—from the French *buste*, "chest" or "bust"—is really an outerwear bra, meant to be admired in its own right, not concealed beneath a blouse.

The gender-bending designer, who's openly gay and has dressed male run-way models in skirts, fishnet stockings, and high heels, was only a boy when he first showed interest in bras—in wearing them, that is. At age ten, he found his grandmother's pale, salmon-pink, latch-up corset in her closet: "I thought, Wow! My God! What is it? How would it fit?" He got hooked on the garment, so to speak, and would ask to lace up his grandmother every time she put on her corset. The fact is little known, but the bustier contraption Gaultier designed for Madonna—a pale, salmon-pink, satin lace-up corset with projectile breasts—was, in fact, a sexy version of his grandmother's undergarment.

"You know the cone bra I made for Madonna," Gaultier told an interviewer. "Well, I made the first one for my teddy bear—*he* had no bra, so I invented one. I did it with paper cones and pins." Gaultier admitted that, from his point of view, the cone bustier was merely "a joke, one of my fantasies that I exaggerated, but, at the same time, it was radical and nice. It got attention." He conceded that while Madonna was wearing the garment her torpedo-shaped breasts were "Well, yes, a little aggressive." The look evoked the sweater girl style of the 1940s—without the sweater.

BREAST IMPLANTS: THE PROSTITUTE CONNECTION; JAPAN, 1940S ◆

*L*adies of the night launched the breast-implant phenomenon.

The full story of breast implants, seldom told, begins in Japan's prostitution underground during and after World War II. Japanese prostitutes servicing American GIs sought ways to enlarge their breasts to increase their profits. The girls realized that American men loved big breasts—and paid more for them, but the diminutive natives of the island country were not naturally well endowed.

To acquire melon-size American bosoms, Oriental prostitutes got their doctors to inject their breasts with various fluids. The first liquid tried was saline solution, then goat's milk; both leaked quickly into the body, deflating the breasts and leaving the girls with massive infections. Next came injections of paraffin wax, which lasted longer; but the treatment was painful, the results lumpy, and the complications more serious.

Determined to have "American tits," the girls allowed their doctors to inject Dow Corning's hottest new product, "inert" liquid silicone, directly into their breasts. Silicone, however, had U.S. military applications, as an insulator, lubricant, and sealant, so the precious chemical was available only on the black market.

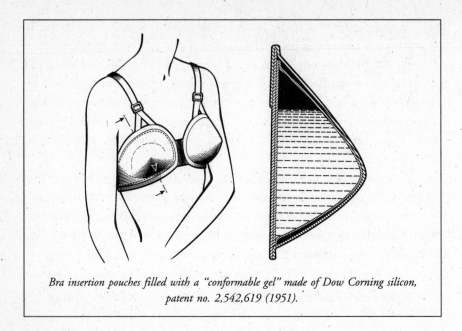

Bra insertion pouches filled with a "conformable gel" made of Dow Corning silicon, patent no. 2,542,619 (1951).

Silicone injections worked. The girls' breasts were immediately larger, still soft and pliant, and the fluid did not seem to leak away from breast tissue into the body. By the mid-1940s industrial-grade silicone had become the hottest black-market item in Japan. Large drums of the chemical were mysteriously disappearing from U.S. military bases. The girls' profits were up, GIs were happy. Word got back to U.S. plastic surgeons that silicone was being used in Japan for cosmetic enhancement. Some American surgeons, most notably in Hollywood, began offering silicone injections to film stars and moneyed socialites.

Word Origins

The word "silicone"—*silic*(o) + *one*—was coined by Dow Corning chemists in 1943 to describe their new polymerized organic compound. They based the name on the glasslike, nonmetallic element, silicon, in the periodic table.

"Silicon" itself had been coined in 1817 from the Latin *silica* + *on* (as in "carbon"). A hard, glassy mineral found in a variety of forms such as quartz, sand, and opal, silica had been around for centuries, going by its Latin name, *silex*, meaning "flint."

"Silex" itself derived from the Indo-European root *skel*, meaning "to cut." Shards of glass were cutting instruments.

FIRST AMERICAN BREAST IMPLANT; 1962 ◆

*B*y the 1950s, several American inventors had designed small bags of silicone—realistic-feeling falsies—that women could insert into their bras. From being worn outside the body to being implanted under breast tissue, and/or muscle, was just one step, which was taken by plastic surgeons Thomas D. Cronin and Frank J. Gerow in 1962, when they implanted the first silicone gel bags into a woman from Houston, Texas.

Dow Corning marketed the new gel bags under the trade name Silastic. Across America plastic surgeons foresaw huge profits, while many small-breasted women saw a ray of hope. In Rockford, Illinois, surgeon Hugh A. Johnson performed more than seventy breast implants and wrote up his results in a journal article:

> *Nothing says it quite so well, "I am feminine," as a nicely formed breast. The flat chested girl is painfully aware of this; with padded brassieres, she is ridiculed by her more generously endowed sisters. The Cronin Silastic breast prosthesis has, however, done much to solve this psychological problem.*

By 1973, more than fifty thousand women had had gel-bag breast implants. Many were leaking. Some women claimed they'd developed medical problems. In 1978, Dow Corning introduced a water-based, "hydrophilic," nontoxic prosthesis, but the company continued to sell its silicone version.

As Herodotus might have said, "The rest is history":

- *1977*—First successful lawsuit; jury awards $170,000 to a woman whose implants ruptured.
- *1982*—Australian physician reports first cases of implant-related connective-tissue disease.
- *1984*—Woman wins first case alleging implant-related autoimmune disease.
- *1988*—FDA requires manufacturers to prove safety of implants.
- *1991*—Jury awards a woman $7.34 million, the largest verdict yet in an implant suit.
- *April 1992*—FDA bans silicone implants, saying manufacturers failed to prove them safe.

- *December 1992*—Jury awards a Texas woman $25 million, the largest judgment to date.
- *April 1994*—Dow Corning and other manufacturers offer a $4.25 billion settlement.
- *May 1995*—Dow Corning files for bankruptcy.

The final verdict on the safety of silicone is in the hands of research scientists. Many women swear their lives have been destroyed by dangerous implants; many lawyers have profited handsomely from those claims. But many medical researchers now believe that "junk science" was to blame for stigmatizing silicone implants—for, in effect, creating a breast-implant fiasco. Fiasco or not, the controversy will continue to plague both science and the courts for some time to come.

HOW TO TELL IF BREASTS ARE REAL ◆

*W*ith breast implants commonplace, especially among models and stars, how can a man tell if a woman's breasts are the real thing?

The single best giveaway is: lack of sidewards slide when the women is horizontal. This means a man has to get a woman flat on her back and barechested to tell. Real breasts, because of their soft tissue, slide sidewards from gravity when a woman is on her back. Since implants are usually anchored by surrounding sutures or embedded under muscle (or both), they don't slide sidewards when a woman is reclining.

Another method is to check for scars around the nipples, under the arms, or directly under the breasts themselves. An absence of scars, however, could mean the woman had an excellent surgeon.

QUIZ ◆ *QUESTION: A man has three girlfriends and decides it's time to get married. He has to choose one. As a test, he gives each $1,000. The first girl spends $900 on clothes and puts the other $100 in the bank. The second one spends $100 and puts $900 in the bank. The third girl banks the entire $1,000. Which girl does he marry?*

ANSWER: The one with the biggest breasts.

CHAPTER 11

Take It Off, Take It All Off

TEDDY TO JOCKSTRAP

> *I don't want people to remember me*
> *for my underpants.*
>
> MARKY MARK

"FETISH"; 1613 ◆

Fetishism is the attachment of erotic feelings to a nonsexual object: a foot might be equated with a penis, a glove with a vagina, silk with smooth skin, fur with pubic hair. Fetishism is almost exclusively a male obsession.

The word "fetish" has a *religious* origin, from the Portuguese *feitiço*, meaning "a relic."

In fifteenth-century Portugal, devout Christians applied the term *feitiço* to saints' mortal remains, rosary beads, and all religious artifacts that had spiritual, or magic, properties. Portuguese explorers to West Africa extended the term to include the indigenous magic charms and sculpted idols of the natives. Anything that worked a miracle or magic was a *feitiço*.

The word itself comes from the Latin *facticius*, meaning "artificial, manufactured," and is the source of our English word "factitious." It is related to the Latin verb *facere*, "to do," and it is in this sense—to do a miracle—

that it entered Portuguese. A Portuguese physician, or an African medicine man, was a *fetissero* (fetisher): he manufactured miracles.

In the early seventeenth century the French borrowed the Portuguese *feitiço* and gallicized it to *fétiche*. This form gave rise to the current English spelling, "fetish" and, less commonly, "fetich."

In the nineteenth century, "fetish" took on sexual overtones in the new field of psychoanalysis. The term came to mean either manufactured items, like articles of clothing, or body parts when they became the object of obsessive displaced sexual interest.

MEN ARE TOGGLE SWITCHES, WOMEN ARE RHEOSTATS: THE ORIGINS OF FETISHISM ◆

*F*etishism is rare among women. This is not to say that they are totally uninterested in jockstraps and jockey briefs. Women are interested in male underwear for the way it handsomely sets off a man's crotch or buttocks—for the effect it adds to his overall appeal or even for its attractiveness of design, use of fabric and color. But women generally are not interested in the garment *without* the man in it; not in the way many men lust after, and are easily aroused by, women's lace panties, high heels, bras, and garter belts—without women wearing them.

Because fetishizing is almost uniquely a male pastime, or sickness (in its extreme), we have come to describe a particular male as being an "ass man," or a "breast man," or a "leg man." Conversely, because fetishism is rare among women—women appreciate the *whole man*—we tend not to characterize a female as being an "ass woman" or a "biceps woman." Women may appreciate a muscular male chest or rock-hard arms—when the parts are attacked to a particular man. Women are turned on by the entire male package; men, quite often, by individual female parts.

This is part of nature's design. A male must be ready to copulate at the moment a female expresses the slightest interest. He may never get the chance again. Or, if he can't get it up quickly, he may have to wait a long time for the next opportunity.

Thus nature has engineered males to turn on immediately, at the faintest invitation, the slightest provocation, at the tiniest glimpse of flesh. The penis is a toggle switch: it's either "on" or "off." There are no intermediate settings. Women are more like rheostats: they can be on "dim," or "bright," or at any glow in between. From nature's standpoint, a penis on "dim" is a useless organ.

To go a step further: men can't fake it, women can—and do. A man on "off" is a dead giveaway. A women on "off" can give a convincing performance at being brightly turned "on." This fact of sex has much to do with the fact that fetishism is a male obsession.

Author John Gray got it right when he said that psychologically "men are from Mars, women from Venus": men like solitude, women like company. In a crisis, men like to withdraw and brood alone, women like to talk things out with a supportive companion. Gray also emphasized that men like sex, women romance. He could have gone further and pointed out that when it comes to arousal, men are like toggle switches, women are like rheostats.

MALE LINGERIE FETISHES •

*M*adonna's cone bustier, which we looked at in the previous chapter, emphasized one aspect of fetishes: excess and exaggeration. The garment's aggressive erectness—hard, conical, pointed, ready to pierce—underscored the long-appreciated correlation between the female breast and the male penis.

How are they similar?

When stimulated, both secrete a milky white fluid. Both are sucked by the partner's lips. Both become hard when excited. Both are most appreciated when they are large, inflated, and firm. Both are a turnoff when they are flabby, deflated, and drooping.

At the Kinsey Institute, where researchers take clothes fetishism quite seriously, an entire shelf is filled with men's monthly periodicals relating eroticism to garments and fabrics. A sampling of magazine titles:

> *Black Garter, Black Lace, Black Satin, Black Silk Stockings* (black is the color of forbidden things), *Lingerie Libertines, Nifty Nylons, Nylon Jungle, Satan and Lace, Silky Sirens, Slip and Garter, Stocking Parade, Velvet Touch.*

The fabrics that appear most often in titles are lace, satin, leather, and nylon. The allure of lace is its peekaboo see-through matrix as well as its delicacy. Satin is often called women's "second skin"; it drapes suggestively over the body. Leather *is* skin, though it once belonged to a cow. Nylon mimics the body's own contours.

Staring at the Kinsey shelf, one can't help but realize that there is no shelf filled with corresponding female literature. What might such titles be? *Butch Jockey Briefs. Banlon Garter Belts. Coarse Woolen Slacks. Smelly Boxer Shorts. Sweaty Jockstraps.* The female equivalent of such male periodical erotica is the fictional genre known as the romance novel. Men peruse the pictures in *Nylon Jungle*; women read the pages of *Love's Violent Passion.* Women want the whole story: exotic settings, yachts, mansions, music, dinner, wine, sex. Men want to get quickly to the climax. One major complaint heard by sex therapists is that men are sexually impatient, eager to climax after too little foreplay. This is why lesbian couples allegedly have the most intense orgasms and why a "quickie" between two gay men can be just that: quick, involving no foreplay *yet* dynamic climaxes for both partners.

UNMENTIONABLES ◆

Knickers. Bloomers. Boxers. Briefs. Panties. Scanties. Teddies. Not that long ago, undergarments were called unmentionables, indescribables, unwhisperables. Even inadmissibles, since evidence for their existence could not be introduced into civil conversation. Words like "breeches" or "drawers" could bring titters of embarrassed laughter from grown women and produce a blush on the cheeks of teenage girls. Little boys chanted a rhyme that could reduce little girls to tears:

I see London, I see France,
I see Mary's underpants.

In 1916, *Vogue* was still referring to lingerie (from the Latin *lineus,* "linen") as "those bashful trifles that are born to blush unseen."

Today unmentionables are mentioned by brand name in TV ads and on the pages of glossy magazines. Indescribables are described in graphic, erotic language. Unwhisperables shout for attention from the bodies of supermodels and prepubescent teens. Nothing about underclothes is inadmissible. Victoria's *real* secret is that the company's name is a tantalizing throwback to the era of Victorian modesty, when a glimpse of gam beneath a petticoat could set a man's heart aflutter and "ankle" was an erotic word.

Before we look at the origins of specific undies, it's important to under-

The bustle may have originated as padding to protect a woman's behind from unwanted pats and pinches.

stand the role of clothing in erotic symbolism. One need not be a psychiatrist to appreciate the sexual intent of two historical female undergarments, the bustle and the girdle.

"Bustle"—German *Bäusche*, "pads" ·

For more than a century, fashionable women wore a rounded framework of padding under the backs of their skirts to exaggerate their rear ends. The bustle look is comical today but could, as styles often do, come back into fashion. The padded effect was not unlike the puffed swelling—and dark reddening—of the female baboon's buttocks when she is sexually aroused and trying to turn on her mate through a routine called "the presentation of the rump."

While a *corset* cinched in the waist and squeezed up the bust, making it more pronounced, the bustle curved and extended the rear end to male fantasy proportions. For centuries, refined women publicly presented their rumps to males. It was the vogue—another example of excess and exaggeration in fashion. Padding and cinching parody the natural female form but have an undeniable effect on the male. They draw his attention to certain body parts that can turn him on. Nature has given him a parts-specific arousal mechanism.

Bustles were immensely popular from the eighteenth century onward. The word "bustle" was first recorded in English in 1786.

But did rear-end padding initially originate to turn men on? Perhaps not. The earliest reference to an exaggerated derriere appeared in 1343, when an English monk, Douglas of Glastonbury, complained:

> *Women wear such tight clothes they invite men to touch their asses; now they must wear long fox-tails sewed into their garments to protect their asses from man's hands. This causes many mischiefs in the realm of England.*

If Douglas is to be believed, women first padded their buttocks to protect them from men's aggressive pinches and slaps. Some fashion historians think that might be the origin the bustle. The fashion then resurfaced centuries later as a sexy affectation—an inversion of its original intent.

"GIRDLE"—MIDDLE ENGLISH *GIRDEN,* "TO ENCLOSE" ♦

For centuries, women wore garments of stretched cloth and "elastic" wool to mold their waists, hips, and upper thighs to men's ideal images of womanhood. A women with too much natural *girth* wore a *girdle*—both words share the same root. The word "girdle" entered English sometime before the twelfth century.

Girdles were an important female undergarment well into the twentieth century. Designer Christian Dior was able to say in the 1950s, "Without foundations there can be no fashion." In other words, unless a woman's natural voluptuousness is not reshaped to some slender ideal by tight undergarments, designer clothes could not exist. Today many women achieve the hourglass shapeliness once enforced by a well-engineered girdle by counting calories, jogging, and gym workouts.

CLOTHING'S SEXUAL SYMBOLISM: FREUD, *THE INTERPRETATION OF DREAMS,* 1900; "FETISHISM", 1927 ♦

Freud wrote the book, so to speak, on sexy clothes and why certain items turn us on. "The desire to see the organs peculiar to each sex exposed," said Freud, "is a fundamental human drive."

Humans like to see other humans naked—we are all would-be voyeurs. Men like to see women naked, but they also like to check out the bodies and genitalia of other men—for comparison's sake and because there is a degree of bisexuality in most people. The equivalent is true for women.

What frustrates our Peeping Tom desire, said Freud, is *clothing*—outer clothing and also underclothing, which is designed to cover up specific erotic regions of the body. Clothes cloak the body and conceal the genitals. Deprived of a glimpse of the "real thing," Freud reasoned, we imbue articles of clothing with symbolism for the body parts they hide from us or suggest to us—parts we wish to see, touch, and possess.

That is also why truly unisex clothing is very rare. Men and women don't like wearing the same styles. Sometimes a foreign stylistic distinction can be subtle to a Western eye: to a Japanese, for example, a man's kimono looks very different from a woman's kimono.

Because men and women imbue garments with sexual overtones, they don't like to see a "feminine" item on a male or a "masculine" item on a female. The signals are confusing. At a deep subconscious level, a man might get turned on by another man's "feminine" garment—something as simple as a soft, pink, linen shirt opened two buttons at the neck. To protect ourselves from this kind of cross-signaling, we tend to react quickly and hostilely toward even the slightest type of cross-dressing. Anger masks or muddles sexual tension.

It is no accident that unisex clothes appeal to young, sexually active and experimental teenagers. "Anything goes" is what the unisex style says and what the wearer wishes to hear.

Clothes and fabrics can easily come to symbolize the body parts they hide or suggest. Here are correlations drawn from Havelock Ellis, Sigmund Freud, and other psychiatrists, to which I've added certain origins:

• *Fur* can symbolize pubic hair. Men and women love to run their fingers through fur and nuzzle their noses in it. But it's mostly women who wear fur; fur coats have never really caught on with men.

Our word "fur" is from the Middle French *fourrer*, meaning "to line a garment" with animal pelts. In the late Middle Ages the robes of royalty were "furred" (lined and trimmed) with the soft hair of animals. Soon people began to refer to animal pelts as "furs." Later the soft hair on a living animal was called "fur."

• *Silk* symbolizes the softness of skin. Women wear silk far more frequently than men.

Our word "silk" is from the Middle English *seolc*, which is thought to have derived from the Greek *sirikos,* from their proper name *Seres,* meaning an eastern Asian people—most certainly the Chinese—who had mastered the weaving of silk.

• **Necktie** symbolizes the phallus. Men wear neckties; some feminists adopted them for a time but gave them up. Watch the way a woman strokes a man's tie, the way she coquettishly tugs on its tip, and walks her fingers up its length. When a man is anxious or frustrated, he fiddles with his tie, rolls it up until it almost disappears from sight, then allows it to suddenly expand to its full length.

The word "necktie" is of relatively recently origin, entering English in 1838; knotted, decorative male neckwear is slightly older. In 1668, a regiment of Croatian mercenaries in the service of Austria appeared in France wearing linen and muslin scarves around their necks. The Croatians used this part of their military uniform to wipe their brows in the desert. Frenchmen picked up the fashion strictly as an affectation, naming ties *cravates,* their name for the "Croats" who inspired the sartorial flair. Since then, neckties have been standard functionless menswear.

• **Lingerie and undergarments** of all kinds symbolize the moment just before undressing. A woman in lingerie—or a man in a T-shirt and briefs —is saying, "I'll be naked any minute now." This is why underwear was called "unmentionables": a garment's name was virtually synonymous with the body part it dared to reveal. Despite designers' attempts to promote unisex underwear, the garments have caught on only with teenagers. Adult men and women like their underwear to look distinctly different. We even use different words: underwear and lingerie.

GAY AND STRAIGHT FETISHISMS ◆

*A*ll of us engage in fetishism to some degree. When a lover departs at sunrise and leaves behind a silk stocking or her perfume's scent on the pillowcase, the item becomes imbued with erotic memories. If, however, the man and the woman had worn identical unisex clothing (or scents), the forgotten object (or imprinted fragrance) might become just that— forgotten. The multibillion-dollar-a-year fashion industry rests on Havelock Ellis's conviction: "The extreme importance of clothes would disappear *at once* if the two sexes were to dress alike." The biggest purchasers of today's unisex fragrances are heterosexual teenagers.

Far more clothes fetishists are heterosexual men than homosexual men.

There's a simple reason for that. A straight man's own clothes are quite different from a woman's—*his* plain white cotton briefs, *her* frilly pink silk panties. But two gay men wear essentially the same garments, maybe even the same brands, in the same size. "Are these my shorts, or yours?" one might ask the other. Heterosexual lovers don't encounter such confusion: "Honey, is this my bra, or yours?" Even if two garments are somewhat similar, like old faded jeans, the sizes are usually different; large for him, small for her. For gays, the lover's clothes are the same as the beloved's.

The Bible states, quite explicitly, "A woman shall not wear that which is a man's, neither shall a man put on a woman's garment; for whoever does these things is an abomination unto God." The text is often read as an injunction against homosexuality and bisexuality, but more accurately it shows that ancient peoples realized that clothing carried sexual overtones.

Fetishism can go too far. For a genuine full-fledged fetishist, the symbol *becomes* the "real thing." A genuine fetishist can reach orgasm with lace panties, even if never worn by a woman. In *Three Essays on the Theory of Sexuality* (1905), Freud assured us—and warned us:

> *A certain degree of fetishism is habitually present in normal love. The situation only becomes pathological when the longing for the fetish passes beyond the point of being merely a necessary condition attached to the sexual object and actually takes the place of the normal aim, and the fetish becomes the sole sexual object.*

MEN IN MINISKIRTS; PRE-3000 B.C.E. ◆

*T*he loincloth, simply and perfectly named, was undoubtedly man's first genital cover; later, he decided to add a back flap to cover his rear end. The garment was of rawhide, split at the sides, and was not unlike a free-flapping miniskirt.

The loincloth probably wasn't an erotic garment initially—it certainly wasn't *underwear*. But in the world of modern fashion, it has resurfaced periodically either as sexy swimwear or beach-party attire. In movies, Tarzan, Spartacus, and Hercules kept the scant leather miniskirt popular for decades. In a way, man's first fashion has never really gone out of fashion.

Why did man decide to cover up his genitals? And then his rear end?

In a word, fashion. Modesty was not a consideration; the loincloth provided little of that since nothing was worn under it. But by wearing *some* article of man-made clothing, man drew a distinction between himself and the naked beasts. The "sophisticated" caveman dressed, if only minimally, while savages from other tribes walked around in their God-given birthday suits.

Clothing, from its inception, also separated people into obvious economic groups. The privileged could afford the fashion of the day; poorer folk dressed in the previous generation's hand-me-downs. In the form of ethnic costumes, clothing was yet another way to distinguish "us" from "them."

What was woman's first attire?

Women in Briefs

Around 3000 B.C.E., in Sumeria, women wore what could be best described as crude "briefs," loincloths drawn up between the legs and tied off. Women's breasts were still bare. Evidence from Babylonian terra-cotta figurines, Assyrian bas-reliefs, and paintings at the palace of Knossos, Crete, attest to briefs as the favorite clothing of female athletes, the "jocks" of their day.

In a sense, women were the first to wear jockey-like briefs, at a time when men paraded around in rawhide miniskirts. Eroticism requires only that the two genders wear different styles; what is worn by the goose in one era can clothe the gander in the next.

THE LAYERED LOOK; EGYPT, 2500 B.C.E. ◆

The first evidence of underclothes comes from Egypt, about 2500 B.C.E. Both the male loincloth and crude female briefs had by now become fashion hand-me-downs, worn only by slaves and low-ranking foot soldiers. Sophisticated, upper-class men and women adopted two-layer clothing, outer- and underwear. Fabric woven of cotton, linen, silk, camel hair, and wool was costly, so the more yardage an individual draped over his or her body, the more obvious the social rank.

The underfabric was tightly woven to make it opaque, thus concealing whatever body parts the wearer wished to hide. The outer fabric was sheer and translucent. While Egyptian outer tunics were cut and draped in various "male" and "female" styles, it was the opaque underfabrics that added sex appeal—is she or isn't she wearing them? The question was probably first asked in ancient Egypt. (Does he or doesn't he cover up his genitals would later be asked of Scotsmen in kilts.)

The Egyptians introduced translucent fabrics and the layered look in clothes.

Thus, while a translucent tunic was lightweight, airy, and comfortable in the desert climate—practical considerations for wearing the garment—it also was sexually suggestive, the first real peekaboo fashion, so to speak.

OPTIONAL UNDERWEAR; DARK AGES TO EIGHTEENTH CENTURY, EUROPE AND AMERICA •

Whatever fashion sense the Greeks and Romans cultivated, it went underground during the Dark Ages. With classical civilization in collapse and fabric in short supply, people wore hand-me-downs. Clothing remained in families for generations, often unwashed. Outer clothing of any sort was a luxury, a heavy cloak or mantel a prized possession. Underwear was literally unmentionable, since it was nonexistent for most people. A man might wrap his diseased or dripping penis in a cloth sack, or a woman might wrap her crotch for a few days a month during menstruation, but bindings of this kind were personal, optional, and not underwear.

To ward off cold, a monk might wear trousers under his tunic; or a wealthy woman might wear pants under her dress. This was layering, not underwear.

During the Middle Ages, as undergarments made a gradual comeback—along with learning and civility—the styles were simple and modest: a loose, heavy chemise for a woman and some type of cotton or woolen drawers for a man. These garments were still optional and were worn beneath baggy, loose-fitting outerwear, which was the style preferred by the Catholic church throughout most of Europe. The most famous undergarment of the period was the *hair shirt,* a garment of penance. Religion taught that clothing was to conceal the body, not draw attention to its parts. Well into the twentieth century, the idea of fashion in Catholic schoolgirls' uniforms was the uniformity of a waistless, below-the-knee, heavy-knit jumper.

Some undergarments in the Middle Ages were designed as an integral part of a particular outfit: male briefs within pants or a bust support as part of a woman's gown. This double-duty fashion posed no particular laundering problem, since most clothes were not regularly washed. There are records of court clothes being periodically spot-cleaned, but they were fully washed only once a year, during the warmest, sunniest days of summer when they could be hung out to dry.

With no central heating, and winters more severe than now, sex between a man and a woman usually consisted of her lifting her skirt only as high as necessary and of him lowering his trousers a few inches in the front. Having sex while dressed did not help to keep clothes clean. Recent films of life during the Middle Ages—say *Rob Roy*, with Liam Neeson and Jessica Lange—show steamy sex scenes with couples fully naked for long stretches, writhing on top of white bedsheets. Historians say this kind of passion was rare not only because of the lack of heating but also because people believed that a "chill"—we'd say a cold bug or flu—was caught from nakedness itself.

THE CORSET; LATE MIDDLE AGES TO 1950S ◆

*T*hrough fashion, said Michel Foucault, the female body has been subjected to various kinds of "disciplinary power." Perhaps the most extreme form of fashion discipline, or bondage, has come from the corset.

Let's look at two word origins:

• **Corset**—from the Old French *cors,* "body"; a close-fitting undergarment, extending from the hips to the breast, tightened with lace, reinforced with stays, worn chiefly by women, to give the torso an hourglass shape. An invention of men. The word entered English in the 1840s, but the garment is much older.

Tightly laced corsets allowed only shallow breathing and caused many wearers to faint.

• **Bondage**—from the Anglo-Latin *bondagium,* "to inhabit"; the sensual experience of safe captivity. To be in sexual bondage is to have no options and be willing to accept physical helplessness. The word entered English prior to the fourteenth century, when it referred to the tenure of a serf or slave to his master.

Only in the twentieth century did the corset become optional and then, for a time, obsolete. It is now back as kinky, voguish S&M attire. The cinching corset disappeared from the modern women's wardrobe in the mid-1920s, when the boyish, tubular, flapper look obliterated all trace of a waistline.

Mysterious Origin

Corsets seem to have first appeared in the late Middle Ages; at least paintings of the period reveal middle-aged women with suspiciously uplifted, pointed breasts and girlishly narrow, adolescent waists. The women were wearing *something* under their outer clothes to achieve those youthful hourglass figures.

Indeed, the function of early corsets was to diminish the waist, lift and emphasize the breasts, and give a woman with a broadening waist a chance to look girlish again. Perhaps the garment was the invention of men who did not want to look at their aging wives and mistresses growing ever broader. Or maybe women adopted the body bondage themselves—the equivalent of our modern-day body contouring by liposuction. Girdling the hips and thighs in tight wraps of fabric was also popular. Since the human torso (female and male) goes from V-shaped in adolescence to pear-shaped in middle age, the corset was in effect an antiaging device.

For centuries, it was mainly queens and noblewomen who were strapped into corsets, or "bodices" as they were also called. The shapes they achieved were sexy. Lower-class women put on weight with age and did nothing about it.

By Victorian times, most women wore some kind of corset. Supported by whalebone stays (Latin *stare,* "to stand"), the garment was now less of an erotic, sexy, upper-class item than everywoman's nod toward modesty. Bound tightly in a corset, she was considered "protected" from the hands of men— the word "stay" also suggests "stay away." If the bound woman was a housewife and mother, her corset was loosely laced. For a mistress, the lacing was tighter. If she were a dominatrix, the lacing was severe.

From its inception, the corset was the single most obvious article of female clothing to be treated as a fetish. Threaded with whalebone stays, a corset stood on its own and thus was a disembodied torso, a bust without a woman present—the very definition of fetish. Fetish periodicals of the 1890s claimed that women had their waists reduced by as much as ten inches—extraordinary discipline and bondage. Scarlett O'Hara, in *Gone With the Wind,* is corsetted down to a sixteen-inch waist.

It is hard for a young person today to realize that women shimmied into corsets well into the middle of this century. Along the way, there were innovations in fabric comfort: rayon corsets in the 1920s, popularized as "artificial silk," brought the "look of luxury" to the mass market. Nylon and stretch Lastex (like latex) corsets in the 1940s. Just before World War II, *Vogue* wrote enthusiastically, "The only thing you must have this season is a tiny waist, held in if necessary by a super-light-weight corset. There isn't a silhouette in Paris that doesn't have cave in at the waist." Rubber elastic corsets were big in the late 1940s and 1950s, when Dior's New Look required every chic woman to have a "tiny, tiny waist."

A leather-clad dominatrix presents herself to the house madam for approval before humiliating a client.

S&M BONDAGE IN MODERN CORSETS ✦

A 1994 article in the magazine *Verbal Abuse* by dominatrix Mistress Angel Stern offered three reasons why women—and an increasing number of heterosexual men—wear corsets:

1. to achieve an idealized shape for one's lover
2. to cross-dress and achieve "gender transformation"
3. to create "erotic discomfort"—such people are "corset masochists."

The age-old corset now plays a major role in the special worlds of S&M (sadism and masochism) and B&D (bondage and discipline). The dominatrix and her slave both don corsets. She, a warrior, wears her tight corset as armor, its extreme and rigid contour a sexual taunt to the slave—who can look but not touch. He, the hostage, is even more tightly corseted, his garment a form of punishment and captivity.

Kinkiness, not fashion, dictates the use of corsets. To S&M aficionados, one of the best-known corset retailers is B.R. Creations, which specializes in fanciful designs in black leather and rubber. "Helpless women with small waists are a sexual turn-on for men," says corset designer Fakir Musafar. "It's also a sexual turn-on for women, if they adjust and take to this body training."

Psychiatrist Wilhelm Stekel (1868–1940) detailed several cases of corset fetishes among married couples. One man obsessed with tiny waists on himself and his wife was "well-educated and respectable, the father of four healthy children, happily married":

> He often tried to lace himself so tight that he would faint . . . He even succeeded in persuading his wife to lace herself, and tried her corset tighter every day himself until her waistline had been reduced about six inches. This also gratified him sexually.

Reshaping the body as a sexual turn-on requires slow, patient, careful progress. To enthusiasts it's called corset training. In *Different Loving: The World of Sexual Dominance and Submission* (1996), Gloria G. Brame details the corset fetish of thirty-nine-year-old Alexis DeVille, a transgender consultant:

> It took about one year to get my waist to 22 inches. It started out almost seven inches larger. It was uncomfortable at times, but you never make it so tight that it's painful. You find that you can hardly breathe at the start. You have to breathe very differently. You tighten until it's slightly uncomfortable, and you see how long you can live with that. The next day you do a little more. . . . It's a very good feeling to be cinched tight and have the laces pulled tight.

THE SMALLEST WAIST IN THE WORLD ◆

Corseting can become a dangerous fetish. *The Guinness Book of World Records* lists the best-known corseting husband-and-wife team as Will and Ethel Granger, an English couple. Will, aroused by delicacy in women, wanted his wife to have the world's smallest waist, and Ethel was more than willing to comply. With patient daily lacing, Will got her waist down to thirteen inches. It is not uncommon for men to admire a tiny female waist: a cinched middle accentuates the fullness of the bust, hips, and derriere. An hourglass figure showcases the body's most erotic zones.

What kind of men and women wear corsets today? Fakir Musafar, who once ran his own corset company, explains:

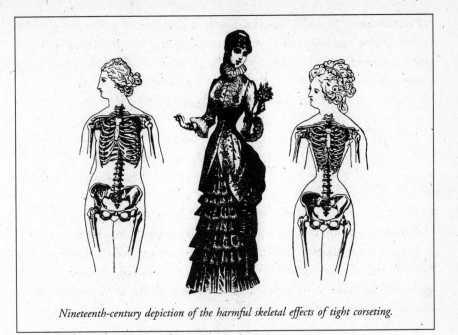

Nineteenth-century depiction of the harmful skeletal effects of tight corseting.

I identified three basic types of people who buy or use corsets. There are corset nonconformists: people who want corsets so that they can change the shape of the body so that it is different from other people's and to realize some kind of aesthetic ideal.

There are corset identificationists: people who primarily associate corsets with femininity and feminine undergarments. They don't particularly have an interest in sculpting the body, but by wearing the corset they seem to have a kind of gender transformation.

Then simply people who are corset masochists: They follow the phenomenon of corset slavery in which the corset becomes an instrument of torture that is applied ruthlessly and regularly to create erotic discomfort.

MODERN CORSETING IDEALS ◆

Corseting fans recognize three different kinds of sexy, idealized shapes, each achieved through slightly different, and increasingly more painful, means:

- **Hourglass figure.** This is the curvaceous shape commonly found on movie goddesses like Mae West and Marilyn Monroe. The hourglass ideal comprises a curvy, diminished waist with full hips and bust. The waist itself is tiny, but the torso is not elongated by corseting. It is the easiest and least painful figure to achieve. "Over time the spine curves gently inward," writes Brame, "while the lower ribs are compressed and pushed upward. An hour-glass corset constricts the intestines and forces them upward and downward from the waist."

• **Wasp waist.** This is the elongated torso look, like a wasp's waist, that was best featured on the late French singer and actress Polaire (1877–1939). A wasp-waisting corset forces the waistline to rise over time, resulting in a long, narrow torso. The spine eventually becomes "bent inward," writes Brame, "the lower ribs yield and are forced upward by the pressure at the waistline, the pelvis tilts, and the buttocks are pushed out and down."

• **Ice-Cream Cone Shape.** This is the severest type of corseting, a combination of the hourglass figure and the wasp waist. It was perfectly exemplified by Florenz Ziegfeld's first wife, actress Anna Held. "The lower ribs collapse completely and the internal organs are stringently compressed," writes Brame. "The ideal result matches full hips with a long, narrow torso."

S&M ◆

*S*adism is a sexual perversion in which gratification is obtained by the infliction of physical or mental pain on others—often upon one's love object. The word entered English around 1888.

Masochism is a sexual perversion characterized by pleasure in being subjected to pain or humiliation—especially by one's love object. The word entered English around 1893.

The term *sadomasochism* combines the two perversions and dates to 1922. Both words have human-interest stories behind them:

"Masochism"—The Lust for Pain

The word "masochism" derives from the name of Leopold von Sacher-Masoch (1836–1895), an Austrian novelist whose personal preoccupation with the sexual pleasure of pain was mirrored in the behavior of his characters. He had been, in a sense, a victim of child abuse.

From early youth, Sacher-Masoch was weaned on tales of violence, gore, and cruelty, told to him by his morbid-minded wet nurse. He particularly loved to hear about the tortures of Christian martyrs and developed a recur-

*Portrait of the Marquis de Sade,
master of cruelty.*

ring dream, which he would have throughout his life, in which he was tortured by cruel, abusive women.

In addition, his hot-tempered father, a local chief of police, would relate the day's crimes in graphic detail—especially sex crimes. The tales of cruel, dominating females torturing hapless men (probably the father's own heated fantasies) captured the boy's imagination, and he began to act out fantasies of his own. He entered into slave-master relationships with many women. Pain at the hands of a beautiful girl brought him to orgasm; humiliation from any woman—particularly his first wife—turned him on.

His writings began to reflect his private sex life. Sacher-Masoch's most widely read novel, *Venus im Pelz*—"Venus in Furs"—displays his obsessive interest in beatings, metal-studded whips, painful corseting, and forced anal penetration. He had a wide collection of sex toys. A well-known literary figure of his day, he was eventually committed to an asylum by his second wife. But even before his death from heart failure, his name had entered medical dictionaries as the term for the psychosexual disorder in which pleasure is derived through the infliction of physical or emotional pain.

"Sadism"—the Pleasure of Cruelty

The word "sadism" derives from the name of an author whose life parallels Sacher-Masoch's in several respects. The Marquis de Sade, the pen name of Count Donatien Alphonse François de Sade (1740–1814), had a brief military career before devoting his life to sexual debauchery and perversion.

Shortly after his marriage into a wealthy family in 1763, de Sade began a series of liaisons with prostitutes, luring them to one of his residences for extended sessions of sexual abuse.

Many times he was caught and, after each scandal became public, jailed. For his flagrant maltreatment of a young prostitute named Rose Keller, he was sentenced to a year's imprisonment. Upon each release, he lured more unsuspecting women into his lairs.

Transferred to the Bastille in 1784, de Sade began to write novels that centered on the sexual compulsions that consumed his life. His most famous novel, *Les Infortunes de la vertu*, "The Adversities of Virtue," dates from 1787 and his collection of stories, *Les Crimes de l'amour*, "Crimes of Love," from 1788.

After the Bastille was stormed in 1789, de Sade was transferred to a lunatic asylum at Charenton. On his release, he resumed writing, offering his plays to the Comédie-Française and penning his infamous "twisted sisters" novels, *Justine* and *Juliette*. In these tales the good, virtuous, selfless sister is debased, abused, and impoverished, while her self-centered, sexually licentious sibling achieves wealth, comfort, and luxury. "Vice is its own reward" was de Sade's theme.

De Sade supported the Revolution but only narrowly escaped the guillotine. His last years were spent in the asylum at Charenton, where he persuaded fellow inmates to perform his plays. He remained a "sadist" to the end.

The men who gave us the words "masochism" and "sadism" both spent time in asylums.

MEN IN CORSETS; 1820 TO PRESENT ◆

*I*n lower Manhattan there is an institution called Miss Vera's Finishing School for Boys Who Want To Be Girls, known to devotees as The Academy. The school's dean of high heels, Miss Dana, will teach any man for a fee—$300 for a two-hour tutorial, $2,000 for a "weekend getaway"—how to properly lace up a corset and walk and sit in the binding contraption. Students are mainly heterosexual male transvestites—middle-aged married men—and male slaves who are into bondage and discipline at the hands of a dominatrix.

It's been estimated that perhaps 90 percent of male transvestites are heterosexual. The other 10 percent, gay men in drag, are more visible and lack reputations, wives, or children to protect.

Men did not always need instruction in putting on a corset. During Victorian times, men throughout Europe used tight-laced corsets to maintain a trim, youthful figure. Today a middle-aged man with a paunch and love handles might have the excess adipose tissue sucked out by a plastic surgeon, but back then men achieved the same look at less expense.

Not all men, of course, wore corsets, but they were advertised in clothing catalogs, and models like the Marlboro or Carlton stated the size waist a man could hope to achieve with a particular garment.

A major retailer, Madame Dowding, of Charing Cross Road in London, advertised men's and women's corsets on the same page. Army men wore corsets to maintain a fit figure *and* rigidly straight posture. Hunters donned a modified corset, a six-inch high "hunting belt" that kept the waist trim and the lower back supported. Athletes, who engaged in strenuous exercise, also wore shortened versions of corsets.

Corseting at School

Male students at boarding schools were occasionally forced to be corseted, in the belief that a waist bound early in life would retain its hourglass shape. Some headmasters, though, were just plain kinky, and some young men, latently inclined to cross-dress, grew to like corset confinement.

A correspondent to the *Englishwoman's Domestic Magazine* wrote of his early indoctrination at a school in 1867, when he was, clearly, a budding young cross-dressing slave:

> I was sent early to school in Austria . . . and I objected when the doctor's wife required me to be laced. I was not allowed any choice, however, and speedily I was laced up tightly in a fashionable Viennese corset. The daily lacing, tighter and tighter, produced inconvenience and pain. In a few months, however, I was as anxious as any of my ten or twelve companions to have my corsets laced as tightly as a pair of strong arms could draw them.

There is written evidence from the Victorian era that women did not like men in corsets, which they saw as effeminate behavior. They preferred "real men" with ballooning waists to svelte men in unisex garments. English dandies, who often continued to contour their waists with corsets long after the fad had passed, claimed they had "bad backs" that needed support. An excellent example of a men's corset is in the Kyoto Costume Institute, Japan. Called The Apollo, it promised to give a man the body of a Greek god. The English corset is flesh-colored to resemble skin, with "Spartan steels" for stays.

Torso corsets are worn today for kinky fun by cross-dressing straight men with female fetishes, as part of their sex play with a dominatrix. Some gay men with penile fetishes wear a "penis corset" as part of sex play. The device is a tube of rubber or leather that can be laced tightly down the length of the penis, keeping the erection under constant pressure, or keeping a soft penis artificially "erect." A penis corset is a stylish version of the penile sheaths worn for centuries by African Bushmen.

NIGHTGOWN; FRANCE, SIXTEENTH CENTURY ◆

*I*n the sixteenth century, when tight-fitting clothing was the vogue, it became a luxury at day's end to slip into something more comfortable. Women got out of their restrictive, whalebone corsets, and men got out of their tightly buttoned-up-the-front woolen waistcoats.

In that era, the term "nightgown" originated in Europe. The term described a full-length, long-sleeved frock that fastened in the front and was essentially unisex. Intended also for warmth in the days before central heating, a nightgown was often made of heavy velvet or wool and lined and trimmed in fur.

For the next hundred and fifty years, men and women wore the same basic garments to bed—though not exactly the same. Even with the utilitarian nightgown, men's garments were simple in style, white or light brown, and totally unadorned; women's came in various styles, colors, and were embellished with lace, ribbon, and embroidery. Had husband and wife crawled into bed wearing identical garments, the history of nightclothes might have ended there. Instead, it branched off into the negligee and pajamas.

Dictionaries also record the first use in the fifteenth and sixteenth centuries of words like *nightcap, nightclothes,* and *nightdress.* People were paying attention to the garments they wore to bed.

The word "negligee" suggests that a woman wearing one should relax and refrain from housework.

WOMAN'S NEGLIGEE; FRANCE, EIGHTEENTH CENTURY •

*I*t was the need to dress differently, for erotic stimulation and for making a gender statement, that produced the negligee for women and, slightly later, pajamas for men.

The term "negligee" arose in the mid-eighteenth century as differences in styles and fabrics between men's and women's nightgowns grew more pronounced. A woman's negligee was a tighter garment than the former nightgown, made in silk or brocade, trimmed with ruffles or lace, and often belted at the waist to emphasize her figure. The negligee was not only for sleeping but also informal wear for lounging at home.

The notion of relaxing in a negligee during daytime hours—and not doing any housework—is inherent in the word's origin: *neglegere*, Latin for "to neglect," compounded from *neg* and *legere*, meaning "not to pick up." A women in a negligee neglected to pick up around the house. The negligee was for leisure or for sleep; not until the 1870s was it called a "nightie."

MEN'S NIGHT SHIRT; EUROPE, LATE EIGHTEENTH CENTURY ◆

*T*he man's plainer, baggier, ankle-length nightgown grew shorter as the eighteenth century progressed. This may have had something to do with the development of central heating, warmer homes, and thicker blankets. But it may also have had to do with urinating at night. A woman sits; she's accustomed to lifting her skirts, petticoats, nightgown, or negligee. A man stands and aims; an ankle-length nightgown, which had to be gathered up and held with the free hand, was an inconvenience. Perhaps too many men peed on them. Whatever the reason, the long nightgown rose up to become a nightshirt, reaching only to mid-thigh.

It was not uncommon for a man to relax at home in trousers and loose-fitting nightshirt. Some men even wore their comfortable bedtime garments during the day as *undershirts*. In this practice, we can see the origin of an entirely new garment.

MEN'S PAJAMAS; LATE EIGHTEENTH CENTURY ◆

*O*ne popular style of lounging trousers, worn beneath a nightshirt, was imported from Persia. Loose-fitting and modeled after the harem pants worn by Eastern women, the trousers were named pajamas, from *pae*, Persian for "leg" and *jama*, "clothing."

The nightshirt and Persian trousers combination—originally uncoordinated in color, fabric, and print—evolved into the more stylized ensemble we know today, with matching top and bottom. Men now went to bed in pants and shirts, comfortable equivalents of their daytime wear; while women retired in long flowing, frilly skirts, also not all that different from *their* daytime wear. The unisex threat posed by the gender-neutral nightgown was no more.

MANDATORY UNDERWEAR; EUROPE AND AMERICA ◆

*A*t some point, most children ask, "Why do I have to wear underwear? Nobody sees it." Mother usually answers, "What if you're hurt in an accident and the doctors have to take off your pants? They'll see you don't wear underwear." The implication is "They'll think you're uncouth" or that your parents are poor. That sentiment on undergarments dates to about the 1830s, when underwear started to become mandatory for all respectable people.

Fashion historians have their own reasons why:

1. Warmth—homes did not always have central heating.

2. Cleanliness—to protect more expensive outerwear from getting soiled with perspiration.

3. To emphasize and support a fashionable figure—certain undergarments can cinch in a waist or push up a bust.

4. To display status and wealth—as with Calvin Klein T-shirts and Tommy Hilfiger briefs today.

5. For pure eroticism—undergarments intimately touch private body parts that our admirers dream of caressing; the root cause of underwear fetishism.

The first reason, warmth, was the concern of those few who choose to wear undergarments during the chilly Middle Ages. The other four reasons developed later and with surprising suddenness.

Fashion historians record a major change in underwear—especially in its favorable acceptance—beginning in the 1830s. Undergarments became not only heavier, longer, and more concealing—a nod to the new Victorian modesty—but also a routine part of daily dress. A respectable person *had* to wear underwear. One didn't leave home without it.

For the first time in history, *not* to wear underclothing implied uncleanliness, coarseness, lower-class disregard for civility, or licentious moral character. Not all men liked the fact that women were now wearing undergarments beneath their skirts; there was less of a chance to catch a "beaver shot." As a journalist wrote in the French newspaper *Gil Blas* in 1890:

> *In my youth, women did not wear undergarments. And our imagination climbed the length of their stockings and seduced us into ecstasies toward those regions as intimate as they are delicious. We did not see, but we knew that we could see, should the occasion arise. But today we know that our view would be irremediably arrested by an obstacle, that our suggestive voyage would end at her drawers of batiste.*

As the opportunity for glimpsing women's private parts decreased, it was replaced by a new voyeurism directed at the sight of underpants. The article of clothing became a fetish item for the vulva. And by *not* wearing underwear, a woman now signaled sexy intentions. A prostitute without underwear displayed her readiness.

The sudden social switch to mandatory underwear resulted from a confluence of three factors:

1. The blossoming of Victorian prudishness and its corresponding dictates of modesty in attire; Queen Victoria ascended to the throne of England in 1837.

2. The introduction of finer, lighter dress fabrics for daytime wear, which in themselves called attention to the contours of the body and made underwear a necessity; and

3. The medical profession's mounting awareness of germs, which, combined with a body chill, could lead to illness.

DOCTORS PROMOTE UNDERWEAR ◆

The medical profession had considerable influence in convincing ordinary people to adopt undergarments, and doctors almost single-handedly started an underwear craze. Physicians advised people against catching a whole body "chill," as if it were as tangible as a virus or bacterium.

Within a few decades, the public was developing an almost pathological fear of exposing any body part except the face to the germ-laden air. By the 1880s, Louis Pasteur had proved the germ theory of disease, and Joseph Lister was campaigning for antiseptic procedures in medicine. "Germs" and "contagion" were among the era's major buzzwords, and the climate, so to speak, called for underwear.

Underwear originally was white, usually starched, always ironed, often scratchy, and made chiefly from cambric batiste, coarse calico, or flannel. Comfort was not a concern; modesty and health were.

Underwear Becomes Erotic

By the 1850s, women's undergarments were being designed with an emphasis on attractiveness. Cotton, both comfortable and absorbent, became a popular fabric. Once underwear began to look appealing, women started to find ways of tantalizingly revealing it—lifting a hemline . . . bending over to pick up a dropped hankie. In the 1880s, ladies' *silk underwear* appeared and, from all reports, it appeared whenever and wherever a woman wished to tease.

Underwear had gone from being optional and unerotic, to mandatory and unattractive, to mandatory and sheer and alluring. Ironically, by making it a necessity, Victorian prudery and the medical profession had guaranteed that every respectable person wore some secret, concealing garment close to his or her private parts.

This certainty allowed the garments to become objects of erotic fantasy and fetishism. In a very real sense, the racy Calvin Klein ads, Victoria's Secret's alluring catalogs and boutiques, and Frederick's of Hollywood's skimpy underwear catalogs owe their existence to a change in attitude about undergarments that began a little more than a hundred years ago.

SCRATCHY WOOLEN UNDERWEAR; ENGLAND AND AMERICA, 1880S ◆

*J*ust when underwear was beginning to become comfortable and erotic, a craze for coarse, scratchy woolen undergarments swept England and America. Once again, the medical profession started the trend.

What came to be called the Wool Movement began in England under Dr. Gustav Jaeger (1832–1917), a moral, prudish former professor of physiology at Stuttgart University. Like most scientists of his day, Jaeger held that masturbation was one of life's odious evils, responsible for all kinds of mental and physical ailments. Men and women would be much healthier if they stopped the self-abuse. What incited masturbation? Nice underwear. Comfortable undergarments, Jaeger argued, caress the genitals and breasts like soft hands, lulling the body into a state of continual arousal and moral laxity. A backlash was beginning against the new, attractive underclothes that people were discussing, buying, and wearing with pleasure.

Dr. Jaeger's remedy: coarse, woolen undergarments that continually itched and scratched. Underwear as penance. Uncomfortable clothes next to the skin, said Jaeger, remind us of the weakness of the will and how vigilantly the body must be tamed.

Oscar Wilde's Underwear

Jaeger also found other health benefits in wearing coarse, porous wool in contact with the skin: it allowed the body to "breathe," to cast off "noxious

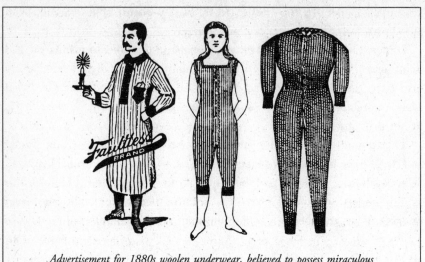

Advertisement for 1880s woolen underwear, believed to possess miraculous health benefits.

exhalations." According to Jaeger's gospel of health, the wool could not be dyed, because dye could leach into the skin.

The Jaeger Company, which manufactured all kinds of woolen underwear—called "health clothing"—nearly put an end to the new, stylish, colorful, silk and cotton undies. Silk, said Jaeger, suffocated the skin entirely; cotton, from plants, was only negligibly more porous. Wool was most fitting for humans because it was a fabric of animal origin. Sheep were mammals, had mammary glands, penises and vaginas, and thus were most like humans.

In England, a "wool health culture" sprang up. Celebrities of the day became some of Jaeger's biggest followers. Oscar Wilde, the era's most notorious dandy and infamous bisexual, wore only woolen undergarments for many years. He enjoyed good health, attributed it in part to wool underwear, and recommended the garments to others.

"Illness of any kind is hardly a thing to be encouraged in others," he wrote in *The Importance of Being Earnest*. "Health is the primary duty of life." One of his most memorable witticisms, in *A Woman of No Importance*, had to do with health: "One knows well the popular idea of health. The English country-gentleman galloping after a fox—the unspeakable in full pursuit of the uneatable." Though Wilde intensely disliked the company of sick people, he believed he possessed—as did others—almost miraculous healing powers.

When friends fell sick, they requested his healing hands at their bedside. On many occasions he advised them to switch to wool underwear.

Like Wilde, playwright and atheist George Bernard Shaw also switched to woolen underwear for its alleged health benefits.

Sexy Underwear from Jaeger Company

The Wool Movement hit America, too. American ladies wore wool corsets, petticoats, and bloomers. Men wore wool long johns under their wool slacks. Boys were put in wool knee-length knickers and knee-high stockings. For more than two decades, the Wool Movement caused underwear discomfort on both sides of the Atlantic. The association of wool with Dr. Jaeger was so strongly established in the public's mind that the compilers of the *Oxford English Dictionary* included as an entry: *Jaeger*, "the proprietary name of an all-wool clothing material manufactured originally by Dr. Jaeger's Sanitary Woollen System Co."

But a new century was beginning, and Dr. Jaeger's own company, after his death, began manufacturing cotton and silk nightclothes and underwear for men and women. The caterpillar and plant fabrics were no longer taboo. Women could purchase panties and corsets in such trendy colors as peach, pink, and ecru. We can only wonder what Jaeger would have thought of his company's advertisement for its "vivacious pantie," which featured a shapely young girl performing a full split in nothing but panties and a shoulder-strapped bodice.

The times had changed, and the Jaeger Company had done a full about-face. It now promoted itself as makers of "the world's most serene under-neaths," and "underneaths" became a new catchphrase. As for the wool underwear craze, the company stated, almost coquettishly: "We found after a time that people were inclined to think that health clothing might be ugly. Today we are leaders in smart underwear." Smart meant sexy.

BICYCLE TRANSFORMS UNDERWEAR; AMERICA, 1890S ♦

*T*he biggest single influence in the redesign of women's underwear —and, to a lesser extent, men's—was the enormous popularity of the "safety bicycle." Essentially the model we know today, the safety bike had equal-size front and back pneumatic tires of rubber and easy-to-apply wheel brakes.

A simplified bicycle had been around for several decades, known as the

The bicycle forced women out of long skirts and into sensible cycling attire.

"bone-cruncher," since a ride on its hard wheels left the peddler aching. But the safety bike—as well as the bicycle built for two and the nickname "bike"—were all new in the 1890s. Bikes were more than trendy, they were sexy. Bikes allowed a young woman to cycle away from home for a clandestine rendezvous with her lover. The bicycle built for two allowed lovers to cycle into the countryside for a romantic afternoon together.

The *Georgia Journal of Medicine and Surgery* reported that the national mania for bicycling produced a gynecological side effect: orgasm. The "pedaling machine," when used at "exhilarating speeds," thrusts the torso forward, "causing the wool undergarments to press against the clitoris, thereby eliciting and arousing feelings hitherto unknown and unrealized by the young maiden." There were many reports in the medical literature of women masturbating on the seats of their bikes. Coarse wool undergarments in contact with the vulva supposedly increased the ease of achieving orgasm.

The era's hoopskirts and horsehair crinoline undergarments were totally inappropriate for biking. A woman cycling in a skirt was a hazard to herself and an eye-opener for men on the sidelines every time she raised a leg or fell off her bike. A man could fall off with only his ego bruised, but a woman in a skirt taking a spill risked her good reputation. Bloomers, baggy trousers gathered at the ankles, became the standard alternative to skirts. Bloomers

*An 1851 caricature of masculine-
looking, cigar-smoking women in
ruffled bloomers.*

were really a divided skirt, but since this skirt could not fly up in the wind
or in a fall, women cyclists were free to wear simpler and more comfortable
undergarments.

A leading physician of the era observed that the combination of bike and
bloomers "converted the lady into a biped and supplied her with a momen-
tum which carried her headlong into the next century."

BLOOMERS: AMELIA JENKS BLOOMER, SENECA FALLS, NEW YORK, 1851 ◆

$\mathcal{A}$ standard dictionary defines "bloomers" as a pair of trousers gathered at the ankles and worn by women with a short belted tunic.
Also, underwear of the same design."

Actually, the underwear preceded the outerwear by several decades but was
never called bloomers at the time.

The first women to wear the pants as outerwear, in the 1840s, was Elizabeth Smith Miller of upstate New York. Had she publicized the fashion,
the pants would probably be known as "Millers." Instead, her friend, Amelia
Jenks Bloomer (1818–1894), an early feminist who lived in Seneca Falls,
New York, foresaw that pants on women could become a revolutionary female fashion.

Bloomer championed dress reform on the grounds that the large hoopskirts of her day were immodest, drafty, and cumbersome not only to ma-

Trapeze artist Jules Léotard popularized skintight hose.

neuver in but also to handle when attending to bodily functions. To make matters worse, the hoopskirt was given added support by layers of stiff linen and horsehair crinoline. A lady could withdraw to a convenience and not emerge for what seemed like hours.

Starting in 1851, Amelia Bloomer, a staunch supporter of reformer Susan B. Anthony, began to appear in public in baggy pants and a short tunic. As more women adopted the style, Mrs. Bloomer turned the trousers into a uniform of rebellion in the women's campaign for the right to vote. Women's pants quickly became known as "bloomers," and earlier undergarments of similar design also were given the name. When the bicycle craze hit in the 1890s, bloomers became the ideal riding attire for women. Today, most people associate the word with ladies' baggy underwear.

Two gramophone hits of the 1890s were "The March of the Bloomers," a militant song, and "Her Bloomers Are Camphored Away," about a woman who gives up the pleasures of daily cycling to raise a family. To become a devoted mother and wife, she packed away her bicycle and baggy pants. By this time, the bike and bloomers were clearly symbols of a young woman's freedom, which this woman chose to forfeit for the sake of her family.

Sensible Attire for Women

In 1880, English noblewoman Lady Harberton founded the Rational Dress Society to promote the cause of "health, comfort, and modesty" in women's dress. The pioneering organization condemned high heels, bust supports, falsies, tightly laced corsets, and all kinds of ballooning crinoline slips. It claimed that men had forced women—either physically or psychologically—into these artificial garments, and Lady Harberton's society encouraged women to rebel against any garment that cramped movement or caused discomfort. The society specified that the total weight of a sensible woman's underwear "should not exceed seven pounds," intolerable by today's standards.

The society also demanded that designers and clothing manufacturers stop changing women's fashions so frequently: "feminine beauty precludes the constant eddies of change which long have typified fashion." Little did Lady Harberton realize that fashions for women—and men—would soon change with the seasons.

LEOTARD; JULES LÉOTARD, FRANCE, NINETEENTH CENTURY ◆

Amelia Bloomer was not the only person in the nineteenth century to start a fashion trend that took its champion's name. Mrs. Bloomer wore baggy pants that concealed her figure; French circus performer, trapeze artist, and renowned lover Jules Léotard (1838–1870) wore skintight hose specifically to show off his manly assets—crotch and rear. We owe our tight Lycra gym attire to his pioneering efforts.

For centuries, horsemen had worn tight, waist-high hose—like modern panty hose—first under their pants to protect their skin from chafing, then later, when weaves became more durable, as outerwear. Léotard adopted the revealing costume as his trademark, astonishing audiences with his acrobatics as well as his anatomy. He was hung by all accounts, proud to show it, and gave his audience something additional to watch as he swung back and forth on the trapeze. Léotard's female fans were legend; they lined up for his autograph at circus tents. When men asked him for advice on courting women, he said, "Put on a natural garb that does not hide your strongest features."

Sleeved or sleeveless, the leotard became the standard dress of acrobats, dancers, and, later, workout enthusiasts. One has only to watch a well-proportioned male ballet dancer on stage—or a shapely woman working out at a gym—to appreciate Léotard's innovation.

"JOCKSTRAP"; 1886 ✦

*A*re men's briefs called "jockey" because men like to think of themselves as jocks? Is a jockstrap only for a jock?

The word "jockey" is northern English and Scottish and is a diminutive of the name Jack, which itself is a nickname for John, James, or Jacob. If dad was "Jack," his junior was usually called "Jockey."

"Jockey" was also the name of a person who professionally raced horses —because he was small in stature, like a "son." The term "jockey" was first applied to a horse racer in 1670. Shortly thereafter, by 1708, people were using "jockey" as a verb, meaning "to maneuver for a position of advantage in any business deal"—hence the phrase to "jockey for advantage." The word also came to mean "cheat" or "swindle."

Thus a man dressed in nothing but jockey briefs could be named Jack, or he might be jockeying for a position of advantage.

For many centuries, "jock" was English slang for "penis." A strap-on pouch that supported the genitals thus became, in 1886, a "jockstrap."

For most of its existence, "jock" was both a four-letter word for penis and a derogatory term for any slow-witted, poorly educated man. We can see how it was eventually applied to athletes.

The term "jock itch" was first recorded in 1950 to describe ringworm of the crotch, tinea cruris.

JOCKEY BRIEFS; AMERICA, 1934 ✦

*I*n 1910, American men welcomed a major underwear innovation: the X-shaped overlapping frontal fly on their undershorts. Called the "Kenosha Klosed Krotch" (because the manufacturing plant was in Kenosha, Wisconsin), the front was constructed of two layers of overlapping fabric, which eliminated the need for cumbersome buttons. This gave the wearer freedom, and men everywhere welcomed the trademarked design.

In 1934, men's underwear was further revolutionized with the introduction of the Jockey brief, named after athletes. The Wisconsin firm of Cooper and Sons, who'd come up with the X-flap, copied the design for white, cotton briefs from a men's white swimsuit that had been popular the previous year on the French Riviera.

The first Jockey style, No. 1001, proved so popular that it was soon replaced by the more streamlined, higher-cut No. 1007, which became known as the classic Jockey brief and had the word "Jockey" stitched around the elastic waistband.

"Hiding the Candy"

In the 1990s, Calvin Klein teamed up with rapper Marky Mark for an ad campaign that would turn briefs as underwear into peekaboo outwear. Klein, beginning in 1982, had begun producing erotic billboard and magazine ads for his line of jockey briefs. The pictures featured nearly naked, muscular young men in white cotton Calvins, their crotches bulging provocatively. "I put balls back into underpants," Klein boasted.

Klein had done just that. In earlier decades, catalogs like Sears's and Montgomery Ward featured men in briefs who appeared to have no genitals at all or lacked what *Penthouse* has called "the overt bulge of masculinity." Great effort was taken to tuck a model's penis and testes tightly between his legs, a technique pioneered by drag queens and known as "hiding the candy." Photographers actually preferred models who had nothing much to hide in the first place. Such models didn't have to be prepped.

Marky Mark had already established a stage look: barechested, jeans falling off his hips, with inches of white briefs exposed. Grabbing his crotch was a trademark gesture. Klein had the rapper photographed with these affectations except for the jeans. The ad was so popular, with girls and gays ripping down billboards from bus stops, that in less than a year both Klein and Chanel had introduced men's designer jockey briefs for women, some styles with fly-crossed crotches. The unisex fad was predictably short-lived.

TEDDY; AMERICA, EARLY TWENTIETH CENTURY ♦

The original "teddy" was a one-piece woman's undergarment, comprising a chemise top combined with loose-fitting panties. Teddies, of silk, lace, or plain cotton, did nothing to contour the body and were popular during the 1920s, when the boyish flapper look was all the rage. Later, thanks to Frederick's of Hollywood, teddies would become skimpier and sexier.

Many arguments have been advanced for the origin of the name "teddy" in relation to underwear:

• Some say the style first arose during the administration of President Teddy Roosevelt (1901–1909) and was named for the era he dominated.
• Others say the name came from "teddy boy" and "teddy girl," names

A "bikini," as depicted in a fourth century Roman mosaic. A nineteenth-century bathing outfit—dangerous when wet.

for British delinquents who committed their crimes in clothing of a dandified Edwardian style (Ted has long been a nickname for Edward).

• Still others claim the name arose because a woman in a teddy is as cuddly as a teddy bear, a stuffed animal that *was* named after an incident involving Theodore Roosevelt and a bear.

"Ted," an Old English term for a "flirt," shares the same Indo-European base as the word "tease." A woman in a teddy is certainly a tease.

BIKINI; FRANCE, 1946 ◆

The underwear known as "bikini briefs" owes its name and shape to a new swimwear design, the bikini, that debuted in Paris in 1946—and to an atom bomb blast over the Bikini Islands.

The first real swimsuits for women appeared shortly after America's entry into World War I. Previously, "*bathing* wear"—a woman couldn't possibly *swim* in it—had been as heavy and cumbersome as street wear. A woman bathed in the ocean in a woolen version of her long skirt and blouse with full sleeves. The new swimsuit was a clinging one-piece affair that had sleeves and reached to just the knees. The revolution was made possible in large measure by the textile know-how of a Danish-American named Carl Jantzen.

Born in Aarhus, Denmark, in 1883, Jantzen immigrated to America and in 1913 became a partner in Oregon's Portland Knitting Mills, which made woolen sweaters, socks, caps, and mittens. Jantzen was experimenting with a knitting machine in 1915, attempting to produce a tighter, lighter-weight sweater with exceptional stretch, when he developed an elasticized rib-knit stitch.

The stitch was suppose to be used in sweaters, but a friend on the Portland rowing team asked Jantzen for an athletic outfit with more "give." His skin-tight, rib-knit stretch suits were soon worn by the entire team. The company changed its name to Jantzen Knitting Mills and adopted the slogan "The suit that changed bathing to swimming."

Swimsuits became even more revealing in the 1920s and 1930s. From backless designs with narrow shoulder straps, women's attire quickly progressed to the two-piece halter-neck top and panties. The bikini was the next step—and through its name, the fashion is forever linked with the start of the nuclear age.

Bikini Atoll Blast

On July 1, 1946, the United States began peacetime nuclear testing by dropping an atomic bomb on the chain of Marshall Islands in the Pacific Ocean known as the Bikini Atoll. The bomb, similar to the type that had devastated Hiroshima and Nagasaki, commanded worldwide media attention.

In Paris, designer Louis Reard was preparing to introduce a daringly skimpy two-piece swimsuit, still unnamed. Reard had drawn up a list of over a hundred possible names for his creation but was dissatisfied with all of them. Newspapers were filled with details of the Bikini bomb blast, and Reard, wishing his suit to command as much media attention as possible, selected a name that was on the public's lips. "The design," he later said, "was itself explosive. A blast."

On July 5, Reard's top model, Micheline Bernardi, paraded down a Paris runway in history's first bikini swimsuit—which stirred more debate, concern, and condemnation than the bomb. In the 1960s, as underwear began to resemble Reard's suit, it was natural to name the slim undergarments "bikini briefs."

KNICKERS; "DIEDRICH KNICKERBOCKER", NEW YORK, 1809 ◆

Today, the word "knickers" stands for two garments, one female, the other male. Knickers are a blousy, loose, underclothing, gathered just below the knees, once worn by women beneath their ballooning crinoline skirts. Knickers are also similar fitting daytime pants once worn by men, particularly young boys—*under*wear for the "fairer" sex, *outer*wear for her rough-and-tumble counterpart.

The name originated as an abbreviation of Knickerbocker, a Dutch surname prevalent among the early settlers of New Amsterdam (New York).

INDECENT EXPOSURE ◆ *In Victorian times, indecent exposure could be something as slight as a woman's bare ankle or leg. Yet it was regarded as respectable and refined for a Victorian woman to display ample cleavage.*

Today it's hard to say what constitutes indecent exposure, aside from exposure by a schoolyard flasher. Starlets present Academy Awards with their nipples nearly visible; Chippendale dancers cover only their genitals. The latter, in a way, is closest to the original Western concept of "indecent exposure," which began with the Greeks.

The Greeks, who adored beauty, did not mind full nudity. What was considered vulgar in public, and a crime of indecent exposure, was a man's erection, or merely the showing of his glans penis. Greek men were uncircumcised. A man was lewd in public if he "stripped the head" or "peeled the shaft" to reveal the glans. This showed blatant sexual intent. A naked retracted penis was inoffensive and natural during sporting events in the nude.

Circumcised Hellenized Jews were teased and taunted at Greek gymnasia, where men worked out naked. Their glans penises were exposed, offensive, and suggested a state of continual arousal. Jewish athletes were considered indecent and, undoubtedly, erotic by some Greek women. Many a young Jewish male underwent a foreskin-stretching procedure that in time gave him back what had been rendered unto God.

As with beauty, indecent exposure is in the eye of the beholder.

The loose, outerwear trousers were worn by early Dutch immigrants. But the garment did not get its nickname until nineteenth-century writer Washington Irving created the fictitious author Diedrich Knickerbocker.

In his humorous two-volume 1809 work, *A History of New York, from the Beginning of the World to the End of the Dutch Dynasty*, Knickerbocker, a phlegmatic Dutch burgher, wrote about Dutchmen clad in breeches that buckled just below the knee. The text contained many illustrations, and American men copied the costume as sportswear, practical for hunting in woods with low brush. Schoolboys were also made to wear knickers, and turning them in for long pants became a coming-of-age rite.

The pants freed the legs from the knees down. By the 1850s, upper-class women had adapted the garment as underwear beneath their crinoline skirts for brisk "healthful" walks, puttering in the garden, or "fossil hunting" (collecting shells) at the seashore, a female fad of the late 1800s.

In England, knickers caught on with noblemen as a trendy, American, risqué fashion. A glimpse of knickers in public set tongues wagging. Eleanor Stanley, maid of honor to Queen Victoria, dashed off this breathless gossip in 1859:

> The new "fast" ladies' fashion is wearing "knickerbockers." I hear that the Duchess of Manchester, climbing hastily over a stile during a paper chase, caught a hoop of her cage, went head over heels, lighting on her feet with her petticoats remaining above her head. They say there was never such a thing to be seen—her underclothing consisted in a pair of scarlet tartan knickerbockers which were revealed to the view of all the world in general and the Duc de Malakoff in particular. Ma chère, c'était diabolique!

In a little more than a hundred years, America has gone from shock at the sight of a lady's knickers to blasé amusement at the sight of Sharon Stone's vagina in *Basic Instinct*.

CHAPTER 12

Va Va Voom!

GIBSON GIRL TO PLAYBOY PET

I used to be Snow White but I drifted.

MAE WEST

AMERICAN FEMALE ICONS: 1890 TO PRESENT ◆

Gibson girl, Ziegfeld girl, vamp, It Girl, Hoochee-coochee girl, Miss Amer- ica bathing beauty, flapper, bombshell, sex kitten, sex pot, sweater girl, glamour girl, oomph girl, sex symbol, pinup, cover girl, Varga girl, Cosmo girl, Barbie, playmate, bunny, centerfold, supermodel.

America has produced a mind-boggling cornucopia of sexy female images in just the last one hundred years. From the wholesome Gibson girl to the busty *Playboy* bunny, each has been immortalized in photography or film and christened with a playful nickname or tantalizing term.

The Egyptians had their wily Cleopatra, the Greeks their love goddess Aphrodite. The Renaissance had its enigmatic Mona Lisa. Seventeenth-century Europeans had their voluptuous Rubenesque beauties. The Bible introduced us to the Mary Magdalene type, and Christianity also gave us the virginal Madonna icon. Each age is remembered today for one or two femmes, or femmes fatales ("deadly women"), who predominated.

Clara Bow, the "It Girl," in the 1920s, when "It" meant sex appeal.

Thanks to photography and film, Americans have created and worshiped more femme icons than all previous centuries combined. Each of our decades has produced *several* new images.

For the most part, men dreamed up these images and named them, and women have worked hard to copy their shapes and costumes. If there is a single attribute that most of these modern images possess, it's "sex appeal" —a relatively new and daring term in English. American men have categorized their women by sexual types and nicknamed them with suggestively playful tags. In centuries past, where a virtue-vice dichotomy prevailed, women came in only two types: good or bad, whores or madonnas, mothers or mistresses.

Before examining the origins of the most popular icons, let's look at terms of endearment dreamed up by men for the objects of their affections:

• *Girl*, from the Middle English *girle*, entered the English language in the thirteenth century, where it initially meant a young person of either sex. For a least a hundred years, a young boy was a *girle*. The word *boy* existed at that time, but it then meant "a male servant."

By the fourteenth century, *girle* meant "a female child" and also "a maiden, a young woman." A young male was now a *boy*. Both "girl" and "boy" were slightly offensive words, considered low-class and off-color.

In the fifteenth century, men began to call an alluring woman a *pretty girl*—"pretty" then meant "artful, clever"—and suggested the girl knew how to catch a man. Because of its sexual overtones, the phrase was not applied to a young female child.

Other "girl" words:

Girlish, 1565—having the characteristics of a girl.

Girlfriend, 1859—a female friend.

Girlie, 1942—a scantily clad woman; the term became popular with reference to pinups like Betty Grable.

• *Gal* was a saucy name for an Irish woman in the late eighteenth century, a modification of the Celtic *caile*, meaning "girl." It was first recorded in English in 1795.

In 1920s America, it came to mean an attractive young woman who was spunky, personable, and held independent views on politics and sex. *What a gal!* was a compliment of high order, implying that the young woman was "a total package" of beauty and brains.

• *Angel*, from the Greek *angelos*, "messenger," was a fifteenth-century endearment for a woman who had not necessarily a comely face but an angelic disposition. She behaved like an angel, even if she did not have a heavenly look.

In time "angel" came to apply to an attractive woman's face. In America, *angel face* dates to 1931, while the somewhat mocking *angel puss* appeared in 1936.

• *A Lovely* dates to late the 1600s and meant a sweet woman of virtuous character, a genuinely nice person. A group of sweet young girls were "lovelies."

In America in the 1930s, the word took on sexual overtones: "She's a lovely" meant she was a great girl to neck or pet with.

• *A Beauty* became a popular term for a pretty girl in the 1820s: *She's a beauty!* It quickly became regional: a girl might be a *Baltimore beauty* or a *Southern beauty* or, also, a *Southern belle*, another popular term of that period.

The fourteenth-century word "beauty," from the Middle English *beaute*, harks back to two Latin words: *bellus*, "pretty," and *bonus*, "good." Life is "pretty good" for a beauty.

• *A Stunner*, 1862, meant a girl of exceptional beauty, possessing both a remarkable face and figure; she was called a *knockout* in the 1920s.

The word "stun," from the Middle French *estoner*, means "to astonish, to make dazed and senseless."

• *Bombshell*, 1930s, was a girl who is stunning or devastating.

The word "bombshell" dates to the early 1700s and was used first in a political context: "the revelation was a political bombshell." It soon came to mean any person or thing that was stunning, amazing, or devastating. In the 1930s, it acquired a strong sexual slant.

• *Chick*, 1927, referred to a girl who was not only good-looking but also modern in her views on dating and necking; a liberated woman of her day.

A *hip chick*, late 1930s, went beyond heavy petting to actual sex.

A *slick chick*, early 1940s, was even more sexually liberated and knew exactly what she liked in her men.

The word "chick" itself arose in the fifteenth century as a shortened form of "chicken," a newly hatched fowl. Thus "chick" implies youth.

• *A Looker*, 1902, was a girl who had both a beautiful face and shapely body. In the 1890s, the term had been a *good looker*.

A looker was decidedly thin; the slender female physique was just beginning to dawn on the twentieth century. As *Vogue* reported in 1908, "The fashionable figure is growing straighter and straighter, less bust, less hips, more waist . . . and a wonderfully long, slender suppleness about the limbs . . . How slim, how graceful, how elegant women look!" Thin was in.

• *Cutie pie*, 1906, was a sweet-looking, pert, bubbly girl, who, by the 1920s, was called just *a cutie*.

By 1912, American women were in the midst of the first national "slimming" craze of dieting and exercise. They had to be thin to fit into the Paris fashions of that year. Fashion writers extolled the "new beauty" in which "thinness triumphs." That year, *Journal des Dames et des Modes*, a new Parisian periodical, warned women, "Men's glances no longer go to anyone but the willowy, slender woman. It is no longer a question of breasts or hips . . . I challenge you to notice a fat woman today."

The word "cute," dating from the early eighteenth century and a shortened form of "acute," originally meant behavior that was "sharp, clever, or shrewd," often in an underhanded manner. This sense of being impertinent or smart-alecky is still alive in the cliché "Don't get cute with me."

• *An Eyeful*, 1920s, referred more to a girl's figure than her face: "She's an eyeful" implied she was stacked.

In the next decade men talked of girls who were "easy on the eyes."

• *Ziegfeld girl*, 1907, originated with Florenz Ziegfeld's *Follies of 1907*, a new kind of musical revue that boasted of displaying "the most beautiful girls ever to walk across an American stage." Each girl was personally chosen

Betty Boop, the quintessential "cutie pie," a sweet, pert, bubbly young woman.

by Ziegfeld, who favored tall, slender, statuesque beauties. The popularity of the Ziegfeld girl contributed greatly toward the thinness trend already under way among American women.

In the past, burlesque girls had been voluptuously plump, with ample buttocks and breasts. Their antics were "burlesque"—from the Italian *burlesco*, "a jest, mockery"—because their acts were a form of grotesque, comic exaggeration. Ziegfeld changed that vogue. As his revues gained in popularity, the girls got thinner, classier, and taller. By the time of the last annual *Ziegfeld Follies*, the ideal female beauty was long, lean, and statuesque in bearing.

• **Dreamboat**, 1936, originated from a hit song of that year, "When My Dream Boat Comes Home." Before the decade was over, an ideal date was a *dream girl*—or just *a dream*.

The word "dream" is an Old English term meaning "joy." A dreamboat is a girl who transports a man to the land of joy.

• **It Girl**, 1927, was a liberated young woman. "It" was a euphemism for "sex appeal," and the term "It Girl" came from a 1927 Hollywood movie based on the mildly titillating best-selling novel *It*, by Elinor Glyn. The star of the film was Clara Bow, billed as the "It Girl."

Before the decade ended with the stock market crash, "It Girl" meant any girl with sex appeal, modern ideas on womanhood, and vivacious gaiety. "We did as we pleased," bragged Clara Bow. "We stayed up late. We dressed the way we wanted. I'd whiz down Sunset Boulevard in my open Kissel with seven red chow dogs to match my hair."

• *An armful*, 1930s, was popularized by Hollywood gossip columnists and suggested a woman with a curvaceous figure. Mae West was an armful.

• *Filly*, 1930s, identified a girl with the friskiness of a young colt.

• *A Dish*, 1936, was a girl who was delectable; her looks and shape set a man's mouth watering.

• *Fox*, 1900, described an energetic, pert girl. The term originated in the South among blacks and became widely known in 1963, when heavyweight boxer Muhammad Ali used it in a *Time* magazine interview.

• *Lolita*, the diminutive of "Lola" (itself a diminutive of "Dolores"), came to mean a sexy, underage nymphet through Vladimir Nabokov's 1955 novel by that name. An account of sexual relations between a twelve-year-old girl and her stepfather, the book scandalized a generation. It was banned in Britain, confiscated by police in France, and lambasted as immoral when published in the United States in 1958.

A "Lolita" was not a passive, helpless victim of an older man but a willing accomplice in their crime. Newspapers used the term in the early 1990s to describe the aggressively sexual sixteen-year-old Long Islander Amy Fisher, who had had a relationship with married Joey Buttafuoco, a car mechanic more than twice her age.

• *Sex kitten*, 1940, was popularized by Hollywood gossip columnists and referred to the sexy purr of a screen vamp seducing her leading man. The word "kitten" has been a diminutive of "cat" since the fourteenth century.

• *Glamour girl*, 1941, was popularized by Hollywood public relations departments as a description of their sexiest stars.

Glamour puss also became popular in the 1940s.

Our word "glamour" is a Scottish variant of "grammar," from the Latin *grammatica*, "learning." Few students today think grammar is glamorous, but the words have a deep occult connection.

In the past, all learning was couched in a language (Latin or Greek) not spoken or understood by the unschooled populace. Scholars were viewed with awe—and not a little suspicion—by ordinary folk, who associated erudition with occult practices and magic. The word "grammar," alternately spelled "glamer" or "glamour," came to mean a "magic spell of enchantment."

As "glamour" passed into more extended English usage, it meant "an elusive, mysteriously exciting attractiveness," something that stirred one's imagination and was colorful and exotic. Eventually the word meant "an

Rita Hayworth epitomized the
American "glamour girl."

attractive or alluring person," one whose beauty worked magic on others.

In this sense, "glamour" was popularized largely by Scottish novelist Sir
Walter Scott, through a favorite phrase of his: *to cast the glamour*, meaning
"to cast an enchantment or spell over someone." A beautiful woman was
"glamorous."

• *Oomph girl*, 1940s, popularized by Hollywood press agents who used
the current term for sex appeal, "oomph"—a sexy allusion to a man's forceful
sigh during intercourse or in eager anticipation of it.

HOOCHEE-COOCHEE GIRL, 1893 •

The origin of the twentieth century's long list of names for sexy
women can be traced back to the spectacular World's Columbian
Exposition, held in Chicago in 1893. The dazzling new wonder of this fair,
was *electricity*, a new kind of power for the new century. One of the fair's
major attractions, an exotic "coochee-coochee" dancer, would generate a
different kind of electricity, a shock felt well into the twentieth century.

Attended by over twenty-one million people, the expo set the country
abuzz with talk of Edison's light bulb, Tesla's electric coil, and Westing-
house's alternating-current dynamo and electric transformer and motor—all
on display. The entire exposition, spread over 686 acres, was lighted by
electricity, and any visitor not impressed with the electric lights could glimpse

the first *Ferris wheel*. Thousands of adults and children stood in long lines for a ride on the monster "bridge on an axle" invented by George Washington Gale Ferris. His wheel was a blatant challenge to the star attraction at the Paris exposition four years earlier, Eiffel's Tower.

Despite the incessant novelty of technological wonders on display, the publicity-grabbing star of the exposition turned out to be a scantily clad dark beauty who did nothing more than shake her hips and grind her pelvis. Sex stole the show—and set the tenor for the dawning century.

Little Egypt, Darling of the Nile

Fahreda Mahzar, billed as Little Egypt, was a sleek Egyptian beauty who had come to America with a troupe of Syrian dancers. Newspaper accounts of the day agree that her *Coochee-Coochee* belly dance outshone the expo's electric novelties. It became the talk of the entire decade. Later called the "hootchy-kootchy," the dance is thought to be named after the state of Cooch Behar in Bengal. Seeking public acceptance through artistic pretension, its promoters billed it as the "Oriental *danse du ventre*," which fooled no one.

Rumor, from coast to coast, was that she danced the coochee-coochee nude; actually the bewitching bellyrina wore a semitransparent skirt. Her writhing antics inspired the fair's public relations man, future New York Congressman Sol Bloom, to compose one of the era's best-selling songs, "The Hootchy Kootchy Dance," which was soon parodied in lyrics like "Oh, they don't wear pants / In the southern part of France."

The fair made Fahreda Mahzar famous and vice versa: seeing Little Egypt became synonymous with going to the fair. She launched a belly dance craze in America, and in a short time there were twenty-two "hootchy kootchy" dancers hip thrusting at New York's Coney Island alone—each claiming to be the original sinner.

Three years later, the real Fahreda Mahzar was arrested by New York City police. In a raid on the famous Sherry's restaurant, she was caught dancing her specialty, this time stark-ravingly naked, at a stag party given by a grandson of P. T. Barnum. Nonetheless, Little Egypt continued to entertain at stag parties, where men paid ten dollars apiece to see what was then a rarity: a nude woman.

The exposure paid well for Little Egypt; Fahreda Mahzar died in 1908, leaving an estate of a quarter of a million dollars. The Egyptian beauty was the first female sex sensation of the twentieth century.

The Gibson Girl, created by illustrator Charles Dana Gibson, was chic, haughty, graceful—and, above all else —beautiful.

GIBSON GIRL; 1890S •

*I*n the Gay Nineties, Victorian elegance and formality waned, replaced by manners, lifestyles, and dress less formal and typically American. It was the first truly *American decade:* and the Gibson girl was, in a very real sense, America's first female icon. She was not blatantly sexy like Little Egypt, who appealed almost exclusively to men, but wholesomely sensual. Social historians call her the "first *real* American woman."

"Gay" in the 1890s meant "carefree, informal." "To get gay" meant to take (hetero)sexual liberties unimaginable just a decade earlier. The "American millionaire" paid no income tax, itself a cause for gaiety.

A stylish woman was still bundled up to the chin and robed to the floor, her feet discreetly hidden in shoes that had to be laboriously fastened with a buttonhook, an inconvenience that would lead in 1893 to the debut of the zipper. Her modish waist was created by an almost impregnable corset that would soon yield to the modern bra.

Into the world of the Vanderbilts, the Astors, and the Belmonts, marched the Gibson girl. Tall and stately, superbly dressed, artful but never wicked, she was an idealized woman, a raven-haired embodiment of every man's dream. Overnight the Gibson girl, which first appeared in the humor magazine *Life,* became the idol and model for a generation of women. She was as much a label of her times as the bobbed-haired flapper would be three decades later.

Before illustrator Charles Dana Gibson synthesized his ideal woman, the image of the American girl was "vague, nondescript, inchoate," as the *New York World* archly reported: "As soon as the world saw Gibson's ideal it bowed down in adoration, saying: 'Lo, at last the typical America girl.'" Though no girl actually resembled Gibson's fantasy, the image was *all-American* and highly influential on a generation.

Previously, idealized women had been European by nationality, Victorian by morality. Gibson's "liberated" creation defined for the world the American ideal of femininity at the turn of the century. With her high pompadour, small waist, and aloof beauty, she became America's first pinup, the undisputed goddess of an era. She influenced fashion right up until the 1920s. She popularized the Gibson girl blouse, a starched, tailored shirtwaist with leg-of-mutton sleeves and a high collar with an ascot tie at the neck. She made popular the dark, floor-length Gibson girl skirt, worn over Gibson girl petticoats. And she introduced women to the "divided skirt," perfect for bicycling. She even popularized the phrase "hourglass figure."

How America Got Its First Pinup ✦

Charles Dana Gibson (1867–1944), born in Roxbury, Massachusetts, was an artist and illustrator. After studying for two years at the Art Students' League in Manhattan, Gibson began contributing stylish pen-and-ink drawings to the weekly humor magazine *Life*. His Gibson girl drawings, characterized by a fastidious refinement of light ink lines, were modeled after his wife. So in demand did he become, that in 1902 *Collier's Weekly* paid him fifty thousand dollars—the largest amount then ever to an illustrator—for one double-page illustration every week for a year. So popular was one series of Gibson girl drawings, "The Education of Mr. Pipp," that it became the basis for a successful play (1905).

From the Gay Nineties until World War I, most American women between the ages of fifteen and thirty yearned to look like the dazzling, self-assured visions that floated through Gibson's drawings. The success of his pen-and-ink ladies astonished their creator, who saw himself more as a social satirist than a fashion trendsetter. His idealized woman, created only to serve as a character in his political and social cartoons, became the center of attraction. "If I hadn't seen it in the papers," he said, referring to the countless references to his creation, "I should never have known that there was such a thing as a Gibson girl."

The American image quickly traveled abroad, through pirated illustrations and romanticized hype. A European commentator exclaimed of America's Gibson girl wanna-bes, "Parents in the United States are no better than elsewhere, but their daughters! Divinely tall, brows like Juno, lovely heads poised on throats Aphrodite might envy." The American etcher Joseph Pennell, after a stroll in Manhattan, remarked, "Fifth Avenue is like a procession of Gibsons."

The commercialization of images was nothing new in the Gay Nineties, and in a short time Gibson licensed his "girls." Glazed on china, etched into silverware, embroidered on pillows and tablecloths, and decaled on whisk-broom holders, the Gibson girl in its day was a phenomenon like Charles Schulz's Peanuts. Before Gibson was thirty-five, he'd published nine volumes of drawings—which also appealed to Americans because they lampooned social climbers, expatriates smitten with all things European, and the foibles of society.

So ubiquitous and influential was the Gibson girl image that its creator was charged with competing against the then-famous Butterick dress patterns, the first—and enormously popular—paper dress cutarounds, which were selling in the Gay Nineties at more than ten million a year. A woman who wished to make herself over was said to be "taking the Gibson Cure."

As sharp a businessman as an illustrator, Gibson made the most of his worldwide publicity. When an automobile manufacturer asked him to create a Gibson girl drawing for an industry advertising contest, offering a cash prize to the winning illustrator but demanding the right to keep the drawings of all loosing artists, he wrote back, "I am running a competition for automobiles. Kindly submit one of yours. If acceptable, it wins an award. If rejected it becomes my property."

THE VAMP: THEDA BARA, 1910S ◆

The 1980s had Madonna and vogueing. The 1910s had Theda Bara and vamping, a sexual dance as much as posture Bara, the original vamp, complained near the close of the decade, "Five uninterrupted years of vamping have drawn my nerves taut."

"To vamp" entered our language and sexual foreplay, the verb fittingly from the Tartar noun *ubry* (via German), "witch"—legendary for casting spells.

Theda Bara (1885–1955) first cast a spell over the nation in 1915 with the release of her film *A Fool There Was*. Billed as the daughter of an Eastern

---

GIBSON MAN ◆ *In illustrations, the Gibson girl was often accompanied by a "handsome swain," who, also to Gibson's surprise, became known as the Gibson man. The icon changed the way in which many American men viewed themselves. Physically patterned on Gibson himself (as well as on the popular author Richard Harding Davis), this escort was strong-jawed, straight-backed, clean-shaven, and resolutely straightforward in manner and address—neither the American "cowboy" type or the "European gent."*

Until the Gibson man appeared, American men had prided themselves on their lush beards and distinguished mustaches copied from European aristocrats—the continental gentleman. Within a short time, the hirsute appearance was out, and clean-cut was in vogue. Bachelors who were Gibson men were encouraged to decorate their apartments in Gibson girl wallpaper and pad their suit jackets to achieve the broad-shouldered Gibson man ideal.

Gibson's male and female icons drew a diffuse young nation, still satisfied with copying its European parent, into sharp focus, establishing a look, feel, and style that were distinctly American.

---

potentate whose name was an anagram for "Arab Death" (Bara Theda), the kohl-eyed Cleopatra (with makeup especially created by Helena Rubenstein) was born Theodosia Goodman in Cincinnati, Ohio. A brief stage career under the name Theodosia de Coppet brought her to Hollywood as a film extra, but her portrayal of the heartless woman who lived only for sensual pleasure rocketed her to stardom. The motto of millions of women was the siren's irresistable *Kiss me, my fool.* Bara's other screen appearances included *Romeo and Juliet* (1916), *Camille* (1917), *Cleopatra* (1917), and *Salome* (1918). Her seductiveness was thought to be a grave threat to public morality, yet she sold out movie theaters across the country.

Vamping brought sex play out of the chaperoned past and into the spirited new century. Perhaps it was defensive rationalization when Theda Bara argued to critics that her portrayal of calculating, coldhearted women was morally instructive to men: "I will continue doing vampires as long as people sin."

Theda Bara, the Vamp, in Cleopatra *(1917)*

"NEW WOMAN"; THE ROARING TWENTIES ◆

The 1920s have been called "the era of self-expression," the time of America's "first sexual revolution." Never before had Americans so recklessly dedicated themselves to trendiness, thrills, self-amusement, and sex—both the sex act and sex talk.

The decade merited its catchy and diverse billings: the Lawless Decade, the Roaring 20s, the Sex Appeal Decade, the Era of Wonderful Nonsense, and F. Scott Fitzgerald's the Jazz Age. The most highly publicized exponent of the new self-expression was the flapper, the emancipated "New Woman" who had finally won the right to vote, drink, and smoke like men—even *with* men. Together with her "sheik"—in raccoon coats or stiff yellow slickers, unbuckled galoshes, in a rumble seat, with hip flasks filled with bathtub gin—they were a sight and a phenomenon, one of many reactions against the advent of Prohibition in 1920.

"SEX APPEAL"; 1920S—A TRENDY NEW TERM ◆

The word "sex," distinguishing male from female, had been around since the fourteenth century, but it got relatively little popular use until the 1920s. Scientists had talked, for instance, of chicks that were "sexed" in the egg, but "sex" remained largely a medical and scientific term.

By 1920, ordinary people were talking about new "sex" discoveries, and "sex" was on everyone's lips in a variety of new terms and phrases:

- **Sex hormones**—substances produced in the gonads or adrenal cortex that affect growth, reproduction, and the development of secondary sex characteristics like facial hair on men and breasts on women.
- **Sex glands**—the gonads and adrenal cortex that produce sex hormones.
- **Sex-linked**—a physical characteristic located on either of the two sex chromosomes, X or Y.
- **Sexology**—the hot new field of scientific study that investigated the interactions between men and women.
- **To have sex** became a popular phrase that turned a noun into a verb.
- **Sex object**—a popular term for a man or woman who had abundant sex appeal.
- **Sex symbol**—the preferred term for a renowned person, usually an entertainer, noted and admired for his or her sex appeal.
- **Oversexed** described a young women who was *too* free with her body. She was a simmering *sex pot*.

Warning to Wives

The entire discussion of feminine beauty changed radically in the 1920s. Around the turn of the century, a woman whose face or figure excited men was said to have "personal magnetism" or "charm," or she was "fascinating." "Femininity" was another favorite euphemism for sex appeal, as a book from the 1890s makes clear:

> *A woman's greatest attraction lies in her femininity. Far above symmetry of form or the most perfect features must certainly be placed that wonderful and mysterious psycho-psychical quality of personal magnetism, which, for lack of a better definition, we will designate as soul-beauty.*

The word the male author was fishing for was "sex appeal."

Florence Courtenay, in *Physical Beauty: How To Develop and Preserve It* (1922), used (and perhaps overused) the new word "sex appeal"—one of its earliest uses—and warned wives against putting on too much weight:

> *The ideal figure is a lithe, well-rounded form, graceful yet not so plump as to be called voluptuous . . . Physical beauty is a definite part of the*

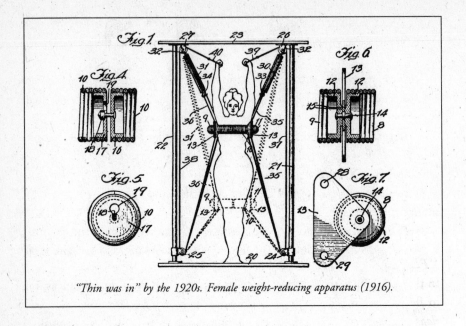

"Thin was in" by the 1920s. Female weight-reducing apparatus (1916).

feminine sex appeal. And a happy marriage depends largely on a normal and happy sex appeal on the part of the women and corresponding sex interest on the part of the man.

FLAPPER; ORIGIN OF THE WORD AND THE WOMAN ◆

Hair bobbed, skirt fringed, stockings rolled, style flippant, she was the free-spoken, gin-swilling, cigarette-puffing, jazz baby who came to epitomize the Roaring Twenties, a free spirit who ushered in a new American woman. Her figure was defiantly boyish, and by bunching her stockings below the knee she blatantly announced to the world that she wore no corset to hold them up. She wielded a cigarette holder like a weapon—which, in the battle of the sexes, it was.

During her brief heyday, she commingled sex and love, redefining each. She gained entry into the male world in the guise of a tomboy, playing at "men's" games while staking out a territory and power base. On the battlefield of the sexes, the flapper was women's Trojan horse.

If her image resembled that of a French prostitute, there was a fundamental reason for it.

FLAPPER ATTIRE: Step-in camisole-knickers in crepe de chine (left), 1925. Crepe de chine camisole-knickers with elastic at knee, 1927.

"Flapper" = Streetwalker

In the mid-1700s, the word "flapper" meant a young, wild duck just learning to fly by flapping its wings. It originated from the Middle English echoic *flappe*, "to swing" while making a slapping sound. By the 1880s, it meant a young girl who wore her hair in a long pigtail (and flapping in the breeze) rather than in the pinned-up vogue of the day.

In France, around the turn of the century, a "flapper" was a streetwalker, a prostitute who dressed in a short skirt and sported bobbed hair. The sight would become familiar to American doughboys during World War I.

By 1910, any sassy, headstrong woman was a "flapper," especially if she espoused a woman's right to drink, smoke, or vote. F. Scott Fitzgerald, in his early short stories, remolded the flapper's image closer to that of the 1920s. But the word and the image existed, in print and pictures, before women began dressing and acting like *jazz babies*.

How to Be a Flapper

The media helped to fan flapper mania, carrying endless stories of flapper exploits, as well as how-to articles on achieving the style. The *New Republic*, soberly straitlaced, made space for a flapper feature, defining the new free spirit:

> *She is frankly, heavily made up, not to imitate nature, but for an altogether artificial effect . . . poisonously scarlet lips, richly ringed eyes. The total weight of her clothes is less than two pounds . . . Jane isn't wearing much this summer.*

What Flapper Jane was not wearing was petticoat, brassiere, or corset.

By smoking and drinking and descending into speakeasies to kick up her heels till dawn, the flapper and her dashing sheik were leaving an indelible mark, as the *Saturday Evening Post* made clear:

> *You may regard the new generation as amusing or pathetic; as a bit tragic, or rather splendid. You may consider their manners crude, their ideals vague, their clothes absurd. . . . But it is useless to deny that these youngsters have a definite bearing on the thought, literature and customs of our day. And particularly do they exert a powerful influence on buying habits and the movement of merchandise.*

SEX TALK ◆ *The Roaring Twenties produced its own sexy buzzwords, or "in" words, and many innocent-sounding expressions had sexual overtones. The period was extraordinarily fertile in phrases for sexy women, courting, dating, and lovemaking. Couples were doing daring new things, behaving in unprecedented ways, and each novelty evoked a new name.*

A sexy flapper, whose shapely legs were gams *(Italian* gambe*) was a* beaut, *or the* cat's meow, *or the* cat's pajamas.

Her lover boy was a jazzbo, jelly bean, *or* lounge lizard, *a word then synonymous with "lady's man" and not yet pejorative.*

He might be either a flat tire *(a bore; perhaps impotent), or* hard-boiled *(tough and without sentiment; the word also has sexual connotations), or* peppy *(full of vim and virility).*

Throughout the course of their blind date, *which might include* heavy necking, *he could become* ossified *(drunk), having consumed too much* giggle water. *After a night of* whoopee *(boisterous, convivial fun, which might end with sex), he might* upchuck *(vomit).*

They could be stuck on *each other.*

A frequent boy petter was a snugglepup *or a* heavy necker, *who often marked his girlfriend with a proud* hickie. *All of this might occur during a* double date *and in a car's* rumble seat, *which gave new meaning to the verb* to park.

If romance soured, perhaps it was because one party was a two-timer, *soon to become an* ex, *though the wounded person might long* carry a torch.

Flappers to be avoided were gold diggers, *interested only in money.*

CONTINUED

A man and woman, each possessing the alluring It *(sex appeal) were known as a* sheik *and* sheba. *And anything a flapper or jellybean liked was* nifty *or* the nuts. *Or* swell *or* swanky *or* ritzy.

Copacetic *meant "excellent."*

Rapture, especially of a sexual nature, was expressed by hot diggity dog. *A young man who thought he might score could shout to himself,* hot diggity.

A stupid girl, perhaps easy to make, was a dumbbell *or* dumb Dora.

At a wild party, the flapper who hoisted her skirt high in a wicked Charleston was egged on by cries of Get hot! Get hot!

At the close of a date, a flapper might say to her "sheik," Thanks for the buggy ride.

To tell him off she'd snap, Go fly a kite.

If her playboy *(or* sugar daddy *made her laugh, she'd giggle,* Ooo, you slaughter me!

Jazz babies never said yes or no, but gave a long, drawn-out Ab-so-lute-ly, Pos-i-tive-ly. *Other times it was a scramble of both:* Pos-a-loot-ly.

The 1920s also saw the heyday of the Greeks (fraternities) and sexually wild frat *parties. A young man who survived* hazing *became a* Joe College, *better yet a* Joe Yale; *a failure was aptly a* Joe Zilch. *The campus, where many students had cars, was quickly becoming a center for moral unrest and* the place to be. *College humor and dirty jokes became the rage across the country:*

She doesn't drink, she doesn't pet,
She hasn't been to college yet.

First Dad: "Do you think your son will soon forget all he learned in college?"

Second Dad: "I hope so. He can't make a living necking."

A magazine of such witticisms, College Humor, *had a circulation of eight hundred thousand. H. L. Mencken said of its youthful contributors, "It takes a year or two of pedagogy to iron out a student of genuinely lively mind. By the time he is graduated he is usually ruined, but while he lasts he sometimes contributes something rich and racy to the national humor."*

MISS AMERICA BATHING BEAUTY; 1921 ◆

*T*he flapper was wild. Miss America was intended to counter that sexy, freewheeling image of young womanhood.

The Miss America Pageant was created in Atlantic City in 1921. Conceived by the town fathers and local newspapermen, its goal was not only to catapult a sweet, wholesome, virginal Miss Nobody into overnight celebrity, but also to promote the seaside resort. Specifically, the creators of the contest wanted to extend tourist season beyond the traditional Labor Day cutoff and well into September. A beauty contest, they reasoned, would keep hotels booked and restaurants full for several more weeks.

The first winner was sixteen-year-old Margaret Gorman, whose measurement were a girlish 30-25-32.

Today, the televised contest is an annual phenomenon, commanding the attention of nearly half the nation's Saturday night viewers. But the first competition was a modest affair, featuring only eight girls. Most of the attention centered on the host, called "King Neptune," who was Hudson Maxim of the armaments-inventing Maxims. Contestants then represented cities (not states) and qualified by winning a hometown "popularity contest." Once in Atlantic City, they participated in a "bathing revue" for which even the all-male orchestra donned swimsuits. That was equality.

The hedonism of the decade made the contest possible and contributed to its rapidly expanding success—and criticism. In its second year, fifty-seven cities sent young hopefuls, which the *Atlantic City Daily Press* boldly described as "piquant jazz babies who shook the meanest kind of shoulders, pink-skinned beauties of all types."

The "Roller Chair Parade" down the famed Boardwalk, reported the *Press*, showed off:

> *Tanned athletic girls, bare of limb, shapely of figure . . . bejeweled favorites of the harem, stately colonial dames in hoop skirts, with black eyes peeping coyly from behind waving fans.*

Several girls flaunted the vogue of bobbed hair, which the judges considered too radical for a truly American Miss. One judge was the artist Norman Rockwell; the evening gown competition was added in 1924.

The contest already served as a vehicle for the new celebrity-creating mill that was motion pictures. In 1922, a motion picture ball was held on the Steel Pier, where "film tests" were made for each contestant, in search of "a girl who'd 'click' in the pictures."

Despite the decade's hedonism, the Miss America contest aroused widespread criticism. The Trenton, New Jersey, Y.W.C.A. worried about the "grave dangers from unscrupulous persons to which the girls were exposed." Before the competition, a spokesperson said, the girls "were splendid examples of innocent and pure womanhood. Afterwards their heads were filled with vicious ideas"—such as money, career, and independence. The *New York Times* damned the contest as a "reprehensible way to advertise Atlantic City."

Bimbo = Dumb Dora = Airhead

When the first few young Miss America winners turned out to be anything but bright, educated, and articulate, contest officials sought out a higher caliber of entrant. "This year the contest will be on a higher plane than ever," promised the *Daily Press* in 1925, "and its fair participants will represent pastors' daughters, school teachers, college girls and femininity generally of the most desirable type."

When criticism of the bathing suit competition did not die down, that revue was dropped—as was the Miss America contest itself in 1927.

The problem was simple. The kind of girl entering the contest was not yet a noble representative of American womanhood but, most often, in the slang of the day, a "dumb Dora." Indeed, when the contest was permanently resumed in 1935, promoters attempted to skirt criticism by instituting a *talent competition* to convince the public that each girl was more than just a body beauty. "In the past," read an official press release, "good looks usually sufficed to win both the coveted trophy and perhaps a stage and screen career. This time there will be no 'beautiful but dumb' Dora."

The next year, Atlantic City Mayor Charles D. White opened the pageant with the reminder, "We are past the time when beauty parades are in the nature of floor shows. . . . This is a cultural event seeking a high type of beauty."

PINUPS; 1940S ♦

*W*hat ain't we got?" asks the chorus of island-stranded sailors in the 1949 musical *South Pacific:* "We ain't got dames." Lacking contact with real women during World War II, soldiers substituted pinups, plastering the colored glossies to the doors of their lockers and the walls of their Quonset huts. Even the inside of a helmet was likely to contain a "girlie picture." The primary female sex symbol of the 1940s was the bathing suit–clad pinup—a separate wartime industry. A GI mania, the pinup made overnight stars of many a shapely young model and Hollywood hopeful.

The phenomenon was also called "Forties Girls," and the most famous pinups came from the motion picture industry. Ironically, the most popular pinup "girl" of the period was Betty Grable, in her mid-twenties, glancing over her shoulder in a tight white swimsuit said to encase the world's "neatest bottom, atop the world's best legs." For that pose of wholesomeness suggesting sex-without-sin, in poster reproductions and in real-life demonstrations, the star earned three hundred thousand dollars in one year.

The term "pinup girl" itself first appeared in the armed forces newspaper *Yank* on April 30, 1943.

Pinup girl Betty Grable, 1940s, famous for her "gams."

Cover Girl

Pinups popped up everywhere. A popular photo of Rita Hayworth, said to be the most "artistic" (sexiest) of the genre, was supposedly affixed to the first atomic bomb dropped on Hiroshima in 1945. Hoping to increase circulation, magazines like *Time* and *Life* latched onto the pinup craze, replacing politicians and generals as cover subjects with *cover girls* like Frances Vornes, dubbed "The Shape" and voted Pinup Girl of 1944.

Film tie-ins were commonplace. A Hollywood feature called *Cover Girl* (1944) featured Anita Colby, who simultaneously held the distinctive position of "feminine director" of Selznick studios. Pinup photos of leggy Jinx Falkenburg were attached to the sides of planes at one air force flight school. Pictures of Chili Williams, famous as the Polka Dot Girl for the pattern on her swimsuit, were distributed to the armed forces by the tens of thousands. Pinups were a home-based war effort. Established stars like Ava Gardner and Lana Turner volunteered to expose their flesh for the fighting boys over seas.

The busty Diana Fluck won her first bathing-beauty contest at age thirteen. Less than two years later, she was a national pinup sensation, with a new name, Diana Dors, and was labeled "the sultry blonde bombshell with the wiggle." Perhaps her most celebrated pinup was a pose in a gondola wearing a diamond-studded mink bikini—the new swimsuit had just debuted in 1946.

VARGA GIRL; 1940S ◆

On October 15, 1940, *Esquire* magazine introduced Alberto Vargas's Varga girl to the world. The painted, airbrushed drawings combined abstract surrealism with popular sex appeal. The Varga girl's waist was so tiny a man could wrap his fingers around it; her enormous breasts stood perfectly horizontal, defying gravity. The impossible physical image was unquestioningly accepted by an eager male audience—and by women in an age when they had no voice in such matters.

Two months later, *Esquire* published a Varga girl calender that sold over three hundred thousand copies through mail order alone. By 1943, more than a million calendars had been sold. Varga girls hung in virtually every barbershop across the country, not to mention army barracks around the world. By the end of World War II, troops everywhere were attesting to the Varga girl's unique importance as a motivator. A combination of barely concealed sexuality and wholesome domestic virtue, she had come to represent everything American soldiers were fighting for.

From 1942 until late 1945, close to six million copies of *Esquire* were printed, without advertising, for distribution to U.S. troops stationed overseas; and three million were distributed to domestic military installations— all free of charge. In 1944, when Postmaster General Frank C. Walker banned the images from the mails, *Esquire*, to remain in circulation, discontinued printing Varga girls. GIs overseas protested en masse, and three young men penned an angry letter to the editor:

> *We would like to know who in hell got the bright idea of banning pictures from your most popular magazine. You won't find one barracks overseas that hasn't got an Esquire Pin-Up Girl. I, for one, have close to fifteen of them. Those pictures are very much on the clean and healthy side, and it gives us guys a good idea of what we're fighting for . . . I wish these high-browed monkeys could spend a year overseas without anything but magazines.*

PLAYMATE; 1950S ◆

*H*ugh Hefner launched *Playboy* in 1953 with a particular market in mind: young, college-educated, and upwardly mobile men whom he described as concerned with "good food, drink, proper dress and the pleasure of female company." The airbrushed Playmates in the centerfold were barer, younger, and prettier than any women previously seen in girlie magazines. Hefner's classic Playmate was an available "girl-next-door fantasy" type, a "child woman" offering her simple, wholesome innocence in a knockout body.

In a stroke of genius, Hefner accompanied each Playmate with a homey autobiographical sketch. No Playmate was ever a golddigger. No Playmate restricted her interest just to handsome men. Every Playmate boasted of having a simple, middle-class background, a nontaxing job, modest ambitions, and, mostly, a burning desire to make some nice guy a loving wife. Later, as the times continued to change, Playmates would show bare nipples and pubic hair, and want to be every reader's mistress.

Vargas Girls in Playboy

In 1956, Alberto Vargas, who'd left *Esquire*, took some of his sexier paintings to Chicago in the hope of getting into Hugh Hefner's sexually more radical magazine. Hefner commissioned a series of *nude* Varga Girls. Vargas produced a five-page layout, and the first nude Vargas girls (the "s" was added for legal reasons, since *Esquire* had rights to "Varga girls") appeared in the March 1957 issue of *Playboy*. The painting proved so popular that in September 1960, Hefner hired Vargas to contribute monthly artwork. His *Playboy* women were more sexually explicit in costume, pose, and playfulness. Artistically, the most distinctive aspect of the artist's work remained his masterful use of the airbrush.

Vargas also contributed the first *black woman* to appear in *Playboy*. When the magazine's photographers, on short notice from Hefner to come up with a black model, could not find an acceptable flesh-and-blood woman, Vargas painted Hefner's African American ideal.

In the 1960s, when *Playboy* began to reveal the pubic hair of its Playmates in "spread shots," Vargas was asked to do the same with his paintings. The request flustered the artist, whose first attempts at airbrushed pubic hair resembled the soft-focus stubble of a man's day-old beard.

In 1986, a selection of Vargas originals sold for $4.6 million. Several paintings within the group sold for $500,000 each, a thousand times the price Alberto Vargas commanded for a commissioned work in 1940.

SKIN MAGS AND HARDCORE SEX; 1970S •

The widespread popularity of wholesome pinup girls, Varga girls, and early Playmates had a seamy downside. Previously, sexy pictures of women most often appeared in a genre called "barbershop" magazines. The models were usually buxsom burlesque queens and hard-edged showgirls, and photo features were interspersed with bawdy cartoons and raunchy jokes.

There was no full nudity, just a risqué playfulness toward sex. The publications also featured mail-order advertisements on breast and penis enlargement, as well as tips on prolonging orgasm. The widespread popularity of pinups and Playmates forced the barbershop magazines to compete by offering more and more bare flesh, ushering in a new breed of kinky skin magazine whose philosophy was "anything goes." Legitimate soft-core sex had bred a hard-core industry.

But there was also an upside to pinups, Varga girls, and early Playmates. Their public acceptance freed the editors of staid, serious magazines, as well as of ladies' magazines, to print more alluring cover poses of less-attired women. And the pictures inside could reveal even more flesh. Pinups and

Playmates also made it acceptable for a film star to pose unabashedly as a sex symbol in legitimate publications. Stars had posed in the near-buff before, of course, but such pictures never made it into mainstream magazines.

According to psychiatrist Karen Horney, pinups and Playmates are a major cause of modern mental distress. Men grow up confused, frustrated, and angry because soft-porn and hard-porn elevate their expectations, setting them up for disappointment in their relationships with real women. Sexually alluring pictures, wrote Horney, continually stimulate a male's desires, frustrate his attempts to satisfy them with facsimiles of the pictured women, cause him to be disappointed in the women he does find available to him, and set up an atmosphere of competition, rivalry, and fear of defeat.

Horney wrote this before the advent of *Playgirl* magazine with its nude male centerfolds, bump-and-grind Chippendale dancers, and male calendar pinups. Would she have felt that these idealized male images frustrate females, elevate their expectations to unrealistic levels, and set them up for disappointment in the kinds of men actually available to them?

WHEN "EXTREME THIN" CAME IN ◆

*W*e have become a culture obsessed with thinness in women, even though most American women are said to be over their medically ideal weight. Thin is in. "Thin feels healthier, looks better, has a better sex life," novelist Fay Weldon says. "Thin has more boyfriends, a bigger house, a higher income, more choices in life—statistics prove it. None of this is fair, it's just true."

Emaciated "superwaif" models like Kate Moss, who look like starving, Third World poster children, were not always the standard of feminine beauty; the extreme thin look is relatively recent.

• Sculpted stone figurines dating from the Stone Age reveal that plump women were revered as goddesses of fertility.

• Greek and Roman men liked their women shapely and voluptuous; a woman too thin was viewed as too boyish—not a *woman*.

• During the Middle Ages, plumpness in a wife was not only a sexual turnon but also considered a sign of health, fitness, and potential success at bearing children. Men placed a premium on a woman's fat reserves.

• Renaissance artists celebrated firm, fleshy women like Botticelli's Venus. Rubens and Renoir made careers out of the soft, feminine beauty of plumpness.

Cross-cultural studies show that in societies where food is scarce, when crop failure is high year after year, people put a premium on plumpness in their women. By carrying extra calories, stored as fat, a woman guarantees she'll live longer to breast-feed and rear children.

But when food resources are abundant to the point of excess—when fast food is at everyone's fingertips—thin women are favored. In such times, extra calories stored as body fat are viewed as a sign of lack of discipline, carelessness, even slovenliness.

Two researchers studied the shapes of store mannequins from the 1920s through the 1990s. Well into the 1950s, mannequins were generally curvaceous and plump, not unlike Botticelli's Venus. They had full breasts, broad hips, and normal-looking arms, even if their waists were unrealistically trim. They were built more like Marilyn Monroe and Jayne Mansfield than bony adolescent boys.

The Jackie Kennedy Look

Starting in the 1960s, with the fashion chic of First Lady Jackie Kennedy, store-window mannequins trimmed down. Their hips became six inches smaller, and their thighs four inches smaller than those of real women at their ideal weight. The mannequins lost so much weight, so quickly, the researchers concluded, that if they were real women they'd have been unable to menstruate or conceive children, and would have had a hard time keeping their bones from becoming brittle.

Over the next two decades, thin mannequins shrunk to "waifs" and then to "superwaifs," the magazine model's ideal of feminine beauty. Few women can achieve that ideal—and live long enough to enjoy its benefits. The unnatural ideal has had devastating consequences in terms of women's self-esteem, as English fashion designer Jasper Conran sums up: "I have never met a woman, however perfect her figure, who is happy with her body. Women subscribe too much to an ideal. They do themselves a disservice."

Throughout most of history, men liked their women to be voluptuously full-figured.

If America and Europe were to suddenly experience a severe food shortage, superthin women most likely would be viewed as sickly and near death. They'd be avoided for their lack of resources in acquiring food or for their "genetic defect" that didn't allow them to store fat. Plump women would be prized for the healthy way their bodies stored precious calories and for their cleverness in acquiring scarce food resources.

Beauty ideals vary from culture to cultures:

BARBIE DOLL BODY; GERMANY, 1950S ◆

*W*hat does the all-American Barbie doll have to do with a shapely German prostitute? A lot. They are one and the same.

Barbie, the most popular doll in history, with gravity-defying breasts, hourglass waist, and perfect long legs, set a new standard for the female figure. She was conceived in the late 1950s by Mattel's Ruth Handler, who named the doll after her teenage daughter. Her daughter, as a child, liked dressing shapely paper-cutout dolls in elaborate costumes. No such doll existed then, or in the mid-1950s: all dolls were angel-faced babies in diapers or simple frocks.

SOUTH AMERICAN INDIAN BEAUTY ◆ *The Sirionó people of eastern Bolivia have a simple criterion for female beauty: a woman's desirability as a wife is based on her body's ability to store fat reserves. She is sexy because she is plump enough to be fertile and make a good mother.*

Allan R. Holmberg lived for a time among them and in The Siriono *(1946) detailed their concept of beauty:*

"Besides being young, a desirable sex partner should also be fat. She should have big hips, good-sized but firm breasts, and a deposit of fat on her sexual organs. Fat women are referred to by men with obvious pride as 'fat vulvas' and are thought to be more satisfying sexually than thin women, who are summarily dismissed as being 'bony.'

"In fact, so desirable is corpulence as a sexual trait that I have frequently heard men make up songs about the merits of a fat vulva.

"In addition, certain other signs of erotic beauty are recognized. A tall person is preferred to a short one. Facial features should be regular. Eyes should be large. Little attention is paid to the ears, the nose, or the lips, unless they are obviously deformed.

"Pubic hair is undesirable and is therefore depilated, although a certain amount of pubic hair is believed to add zest to intercourse.

"A woman's vulva should be small and fat, while a man's penis should be as large as possible."

Mattel plays down the connection, but the model for Barbie was a seductive German sex doll, Lilli, manufactured in the mid-1950s. The doll, in turn, had been based on a 1952 racy German cartoon character, also named Lilli, a golddigger by trade, who appeared in a postwar German tabloid.

In *Forever Barbie* (1994), M. G. Lord gives Barbie's full biography:

Barbie was knocked off from the "Bild Lilli" doll, a lascivious plaything for adult men that was based on a postwar comic character in the Bild Zeitung, *a downscale German newspaper similar to America's* National Enquirer.

The doll, sold principally in tobacco shops, was marketed as a sort of three-dimensional pinup. In her cartoon incarnation, Lilli was not merely

---

ISLAMIC IDEAL OF FEMALE BEAUTY ♦ *Hārūn ar-Rashīd, born near modern Teheran, Iran, around 765 C.E., was the fifth caliph of the 'Abbasid dynasty. he ruled Islam at the zenith of its empire with a luxury memorialized in* The Thousand and One Nights, *otherwise known as* The Arabian Nights of Entertainment. *He conducted an opulent court in the then-new capital of Baghdad and was a connoisseur of beautiful women. According to a court observer:*

"To be relished by men, a woman must have a perfect waist, and be plump and lusty. Her hair should be black, her forehead wide, her eyebrows of Ethiopian blackness, her eyes large with the whites in them very limpid.

"With cheek of a perfect oval, she will have an elegant nose and a graceful mouth; lips and tongue vermilion. Her breath will be of pleasant odor, her throat long, her neck firm. Her breasts must be full and firm, her belly in good proportions, and her navel well-developed and marked.

"She must have the thighs and buttocks hard, the hips large and full, a waist of fine shape, hands and feet of striking elegance, plump arms and well-developed shoulders. If one looks at such a woman from the front, one is fascinated. If one looks from behind, one dies of pleasure.

"Looked at sitting, she is a rounded dome. Lying down, she is a soft bed. Standing up, she is the staff of a standard.

"She hides her secret parts. She is always elegantly attired, perfumes herself with scents, uses antimony for her toilet, and cleans her teeth with the bark of the walnut tree, which reddens the lips and gums.

"Such a woman is cherished by all men."

---

a doxie, she was a German *doxie—an ice-blond, pixie-nosed specimen of an Aryan ideal—who may have known hardship during the war, but as long as there were men with checkbooks, was not going to suffer again.*

Lilli was an exhibitionist and a floozy, with the body of a Varga girl. Scantily clad, she flung herself at wealthy men. In one typical cartoon, Lilli appeared at a female friend's apartment concealing her naked body with a newspaper. The caption read: "We had a fight and he took back all the presents he gave me."

HINDU CONCEPT OF FEMALE BEAUTY ◆ *Once again, plumpness plays a part in the sexual attractiveness of females. The Hindu man, as psychiatrist Havelock Ellis reported, likes his women to have a particularly full face and belly:*

"Her face is pleasing as the full moon. Her body is well clothed with flesh and as soft as the mustard flower. Her skin is fine, tender, and fair as the yellow lotus, never dark colored.

"Her eyes are bright and beautiful as the orbs of the fawn, well-shaped and with reddish corners. Her bosom is full and high. She has a good neck; her nose is straight and lovely, and three folds or wrinkles cross her middle—above the umbilical region.

"Her vulva resembles the opening lotus bud, and her love-seed is perfumed like the lily that has newly burst. She walks with flamingo-like gait, and her voice is low and as musical as the Kokila bird."

In another cartoon, a policeman warns Lilli that her two-piece bathing suit is illegal on the boardwalk. "Oh," flirts Lilli, "and in your opinion which part should I take off?"

The German cartoon debuted on July 24, 1952, and was soon fashioned into a busty doll in stiletto heels. Lilli was definitely a "doxi" (or "doxy")—from the Dutch *docke*, meaning "doll," and British slang for a prostitute or mistress.

Sculpted by German doll designer Max Weissbrodt, Lilli was never intended for children. Men who bought the dolls or were given them as gifts often placed Lilli on a car dashboard. "She was a pornographic caricature, a gag gift for men," writes Lord.

Like Barbie, Lilli had an outfit for every occasion, but the occasions were not those which nice girls attended. In her lace teddy, Lilli was "the star of every bar," one ad boasted. Lilli wasn't just a symbol of sex, concludes Lord, "she is a symbol of illicit sex."

The Americanization of Lilli

Ruth Handler saw her first Lilli doll while on a family vacation in Switzerland. "We were walking down the street in Lucerne and there was a doll,"

Wer mit Liebe schenkt — an Lilli denkt

PROMOTIONAL AD: *"Whoever gives with love—thinks of Lilli."*

she said, "an adult doll with a woman's body." She immediately realized that the body was exactly what she'd envisioned for her own creation. Purchasing a Lilli doll for herself (and two for her daughter Barbie), Ruth Handler brought it back to America and instructed her designers to duplicate the body. One engineer, Jack Ryan, described Lilli as "a hooker or an actress between performances."

As an Americanized Lilli, Barbie made her debut at the toy fair in New York City in the winter of 1959.

The eleven-and-a-half-inch doll, promoted as "the only anatomically perfect doll manufactured today," received mixed reviews. Buyers, mostly men, offered opinions from "Fashion dolls are dead," to "Mothers aren't going to buy a doll with breasts." Sears found Barbie "too sexy" to stock.

Ruth Handler, convinced she had a potentially hot-selling toy but concerned with the negative reception, contacted her supplier and cut back on the number of dolls being manufactured—a mistake she'd quickly regret. Barbie was more than a hit; she was a marketing phenomenon. The craze for the curvaceous "Teenage Fashion Model" with an enviable wardrobe, hoop earrings, hot red fingernails and toenails, pointed eyebrows, and pouty lips seductively delineated was immediate—and nonstop. Mattel spent the next three years struggling to meet back-orders because of its initial production cutback.

Two Lilli dolls. The advertisement reads: "Whether more or less naked, Lilli is always discreet."

By the mid-1960s, the doll was selling in the millions and her clothing manufacturer could barely keep up with demands for Barbie dresses, minks, gowns, swimsuits, and sequined bolero jackets. Her chic clothes were never cheap; a complete wedding trousseau cost thirty-five dollars. There was a Barbie magazine and Barbie fan clubs across the United States and Europe; and the shapely figurine was smuggled into several Muslim countries where she was not dressed in a veil.

Ironically, her most vocal critics initially were men. One writer found her "a predatory female," another "the perfect bitch." Feminists would later view her as "the perfect bimbo," "an airhead," and fault her for providing young girls with unrealistic goals in physical measurements and perpetual beauty.

Shortly before Christmas 1964, when the doll was *the* gift for girls, the *Saturday Evening Post* lambasted her as the ultimate material girl:

Anyone looking for deeper values in the world of Barbie is looking in the wrong place. With its emphasis on possessions and its worship of appearances, it is modern America in miniature—a tiny parody of our pursuit of the beautiful, the material, the trivial.

Lilli comic strip: "How can you marry a man with lots of money? As soon as you marry him, it will be gone."

The original three-dollar doll is now a thousand-dollar collectible. As an American pop culture icon, Barbie was sealed into the 1976 bicentenary time capsule, to be opened a hundred years hence. How will her shapely figure and dated wardrobe be reviewed then? As incidental social memorabilia? Or as our own time's high standard of feminine shapeliness?

CHAPTER 13

ℐuts and ℰggs

"Cum" to "Cummerbund"

*The only known aphrodisiac
is variety.*

Marc Connolly

"Balls"; America, Mid-Nineteenth Century ◆

As a colloquialism for "testes," "balls" is of recent origin. The term appeared in the middle of the nineteenth century as an abbreviation of *ballocks,* which for a thousand years had been Standard English for male testes. An older English word was *ballucas,* from the Indo-European root *bhel,* "to swell"—also the root of our word "bowl." A bowl is half of a hollowed-out ball.

In the American Midwest, "ballocks" (sometimes spelled "billox") was a popular word for testes as recently as the middle of the twentieth century. A favorite child's rhyme joked:

*Yankee Doodle had a cat,
And he was full of frolic,
And all the mice and rats
That came around,
They grabbed him by the ballocks.*

Ballsy, which describes a man—and nowadays a woman—who is aggressive and gusty, was first recorded in 1959, though equivalent expressions, like "he's got balls" or "she's got balls," are older. As comedian George Burns used to joke, "If my aunt had balls, she'd be my uncle."

Men might actually live longer if their testes were removed before midlife, a fact little known and less acted upon. During a period when castration was the penalty for rape, studies showed that prisoners castrated in their twenties and thirties lived on average thirteen years longer than their intact inmates. Testosterone is a ticking time bomb.

Similar life-extension results were reported in former East Germany among imprisoned rapists who had been chemically castrated with injections of female hormones. Their *cojones* shrunk and they sprouted shapely breasts and voluptuous buttocks—and, consequently, were irresistible to fellow inmates, who raped them, putting a new spin on Cicero's injunction "Let the punishment fit the crime."

Doctors now treat men at high risk for heart attacks with small doses of estrogen, extending their lives by, in effect, reducing the influence of testosterone.

BLUE BALLS; ENGLAND, PRE-SEVENTEENTH CENTURY ◆

The term "blue balls" refers to a painful ache and darkening of the testes that can occur when a young man, say on a hot date and with high hopes of scoring, does not reach orgasm after lengthy arousal. The skin of the scrotum actually darkens to a deep purple.

Most men believe that a frustrated orgasm is the only cause of this syndrome. But the scrotum can turn a purplish blue, and the testicles severely ache, after three or four ejaculations over a short period of time. There is a simple reason: before ejaculation, a great deal of blood is pumped into the testes. As long as sexual arousal remains high, with or without orgasm, the dark red blood, high in purplish hemoglobin, cannot drain away; consequently the entire region becomes dark and overexercised, as an overworked muscle can turn red and ache.

The term "blue balls" is at least four centuries old and first appeared in England as "blue ballocks."

"TESTIS"—"I BEAR WITNESS" ◆

*T*estis," a single male testicle, is also the Latin noun for "witness." Our verb "to testify" derives from the Latin *testis*.

"Testis" entered the English medical vocabulary in the early eighteenth century. For the previous two hundred years, anatomists had been using "testicle" to describe the male reproductive gland.

Today we take an oath by placing a hand on a Bible, but in ancient times testimony was validated by grasping the testicles of a witness; he let go of his friend's testes only when he'd finished testifying. This was male bonding put to practical purpose. Back then, before there were Bibles to swear on, women did not take oaths except for servitude in marriage.

The Israelites employed this intimate ball-in-a-hand protocol, which had no sexual overtones. It appears several times in the Bible:

• When Abraham sent his servant to find a suitable wife for Isaac, the old man had him put his hand under Abraham's thigh and swear on his testicles to fulfill his mission:

And the servant put his hand under the thigh of Abraham his master, and swore to him concerning that matter. Genesis 24:9.

• When Joseph's father was dying, he asked his son to put his hand beneath his thigh and swear on his testicles that he'd be buried in the family tomb:

And the time drew nigh that Israel must die, and he called his son Joseph, and said to him, If now I have found grace in thy sight, put, I pray thee, thy hand under my thigh, and deal kindly and truly with me; bury me not, I pray thee, in Egypt. Genesis 47:29.

GROPING ONE'S CROTCH ◆

A man might also testify by grasping his own testes for the duration of his oath. The holding of two testes bore witness to a man's sincerity: he clutched in his palms his most prized possession, the essence of his virility.

For many centuries, a Roman Catholic priest could not be promoted to the rank of bishop if he had only one testis. And, too, a man without testes—either a eunuch or a man whose testicles had not descended at puberty—could not receive the sacrament of Holy Orders. The priesthood was closed to ball-less men; now it is closed only to women.

In Old Testament times, eunuchs, castrated for any number of military or medical reasons, were less worthy than Israelites with intact testes. The Bible has a lot to say about men's balls, called "stones" in some translations:

• According to Deuteronomic law, ball-less men could not participate in temple rituals or become priests:

He that is wounded in the stones, or hath his privy member cut off, shall not enter into the congregation of the Lord. Deuteronomy 23:1.

• So fastidious were Hebrew lawmakers about male genital perfection in the presence of God that a castrated animal was unsuitable as a sacrificial offering:

You shall not offer the Lord that which is bruised, or crushed, or broken, or cut. Leviticus 22:24.

• If two male Israelites were brawling and one man's wife reached out to help her husband by seizing his opponent's genitals, she was punished by mutilation—the offending hand was cut off:

When men strive together one against the other, and the wife of one draws near to deliver her husband out of the hand of him that attacked him, and puts forth her hand, and takes him by the secrets: Then thou shall cut off her hand, and thine eyes shall not pity her. Deuteronomy 25:11–12.

Today, in parts of Latin America, Eastern Europe, and Africa, men still take solemn oaths by touching their testes. In some cultures men touch their balls in the superstitious belief that it brings good luck—an act athletes sometimes engage in.

This touching, a trademark among rap singers, underscores the biological fact that the gonads are what make a man "male." In the womb, they produce testosterone, which shapes the male brain, musculature, and genitalia. At puberty, they produce the sex hormones, or androgens (*andros*, Greek for "male"), that virilize a boy, gifting him with a beard, the physical stature of a man, and the sperm that can turn him into a father. The testes are *the* crucial part of the male sexual anatomy; the penis is primarily a delivery system.

"Scrotum"; 1597 ♦

*S*crotum," the name of the fleshy sack that holds the testes, is from the Latin *scorteus,* "of leather," an allusion to the sack's leathery texture. First recorded in its anatomical context in 1597, the word is also related to the Latin *scrautum,* "quiver," a sack in which arrows are kept. Picturesquely, sperm can be viewed as arrows of love fired off from a man's prize weapon.

The human eyelid and the skin of the scrotum are the only body parts with virtually no subcutaneous fat.

Every boy soon learns that his balls are not always balanced in his scrotum; the left one usually hangs lower than the right—perfectly adjacent balls would always be colliding. And, too, the balls dangle away from the trunk to maintain a temperature three or four degrees Fahrenheit lower than the rest of the body, the point at which sperm are best produced. A hot bath can leave a man's sperm dazed and lethargically unreproductive.

At the other extreme, to protect the sperm in cold weather, the balls are raised and squeezed tightly against the trunk by the sack's "cremasteric" muscles—from the Latin *crematus,* "burned" also the origin of our word "cremate."

"Semen"; Fourteenth Century ♦

*S*emen" is the name of the viscid, whitish fluid of the male repro- ductive tract, consisting of spermatozoa suspended in secretions from accessory glands. The word, first used in its anatomical context in the four- teenth century, is Latin for "seed" or "germ." From the same source comes our verb "disseminate," to "scatter seed."

Many terms are related to "semen":

• When you attend a *seminar,* you are at a gathering of thinkers who germinate, or hatch, new ideas.

• *Seminal* thinkers are people who give birth to highly novel ideas, new seeds of thought.

• *A seminary* originally meant a "seed plot, or nursery"—a place where

THE POPE'S BALLS ◆ *In* Lives of the Popes *(1479), Bartolomeo Platina reported that for some time all papal nominees had to have their testes felt before being installed as the new pope. This was to prevent any woman usurper from ascending to the throne, a fear that had grown out of rumors that one or more earlier popes had been women.*

Platina tells of one ninth-century pope, "John," who was discovered to be a woman: "She disguised herself when young as a man and traveled with her male lover, a scholar. In Rome, she met with few who could match or exceed her knowledge of Scriptures. By her learning and brilliant readings she gained great respect . . . and was chosen pope by common consent."

Unfortunately, says Platina, the pope became pregnant by one of her manservants. "She hid her big belly for quite a while until one day, when she was going to the Lateran Church, her labor came upon her and she died upon the spot. She had presided two years, one month, and four days, and was buried without any pomp."

To prevent such a travesty from recurring, Rome's cardinals introduced the "porphyry chair," a throne of purple stone with a hole in the center. "When any new pope is first seated," explained Platina, "the youngest deacon reaches up through a hole in the chair's seat and touches the pope's genitals."

Is the story of the ninth-century "John" true?

It's hard to say for sure. Officially, there were at least two popes named John in the ninth century. One was an antipope, enthroned in 844 by the people of Rome after violent demonstrations against outrages in the papacy. Eventually dethroned (and nearly murdered), he was dispatched to a monastery and nothing more of his fate is known. Another, John VIII, elected in 872, was the first pope to be assassinated—poisoned by his relatives and then clubbed to death. Amid such skulduggery, there just might have been a woman pope.

something develops and grows. That's why young theological students are called *seminarians:* they are "seeds" for the next generation of priests.

Semen is ejaculated as a liquid and immediately gels; then, after five minutes, it reliquifies. The transformation is due to enzymes. The gel state protects the delicate sperm until it is safely in the vaginal tract, then the liquid state assists the sperm's upward motility toward the oviducts.

Men with Mr. Universe bodies, who get muscular by taking steroids, usually have wimpy sperm. Steroid shots or pills can paralyze the pituitary gland, which plays a vital role in sperm production. Thus, big muscles can mean bad sperm, while a wimp type can have potent sperm.

"SPERM"; FOURTEENTH CENTURY ◆

*S*perm," both the singular and plural for the male gamete, is from the Greek *sperma,* the "seed" or "germ" of a plant or animal. The word was first recorded in its anatomical context in the late fourteenth century.

Spermicide, an agent that kills sperm, is formed by adding the Latin *caedere,* "to strike down or slay."

A sperm whale's testes weight about 27 pounds; those of a blue whale are about three feet long and weigh 110 pounds. Yet the individual spermatozoa of whales and men are about the same microscopic size.

Relative to body weight, the Japanese dolphin has the largest testes of all mammals.

Sperm are microscopically tiny and make up only 3 percent of the average human ejaculate. The other 97 percent consists of fluids manufactured in the "prostate" gland—from the Greek *prostatis,* "one that stands before"—and the seminal vesicles. These fluids are squirted behind the sperm as it passes the gland. Thus the forward part an ejaculate—what is contained in the initial spurt—is richer in sperm than the trailing end. Once all the fluids combine with the sperm, the mixture is called "semen," something of a misnomer. Semen is more than just "seed."

While some people who engage in oral sex do not like the taste of semen, others find it sweet-tasting: it contains the sugar fructose, in varying amounts, and can be influenced by diet.

The thick viscid fluid has a nutritional value of about six calories per average ejaculate.

SPERM FACTORY ◆ *Each minute of his life a man makes fifty thousand sperm. Each hour he makes three million sperm. Each day of his life he makes a total of seventy-two million sperm, give or take a few million. This prodigious manufacturing starts around puberty and, with a slight falloff due to environmental pollutants and age, continues to the grave.*

A woman, on the other hand, produces one egg every twenty-eight days and stops altogether at menopause. An egg is rare; sperm are nearly countless and commonplace. Women, one might say, are far more biologically efficient—or precious—than men.

In the average ejaculate, a man releases three hundred to five hundred million sperm. By comparison, a gorilla ejaculates fifty million sperm; and a chimpanzee, man's closest primate relative, shoots off six hundred million. The horse tops these numbers, producing about thirteen trillion sperm per ejaculate.

The number of sperm produced is related to the size of a man's testicles. So if a man were inclined to boast, he might want to skip the size of his penis and stress the size of his balls.

SURVIVAL OF THE FITTEST ◆

Semen is alkaline; vaginal fluids are more acidic. It is thought that sperm's alkalinity protects it from the hostile environment of the vagina, whose acids help ward off bacteria. Semen also contains a powerful antibacterial agent for an extra measure of safety.

This is not overkill, since only about two hundred sperm out of five hundred million ejaculated survive the journey up the vagina, through the uterus, and into the oviduct. Many sperm never make it past the physical barrier of the cervix. Others become exhausted swimming across the vast uterus, which, considering the length of sperm, is comparable to tadpoles crossing the Atlantic Ocean. Others get waylaid and enter the wrong oviduct—the one without an egg. Many get confused and swim backward or sideward; to win the race and capture the coveted egg, sperm must swim unswervingly forward—and fast.

Hardy sperm, which swim at the rate of three milliliters per minute, can

The maypole was a phallic symbol. Dancing around it increased a couple's fertility.

survive from two to seven days in the female reproductive tract (it may take this long for one sperm to find the single egg). Slow swimmers don't have a chance. In fact, given the odds, it's amazing conception takes place at all.

Perhaps as many as a hundred survivors will spot the egg, and then all hell breaks loose. There is a frenzy of competition, relentlessly violent and savagely aggressive, which has been compared to the behavior of men themselves in large groups. A hundred sperm after one egg are not unlike a hundred men chasing after one woman.

There can be only one winner. Wriggling in a tumult, sperm collide with each other as they batter the outer wall of the egg. Each sperm releases a chemical that it hopes will eat through the coating at its own location. Eventually tiny holes appear in the wall and, in a flash, a few lucky sperm dash inside—losing their tails in the scrimmage. Each sperm is now nothing but a head—but a determined head. These semifinalists now engage in an even fiercer battle to break through the innermost wall of the egg, the final bastion, to arrive at the coveted nucleus.

A tough membrane protects the female's DNA. Only the strongest single sperm out of the five hundred million ejaculated will break through this formidable barrier. "Winner takes all" is the genetic game, the champion sperm fusing its nucleus with the nucleus of the egg. Each nucleus contains twenty-three chromosomes, *half* the number needed to make a new human being.

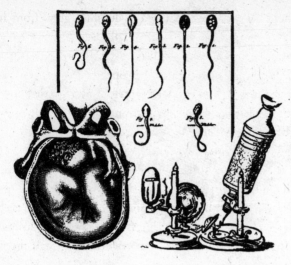

The microscope proved that a fetus developed from more than sperm—women would eventually get credit for contributing eggs.

DISCOVERY OF SPERM; ANTONIE VAN LEEUWENHOEK, NETHERLANDS, 1677 ◆

*E*ven young schoolchildren know that in order to make a baby—a baby chick, a baby bunny, or a human infant—the father's sperm must implant itself into the mother's egg. But this major reproductive principle was confirmed only in the nineteenth century.

Early physicians did not even guess that conception required the union of a sperm and an egg. For centuries, no doctor suspected that a female egg, other than calcium-shelled bird eggs, even existed. Men, and only men, were responsible for the continuation of the species. Physicians assumed that the male ejaculate contained *homunculi,* or "tiny people," fully formed, who grew into human beings after being deposited in the uterus. The male thus played the most important role in reproduction, a state of affairs readily accepted in the male-dominated societies of earlier times.

A mother's womb was thought to nurture a "tiny person" until he or she was ready to be born, but it was believed that the mother made no essential contribution. If a child eventually resembled the mother, that was due to the "influence of the womb." For centuries, all contraceptive methods were a means of halting the march of homunculi up the vaginal canal and into the nurturing womb.

How could a father, a male, produce a daughter, a female? Albertus Magnus, also known as Albert the Great (c. 1200–1280), held that a female fetus developed from a father's "weak" seed, while a male child grew from his "strong" seed. No one, of course, had yet seen a "male seed."

In 1677, Antonie van Leeuwenhoek, a Dutch haberdasher, constructed his first quality microscope. A tireless inventor, he continued to ply his trade while grinding glass in his spare time to make lenses of ever greater power and clarity. In producing microscopes of high resolution, he almost single-handedly established the field of microbiology.

Continually sliding new specimens under his lenses, Leeuwenhoek observed that aphids reproduced by parthenogenesis, or "virgin birth," in which female eggs hatch without male fertilization. Using his own blood, he gave the first accurate description of red blood cells; and using his own saliva, he recorded the myriad bacteria that inhabit the human mouth. Using his own ejaculate, which drew cries of immorality, he discovered sperm, half the reproductive story.

Mysterious Medical Student

Leeuwenhoek's interest in seminal fluid was prompted by a young medical student whose identity haunts the annals of science. Perhaps he was named Ludwig Hamm, or van Ham, or von Hammen—no one knows for certain.

One day in 1677, the student, who was attending the University of Leiden, showed Leeuwenhoek a bottle containing semen. The fluid, he said, came from a sick man who suffered excessive nocturnal emissions, and it looked very strange under a microscope.

"In what way?" Leeuwenhoek asked.

"It's alive," the student exclaimed. "It's swarming with little, tailed animals. Perhaps these are what have made the man sick."

The master microscopist placed a sample on a slide and saw hundreds of writhing "animalcules." Had they caused the man's sickness? Or did every male ejaculate contain such curious creatures? At that point the young "discoverer" of sperm walked out of the history of science, never to be mentioned again.

Leeuwenhoek's curiosity was aroused. In need of a semen sample from a *healthy* man, he became his own guinea pig. He went on to collect semen from hospitalized patients, healthy students at the university, and distinguished scientists in London's Royal Society. Famous men freely offered up their sperm to be scrutinized. Today, of course, the medical collection of sperm is commonplace; a man is given a pornographic magazine, a sterile vial, and assigned to a solitary cell. But centuries ago the idea of grown men masturbating into glass bottles for the sake of science caused public outrage.

Under magnification, Leeuwenhoek observed that "seed" resembled swimming tadpoles, not perfectly formed "tiny people." No one was quite sure what to make of the squirming objects in seminal fluid; the organisms' tails were six times the length of their bodies. Leeuwenhoek concluded that they had to play a major role in the fertilization of the egg:

> I have seen so excessively a great quantity of living animalcules that I am much astonished by it. I can say without exaggeration that in a bit of matter no longer than a grain of sand more than fifty thousand animalcules were present, whose shape I can compare with our river eel. These animalcules move about with uncommon vigor . . . and astonish my eye.

DISCOVERY OF THE EGG; REGNIER DE GRAAF, HOLLAND, 1672 ◆

By the seventeenth century, some thinkers, following the ideas of Aristotle, argued that a women's menstrual blood was used to form the material substance of the fetus: its flesh, blood, and bones. For these men, a woman played a substantial role in the formation of the baby: she supplied the building materials.

Nonetheless, it was the seminal fluid of the male that served as the "organizing agent" that directed the assemblage of the fetus. This "agent" was not unlike the later concept of genes and DNA, life's blueprint.

When the Dutch anatomist Regnier de Graaf peered down the tube of an early microscope in 1672, he discovered that the female "ovaries," identified a century earlier, produced eggs. These eggs did not have shells. De Graaf claimed that the eggs traveled down the "Fallopian" tubes to the womb. But most doctors at the time—all men—refused to believe that a woman could contribute to half the formation of a fetus. The "eggs," they said, merely nurtured the male seminal fluid in some unexplained way.

(Today we know that what de Graaf saw were not eggs but *Graafian follicles,* small protective sacs of fluid in the wall of the ovary in which the eggs grow.)

In de Graaf's time, a few biologists—most notably English physician William Harvey, discoverer of the circulatory system—reasoned that since ho-

AUTOFELLATIO ◆ *Teenage boys have always experimented with tasting their own sperm. Some, in contorted positions, attempt to ejaculate into their mouths. Others attempt to perform fellatio on themselves. One of the most remarkable cases of autofellatio was witnessed by a U.S. Army doctor, Joseph Richard Parke, in 1908.*

A mother had brought her fifteen-year-old son to Parke. The boy, by years of training, had succeeded in making his spinal column so flexible that he could quite easily suck himself off. The mother wanted the boy "cured"—broken of the habit. Parke wrote:

"In order to convince myself that the thing [autofellatio] was possible, I asked him to put his penis into his mouth. He did not hesitate to do so, apparently regarding the act as of little consequence. When he did so the old passion revived, and absorbed him irresistibly.

"Whether the reader regard the part played by me as morally culpable, or professionally justifiable, I at least had the novel experience of witnessing an act of mouth-stupration by a boy—self-performed—in my own private consulting room.

"He lay on a couch; and as the climax of the orgasm approached, apparently forgetting my presence, and every other consideration, he resigned himself with utmost abandonment to the delirium of his pleasure, rolling, gasping, writhing, and resembling nothing so much as some sort of animal, curled up in a ball, enduring its death agony.

"He was afterward committed to a sanitarium for the treatment of such cases."

munculi did not exist in the male ejaculate, the female egg must contain the embryo in a preformed state, which just needed to grow to size in the womb. Harvey and his followers championed the "egg theory," or *ovulism*, summed up in their motto *Omne vivum ex ovo*, "All life comes from the egg."

Thus, for a time, women got *all* the credit for propagation of the species. For Harvey, a father sowed no significant "seed" in the womb, the mother's egg just hatched there; the egg was a slumbering creature awakened by a touch from seminal fluid.

By the end of the seventeenth century, any anatomist could gaze down the barrel of his microscope and see "eggs" and sperm. But, astonishingly, no one connected the dots to arrive at the complete picture of sexual reproduction: one sperm, one egg.

• **Egg** is from the Old English *aeg*, where it strictly meant a calcium-shelled bird's egg—not a woman's egg from her ovaries, as yet undiscovered. The Indo-European root of *aeg* is *owjom*, which gave rise to the Latin *ovum*, for a bird's egg. The spelling "egg" entered English around the fourteenth century.

• **Ovary**, either of the pair of female reproductive glands producing eggs and, in vertebrates, sex hormones, is from the Latin *ovum*, "egg." The spelling "ovary" entered English in the mid-1600s.

FALLOPIAN TUBES; GABRIELLO FALLOPIO, ITALY, 1561 •

*I*n the sixteenth century, the Italian anatomist Gabriel Fallopius (the Latin form of Gabriello Fallopio), while dissecting cadavers, had described two slender tubes that connected the "ovaries" to the uterus, later named the *Fallopian tubes*. Fallopio suspected that the five-inch-long tubes served some important reproductive function—but wasn't sure what.

Born in Modena, Italy, around 1523, Fallopio served as a canon of the cathedral of Modena. Later he turned to the study of medicine and in 1549 became professor of anatomy at the University of Pisa. Human cadavers were then easy to obtain, and Fallopio performed an exhaustive observation of the body. He described many of the major nerves of the head and face, and the semicircular canals of the inner ear that are responsible for maintaining body equilibrium.

Enamored with female anatomy, he is responsible for naming several major female structures:

• **Vagina**, Latin for "sheath." Prior to Fallopio's time the vagina went by several intriguing names, as we saw in an earlier chapter.

• **Placenta**, the vascular disklike organ that connects the embryo to the uterine wall via the umbilical cord; Latin for "flat cake."

• **Clitoris**, the small, hooded, erectile organ at the upper end of the vulva. Fallopio knew that it was extremely sensitive in females. But he did not know—nor would any doctor until late in the twentieth century—that it was *the* major organ for female sexual orgasm.

Fallopio described his dissection of cadavers in his only major work, *Observationes anatomicae* (1561).

Many of the details of sexual reproduction have been discovered in just the last few decades. Fallopio might have been pleased to know that the tubes named after him are the primary environment where fertilization of the egg takes place. The mucous membrane lining the tubes gives off secretions that help transport the sperm upward, and the egg downward, keeping both alive until they meet.

Sperm and Egg Union; Lazzaro Spallanzani, Italy, 1779 •

The basis of sexual reproduction was first described by an Italian physiologist, Lazzaro Spallanzani. Suddenly, the copulation of man and a woman, which had been going on for millions of years, was understood. Nature had designed the two sexes and their intriguingly different body parts—penis and testes, uterus and ovaries, sperm and egg—for the well-orchestrated composition of a new life. Parents who may feel awkward explaining the "birds and the bees" to their children may take some comfort in the fact that *nobody* understood how sex worked until around the time of the American Revolution.

This monumental discovery in sexology, which created the discipline that goes by that name, was made by a chaste, celibate Roman Catholic priest. During the previous century, some anatomists thought that spermatozoa, which had been observed, were environmental contaminants picked up once the milky seminal fluid left the penis and hit the air. Others, like German anatomist Johann Friedrich Blumenbach (1752 to 1840), classified sperm with simple single-celled protozoa.

In 1779, Spallanzani performed some of biology's most critical experiments. He showed for the first time, under carefully controlled conditions, that physical contact between the male seminal fluid and the female egg was necessary if the egg was to develop into a fetus.

A Priest Collects Sperm and Eggs

Born in 1729 at Scandiano, Italy, Lazzaro Spallanzani studied mathematics, philosophy, and languages at a Jesuit seminary in Reggio. After graduation he entered a seminary and eventually took holy orders. For a time he supported himself as a priest in Modena, while conducting experiments with sperm and eggs. His religious beliefs, among other things, prevented him from collecting and working with human sperm. He wondered, though, if every human sperm in an ejaculate had a soul and, if so, what happened to the innumerable souls in wasted semen—his own included. If every sperm had its own soul, masturbation and contraception were grave evils indeed.

By Spallanzani's time, many biologists believed in "remote fertilization," in which the egg could be stimulated to develop without contact with seminal fluid. If an egg were exposed to invisible "spermatic vapor," *aura seminalis,* it would develop into an embryo—so their theory went. Since male vapor —not unlike a ghost—could not be seen, its existence was a matter of faith.

There was also some worry that this ghostly vapor, once released from an ejaculate and airborne, might waft up the legs of some unsuspecting female, causing an unwanted pregnancy. No one knows how many unmarried women at the time may have credited their pregnancies to spermatic ghosts.

Spallanzani, as professor of natural history at the University of Pavia, believed in spermatic ghosts. He attached freshly laid toad spawn (eggs) to a watch glass and inverted it over another watch glass containing toad seminal fluid. He thus had an enclosed system in which the eggs and seminal fluid were separated, and where the invisible ghostly male "vapor" could migrate to stimulate the eggs.

Nothing happened; no eggs turned into tadpoles. But when the priest mixed eggs directly into seminal fluid, the physical contact produced tadpoles.

Toads in Trousers

How did Spallanzani obtain frog seminal fluid? Believe it or not, he dressed male frogs in tiny taffeta trousers and placed them in the company of naked female frogs. He waterproofed the pants with a light coating of candle wax. Aroused, the males mounted the females and ejaculated into their pants, then Spallanzani collected his samples. In showing that seminal fluid caused unfertilized eggs in vitro to develop into tadpoles, Spallanzani was one of first scientists to achieve *artificial insemination* in a laboratory under controlled condition.

Heady from his success, Spallanzani was determined to show that sperm-

*The study of male and female toads revealed that both sexes make equal
contributions to the production of offspring.*

egg sexual reproduction also occurred in mammals. The priest masturbated
a male dog, then artificially inseminated a bitch, which he kept in an isolated
room—to dispel once and for all the "vapor" theory of insemination. The
bitch had pups. Mammals, Spallanzani concluded, like frogs, propagated by
sexual reproduction.

Spallanzani made many attempts to crossbreed cats and dogs and failed,
for reasons that are well understood today: DNA is species-specific.

IMPLANTATION OF SPERM INTO EGG; HERMANN FOL, SWITZERLAND, 1877 ❖

Although Spallanzani suspected that something in the seminal
fluid—most likely spermatozoa—was essential for fertilization, he
could not confirm the role of sperm.

In 1824, French chemist Jean Baptiste Dumas demonstrated that sperm
advance toward a single egg and "touch" it in order to produce offspring.
But no one had microscopically witnessed the act of implantation. Indeed,
most scientists did not even suspect that the *fusion* of sperm and egg was the
secret of sexual reproduction.

In 1840, English embryologist Martin Barry suggested that the essential
requirement for successful fertilization was penetration of "one or more"
sperm into an egg. Barry was uncertain of the number of sperm needed to
turn an egg into an offspring. Did many sperm penetrating an egg produce
a male? Would a single sperm and egg yield a female, the "weaker" sex?

The clinging together of a *single* sperm and a *single* egg—in toads—was
first observed in 1854 by English entomologist George Newport. But New-

MALE-FEMALE EQUALITY ♦ *Why in humans, and in many species familiar to us, are males and females produced in nearly equal numbers? (Actually, males are slightly more common than females at birth, but differential mortality of males leads to a female majority in later life.) After all, one man can impregnate many women.*

If, say, one male can mate with nine females, and the population contains 100 individuals, why doesn't nature makes ten males and ninety females? Many men think they would prefer such odds.

If Darwinian natural selection existed to favor only large populations, then this scheme of male-female imbalance might work. But natural selection works by the struggle of individuals to maximize their own reproductive success.

In a world in which ten males inseminated ninety females, most of the offspring would be siblings or half siblings. Many children would have different mothers but share the same father. The mating of brothers and sisters, or half brothers and half sisters, is dangerous because bad genes get to express themselves and weaken the population. Thus a single father would not be maximizing his reproductive DNA success by producing generations of closely related males and females.

Consequently, a large number of different males exist—in a nearly one-to-one ratio with females—to ensure that future generations are not fertilized by their siblings. In insect species where "sib mating" is commonplace, females can, and often do, greatly outnumber males.

port's microscope was not powerful enough to allow him to learn what happened after the two units touched.

It was not until 1877 that Swiss biologist Hermann Fol actually observed the *entry* of a sperm into an ovum—of a sea urchin—thereby demonstrating how pregnancy actually occurs.

At the same time, German zoologist Oskar Hertwig observed that once fertilization took place, the egg immediately formed a shell that prevented competing sperm from entering—and within minutes the fertilized egg began to divide. Since only the head of the spermatozoon made it into the egg (the

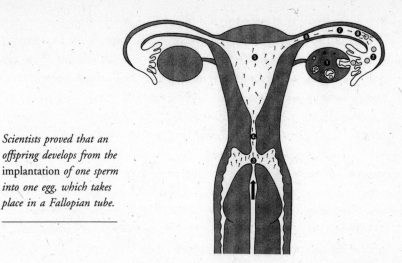

Scientists proved that an offspring develops from the implantation of one sperm into one egg, which takes place in a Fallopian tube.

tail dropped off), Hertwig concluded that the head of the sperm was the *nucleus* of the cell, and that "fertilization is based on the fusion of sexually differentiated cell nuclei."

Thus, little more than a century ago, science proved that an offspring is produced by the process of fusion: one sperm implants itself into a single egg.

Chromosomes and DNA

In 1895, German cell biologist Theodor Boveri counted the chromosomes (Greek *chroma,* "color" + *soma,* "body") in cells and concluded that half of an offspring's genetic endowment is contributed by the father, half by the mother. For the first time in history, the two sexes were shown to make equal contributions to a new life.

Soon thereafter, scientists realized that there were two basic kinds of chromosomes: autosomes, which control the inheritance of all characteristics except sex-related ones, are controlled by the second type, sex chromosomes. Humans have twenty-two pairs of autosomes and one pair of sex chromosomes—an X in the female, and a Y in the male.

Finally, in 1944 a group of American bacteriologists, led by Oswald T. Avery, demonstrated that the fundamental material of heredity, which exists within the genes that make up the chromosomes, was deoxyribonucleic acid, *DNA.* The science of modern genetics was born.

KICKED IN THE NUTS ◆ *Every boy learns early in life how painful it is to have his testes struck hard. The pain radiates instantly from the testes deep into the abdomen, registering like an intense stomach ache. There's a reason for that.*

The testes are rich in nerve endings. The tiniest pinprick to a gonad is painful—even the thought of having his gonads assaulted makes a man flinch. During embryonic life, the testes form in the abdomen, near the stomach and kidneys. The nerve and blood vessels of the testes remain attached there even after the gonads descend to hang freely in his scrotal sac. That's why a kick to the balls feels like a punch in the stomach. To rephrase the cliché: there are indeed more ways to a man's stomach than through his mouth, and one is through his balls.

On the other hand, the nerves of the scrotum are related to the ones that connect the skin of the thigh to the spinal cord. Thus lightly stroking a man's inner thigh is as pleasurable and erotic to him as stroking his scrotum.

MISCONCEPTIONS ABOUT BIRTH FROM AROUND THE WORLD ◆

*S*cience has exhaustively detailed the dance of conception, but throughout the world many peoples still harbor their own traditional ideas about birth. Yale medical anthropologist Carol Laderman has surveyed these notions:

• **Frequent Sex.** The Mount Hagen people of New Guinea in the South Pacific believe that a child is formed from stored menstrual blood and semen. During gestation, the father helps form the child's body by frequent acts of intercourse. The more sex the couple has, the more robust the infant will become.

• **Mutual Orgasm.** The Mori of the island of Celebes in Indonesia consider one act of coitus sufficient for procreation—but only if both man and woman achieve orgasm. It is a shared orgasm that causes a mingling of the sexual fluids that yields an offspring.

• **Holy Spirit.** The Trobriand Islanders off eastern New Guinea believe that a woman conceives without male assistance. Penetration by the husband merely "opens the way" so that a heavenly "spirit of birth" can freely enter his wife's unobstructed vaginal passage and impregnate her.

• *Male Conception.* The Malays of southeast Asia maintain that human nature is a combination of animal instincts and rationality. Men, they claim, are more rational than women, so a baby forms in its father's *brain.*

A father is pregnant for forty days, while the fetus travels from his brain to his liver, the "center of emotions." The father-with-child experiences strange food cravings similar to those his wife will later experience. After the baby has absorbed its father's rationality and emotions, it travels to the tip of his penis and is shot into the mother's womb.

• *Tasty Testes.* In many parts of the world, men wishing to father children try to increase their odds by eating sheep or bull testicles. Testicles are also believed to be an "aphrodisiac" (from Aphrodite, the Greek goddess of love), which increases the eater's sex drive, allowing him to copulate repeatedly. Even better than eating animal testes is to swallow the balls of prisoners captured from neighboring tribes.

"Cum", "Come"; England, Post-Sixteenth Century •

A come-on is an inducement, often of a sexual nature. A *come-hither* look is a flirtatious invitation. A *comely person* is a handsome man or beautiful woman. A *comer* is a person who shows promise of success—or a man who shoots off a heavy load of cum; he's also a cummer. *To come off* can mean to reach orgasm prematurely. *To come out* means to make one's homosexuality public knowledge. A *comeback* is a witty retort.

"Come" is a rich word. It has many nonsexual uses, but most of them can, through a slightly altered context, become sexually charged. How did such an ancient, practical, and innocent four-letter word *come* to be so erotic? Even its past tense, *came,* is sexually charged.

The verb "come" is from the Old English *cuman,* meaning "to go" from a place thought of as "there" to a place thought of as "here."

In Shakespeare's era, the written word flourished; and through the invention of the printing press more than a hundred years earlier, books were becoming commonplace. Writers who addressed the subject of sex searched endlessly for euphemisms for bawdy or sexually explicit words, which could not be printed. At some point early in the seventeenth century, the phrase "to come at" became associated with sexual intercourse; an aroused man "came at" his lover or, in a gentler sense, "came unto" her. Readers knew that the euphemism meant "to copulate."

During this period a sweet, thick, milky-white, English honey became known as "coome." It may have been an innocent name, but most likely it wasn't: the male ejaculate was already being called "coome"—or "come."

But the erotic word, meaning both coitus and ejaculate, was hard to spot on the written page, since "come" had so many innocent, nonsexual meanings. It could appear in a novel hundreds of times and never have a sexual shading. Linguists believe this is why writers began to spell the word "cum"—to make it jump off the page. Horny eyes scanning a book for sexual highlights could easily spot the titillating spelling.

CUMMERBUND = LOINCLOTH ◆

When a man wears a tuxedo, he usually wraps a cummerbund around his waist. He probably doesn't know that the word predates the tuxedo—which originated as formal dress in Tuxedo Park, New York, in 1886—and is sexually charged.

Centuries ago, in Persia, a *kamarband* was a wide cotton cloth that a groom wrapped around his loins during the marriage ceremony. By tightly binding his penis and testicles he was displaying his modesty—and perhaps his virginity—to his bride-to-be. We might say that he would not yet "come onto her" or "cum." Once the couple was pronounced husband and wife, the man unwrapped his privates by ceremoniously removing the *kamarband*: *kamar + band*, "loin" + "band."

With the passage of time, many customs lose their original intent and become meaningless formalized practices. This happened with the *kamarband*. By the time the British had settled in the Middle East, the loincloth of modesty was worn by future husbands merely as a decorative *waistband*: it had moved up from the groin. The British spelled the word "cummerbund," which was something of a transliteration, but that spelling is coincidentally significant. The English verb "cumber" means to hinder by obstruction or interference—just what the band of modesty was once intended to do.

NEW YORKERS VERSUS LOS ANGELES MEN ◆ *The city in which a man lives may have something to do with his sperm count. Environment and/or diet may be a factor.*

A 1996 study of sperm counts in several American cities found that the highest levels, or most potent men, lived in New York City. New York males had an average of 131.5 million sperm (per milliliter of semen), while, for instance, Minnesota men had 100.8 million and Los Angeles men only 72.7 million.

Dr. Harry Fisch of Columbia Presbyterian Medical Center (himself a New Yorker) conducted the study and admitted to being puzzled by the results. Fisch's work was published in Fertility and Sterility, *and an independent study from Seattle later arrived at similar conclusions.*

Just two months before Fisch's work was published, *the* British Medical Journal *reported that men born in the 1970s had 25 percent lower sperm counts on average than men born in the 1950s. Environmental pollutants were thought to be the culprit, and the scientists who had conducted the study predicted that the average male, living in an industrial country, would fall below the fertility threshold by the middle of the next century. A dire forecast.*

"In reality, there is no decline in the fertility of men," Fisch argues. "There's been so much hysteria and speculation of late." In fact, Fisch's sperm count levels are about the same as those found by researchers in the 1940s. "There's really been no change in the past fifty years," he says confidently.

Are environmental toxins wreaking havoc with human sperm? Dozens of animal species—Florida alligators, Lake Michigan mink, Baltic Sea fish—have suffered documented cases of shriveled penises and testicles, "feminized" male behavior, and infertility problems, all from pollutants. Are humans in for the same troubles? Only time will tell. At stake is nothing less than the human species' ability to reproduce itself.

WHY DOES ORGASM EXIST? ◆

*M*en and women enjoy orgasms. Do cats and dogs? Does a male fish like to ejaculate? Does a female fly enjoy being mounted?

The simpler the creature, the more difficult it is to determine whether its sexual copulation is pleasurable, much less intensely orgasmic. Nonetheless, so many mammals court sex so aggressively it must offer some pleasurable reward. Scientists use terms like "estrus frenzy" or "ejaculatory reflex." Only for humans do they dare use "orgasm," an interesting word:

Orgasm derives from the Greek *orgasmos,* meaning "to swell as if with moisture," which is exactly what an excited penis does; it swells with blood. To the Greeks, *orgasmos* also meant "lust."

The Indo-European root of the Greek word is *werg,* "to swell with sap or anger." The Sanskrit equivalent is *urja,* meaning "violence and vigor"—an apt description of copulation at the moment of climax.

The spelling "orgasm" entered English around 1763.

Human males definitely experience orgasms; females, studied less than males, can often achieve it. The real question is why human females have orgasms at all.

There are two schools of thought on the question.

One holds that women have orgasms because men do. Female orgasm may be more a social than sexual function. If nature had really wanted women to experience orgasm every time, it would have designed her genitals in a simpler, more sensitive fashion. The clitoris would be larger and more conveniently situated for easy stimulation during intercourse.

The second school of thought holds that female orgasm has a reproductive purpose though no one is sure exactly what it is. One belief is that orgasm influences the motion of the vagina and uterus to facilitate the mobility of sperm. If true, a women who experiences regular orgasms has a higher chance of becoming pregnant. Conversely, an inorgasmic woman might remain infertile—though obviously women can and do conceive without achieving orgasm, as in rape, for instance.

Have human females lost some earlier facility for orgasm? Some sex researchers believe that might be the case. Their speculation is based on the fact that human females, unlike species that experience periods of reproductive "heat," can have intercourse at any time, whether or not they are fertile. Thus, much of human female sex is social, performed for pair-bonding purposes, or to release bottled-up daily tension, or a wife is merely submitting to her husband's demands. Over time, orgasm took a backseat to these other factors.

MALE ORGASM—THE BIG O ◆

*T*echnically speaking, *orgasm* is a nervous-system response, while *ejaculation* is a reproductive one. Boys as young as seven can experience orgasms with no ejaculate. On the other hand, very old men can ejaculate without orgasm.

The Big O is not always so big even for young men. A teenage boy who masturbates several times within a short period soon realizes that each orgasm decreases in pleasurable intensity, and each ejaculate is less in volume. Hold back sex for several days and the Big O is Jumb-O.

Men know that an orgasm can be a powerful muscle relaxant, a great way to relieve stress. There is a physiological reason for this, which also explains why men fall asleep so easily after sex. Here's what happens to a man during orgasm:

Thirteen Stages of Male Orgasm
1. The shaft of his penis reaches its maximum length, width, and rigidity.
2. The head of the penis, or glans, swells and darkens due to vasocongestion of blood.
3. The opening at the tip of the penis widens and is moistened with fluid from the Cowper's glands.
4. His testes enlarge by 50 to 100 percent of their normal size. They rise and rotate to come into close contact with his body.
5. His blood pressure shoots from an average systolic of 120 to as much as 220.
6. His heart rate accelerates from 70 beats a minute to over 150—and may soar to 180.
7. His breathing rate increases by a factor of three, becoming rapid and shallow.
8. His body muscles are in a state of high tension. His face grimaces, hands claw, toes curl, feet arch, and his vocal cords can emit some inhuman, animalistic cries.
9. All rational thought processes in the brain are swamped by the sensation of intense pleasure. He's all boner and no brain.

WHEN DO GIRLS BECOME FERTILE? ◆ *We say a girl becomes fertile at puberty, after her first menstruation, but that is not exactly true. Puberty, especially in females, is not a single event but a complex process, a period of sexual maturation.*

Conception is impossible without the presence of several hormonal conditions, which are not usually present at the time of the first menstruation. Furthermore, to bring a fetus to term requires even more complex hormonal chemistry, which a very young girl, even if she conceives, still may lack.

For most girls, there is an appreciable period following the first menstruation when they are infertile, known as the adolescent sterility period. In some females it can last two years or longer. However, no sexually active girl should be lulled into a sense of false security, since the window of infertility can vary widely.

10. His nipples swell, harden, and, in some men, become highly sensitive to touch.

11. A sex flush of blood fans out over his body, reddening his skin, especially the face, chest, and buttocks.

12. The erectile tissues in his nose, similar to erectile tissues in his penis, swell; some men, to breathe, experience an attack of sneezing.

13. The instant after orgasm, sweat breaks out over his body, especially on the palms and feet. Some men are drenched with perspiration.

After that workout, who wouldn't be exhausted and ready for sleep?

CHAPTER 14

ℬattle of the 𝒮exes

DOUBLE STANDARD TO EQUAL RIGHTS

Nobody will ever win the battle of the sexes.
There's too much fraternizing with the enemy.

HENRY KISSINGER

"SEXISM"; 1968 ◆

𝒮exism is probably as old as human sex itself, but the word "sexism" has been around for only thirty years. According to the *Merriam-Webster Collegiate Dictionary*:

- *Sexism*, 1968, [*sex* + *-ism* (as in *racism*)]. (1) prejudice or discrimination based on sex; especially discrimination against women. (2) behavior, conditions, or attitudes that foster stereotypes of social roles based on sex.
- *Male chauvinist pig* is another 1960s term, though *chauvinism* was coined more than one hundred years earlier, based on Nicolas Chauvin, a character noted for his excessive patriotism and devotion to Napoleon in Théodore and Hippolyte Cogniard's 1831 stage work *La Cocarde tricolore*.

Men have done some pretty dreadful things to women in the name of sex. They locked wives in chastity belts. They over-praised virginity so that every woman with a normal sex urge felt like a whore. They created a double standard between the sexes. They denied women the right to vote on the assumption that their brains were smaller than their breasts.

Every man at some point in his life has probably made a dirty sexist dig:

"I never turned over a fig leaf that didn't have a price tag on the other side." Saul Bellow.

"No man should marry until he has studied anatomy and dissected at least one woman." Honoré de Balzac

"When a woman becomes a scholar, there is something wrong with her sex organs." Friedrich Nietzsche.

"Women and people of low birth are very hard to deal with. If you are friendly with them, they get out of hand, and if you keep your distance, they resent it." Confucius.

"A woman carrying a Torah is like a pig at the Wailing Wall." Rabbi Yehuda Meir Getz.

Today feminists hurl their own barbs:

"If they could put one man on the moon, why can't they put them all?" Rosanne Barr.

"Can you imagine a world without men? No crime and lots of happy fat women." Nicole Hollander.

American anthropologist Margaret Mead, who studied the war of the sexes in various cultures, came to two conclusions: (1) "Mothers are a biological necessity; fathers are a social invention." (2) "A man's role is uncertain, undefined, and perhaps unnecessary. By a great effort man has hit upon a method of compensating himself for his basic inferiority."

THE RIGHT TO VOTE; 1920 ◆

*M*ost young people today don't realize how recently women won the right to vote—"suffrage," from the Latin *suffragium*, "a vote."

For centuries, women's minds were considered to be child-like, cluttered with too many nonsensical notions and romantic fantasies to grasp the intricacies of "hard" subjects like science, medicine, and politics. A wife was a man's *property*, and it was the father who *owned* the children: he could sell them, or trade them.

The first nation to recognize women as the voting equal of men was New Zealand in 1893. Seeing no national deterioration on the island, nearby Australia allowed its women to vote in 1902. Finland came next (1906),

With the suffrage movement women said they'd had enough of being treated as second-class human beings.

followed by Norway (1913). Women then won the right to vote in Soviet Russia, Germany, Austria, Poland, and Czechoslovakia. Finally, in 1920, American women were considered smart enough to assist in electing president and vice president.

American women had been fighting for that right for about seventy years. Why did it take so long? Here's a sampling of the opposition they came up against:

"Nothing could be more anti-Biblical than letting women vote." Harper's Magazine, *November 1853*

"Give women the political right to vote and be voted for, render it feasible for them to enter the arena of political strife . . . and what remains of family union will soon be dissolved." Catholic World, *May 1869.*

"Sensible and responsible women do not want to vote. The relative positions to be assumed by man and woman in the working out of our civilization were assigned long ago by a higher intelligence than ours." Former President Grover Cleveland, 1905

Women had been treated so dreadfully by men for so many centuries that many women felt they actually *were* too dumb to vote. In March of 1892, Mrs. Elizabeth Lynn Linton wrote:

The Women's Suffrage Movement is an epidemic of vanity and restlessness—a disease as marked as measles or smallpox. . . . Hereafter this outbreak will stand in history as an instance of national sickness, of moral decadence, of social disorder.

In France, women didn't get the right to vote until 1944; in Italy and Japan, not until 1945. Canadian women didn't get the right to vote until 1948, and Mexican women had to wait until 1953. In Saudi Arabia, women still can't vote.

Let's look at the origins of some negative words that have been used on women:

"BITCH"; ENGLAND, VICTORIAN ERA ◆

*B*itch" is from the Old English *bicce,* meaning a "female dog" or any other carnivorous mammal. It is also a contemptuous term for a bad-tempered, malicious, or promiscuous women—as judged by the name-caller. A "bitch" is a man-eater.

Until the Victorian era, "bitch" was not a bad word. A female dog was a "bitch." A fun-loving woman might affectionately be called a "pleasant bitch" or even an "agreeable bitch"—the latter phrase was used as a compliment by Jonathan Swift as late as 1713. African American men at one time called their wives and girlfriends "black bitches" with no disrespect intended. For centuries, a male clown or court jester could be called a "comical bitch."

According to the *Oxford English Dictionary,* the taboo against the word "bitch," in particular in regard to women, began in the nineteenth century: "Not now in decent use; but formerly common in literature."

In 1841, four years after Victoria became queen, the *OED* dropped all definitions of "bitch" because the word had become street slang. Many upper-class British stopped calling their female dogs "bitch" and used terms like "lady dog," "she dog," and "doggess"—like "goddess." The great eighteenth-century British lexicographer Samuel Johnson wrote that one day his mother insulted him by calling him a puppy—"I asked her if she knew what they called a puppy's mother?"

"Bitch Goddess"

Linguists are not certain why "bitch" passed from being a benign word, often an endearment, to a taboo. Some theorize that its explosive sound made it ideal for firing off as a slur. The psycholinguistics of all curse words require that they carry maximal energy on minimal sound, a spiked waveform characteristic of consonants. This gives the word energetic punch, making it "explosive."

The word "bitch" was first recorded as a verb—"to chronically complain about something"—in 1823.

Bitch goddess, first recorded in 1906, originally meant "worldly success." Today it characterizes a particularly "bitchy" woman.

"BIMBO"; AMERICA, THE ROARING TWENTIES ◆

The Jazz Age produced scores of catchy, flashy words for females, and it is during this period that "bimbo" came into use. First it meant a tramp or prostitute, then a promiscuous flapper, and finally a dumb woman—or at least perceived as dumb. During Prohibition, when the Sicilian Mafia got a toehold in America, many Italian terms entered the language. It's thought that "bimbo" is from the Italian *bimbo,* "baby."

The term became popular during the 1930s, through the detective novel. The genre helped perpetuate the stereotype of the beautiful but dumb blonde who is taken out for a night on the town in exchange for sexual favors. The phrase "I am not a bimbo" enjoyed a certain popularity in the 1980s.

English novelist P. G. Wodehouse departed from the typical use of the word in *Full Moon* (1947), mentioning male "bimbos who went about the place making passes at innocent girls after discarding their wives."

"BATTLE-AX"; POST-FOURTEENTH CENTURY ◆

A "battle-ax," we say, is an ugly woman, whose face looks like it's been axed in a battle of the sexes; she may also be sharp-tongued and domineering, usually past childbearing years. She may also be big and powerful.

In the fourteenth century, a "battle-ax" was a broadax that had long been used as a weapon of war. Over time, a damaged or grotesque human face was said to be "battle-axed," which gradually evolved into the put-down "battle-ax."

A story surrounding the word's homegrown origin is related by Hugh Rawson in *Wicked Words:*

The word "floozy" means "tasteless, showy" and has long implied that a woman was morally loose.

Legend has it that the term honors the women who produced Battle-Ax Cut Plug chewing tobacco at the processing plant in Lexington, Kentucky, around the turn of the century. Little red axes adorned the tin tags attached to the plugs and the women workers, being of a rather rough-and-ready nature, came to be known to the local gentry as battle-axes.

"DITZ"; AMERICA, 1960S ◆

To call a woman a "ditz" is to imply that she's empty-headed. The slang seems to be of recent origin, going back no further than the 1960s, when it first appeared in print. It may be a variant of "dizzy," a popular 1920s expression—as in "She's a dizzy blonde."

Interestingly, there is a gender bias to "dizzy." Applied to a man, the term can be an endearment, as it was for jazz musician Dizzy Gillespie and baseball player Dizzy Dean.

"Ditz" may also have come from "ditty"—Middle English *dite*—a simple song or silly limerick.

"FLOOZY"; AMERICA, 1910S ◆

A "floozy" is a cheap, flashy, low-class women who may or may not be a prostitute—the implication is that she's morally loose. It's an early twentieth-century word, thought to come from the British *flossy*, meaning "tasteless" and "showy."

"HUSSY"; ENGLAND, 1505 ♦

A "hussy" is a bawdy, saucy minx, a young woman who is sexually playful and may very well "put out." The term originated from the legitimate Middle English *huswif,* meaning "housewife," or the mistress of a household: *hus* = "house" + *wif* = "wife."

A *huswife* was frugal, strict, and ran all the domestic aspects of family life. The word—and the variant "hussy"—applied mainly to lower-class house-wives, but by the seventeenth century "hussy" had become a rude address for any woman perceived as bossy and authoritative. Later, it took on sexual overtones, as in "shameless hussy."

Today "housewife" itself has come under attack as sexist; a woman who chooses to stay at home to devote herself to child rearing and running a household is properly called a "homemaker." A homewrecker is a hussy.

"TAIL"; ENGLAND, PRE-SIXTEENTH CENTURY ♦

A sexually desirable woman is a "tail," and intercourse with her is getting "a piece of tail." In the eighteenth century, a prostitute was called a "tail."

The word is, in a way, a curious male projection of his desire for a woman onto that woman herself: *penis* is Latin for "tail."

Shakespeare used the word "tail" to mean both "penis" and "vagina" in the same exchange, as we saw in the bawdy banter between Petruchio and Katherine in *The Taming of the Shrew.* Petruchio teases, "Who knows not where a wasp does wear his sting? In his tail [penis]." Katherine chides, "Yours, if you talk of tails [penises]. And so farewell." Petruchio retorts, "What, with my tongue in your tail [vagina]?"

Shakespeare also loved to pun on the words "tail" and "tale," giving a sexual undercurrent to an otherwise straightforward sentence, as in *Othello*:

CLOWN: Why, masters, have your instruments [genitalia] been in Na-
ples, that they speak i' th' nose thus? [An allusion to syphilis, the
"Neapolitan disease"].
MUSICIAN: How, sir, how?
CLOWN: Are these, I pray you, called wind instruments [a pun on
fellatio]?
MUSICIAN: Aye, marry, are they, sir.

CLOWN: O, thereby hangs a tale [tail].

MUSICIAN: Whereby hangs a tale, sir?

CLOWN: Marry, sir, by many a wind instrument that I know.

As Norrie Epstein makes clear in *The Friendly Shakespeare*, "There is no denying it: Shakespeare was not merely bawdy—the usual term used to convey full-blooded Elizabethan lustiness—he was stunningly vulgar"—and immensely popular with audiences. Today we often think of Shakespeare as highbrow, but in his own day the Bard was enjoyed—and his raunchy wordplay well understood—by people of all classes. Unfortunately, in high school texts, the sexual fun and games in Shakespeare's plays receives a vague asterisked explanation: "bawdy Elizabethan pun"—as if an explicit explanation would shock today's sexually active students.

"TAMALE"; MEXICO, 1850S ◆

The word "tamale" is Mexican Spanish, from the Nahuatl *tamalli*, meaning "steamed cornmeal dough." The food item is made of ground meat seasoned with chili, rolled in cornmeal dough, wrapped in cornhusks, and steamed. The word entered English usage in the 1850s, and from the start it had sexual overtones. A tamale is to be eaten, and so is a delectable woman.

Mexican Americans also popularized calling a woman a *hot tamale* and, more recently, a *taco belle*. Men have always thought of the pleasures of eating and of women in the same gestalt, satisfying both gastronomic and libidinal appetites.

"TART"; ENGLAND, POST-FIFTEENTH CENTURY ◆

The British gave us "tart" for a morally loose woman and also a professional prostitute. The highly suggestive word is from the Middle English *tarte*, a small pastry shell (read "vagina") filled with jam and sweet cream (read "semen" or "a woman's own sexual juices"). A tart is also a pie, and "pie" has long been a euphemism for female genitalia—as in "hair pie." Pastry chefs today make all kinds of tarts, filling frilled or fluted doughs with creams, custards, and puddings. The dessert tart arrives linguistically packed with both calories and double entendres.

Tarts have been getting sweeter over the centuries. At one time, a rhubarb

Two "tarts" stage an erotic show for a paying voyeuristic client.

tart, made with little or no sugar, was indeed *tart*—"sharp in taste, sour." That word comes from a different Middle English term, *teart,* meaning "sour" or "acidic." It's also been suggested that calling a woman a "tart" might have originated from the act of cunnilingus, since vaginal juices, which are protectively antibacterial, are acidic in nature and can be "tart."

Tart up, meaning to dress up excessively or in a fancy style, originated in the 1930s.

"FOX"; POPULARIZED IN THE 1960S ◆

For centuries men have been calling a sexy woman a "fox"—and a "beaver" and a "bunny"—or, if she's unattractive, a "cow" or a "dog." The list of animals is long. In each case there is some animal trait, either appearance or behavior, that explains the association. With "fox," the association may be with the animal's large bushy *tail,* since that word is packed with sexual meanings. Or it may be because the fox has delicate features and is smart, clever, and elusive.

It may also be due to the fundamental meaning of "fox"—from the German *Fuchs* (which sounds something like "fuck"), whose Indo-European base, *puk,* meant "thick-haired and bushy"—an apt description of pubic hair. Is a woman a fox because she has a bushy vagina?

In the United States, heavyweight boxer Muhammad Ali helped popularize

---

LAST CALL SYNDROME ◆ *Around closing time, a bartender an-nounces a "last call" for drinks. It is also the last desperate interval for customers to hitch up for the night. It turns out that at closing time men and women regard each other quite differently.*

Researchers studied more than two hundred customers in a bar between the hours of 9 P.M. and midnight. They regularly asked clients to rate the sexual attractiveness of members of the opposite sex from across the room. A woman's perception of a certain man's desirability did not significantly change as the hours ticked toward closing time.

Men, however, perceived women as getting increasingly attractive as the evening passed and last call drew near. A woman who had been rated "undesirable" at 9 P.M. was, by midnight, "acceptable." Many average-looking women had, in three hours' time, become "foxes."

Had the men gotten drunk? Is that what lowered their standards?

The researchers tested that possibility. Whether a man had one drink or six, his perception of a particular woman's sexual attractiveness increased steadily as midnight approached. Booze had nothing to do with it. What counted was the possibility of scoring that night.

---

the word in the 1960s, using it in many of his rhymes delivered in the ring. A French film, released here in 1958 as *The Foxiest Girl in Paris*, also used the word in its title.

"VIXEN"; SIXTEENTH CENTURY ◆

To call a woman a "vixen" is to imply that she's loud, formidable, and shrewish. A vixen is a female fox, with the word coming from the Middle English (southern dialect) *fixen*, "she-fox." In protecting her cubs, a vixen can be formidable, and perhaps through this association the word was applied to women. A sexy, desirable girl is a "fox" (the male animal's name), but an off-putting shrewish girl is a "vixen" (the female animal's name). Is this a sexist use of slang?

The term "vixen" can also describe a stylish, sexy, attractive woman who might be playfully aggressive—very much like a "fox."

"JAP"; AMERICA, 1970S ◆

*T*his acronym for Jewish American Princess, which implies a rich, spoiled, sexually cold woman, became popular in the 1970s. As Bruce Jay Friedman wrote in *The Lonely Guy's Book of Life* (1978), "The big news is The Return of the Jewish Woman, or Jewish-American Princess, as it were. Many have been to Tibet. Others have faithfully attended Masturbation Class. A lot of them kiss back."

The term, which began as a joke, turned into a hurtful slur. "The humor began to wear thin," writes Hugh Rawson in *Wicked Words*, "and JAP jokes were the subject of a 1987 Conference on Current Stereotypes of Jewish Women, sponsored by the American Jewish Committee. Speakers asserted that the jokes were rooted in anti-Semitism as well as sexism."

"What had started as humor has escalated into attacks," Susan Weidman Schneider told the conference audience. "Imagine for a moment that you are an 18-year-old female Jewish student at a college football game. And when you get up to get a soda you hear someone yell 'JAP! JAP! JAP!' Then the cry is picked up by everybody sitting in the stadium. *JAP! JAP! JAP!*'"

MADONNA-WHORE SYNDROME; ANTIQUITY TO PRESENT ◆

*M*any men wrestle throughout their lives with the so-called madonna-whore syndrome: the idealization of woman as "virgin, wife, and mother" versus the eroticization of woman as "hussy, whore, and tease." Much of the pornography industry is built on this dichotomy, which also underlies a good deal of the violence that men inflict on women.

Religion's Role

The view of women as temptresses, sinners, necessary evils, and second-class citizens is ancient in most patriarchal societies. In the Western world, it reached a frightening peak and became misogyny in the early centuries of Christianity. With Jesus Christ's birth *mother*—also a lifelong *virgin*—held up as the idealization of womanhood and the model to which every Christian woman should aspire, a woman was supposed to bear children but never sully herself with sexual thoughts or pleasures. This impossible "virgin-mother" image, which contradicts the biology of nature, has generated repercussions that still resonate.

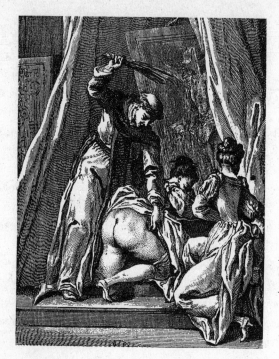

*"The Flagellation of the
Penitents," Charles Monnet
(1732–1808).*

Until quite recently, for instance, the Catholic church maintained that the
only reason for a husband and wife to have sex was to conceive a child. In
the late 1960s, when American women were burning their bras in the wom-
en's liberation revolution, Pope Paul VI addressed an audience of obstetri-
cians and gynecologists in Rome, telling them how their profession must
view each and every woman:

> *Woman is a vision of virginal purity which restores the highest moral
> and emotional sentiments of the human heart . . . She is the creature most
> docile, singing, praying, yearning, weeping, she seems to converge naturally
> towards a unique and supreme figure, immaculate and sorrowful, which a
> privileged Woman, blessed among all, was destined to become, the Virgin
> Mother of Christ, Mary.*

In stating that every living woman "seems to converge naturally towards"
the immaculate Virgin Mary, the pontiff reinforced the centuries-old impossible role of woman as virgin *and* wife/mother—the madonna-whore
syndrome.

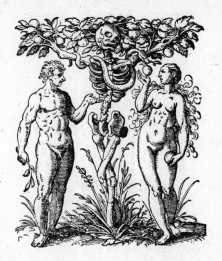

Macabre representation of the "Tree of Knowledge and Death," in which a woman's sin brings spiritual death upon the human race.

Over the ages, the dichotomy helped give rise to the double standard between the sexes.

DOUBLE STANDARD; ANTIQUITY TO WOMEN'S LIB ◆

*W*omen's studies programs look back over history and record men's attitudes toward women—some favorable, many unfavorable. In seeking to answer the modern question of what roles women should play in society, feminists scour the pages of the past for a perspective on the way men have thought about the "fairer sex," the "weaker sex."

How did the double standard—one category of rights and privileges for men, an inferior one for women—come about?

The answer in part can be found by taking a chronological march through time looking at influential men's attitudes toward women. This is done in considerable detail by Rosemary Agonito in *History of Ideas on Women* (1977).

Moses, c. 1300 B.C.E.
Woman as God's afterthought; the origin of sin and downfall of humankind.

The concept comes from the Book of Genesis, which relates the story of the creation of Eve from Adam's rib and her subsequent disobedience in eating from the tree of forbidden knowledge. Ecclesiasticus, a book of proverbs in the Apocrypha, sums up the female gender:

Plato, Greek philosopher.

Woman is the origin of all sin and it is through her that we all die.

Plato, 427–347 B.C.E.
Woman as man's equal in matters of state but not of sex:

> *Men and women are to have a common way of life . . . common
> education, common children; and they are to watch over the citizens in
> common whether abiding in the city or going out to war; they are to keep
> watch together, and to hunt together as dogs do; and always and in all
> things, as far as they are able, women are to share with the men . . . In
> so doing they will do what is best, and will not violate, but preserve the
> natural relations of the sexes.*

Aristotle, 384–322 B.C.E.
Woman as a mutilated and incomplete man—a "defective male."

For Aristotle, women lacked the force to create human life, which sprang
solely from the male ejaculate, and matured and was nourished in the female
womb. The male, not the female, created life, an error that would go unchallenged for eighteen centuries. Although Aristotle was a devoted pupil of
Plato, he held the pre-Socratic view that woman was "colder" than man and
therefore had less of a soul, and was less capable of rational thought, and
consequently subordinate to the rule of men:

"Phyllis Riding Aristotle," Hans Baldung Grien, 1513.

The nature of man is the most rounded off and complete, and consequently in man the qualities or capacities are found in their perfection. Woman is more compassionate than man, more easily moved to tears, at the same time more jealous, more querulous, more apt to scold and to strike . . .

She is, furthermore, more prone to despondency and less hopeful than the man, more void of shame or self-respect, more false of speech, more deceptive, and of more retentive memory [i.e., a woman never forgets a slight]. She is also more wakeful, more shrinking, more difficult to rouse to action, and requires a smaller quantity of nutriment . . .

Out of these two relationships between man and woman, master and slave, the family first arises . . . As the poet says of women, "Silence is a woman's glory," but this is not equally the glory of man.

Plutarch, c. 46–c. 120 C.E.

Woman as more virtuous than man but like a child.

For Plutarch, a husband must own all property and act as both his wife's father *and* mother, since a female never grows up to be a real adult. It never seems to have dawned on Plutarch that it was society that never allowed women to grew into adults.

HUSBAND: *For father thou and mother art to her;*
She now is thine, and not the parent's care.

The conversion of Paul—after which he gave up sex and wrote of women as temptresses.

WIFE: *And you, my honored husband, are my guide,*
And tutor in philosophy beside,
From whose instructions I at once improve
The fruits of knowledge and the sweets of love.

Saint Paul, d. 67 [?] C.E.; Apostle
Woman as wife and mother, subservient at all times.

If a man cannot live an ideal, sexless life, said Saint Paul, "better to marry than to burn":

> *It is good for a man not to touch a woman. Nevertheless, to avoid fornication, let every man have his own wife . . . The wife hath not power of her own body, but the husband: and likewise also the husband hath not power of his own body, but the wife.*
>
> *The man is not of the woman; but the woman of the man. Neither was the man created for the woman; but the woman for the man.*

Tertullian, c. 160–c. 230 C.E.; Theologian
Woman as "a temple built over a sewer."

> *Woman! You are the devil's doorway! You lead astray one whom the devil would not dare attack directly.*

Saint Jerome, monk and scholar, had a highly active libido.

Saint Ambrose, c. 340–397 *C.E.*; Bishop of Milan, Church Father

Virginal woman as the highest ideal.

Chaste and celibate, Saint Ambrose held equally harsh views of women— even married women:

> *I do not condemn marriage, only I consider chastity higher. The former is permissible, the latter I admire.*

Saint Jerome, c. 340–c. 420 *C.E.*; Monk, Scholar, Church Father

Woman as temptress.

Saint Jerome fought a lifelong battle with his active libido:

> *My face was pale and my frame chilled from fasting, yet my mind was burning with the cravings of desire, and the fires of lust flamed up from my flesh . . . I'd gone into the desert to be alone with wild beasts and scorpions, but in my mind woman followed.*

Unable to get women off his mind, he condemned them.

Saint Augustine, 354–430 *C.E.*; Bishop of Hippo

Woman as man's greatest spiritual obstacle to salvation.

For Christianity's most prominent church father, woman had three roles on earth. As temptress, she was an instrument of the devil; as wife, she was the property of her husband; as mother, she was an instrument in God's great design for the continuance of the species:

> *God, then, made man in his own image. He created for him a soul endowed with reason and intelligence, so that he might excel all the creatures of the earth, air, and sea, which were not so gifted. And when he had formed the man out of the dust of the earth . . . He made also a wife for him . . .*
>
> *For not without significance did the apostle say, "And Adam was not deceived, but the woman being deceived was in the transgression": but he speaks thus, because the woman accepted as true what the serpent told her, but the man could not bear to be severed from his only companion, woman, even though this involved a partnership in sin. He was not on this account less culpable, but sinned with his eyes open.*

Saint Thomas Aquinas, c. 1225–1274; Church Doctor
Woman as a "derivative being," a "defective male."

Aquinas adopted Aristotle's idea: a woman does not produce human life but merely allows the "male seed" to grow to term in her womb. A male child is produced by "perfect seed," whereas a female child comes from either "defective seed" or copulation in a windy climate. Aquinas's theology provided the Catholic church with its official philosophy for centuries:

> *It was necessary, as the Scripture says, for woman to be made as a help to man; not, indeed, as a helpmate in other works, as some say, since man can be more efficiently helped by another man in other works; but as a help in the work of generation.*
>
> *Some living things do not possess in themselves the power of generation . . . Among perfect animals the active power of generation belongs to the male sex, and the passive power to the female.*
>
> *As regards the individual nature, woman is defective and misbegotten, for the active force in the male seed tends to the production of a perfect likeness in the masculine sex; while the production of woman comes from defect in the active force or from some material indisposition, or even from some external influence; such as that of a south wind, which is moist.*

Francis Bacon, 1561–1626; Philosopher and Statesman

Woman, marriage, and parenthood as man's greatest impediments to real achievements in life.

The homosexual English philosopher and statesman was extremely hostile toward women, a sex "without merit." Bacon chose celibacy for himself, as recommended by Saint Paul.

During Bacon's era, brutal laws made a wife the exclusive property of her husband, even if he should turn out to be a drunkard and abuser. Bacon suggested that men should avoid even conversation with women, sparing themselves the temptation of feminine wiles—and subsequent fatherhood. In Bacon's eyes, the only good thing a wife and children could do was teach a man discipline:

> *He that hath wife and children hath given hostages to fortune; for they are impediments to great enterprises, either of virtue or mischief. Certainly the best works, and of greatest merit for the public, have proceeded from the unmarried or childless men, which, both in affection and means, have married and endowed the public.*
>
> *The most ordinary cause of a single life is liberty, especially in certain self-pleasing and humorous minds, which are so sensible of every restraint, as they will go near to think their girdles and garters to be bonds and shackles. Unmarried men are best friends, best masters, best servants.*

David Hume, 1711–1776; Scottish Philosopher and Historian

Woman has a greater moral obligation than man.

Woman, having the weaker sex drive, has a greater moral responsibility to remain faithful to her husband. Man, with the higher sex drive, can be expected to wander, though he should not.

For Hume, as for English philosopher and political theorist Thomas Hobbes (1588–1679), a husband, in order to be a good, supporting father, must have absolute certainty that the children his wife bears are biologically his—and not another man's. Without this assurance, no man would make all of the many sacrifices necessary to shelter, support, and educate offspring. Thus a woman must never, ever cheat.

The dilemma thus presented to every wife is sexually submit to your husband in order to become pregnant, but have absolutely no sexual feelings ever for any other man. For Hume and Hobbes, this is achieved by instilling in young girls—from the earliest age, when their minds are most impressionable—a burning desire for motherhood and a total commitment to marital fidelity. Thus emerges the philosophical basis for a "double standard" between the sexes. Hume recognizes that it may not be "just" [equitable] for women, but it is necessary for society:

> As to the obligations which the male sex lie under, with regard to chastity, we may observe, that according to the general notions of the world, they bear nearly the same proportion to the obligations of women . . . 'Tis contrary to the interest of civil society, that men should have an entire liberty of indulging their appetites in venereal enjoyment. But as this interest is weaker than in the case of the female sex, the moral obligation, arising from it, must be proportionally weaker.

Immanuel Kant, 1724–1804; German Philosopher
Woman's greatest attribute is charm, which education diminishes.

For Kant, neither man nor woman is complete; they must come together in marriage to form "a single moral person." The "sublime" male brings to the union a rational mind and desire for learning and self-improvement. The "beautiful" woman contributes gentleness, taste, discretion—and, most of all, charm, her greatest gift. It is with charm that a woman wins a man and keeps him. So important is feminine charm, that Kant warns women against acquiring too much education, since learning diminishes charm and drives men away.

"Even woman's vanity cannot be condemned, since it enhances her charm," writes Rosemary Agonito in *History of Ideas on Woman*, in discussing Kant. "Women have no sense of duty because they live by feelings, while men live by reason. Morality in women amounts to a feeling of propriety, Kant says, avoiding evil because it is ugly, not because it is wrong."

Although man is the noble and sublime gender in Kant's eyes, any woman can acquire a small degree of nobility and sublimity by treasuring her man.

From Kant's *Observations on the Feeling of the Beautiful and Sublime*:

> He who first conceived of woman under the name of the fair sex *probably wanted to say something flattering, but he has hit upon it better than even he himself might have believed . . .*
> Women have a strong inborn feeling for all that is beautiful, elegant, and decorated. Even in childhood they like to be dressed up, and take

pleasure when they are adorned . . . They love pleasantry and can be entertained by trivialities if only these are merry and laughing . . . They have many sympathetic sensations, goodheartedness, and compassion, prefer the beautiful to the useful, and gladly turn abundance of circumstance into parsimony, in order to support expenditure on adornment and glitter.

They have very delicate feelings in regard to the least offense, and are exceedingly precise to notice the most trifling lack of attention and respect toward them. In short, they contain the chief cause in human nature for the contrast of the beautiful qualities with the noble, and they refine even the masculine sex . . .

The virtue of a woman is a beautiful *virtue. That of the male sex should be a* noble *virtue. Women will avoid the wicked not because it is unright, but because it is ugly; and virtuous actions mean to them such as are morally beautiful. Nothing of duty, nothing of compulsion, nothing of obligation! . . . They do something only because it pleases them . . . I do hardly believe that the fair sex is capable of principles, and I hope by that not to offend, for these are also extremely rare in the male.*

Georg Hegel, 1770–1831; German Philosopher

Woman as wife and mother; husband as the absolute ruler of the household.

For Hegel, every woman's role is to shed any feelings of individuality and integrate herself totally into the role of obedient wife and devoted mother. Woman is a being created for total self-sacrifice and self-negation. She must suppress any notion about entering the male realms of politics, education, and science; lacking rational and analytical skills, she's doomed to failure. Only men can think abstractly; women are a bundle of feelings and opinions—not ideas.

Like woman, man must suppress his individuality but to a lesser degree. He does this for the benefit of the state and society as a whole, by becoming a statesman or a scientist—*his* chief roles in life. Fatherhood is his sideline vocation:

> *Women can, of course, be educated, but their minds are not adapted to the higher sciences, philosophy, or certain of the arts. These demand a universal faculty. Women may have happy inspirations, taste, elegance, but they have not the ideal.*
>
> *The difference between man and woman is the same as that between animal and plant. The animal corresponds more closely to the character of*

man, the plant to that of the woman. In woman there is a more peaceful unfolding of nature, a process, whose principle is the less clearly determined unity of feeling.

If women were to control the government, the state would be in danger, for they do not act according to the dictates of universality, but are influenced by accidental inclinations and opinions. The education of woman goes on one hardly knows how, in the atmosphere of picture-thinking, as it were, more through life than through the acquisition of knowledge. Man attains his position only through stress of thought and much specialized effort.

Søren Kierkegaard, 1813–1855; Danish Religious Philosopher

Woman, like man, is a collection of infinite possibilities.

In existentialist philosophy, experiences and choices make a person what he or she is. There are no absolutes, no stereotypes. Subjective reality is the only reality. Given ample freedom, a woman can become whatever she wants to be:

Therefore woman cannot be exhaustively expressed by any formula but is an infinity of finitudes. He who is bent upon thinking her idea is like one who gazes into a sea of nebulous shapes which are constantly forming, or like one who is bewildered by looking at the billows with their foaming crests which constantly elude him; for her idea is only a workshop of possibilities, and for the erotic these possibilities are the never-failing source of enthusiasm.

Arthur Schopenhauer, 1788–1860; German Philosopher

Woman as the weaker sex, gifted with cunning.

All women, in all respects—biological, emotional, intellectual—are inferior to men. Women are by nature silly, childish, willful, and spiteful. They cannot reason clearly or think abstractly at all. Because they cannot even distinguish right from wrong, they must constantly obey men and live by men's rules.

Because women are physically smaller and weaker than men, nature has compensated them with one attribute: cunning. Women are thus masters of pretense and deception, skilled at conniving to get their way in petty things.

German philosopher Schopenhauer argued that a woman's greatest "gift" was cunning; with the promise of sex she could get a man to do almost anything.

No woman is really attractive; most, in fact, are ugly. Women must paint their faces and powder and perfume their bodies in order to attract men, which they do through camouflage and deception.

Schopenhauer is one of history's great misogynistic philosophers. His contempt for women—or fear of them—is unparalleled, even by Christianity's greatest anti-woman saints.

"Women's deficiency in love makes her hate her own sex and unable to love her own children on any level other than the purely instinctive," Rosemary Agonito writes of Schopenhauer's views. "She is capable only of genuinely loving man, since this is her whole goal in life."

Schopenhauer's classic essay *On Women* is so intensely hateful, so relentlessly misogynistic, that one can only laugh—or cry to think that many men in Schopenhauer's day agreed with his ideas. Virtually every negative stereotype ever written about women appears in this essay—and Schopenhauer dreamed up a few new ones as well:

> *With young girls Nature seems to have had in view what, in the language of the drama, is called a* striking effect; *as for a few years she showers them with a wealth of beauty and is lavish in her gift of charm, at the expense of all the rest of their life; so that during those years they may capture the fantasy of some man to such a degree that he is hurried away into undertaking the honorable care of them, in some form or other, as*

long as they live—a step for which there would not appear to be any sufficient warranty if reason only directed his thoughts.

Accordingly, Nature has equipped women, as she does all her creatures, with the weapons and implements requisite for the safeguarding of her existence, and for just as long as it is necessary for her to have them. Here, as elsewhere, Nature proceeds with her usual economy; for just as the female ant, after fecundation, loses her wings, which are then superfluous, nay, actually a danger to the business of breeding; so, after giving birth to one or two children, a woman generally loses her beauty; probably, indeed, for similar reasons.

And so we find that young girls, in their hearts, look upon domestic affairs or work of any kind as a secondary importance, if not actually as a mere jest. The only business that really claims their earnest attention is love, making conquests, and everything connected with this—dress, dancing, and so on . . .

It is only the man whose intellect is clouded by his sexual impulses that could give the name of "the fairer sex" to that under-sized, narrow-shouldered, broad-hipped, and short-legged race. Instead of calling them beautiful, there would be more warrant for describing women as the unaesthetic sex. Neither for music, nor for poetry, nor for fine art, have they really and truly any sense or susceptibility; it is a mere mockery if they make a pretense of it in order to assist their endeavor to please . . .

That woman is by nature meant to obey may be seen by the fact that every woman who is placed in the unnatural position of complete independence, immediately attaches herself to some man, by whom she allows herself to be guided and ruled. It is because she needs a lord and master. If she is a maiden, it will be a lover. If she is a widow, a priest.

Charles Darwin, 1809–1882; Naturalist and Evolutionist

Woman as man's evolutionary equal—but nature has afforded each sex a separate and distinct role.

For centuries before Darwin posited his theory of evolution of the species, philosophers and theologians had pointed to the Book of Genesis as proof that God had created woman as an afterthought, as a "derivative being." Darwin offered impressive evidence that creation was not a mere four thousand years old, as biblical scholars maintained, but millions of years older.

Charles Darwin viewed women as men's "evolutionary equal."

Man and woman came into being simultaneously and evolved side by side —but not with identical skills. Natural selection, said Darwin, made men strong, brave, competitive, and intelligent; whereas women, who have to nurture offspring, were made compassionate, affectionate, self-sacrificing, and dependent:

> *Man is more courageous, pugnacious and energetic than woman, and has more inventive genius. His brain is absolutely larger, but whether or not proportionately to his larger body, has not, I believe, been fully ascertained . . .*
>
> *Woman seems to differ from man in mental disposition, chiefly in her greater tenderness and less selfishness . . . Woman, owing to her maternal instincts, displays these qualities towards her infants in an eminent degree; therefore it is likely that she would often extend them towards her fellow creatures.*
>
> *Man is the rival of other men; he delights in competition, and this leads to ambition which passes too easily into selfishness. These latter qualities seem to be his natural and unfortunate birthright . . .*
>
> *The chief distinction in the intellectual powers of the two sexes is shown by man's attaining to the higher eminence, in whatever he takes up, than can women—whether requiring deep thought, reason, or imagination, or merely the use of senses and hands . . . the average mental power in man must be above that of woman.*

Ralph Waldo Emerson, 1803–1882; Poet, Essayist
Every woman should have the right to vote.

Women's suffrage in America began at the woman's rights convention held in Seneca Falls, New York, in 1848—at a time when most American men felt that women simply did not have the intelligence to elect a president or begin to understand proposed legislation.

One of the most prominent speakers on behalf of women's rights was Ralph Waldo Emerson, who addressed the 1855 National Woman's Rights Convention in Boston:

> *Women are . . . civilizers of mankind. What is civilization? I answer, the power of good women . . . The starry crown of woman is in the power of her affection and sentiment, and the infinite enlargements to which they lead . . .*
>
> *The times are marked by the new attitude of Woman; urging, by argument and by association, her rights of all kinds—in short, to one-half of the world—as the right to education, to avenues of employment, to equal rights of property, to equal rights in marriage, to the exercise of the professions and of suffrage.*

Friedrich Nietzsche, 1844–1900; German Philosopher
Woman may be fun to play around with, but she is a dangerous toy.

The prospects of equal rights for women terrified Nietzsche. For the atheistic philosopher, man was master, woman slave. Men set the rules, women followed them. Men were strong, women weak. Men courageous, women timorous. Men, noble and proud; women, humble and self-loathing. For Nietzsche, women should be bred and trained to serve and entertain men.

Man's one weakness is his sexual desire for women, and women exploit this flaw to the hilt. Indeed, woman's lifelong work is tempting men, in order to bear children and be comfortably kept. Society must therefore produce a breed of Supermen, who are immune to feminine wiles, and copulate merely to continue the species:

> *Everything concerning woman is a puzzle, and everything concerning woman has one solution: it is named pregnancy. For woman, man is a means, the goal is always the child. However, what is a woman for man?*
>
> *The real man wishes for two things: danger and recreation. Hence man wants woman as the most dangerous plaything. Man should be brought up*

*for the purpose of war and woman for the relaxation of the soldier: every-
thing else is foolish . . . Let your hope ask: May I give birth to a
Superman!*

*The soul of a man is deep; his stream thunders through underground
caverns; woman guesses his power but is unable to understand it . . . Do
you go to women? Do not forget the whip!*

Bertrand Russell, 1872–1970:
English Philosopher and Activist
Woman should be liberated to follow her desires.

Russell believed that Christianity, with its repressive view of women and
sex, had turned women into second-class citizens who desperately needed to
be liberated. Russell championed a woman's right not only to vote but also
to sexually govern her own body—to do with it what she wished. He deplored the "double standard" for men and women:

> *Saint Paul introduced an entirely novel view of marriage, that it existed
> not primarily for the procreation of children, but to prevent the sin of
> fornication ["Better to marry than to burn"] . . . Paul's views were em-
> phasized and exaggerated by the early Church [and] did a great deal to
> degrade the position of women . . .*
>
> *Since woman was the temptress, it was desirable to curtail her oppor-
> tunities for leading men into temptation . . . It is only in quite modern
> times that women have regained the degree of freedom which they enjoyed
> in the Roman Empire . . .*
>
> *It is evident that so long as many men for economic reasons find early
> marriage impossible, while many women cannot marry at all, equality as
> between men and women demands a relaxation in the traditional standards
> of feminine virtue. If men are allowed prenuptial intercourse (as in fact
> they are), women must be allowed it also.*

Sigmund Freud, 1856–1939; Father of Psychoanalysis
Woman as a castrated man, consumed with "penis envy."

Freud's ideas on women and sex have had a tremendous influence on our
century. He believed that all children go through a "phallic stage". A young
girl, argued Freud, was satisfied with her clitoris until she glimpsed her first
penis; then she grasped the true measure of her inferiority. She envied the
penis, believed she'd once had one but had been castrated—by her mother

For Freud, women suffered "penis envy."

and for some unknown offense—and, wishing to be a male again, attached herself to her father.

According to Freud, a "healthy" woman grows in time to accept her castrated state and even to embrace her femininity. But deep down, she will always long for a penis (read "every woman needs a man"). A woman who cannot adjust to having been castrated compensates later in life by adopting a "male role"—say, as a CEO, an MD, or a Ph.D.

Only someone with a penis himself would have come to these conclusions, and only an audience of penis owners would have so readily accepted the concept. Had the psychiatric profession then not been almost exclusively male, many of Freud's phallic ideas might well have died on the vine:

> With their entry into the phallic phase [of childhood] the differences between the sexes are completely eclipsed by their agreements. We are now obliged to recognize that the little girl is a little man. In boys, as we know, this phase is marked by the fact that they have learned how to derive pleasurable sensations from their small penis and connect its excited state with their ideas of sexual intercourse.
>
> Little girls do the same thing with their still smaller clitoris . . . all masturbatory acts are carried out on their penis-equivalent . . . in the phallic phase of girls the clitoris is the leading erotogenic zone. But it is not, of course, going to remain so. With the change to femininity the clitoris should wholly or in part hand over its sensitivity, and at the same time its importance, to the vagina. This would be one of the two tasks which a

woman has to perform in the course of her development, whereas the more fortunate man has only to continue at the time of his sexual maturity the activity that he has previously carried out . . .

That is all I have to say to you about femininity. It is certainly incomplete and fragmentary and does not always sound friendly. But do not forget that I have only been describing women in so far as their nature is determined by their sexual function. It is true that that influence extends very far; but we do not overlook the fact that an individual woman may be a human being in other respects as well."

Ashley Montagu, b. 1905; Anglo-American Anthropologist
Woman as the smarter, fitter, overall superior gender.

"The evidence indicates that woman is, on the whole, biologically superior to man," wrote Ashley Montagu. In 1953, Montagu published his groundbreaking book *The Natural Superiority of Women.* Its premise is simple: men have labeled women inferior for centuries because men have been jealous of woman's capacity to give birth, to create life, to perform the greatest act a living creature can perform, propagation of the species. Out of envy, men have debased and bullied women, and labeled childbirth, a joyous miracle, a disgusting and painful travail—which it then became for women. Men used childbirth to frighten and belittle women. According to Montagu, women don't suffer penis envy; men suffer birthing envy.

Women are even physically stronger than men, claimed Montagu. Men have taken to measuring strength in terms of muscle power alone, but women excel in stamina and pain endurance.

Women on the average are smarter too, argued Montagu—when they are allowed to be educated, which men long denied them.

Men are the superior gender only when they are allowed to define the criteria of superiority. Montagu went one step further: woman is a creator and fosters life; man is a warrior and destroys it:

Man's jealousy of woman's capacity to bear children is nowhere better exhibited than in the Old Testament creation story in which man is caused to give birth (from one of his ribs) to woman . . . Their envy of woman's physiological powers causes them to feel weak and inferior, and fear is often added to jealousy. An effective way for men to protect themselves against women, as well as to punish them, is to deprecate their capacities by deprecating their status.

One can deny the virtues of women's advantages by treating them as disadvantages and by investing them with mysterious and dangerous properties (like menstrual blood). By making women objects of fear and something to be avoided as unclean, one can lower the cultural status of women by simple inversion. Their biological advantages are demoted to the status of cultural disadvantages . . .

In all societies women have played a much more important role than their menfolk have been generally inclined to admit. After all, if one is afflicted with feelings of inferiority—as the male is with respect to the female—a strong overcompensatory tendency to play cock o' the roost is likely to develop. It is difficult to admit, even though the dark suspicion may have dawned on one, that women are one's equals, and—perish the thought—they certainly are not one's superiors . . .

The natural superiority of women is a biological fact, and a socially unacknowledged reality. The facts have been available for more than half a century, but in a male-dominated world, in which the inflation of the male ego has been dependent upon the preservation of the myth of male superiority, the significance of those facts has simply been denied attention.

Men's envy of women's capacity to give birth, to create a new life, is evident in the madonna-whore syndrome. Man, in his mind, divides woman into two mutually exclusive categories for his own purposes. The whore satisfies his sexual lust; the virgin, by *not* bearing children, calms his birthing jealousy.

WOMEN ON MEN; 1963 TO PRESENT ◆

*T*he first shot in the women's liberation movement was fired in 1963 with the publication of Betty Friedan's *The Feminine Mystique*. The title referred to the sad, false, dehumanizing ideal to which women—then and in the past—were forced to conform.

We've just surveyed what history's philosophers and theologians have said about women over the centuries. Betty Friedan argued that women had it no better in the early 1960s. Their oppressors then were men in the media, advertising, business, government, and education who produced idealized images of women that few women could live up to. Friedan compared the housewife of the 1950s with a prisoner in a Nazi concentration camp, both dehumanized by their slave status. Both were deprived of freedom, individual identity, and self-respect; and both were imprisoned—in a home and in a cell—where their primary concerns were "simple animal needs": food, cleaning the nest, breeding the next generation. No woman was allowed outside of her home/cell to breathe the fresh air of ideas, creativity, national events, or the world at large.

Friedan, who'd been a magazine writer, claimed that in numerous interviews with housewives she'd come to realize that all suffered from a "problem that has no name":

> *Just what was this problem that has no name? What were the words women used when they tried to express it? Sometimes a woman would say, "I feel empty somehow . . . incomplete." Or she would say, "I feel as if I don't exist." Sometimes she blotted out the feeling with a tranquilizer. Sometimes she thought the problem was with her husband, or her children, or that what she really needed was to redecorate their house, or move to a better neighborhood, or have an affair, or another baby.*
>
> *Sometimes she went to a doctor with symptoms she could hardly describe: "A tired feeling . . . I get so angry with the children it scares me. I feel like crying without any reason." (A Cleveland doctor called it "the housewife's syndrome.") A number of women told me about great bleeding blisters that break out on their hands and arms. "I call it the housewife's blight," said a family doctor in Pennsylvania. "I see it so often lately in these young women with four, five and six children who bury themselves in their dishpans. But it isn't caused by detergent and it isn't cured by cortisone."*
>
> *It is no longer possible to ignore that voice, to dismiss the desperation of so many American women. This is not what being a woman means, no matter what the experts say.*

In 1970, Australian-born writer Germaine Greer published *The Female Eunuch*, which became a huge best-seller and made its author the "high priestess of Women's Lib." Greer applied the ideas of sexual liberation and sexual freedom, long a male's domain, to the position of women, arguing that equality could be achieved only if women could free themselves from sexual repression. She championed "clit power," pointing out that "men love their cocks" and questioning why women are taught to be ashamed of their privates? "Lady, love your cunt!" she cheered. Many took up the call.

UNITED NATIONS GENERAL ASSEMBLY: "DECLARATION OF WOMEN'S RIGHTS"; NOVEMBER 7, 1967 ◆

*I*n 1967, women from around the world met at the United Nations in New York to reclaim some of the power they'd lost to men over the centuries. What they wanted most was recognition that they were not inferior to men—and maybe a constitutional amendment to that effect. They knew the fight would be hard. The goals of the conference—expressed in the Declaration on the Elimination of Discrimination Against Women— were to reclaim human dignity and self-worth, to fight sex discrimination, and to promote equal rights in all areas of life:

> *The General Assembly . . .*
>
> *Considering that discrimination against women is incompatible with human dignity, and with the welfare of the family and of society, prevents their participation on equal terms with men, in the political, social, economic and cultural life of their countries, and is an obstacle to the full development of the potentialities of women in the service of their countries and humanity,*
>
> *Solemnly proclaims this Declaration:*
>
> *. . . Discrimination against women, denying or limiting as it does their equality of rights with men, is fundamentally unjust and constitutes an offense against human dignity.*
>
> *. . . Equal conditions of access to, and study in, educational institutions of all types, including universities, vocational, technical and professional schools.*
>
> *. . . The right to equal remuneration with men and to equality of treatment in respect of work and of equal value.*
>
> *. . . Parents shall have equal rights and duties in matters relating to their children. In all cases the interest of the children shall be paramount.*
>
> *. . . Women shall have equal rights with men during marriage and at its dissolution.*
>
> *. . . The right to vote in all elections and be eligible for election to all publicly elected bodies.*
>
> *. . . The right to hold public office and to exercise all public functions . . .*
>
> *Governments, nongovernmental organizations and individuals are urged, therefore, to do all in their power to promote the implementation of the principles contained in this Declaration.*

CHAPTER 15

Love for Sale

"HOOKER" TO "HUSTLER"

All actors are whores,
we all sell our bodies to the highest bidder.

WILLIAM HOLDEN

WHAT PROSTITUTION IS—A BROAD VIEW ◆

*S*ome would argue that we are all "whores" at one time or another. Most people have done something that they wouldn't have done if they weren't getting paid the right price for it—and the price need not always be money:

> *The only reason I'm in Hollywood is that I don't have the moral courage to refuse the money.* —Marlon Brando
> *I made appearances at cocktail parties in Florida for five hundred dollars a pop, pretending to be an old friend of the host.* —Mickey Rooney
> *I do everything for a reason. Most of the time the reason is money.* —Suzy Parker
> *I did it for the loot, honey, always the loot.* —Ava Gardner
> *I went into the business for the money, and the art grew out of it.* —Charlie Chaplin

On hunts and during war, men often were accompanied by "temporary" wives.

I've done the most unutterable rubbish all because of money. I didn't need it.
The lure of the zeros was simply too great. —Richard Burton
People think I sit here and push buttons and get things accomplished. Well, I
spent today kissing behinds. —Harry S. Truman

In other parts of the world, customs that Americans would view as sexual prostitution have been, and in some cases still are, seen as practical and acceptable:

• **Temporary Wife.** In areas of Outer Mongolia, a traveling merchant, who could be gone from his wife and children for weeks at a time, would take a prostitute with him on his rounds. As sexual companion, she satisfied his urges and was well paid for her efforts. "Temporary wife" was her title.

• **Wife and Servant.** Among some American Indians, it was customary for a hunter, who might be gone from his family for days at a time, to take a single, young woman on his expedition. She not only satisfied his sexual needs but also performed wifely chores in the tent and around the campsite and was paid at the end of the hunt with a meaty portion of the catch.

• **Ex-Wives.** The Creek Indians recruited their traveling women from ex-wives of the clan who had been abandoned by their legal husbands. A cast-aside wife or attractive young widow unable to support herself eagerly sought work as a man's female traveling companion.

• *Male Lovers.* Among the Tlinget of Alaska, wives of wealthy men were allowed to take an additional male lover, provided he was a kinsman. The lover was paid for his services by the husband, and his function was to keep the idle, rich woman sexually sated and confined to her igloo while the husband was on hunting expeditions. The husband had peace of mind in knowing that his wife was at home, happy, and protected by a kinsman.

• *Sacred Whores.* In the Near East, a class of women known as sacred prostitutes served as priestesses. A girl's parents chose the career for her. Holy whores ran regional religions, lived in temples, and offered sexual services—and blessings—in exchange for cash or jewelry. The money they earned went to maintaining the temple and kept the religion thriving.

All of these instances involved the exchange of sex for money or goods, but not one of them bore the stigma associated with prostitution. How and why did the Western attitude toward sex for money change so severely?

Some word origins first.

"WHORE"; ENGLAND, ELEVENTH CENTURY ◆

Today the term "working woman" is a badge of honor and independence. But for many centuries the only cash "work" for a woman in a man's world was the selling of her personal and private wares.

The slur "whore" is dated to eleventh-century England and is from the Anglo-Saxon *hore*, "adulterer." It is related to the Latin *carus*, "dear"—as well as to our word "charity"—through the Indo-European root *karo*, meaning "to be fond of," "to desire."

As a verbal taboo, "whore" has gone in and out of fashion. Shakespeare freely used it on many occasions. Noah Webster deleted every "whore" reference from the family Bibles he published in the 1830s.

In 1926, when John Ford's play *'Tis Pity She's a Whore* (1633) was revived in New York, newspapers refused to print the title in full, shortening it to *'Tis Pity*. The Performing Arts Company at Michigan State University advertised their 1967 production as *'Tis Pity She's a* ———.

The word offered Dorothy Parker one of her most memorable lines, "You can lead a horticulture, but you can't make her think."

Scores of colorful synonyms capture the essence of the world's "oldest profession"—and "oldest professional":

• **Lady of the night**, dating from at least the 1700s, suggests the hours during which she did her work.

• **Streetwalker**, from the 1590s, suggests where she plied her trade or lured clients.

• **Painted woman**, from at least the 1500s, tells us much about her facial appearance and how it differed from that of an unpainted housewife.

• **Woman of the town**, from the 1850s, signifies her notoriety among townfolk.

• **Menace to decent women**, from the 1850s, suggests how her married female competition regarded her.

• **Fallen woman**, popular in the 1870s, tells us how society's morally upright regarded her as having suffered a "fall from grace." Other euphemisms of the period were *social evil*, *woman of ill repute*, and *menace to society*.

• **Jezebel** is an ancient, biblical reference to the infamously wicked wife of Ahab, king of Israel.

• **Lady of easy virtue**, first recorded in America in 1809, in Washington Irving's *Knickerbocker's History of New York*, implies that whatever virtue a woman had was willingly surrendered.

• **Trollop** is from the fourteenth-century English *troll*, meaning "to move back and forth," as in dragging a line and lure to catch fish—in this case the "fish" being a man.

• **Strumpet**, from the fourteenth century, derives from the Latin *stuprum*, meaning "dishonor."

• **Slut**, from the fifteenth century, is from the Middle English *slutte*, meaning a "slovenly woman." Only later did it come to mean a sexually loose female.

"WHOREHOUSE"; ENGLAND, FOURTEENTH CENTURY ◆

*I*n 1978 the head of New York City's Department of Transportation refused to accept bus advertisements for the popular musical comedy *The Best Little Whorehouse in Texas*, which included the line, "Come to the Whorehouse." As we've seen, the word "whore" originated in the eleventh century; "whorehouse," the place of business, appeared about three hundred years later.

• **Bawdy house**, first recorded in the 1550s, took its name from prostitutes being called *bawds*, from the Old High German *bawd*, meaning "bold."

From "Jezebel" to "strumpet," ladies of easy virtue have gone by many colorful names.

• **Brothel**, from the Old English *breothan*, meaning "to go to ruin," was the name of a prostitute in the fifteenth century. In the following century, it came to mean a prostitute's place of work.

• **Bordello** was first recorded in English in Ben Jonson's comedy *Every Man in His Humour* (1598). The word is Italian, from the Old French *bordel*, meaning a "small house."

• **House of assignation**, from the 1830s, meant a large, elegant brothel.

• **Stag party** in the 1850s meant merely a bachelor's blast; around 1910 it acquired the connotation of a party where prostitutes performed sex acts.

"Harlot"; France, Thirteenth Century ◆

"Harlot," long a polite euphemism for "whore," is one of those rare words that has undergone a male-to-female sex change. Dating from the thirteenth century, and deriving from the Old French *herlot*, meaning "rogue" or "vagabond," it was originally a masculine term for any down-and-out beggar. The term expanded to include male buffoons and clowns, then male jugglers and itinerants, and finally male servants and any regular "good guy."

In the 1430s, female jugglers, dancers, and actresses began to be called harlots—then female artists of any kind. The more "feminine" the word

Looking the girls over in a better-class brothel in Paris, 1910.

became through association, the less it was used by men on themselves. By the sixteenth century, a harlot was a female prostitute and all the previous meanings of the word had vanished. Why? Most likely because standard Bibles of the period, including the Geneva Bible of 1560, the version used by Shakespeare, had dropped "whore" and "strumpet" for the gentler "harlot," as in "How is the faithful city become a harlot!" (Isaiah 1:21).

"Hooker"; America, 1860s ◆

*H*ooker" is believed to be associated with General Joseph ("Fighting Joe") Hooker of Civil War fame. To bolster morale, General Hooker supposedly allowed prostitutes access to his troops in camp, where they became known as "Hooker's girls." When a section of Washington, D.C., on Lafayette Square was set aside for brothels, it acquired the name Hooker's Division or Hooker's Row, and the local strumpets and harlots became known as "hookers."

Prostitution is a seamy side of the Civil War that is not taught in schools. To make a quick buck—or merely to survive—an enormous number of young women sold themselves to the hundreds of thousand of troops passing through cities or stationed in temporary camps throughout the south. Military records kept by the Union Medical Corps showed that 202,000 cases of venereal disease were diagnosed among 531,000 soldiers—a whopping 38 percent.

Many documents relating to prostitution during the Civil War are at the Kinsey Institute for Research in Sex, Gender, and Reproduction. Much of the material consists of letters home written by fighting men. Some of the prostitutes they describe were white, others black. Black girls often cost more because men believed they provided more pleasure. Harris Levin, a soldier in Company L of the Second Virginia Reserves, wrote in the fall of 1864:

Several nights a week our lonely post is visited by two sisters who are rentable for riding. They visit the boys at Brooks and Semes also, as they lived at Hatcher's. Amanda is about fifteen and my favorite. She has never asked for more of me than a good poking, but does of the others. But her sister Carrie will ask pay for her accommodations to me, so you know which I choose.

Sometimes they bring a nigger with them and the gentlemen prefer her. But I have never had wealth enough to acquire such tastes.

Also in 1864, a young employee of the U.S. Sanitary Commission wrote home to his father deploring the number of prostitutes in City Point, Virginia:

This is a whole city of whores. Yes, father, a whole city . . . At pay time, the lines before these [whore] houses are appalling and men often fight each other for a place. The average charge is $3 and on pay days some make as much as $250/$300. Though between pay periods, it is said they will take their time and do many special things and charge amountingly.

Some of these hussies, during their indisposed periods, sell their services to the men to write letters for them to their loved ones back home. How foul. A mother, a wife or sweetheart receiving a letter penned by these soiled hands.

I have not yet been able to reach [General] Grant to protest these matters. Though he has ordered our men not to rape the rebel women, under penalty of death, two have so been executed since I have been here. I have talked with Bowers and he tries to defend the village [of prostitutes] as necessary in view of that order. Think of it father, he implies our devoted soldiers would become rapers and satyrs if not for these creatures.

*An 1879 newspaper
illustration of a whorehouse
in Chicago's red-light district.*

"TENDERLOIN DISTRICT"; NEW YORK CITY, 1880s ◆

A Manhattan police officer, Alexander Williams, is thought to be responsible for the phrase "tenderloin district." As the story goes:

In 1876, Williams was assigned to New York City's old 29th precinct, extending from 23rd Street to 42nd Street west of Broadway. The vice-ridden area was notorious for its graft and prostitution. Williams liberally helped himself to illegal cash and boasted that his new assignment allowed him to switch from eating cheap, tough chuck steak to expensive tenderloin cuts. Soon, among police, "tenderloin" meant any vice-filled neighborhood where easy cash could be picked up; and, probably because "loin" has sexual connotations, the word "tenderloin district" quickly came to mean an area filled with prostitutes.

• **Red-light district** dates from the 1890s. Prostitutes have always burned candles or oil lamps in the windows of brothels to get the attention of prospective clients. But the term "red light" is thought to refer to the early use of Thomas Edison's electric bulbs which brothels covered with shades and fabrics of red—the color of heat and passion.

• **Cat house** became a popular term for a bordello during World War I, but the term predates the war: *cat* and *pussy* were old slang terms for vagina.

• **Call house** in the 1920s meant a brothel where men came to "call on" girls. A woman who worked in the house was a *call girl*. By the 1950s, once

> **PROSTITUTION BETTER THAN ADULTERY** ◆ *Solon (c. 640–*
> *c. 559 B.C.E.), the Athenian statesman and lawgiver, arranged for the*
> *importation of young prostitutes from Asia Minor and saw that Greek*
> *brothels paid taxes to the government. Under his influence, the prices on*
> *prostitution were fixed very low so that all freemen could easily afford*
> *whores. Adultery was a criminal offense, prostitution was not. A wife was*
> *cherished, a whore disposable.*
>
> *Solon railed against Athenian men who committed adultery. So did the*
> *first-century B.C.E. Roman philosopher Xenarchus; a man had no excuse*
> *for having sex with another man's wife because:*
>
> *"There are very fine-looking girls at the brothels. You can see them*
> *standing outside, breasts bared in the sunshine, almost naked, lined up*
> *conveniently one after the another. From these, anybody can pick out a*
> *favorite: fat or thin, curvy, lanky, bent over. Young or old. Firm or lush.*
>
> *"You have no need to prop a ladder to climb in secretly [to a married*
> *woman's house], and you don't have to crawl in through the smoke hole,*
> *or be smuggled in under a pile of straw. You don't need married women.*
> *These young girls on the street nearly drag you in. They call out 'daddy' to*
> *older men, and 'lover boy' to younger ones. You can have her cheap, and*
> *without risk, available day and night—and any way you want her.*
>
> *"With married women, you can never have them easily; you are always*
> *afraid, risking your life. Oh, Aphrodite, how can men go after married*
> *women once they know the laws?"*

telephones were commonplace, *call girl* meant a prostitute who could be contacted by phone.

THE WORLD'S OLDEST PROFESSION; SIX MILLION YEARS AGO ◆

*P*rostitution is not called "the world's oldest profession" for nothing. It *is* the oldest cash-for-commodities transaction for which records exist. It is safe to assume that it predates recorded history.

Prostitution is also the oldest evidence of supply-and-demand economics:

men demanded the goods and women supplied them. In a man's world, women were commodities, exchanged like cattle or crops. Thus it is not surprising that the oldest recorded acts of prostitution were heterosexual.

Anthropologists, surveying our hunter-gatherer ancestors, believe that campsite mothers bartered sexual favors for food and protection for themselves and their children. The strongest men fed and protected the "sexiest" women—those who remained sexually receptive for the longest periods. In this way, the genes for longer and longer estrus, or sexual heat, in the protomodern female eventually produced year-round female sexual receptivity. This explanation for the emergence of continual estrus suggests that heterosexual prostitution is deeply ingrained in our species. By having to wean and rear children, a woman was unable to hunt. To protect herself and her young, she offered sex as a way to get a man—and keep him.

Animal Prostitutes

Most people don't think of animals in terms of "selling" sex, but many species do just that. Female primates, for instance, will offer sexual services—"presentation" of the rump—in return for food or protection from a champion male. In times of warfare between monkey clans, even a young, defenseless male will offer his rump to an older, larger male in return for protection from attack. Throughout the animal kingdom, all kinds of females use sex to get what they want or need, and males of all sorts—including humans—seem content with this kind of bartering.

How Human Prostitution Arose— Four Views ♦

*O*ver the last two centuries, with advances in evolutionary biology and psychology, several theories have been offered to explain how the business of prostitution arose in human society:

Men Have Always Ruled the World and Taken What They Wanted

This theory was offered in 1861 by British jurist and legal historian Sir Henry Maine. Patriarchy was the original—and universal—system of social organization, he argued. The family began as the basic social unit, with the male parent holding supreme authority in his household. From this small fiefdom of male power, authority eventually extended outward to clans run by elected males, then to city-states run by male warriors and high priests, and finally to nation-states ruled by kings and generals. Men always had the power; women were always subordinate. Prostitution arose as a male prerogative, and a class of single young women arose to satisfy male demands.

Prostitution Existed Before the Family

This theory was offered by several sociologists in the last century. Among early hunter-gatherers, there was neither a patriarchy nor a matriarchy. Men and women existed in a state of sexual license. Free sex was everywhere. All women were prostitutes—so were all men. Sex was barter.

There was as yet no stable family. Women took care of their infants; but men, inseminating one woman after another, did not hang around to rear their offspring. Since father was unknown, mother made all the decisions and answered all the questions of ownership and inheritance. A matriarchy arose.

But it didn't last long. With the advent of agriculture, and the subsequent ownership of farmland, a man and a women settled down to raise a family on their plot. Since the male was physically stronger, the woman fell under his domination in all things. The matriarchy disappeared, replaced by a patriarchy. The natural superiority of woman—because in nature she is more closely connected with procreation and offspring—was superseded by the unnatural primacy of man.

Man held it on the basis of superior physical strength. Out of this gender inequality, prostitution arose. Women never wanted to be prostitutes; men had just economically rigged society so that some women had to sell sex to survive.

Secular Prostitution Is a Direct Descendant of Sacred Prostitution

For sociologist Robert Briffault (1876–1948), women initially had all the power because, as childbearers, they were closer to nature than men. In the days when nature was worshiped, women were earthly goddesses who wrote laws and ran economic and political life. Men may have shared in the power, but it was the high priestess—or temple goddess—who was believed to be married to the heavenly god of all creation.

Because female goddesses did not marry, they could take any number of men as lovers. Thus arose the well-documented phenomenon of the sacred

A prostitute tolerates a client's whipping whim—an engraving from 1776.

prostitute, who ran religions. A man who paid for sex with one was "communicating with nature."

In the Middle East, the sacred prostitute fell with the rise of male monotheistic Judaism. One male God replaced many female goddesses (and gods), beginning around 1300 B.C.E. Around this time, Moses is supposed to have written down the first five book of Hebrew Scripture.

How did it happen?

Several biblical scholars claim that the Fall in Genesis, Eve's temptation by Satan, was concocted by Levite male priests, belonging to Moses' clan, to wrest the reins of religious power from women. Eve, who metaphorically is *all* women, is cast as a temptress, the easy handiwork of Satan. She sins, then tempts Adam into sinning, and God punishes all of humankind with toil, pain, sickness, and death. By denigrating females, the Fall myth successfully suppressed worship of female goddesses. The Levite priests filled the void with their own monotheistic male God and their own exclusive male priesthood. The Fall in Genesis was, in effect, the fall of goddesses, of matriarchal worship, and of the female priesthood. After the Fall, the books of the Old Testament treat childbirth and menstrual blood as dirty things that men should avoid.

Sleazy secular prostitution, argued Briffault, was a direct descendant of the once holy efforts of sacred prostitutes.

It is known that for centuries after the fall of goddesses, brothels continued to be called "abbeys" (from the Latin *abbatia*), a reference to their once sacred status.

Prostitution Exists Because Some Men Are Sexually Satisfied Only by Whores

This was basically Sigmund Freud's view. Man's primitive impulse is for sex with many different, and young, women: *different*, because man continually needs new stimuli; *young*, because they make fitter, longer-lived mothers.

But, said Freud, "Civilization has been built up . . . by sacrifices in gratification of the primitive impulses." Nonetheless, the impulses are still there, stronger in some men than others. A more civilized man has "tender" sexual impulses and achieves sexual satisfaction with a moral, loving woman with whom he constructs a relationship. Other men, though, with primitive impulses—and perhaps a lack of self-worth—can achieve intense sexual gratification only with an anonymous women whom they regard as inferior. Even if society did not stigmatize prostitutes, these men would have to condemn them as inferior.

However, the argument continues, all men, deep down, really enjoy at times anonymous sex with "forbidden" women—a naughty quickie; an orgasm that does not include issues of love, lengthy foreplay, and concern for a partner's sexual satisfaction; copulation that is purely a selfish sex act.

For Freud, the "bad" prostitute exists so that the "good" wife and mother can be viewed on a pillar of virtue. Without the whore, the madonna would not be as pure and desirable.

MARY MAGDALEN: PROSTITUTE OR FIRST EVANGELIST? ◆

*W*ith her long, fiery red hair and body draped in a scarlet robe, Mary Magdalen is, in Christian theology, the quintessential whore. Our predominant image of her—the first woman to enter Christ's ministry as well as the first person to see the risen Savior—is of a beautiful, repentant prostitute, kneeling at Christ's feet, weeping for her vices.

This is, too, the essence of the age-old, male-inspired image equating feminine beauty, sexuality, and sin. For nearly two thousand years, the traditional conception of Mary Magdalen has been that of the good-hearted

SEXY ORIGINS AND INTIMATE THINGS

A WHORE'S TRICKS ◆ *Lucretius (c. 96–c. 55 B.C.E), the Roman poet and Epicurean philosopher, taught that whores practice special hip movements to avoid pregnancy. In fact, one way to tell a respectable wife, interested in breeding and raising a family, from a whore, interested only in pleasure and money, was from her positions and movements during lovemaking:*

"Sexual position means everything. Wives who imitate the manner of wild beasts and quadrupeds—breasts down, haunches up—generally conceive better since the male seed can more easily reach the proper place.

"It is not at all necessary for wives to move in any way during intercourse. For a wife prevents and battles pregnancy if in her joy, she answers the man's lovemaking with her buttocks, and her soft breasts billow forward and back. For she then diverts the ploughshare out of the furrow and makes the seed miss its mark.

"Whores practice such movements for their own personal reasons. They do it to avoid conception and pregnancy; and also to make the lovemaking more enjoyable for men, which obviously isn't necessary for our wives."

prostitute who, having heard Christ's message, found strength to repent for her past and devote her life and love to him.

When Christ sat to eat at a Pharisee's house, an unnamed woman (traditionally identified as Mary Magdalen) appeared:

Behold, a woman of the city, which was a sinner, when she knew that Jesus sat at meat in the Pharisee's house, brought an alabaster box of ointment,

And stood at his feet behind him weeping, and began to wash his feet with tears, and did wipe them with the hairs of her head, and kissed his feet, and anointed them with the ointment.

When the Pharisee which had bidden him saw it, he spoke within himself, saying, This man, if he were a prophet, would have known who and what manner of woman this is that touches him: for she is a sinner (Luke 7:37–39).

388

Mary Magdalen (with long, uncovered hair, the sign of a prostitute), Salome, and Mary, the mother of James, at Christ's empty tomb.

In her scholarly biography *Mary Magdalen* (1993), Susan Haskins presents a convincing case that Christ's first female follower was no prostitute and probably not the unidentified woman in Luke who washes Christ's feet. Examining every appearance and inference of Mary Magdalen in the Gospels, Haskins concludes that Mary's "seven devils," to which both Luke and Matthew ambiguously refer, were not the seven deadly sins (which were codified centuries later) but various symptoms of "mental disorder." Perhaps they were nothing more than the frustration and anger that came from being an independent, unmarried, inquisitive woman in a man's world.

In a time where every woman received her identity and validation through a man by becoming a wife and a mother, Mary Magdalen was beautiful and chose to remain single. Might her "whoring around" have been merely wishful male thinking? Gender slander? Haskins shows that the Greek word for "harlot," *porni*, is used with great inconsistency in the Four Gospels. Mary is sometimes called a *amartoli*, Greek for "sinner," in which the sin can be theft, broken vows, murder, prostitution, or demonic possession (read "mental illness").

Jesus Christ, suggests Haskins, "cured" Mary Magdalen's troubled, independent mind—that is, he accepted her as an equal to men; he acknowledged her worth as a human being, irrespective of being a wife or mother. Later church fathers, says Haskins, were troubled by Christ's close personal relationship with a single, beautiful woman, as well as by her prominent role in the Easter Sunday redemption story, the central truth of Christianity. Thus, they fostered the myth of Mary Magdalen as a sinning whore turned into a chaste devotee. It is easier to explain Christ's relationship with Mary Magdalen if she was a repentant sinner than if she was a free-spirited, beautiful devotee.

Today, many biblical scholars feel as Haskins does. In 1990, a prominent Lutheran minister delivered a sermon in New York City on Mary Magdalen's feast day, July 22:

> There is certainly no biblical basis for identifying her as the reformed prostitute or that she had long red hair [long a male symbol of a harlot]. The sole characteristic that stands out about Mary is the fact that she is not identified [in the Gospels] as the mother or the wife of some man. She has the audacity to stand completely on her own as a person. For as long as this parody of Mary Magdalene stands, the church provides a continued obstacle to its own and the world's understanding of female social equality.
>
> This feast which honors Mary of Magdala for what she really is could be a key to a new level of Christian sexual consciousness. All we need do is proclaim honestly the true role this woman had in the story of the redemption. Recognize her as a full member of the revolutionary community created by the One who considered men and women equal . . .
>
> Jesus valued her as a unique person in whom the life and power of God flowed with the same degree of intensity as it did in Peter, James or John.

WHORES TO THE HOLY LAND; THE CRUSADES, 1095–1272 ◆

*P*rostitution has played a large part in every major war; it is the silent, untold story. The Holy Crusades, despite their religious purpose, were no different. During the eight major Crusades to recapture the Holy Land from the "infidel" Turks, hundreds of thousands of men were without their wives and girlfriends for months at a time. Hordes of prostitutes followed the men as camp hangers-on.

King Richard the Lionhearted, himself bisexual, was outraged that his troops wasted so much money on whores. He did not mind that the men had sex with prostitutes—just that they were willing to pay so much for the best girls.

The Holy Crusades created a boom in prostitution.

The number of prostitutes following the crusaders ran so high that Pope Clement III (1187–1191) pleaded that no women be allowed to accompany troops except the oldest and ugliest laundresses and cooks.

Arab historian Imad al-Din, who wrote an account of Saladin's attempt to recapture the Holy Land in the 1180s, painted a colorful picture of camp whores. His mind is particularly fertile when it comes to coining metaphors for the act of copulation:

> *They arrived by ship, three hundred lovely Frankish women, full of youth and beauty, assembled from beyond the sea and offering themselves for sin. They were all licentious harlots, proud and scornful, foul-fleshed and sinful, making love and selling themselves for gold.*
>
> *They dedicated as a holy offering that which they kept between their thighs. They were openly licentious and devoted to relaxation. They plied a brisk trade in dissoluteness.*
>
> *They made them targets of men's darts. They offered themselves to the lances' blows. They were the places where tent pegs are driven in. They invited swords to enter into their sheaths. They made javelins rise toward their shields. They excited the plough to plough. They caught in their nets the horns of budding rams. They gave the birds a place to peck their beaks. They caught lizard after lizard in their holes. They guided pens into ink-wells, torrents to the valley bottom, streams to pools, gold ingots to crucibles, firewood to the stove, guilty men to low dungeons . . . They claimed all*

this was an act of piety toward men who were far from home and their wives.

"PIMP"; FRANCE, PRE-FIFTEENTH CENTURY ◆

*T*he man who solicits clients for a prostitute is a "pimp," a word of unclear origin. Some believe that the term derives from the Old French *pimpreneau*, meaning "a knave, rascal, scoundrel." Others point to a South African expression, *impimpsi*, for any lowlife or stool pigeon. But the African word may well be the common English "pimp" given a later Swahili prefix, *im*, and suffix, *si*—a twentieth-century coinage.

The best bet is that "pimp" originated with the Middle French *pimper*, "to allure, to dress smartly." Pimps, lower-class men with lots of cash, have been known for their outrageously stylish attire.

The spelling "pimp" was first recorded in 1666 in Samuel Pepys's diary.

◆ *John*, a man who pays for the services of a prostitute, became popular in the 1930s, though the word is older. Some linguists date it to the mid-1800s, when the term meant any man who was an easy mark, for a shyster or a prostitute.

"HUSTLER"; 1924—MALE PROSTITUTION ◆

A female prostitute is called a "whore" or "harlot." Her male equivalent goes by the term "hustler." The word, dating from 1825, is from the Dutch *husselen*, and meant "to shake up" (as with a pocket full of coins) or "to obtain money aggressively or dishonestly." First applied to a male prostitute around 1924, "hustler," as well as the activity it describes, has a less colorful history than harlotry—or at least male authors have not written as extensively about male prostitutes.

Sophocles, the fifth-century B.C.E. Greek playwright, bought boys for sex. So did English explorer Sir Richard Burton, American songwriter Cole Porter, and film director George Cukor. In their memoirs, playwright Tennessee Williams and novelist Gore Vidal confessed that it was standard practice for them to buy young men.

Irish dramatist Oscar Wilde, a married man, sought out lower-class boys

A pimp and his whores fleece a would-be client.

and bragged that he bought sex from five boys in one night. "I kissed each one of them in every part of their bodies," he boasted to a friend. "They were all dirty and appealed to me just for that reason."

French writer Jean Genet admitted to having hustled early in life, as did gay writer John Rechy. Going farther back, Socrates' disciple, Phaedo of Elis, spent a good deal of his youth as a hustler. Male prostitution is probably as old as the female variety.

A Short Career

Male prostitution has always been less of a formal institution than female sex-for-cash. The sacred prostitutes of the Near East, the geishas of Japan, and the mistresses of European noblemen sold their bodies to obtain power, social freedom, and economic success in a man's world. As American prostitute Dolores French described her own experience (1988), "Best of all, I was in control. By living off the money men gave me for sex, I was able to achieve the independence from men my mother had always wanted me to have."

Male hustlers, on the other hand, who also sell their bodies to men (there are few historical accounts of male brothels for upper-class women), don't seem to rise up the social and economic ladder as much as their female counterparts. Studies show that most hustlers are young men in their teens and early twenties, mostly heterosexual or bisexual men eager for a quick buck. The boys are often homeless and willing to barter their bodies for a

Horatio Alger helped rehabilitate teenage runaways and, in the process, sexually abused many boys—an aspect of the "Horatio Alger story" seldom told.

meal, a night's lodging, or drug money. Their clients can be older homosexual men, who refer to hustlers as "trade," or married men.

Male hustlers, on the average, tend to get out of the business faster than female prostitutes. Straight boys may tire of the practice, while gay boys may fall in love with a male client and leave the profession—profitably. While youth is an important commodity for a female prostitute, it is even more highly prized in the male hustler. A male prostitute's working life is extremely short.

A "Horatio Alger" Story

Few people realize that American novelist Horatio Alger (1834–1899), who popularized the rags-to-riches story in which a waif works his way up the ladder of success, bought male hustlers. Anyone who uses "a Horatio Alger story" as an expression of the American dream should be acquainted with the facts.

As a minister of a Unitarian church in Brewster, Massachusetts, Alger was charged in 1866 with soliciting sex from parish boys. A church committee reported, "We learned that the Reverend Horatio Alger, Jr., has been practicing on young boys . . . deeds that are too revolting to relate":

That Horatio Alger, Jr., who has officiated as our Minister for about fifteen months past has recently been charged with no less magnitude than the abominable and revolting crime of unnatural familiarity with boys.

Whereupon the committee sent for Alger and to him specified the charges and evidence of his guilt, which he neither denied or attempted to extenuate, but received with apparent calmness of an old offender—and hastily left town on the very next train for parts unknown.

Alger headed straight to New York City, known even then for its large number of homeless male teenage runaways.

In 1867, he began to write stories for boys and to take in homeless waifs. He published *Ragged Dick, or Street Life in New York with the Boot-Blacks* about an urchin's rise from squalor and thievery to respectability and financial success by luck and pluck—and help from older men. Alger became an overnight success. Social reformers, working to help the plight of orphans and homeless teens, helped publicize his stories.

Alger spent much of his later life working tirelessly to improve the conditions of homeless boys, runaways, and male orphans. He took a charitable interest in the Newsboys' Lodging House, which could accommodate 250 boys. By 1869, over eight thousand of them had passed through its doors—and some smaller number through the ex-reverend's bedroom door.

In demand on the New York social scene, Alger always traveled about town in the company of one or two of his favorites. Today this would raise eyebrows, but back then no one questioned Alger's obsessive interest in young boys, his overnight campouts with them, his effusive descriptions of their beauty and robustness, or his informal adoption of two brothers, Tommy and John Down. Having learned how to be discreet, Alger never again raised a hint of scandal.

Alger's stories remained popular throughout the 1920s, favored by businessmen, ministers, educators, and parents who saw in the rags-to-riches formula confirmation of the American dream. Few people realize that there is a sexual element to the true Horatio Alger story.

LEGAL MALE PROSTITUTION ◆

*I*n Oman, a small Muslim country on the southeastern coast of the Arabian Peninsula, young effeminate males legitimately serve as prostitutes. They're called *xaniths*. To the Omani, the genitals are not what determine who's a man or a woman, but the role a person plays in the sex act. An active partner is a "man," a passive partner is a "woman." Male prostitutes are "women," and they are also considered a "third sex."

With real Omani women robed and secluded from most of society, the *xanith* serves a respectable function. A boy, who is usually somewhat effeminate, practices his trade of prostitution and can earn a good living at it. Later, if he wishes, he may marry a woman and father children.

Under Islamic law, a *xanith* enjoys all the rights and freedoms of a man: he goes by a masculine name and accompanies other men to the mosque for ritual worship. But in communal compounds, he performs a woman's household chores, and on festive occasions he joins with women in singing and dancing. In a 1982 article in *Science Digest*, "The Erotic Sorcerers," Charles and Cherry Lindholm detail his role:

> His appearance reflects his ambiguous sexual status. He wears the man's long tunic, but tightly belted at the waist like a woman's. His hair is neither long like a woman's nor short like a man's, but of an intermediate length. He goes bareheaded, although both men and women cover their hair. Interestingly, he is legally prohibited from wearing women's clothes and can be imprisoned and flogged if he does so.

The harshness of the punishment for a male prostitute who dons female clothes indicates the real importance of the *xanith*'s role in Omani society. As a male prostitute, he serves to protect the virtue of Omani women, who, ideally at least, are supposed to be absolutely pure and isolated in their homes. Virtually their sole purpose in life is to bear children.

In Oman, there are a few female prostitutes, but their services are expensive and illegal. Young male prostitutes are plentiful, cheap, and sanctioned by law. If a *xanith* were to dress as a woman, he would no longer be preserving women's purity since he would be sullying their image in public.

Norwegian anthropologist Unni Wikan estimated that one out of fifty Omani men is a *xanith*. Several factors contribute to the continuance of male prostitution. One is the sexual unavailability of women. Another is economic: poor people in Oman have very few ways to learn a living. Being a *xanith* provides a man with *two* paying occupations: prostitute and domestic servant. Being a "third sex," he can work in numerous capacities that are off-limits to women. Omani women cannot even be seen by men who are unrelated to them.

Work as a male prostitute can pay off in the end. After several teenage years working as a *xanith*, a heterosexual male can have saved enough money to buy a bride, which is very costly in Oman. He may then entirely drop his role as a male prostitute and assume the role of a respectable married man and father. In a sense, being a *xanith* can serve as a legitimate method for achieving upward mobility in Omani society.

More Love for Sale

PEEP SHOW TO PHONE SEX

*If the First Amendment means anything, it means that
a state has no business telling a man, sitting alone in his own house,
what books he may read or what films he may watch.*

JUSTICE THURGOOD MARSHALL

PEEP SHOW BOOTH; 1960S ♦

*H*ugh Hefner (*Playboy*) and Larry Flynt (*Hustler*) are more famous, but Cleveland businessman Reuben Struman has really dominated the production and distribution of porn in the United States—and throughout the world. A business rival once complained that the mild-mannered, soft-spoken Struman did not simply control the adult entertainment industry; he *was* the industry.

Struman is credited with inventing the simple but extraordinarily lucrative peep show booth. Starting in the 1960s, he began to enclose coin-operated projectors in small, private booths with a screen and a door that could be locked. He gave men the opportunity to view explicit sex films in relative secrecy.

After installing peep shows in his own porn magazine stores, he leased booths to other adult bookstore owners. Finally he began to manufacture booths and started a company to maintain them. The huge demand for sex

A "whipping club" in England where men "peeped" on women whipping other women.

films to show in Struman's coin-operated booths helped establish the nation's adult film industry.

Men have been peeping at women for centuries:

• **Peephole**, meaning a crevice or hole in the wall through which a man watched a woman undress, dates to 1681.

• **Peep show** dates to 1851 and the early days of photography. Men would pay a nickel to slip behind a curtain or screen and view racy stills of nude and semiclad woman.

"PEEPING TOM"; 1796 ◆

*T*he term "peeping Tom," meaning a pruriently prying person, or voyeur, dates to about 1796, though the "Peeping Tom" of legend may go back to the story of the eleventh-century Lady Godiva of Coventry

According to the tale, Lady Godiva's husband, Leofric, earl of Mercia and lord of Coventry, imposed a heavy tax on his subjects, who were already poor. A pious woman, Lady Godiva sympathized with the people and implored her husband to rescind some of the taxation. He agreed but imposed one condition: she'd have to ride through the marketplace stark naked.

When she accepted the dare, he imposed a decree on the townsfolk: during his wife's ride, all citizens had to stay indoors and keep their shutters drawn.

All did except for Tom, the city tailor. Here the legend bifurcates into two different endings. In one version, Tom is a true voyeur and can't resist "peeping" at the naked Lady Godiva. In the other, Lady Godiva's horse neighs as it passes Tom's window and he impulsively peeks out to look at the horse more than the woman. In both versions he's struck blind.

In a third telling of the legend, a more moralistic version, he's struck dead.

"PROSTITUTE" AND "PORNOGRAPHY" ◆

*T*he verb "to prostitute," first recorded in 1530, is from the Latin *prostitutus*, made up of its most elemental terms from *pro* (before) + *statuere* (to station). It suggests that a streetwalker stationed herself, or himself, at a specific location in a town. "Prostitute" was first recorded as a noun in 1613.

A person who writes about prostitutes was first called a *pornographer* around 1850—from the Greek *porni*, "prostitute" + *graphos* "writer."

The term for the depiction of erotic pictures or words, *pornography*, was first recorded around 1864, though the pornography industry is much older. It's never been as prosperous as it is today: according to *Adult Video News*, a trade publication:

• The number of hard-core video rentals rose from 75 million in 1985 to 490 million in 1992 and climbed to 665 million, an all-time high, in 1996.

• In 1996, Americans spent more than eight billion dollars on hard-core videos, peep shows, live sex acts, sex toys, computer porn, sex magazines, and adult cable programming, an amount much larger than Hollywood's domestic box-office receipts and larger than all the revenues generated by rock and country music recordings.

• Americans now spend more money at strip clubs and peep shows than at Broadway, off-Broadway, regional, and nonprofit theaters; at the opera; the ballet; and jazz and classical musical performances combined.

• A well-run strip club makes five million dollars a year. There are about twenty-five hundred strip clubs in America.

• A top porn stripper earns twenty thousand dollars a week just dancing at a club.

• Internet porn is rapidly gaining in popularity. For instance, *Playboy*'s Web site, which offers free glimpses of its Playmates, averaged about five million "hits" a day in 1996. This gives a new meaning to men "hitting" on women.

Porn has become so commonplace that we can easily forget how strictly it was prohibited just three decades ago. Sociologist Charles Winick estimates that the sexual content of American culture has changed more in the last two decades than in the previous two centuries. The Internet promises to combine the video store's diversity of porn choices with the secrecy of purchasing through the mail. "On-line sex" is the new porn wave of the twenty-first century.

"STAG" ENTERTAINMENT; 1840S •

*I*f a party or movie is "stag," it's restricted to men. The word "stag" arose before the twelfth century from the Old English *stagge*, which first meant a "drake," or male duck, then an adult male red deer. A stag is always a male animal.

"Stag" started to be attached to the human male animal in the 1840s. It meant male-only entertainments such as a party at which a stripper danced or, later, a group viewing of nude photographs. A gentleman invited to a "stag party" might enjoy nothing more than perusing a half dozen grainy, black-and-white stills of a middle-aged Rubenesque woman wearing only stockings and heels. Men previously had viewed artists' drawings of nude women; now they ogled "live pictures" of real woman. "Photo porn" had been born.

Not long after Thomas Edison pioneered moving pictures, "stag movies" became the hot male-only entertainment. The dim, flickering nudity and mild passion of *The Dolorita Passion Dance* and *The Kiss* of the 1890s quickly passed to the amateurish but truly pornographic "stag shorts" of the 1930s.

As films got longer, more daring and professional, other terms arose:

• *Adult movies*, 1940. The first "adult movies" were available for viewing only in peep show arcades. By the next decade, adult movies could be purchased through the mail for private viewing at a home stag party—for those who had their own projectors.

• *Blue movies*, 1950. While the term "blue movies" arose in the 1950s, the adjective "blue," meaning "indecent or obscene" was borrowed from the 1860s, where it referred to off-color language. Why "blue?"

The adjective "blue" precedes many respectable words: "blue book" (1836), a register of socially prominent persons; "blue coat" (1593), an officer of the law; "blue ribbon" (1651), an award for preeminence; and "bluestocking" (1790), as in "Bluestocking societies," eighteenth-century clubs for women having intellectual and literary interests.

Most linguists agree that "blue" got its off-color connotation with the passage in the 1620s of the extremely rigorous "blue laws" designed to regulate morals and conduct in colonial New England. The "blue laws" especially regulated what amusements people could engage in on Sunday, the Lord's Day. It's said that the laws were dubbed "blue" because they were originally printed on blue sheets of paper, which were posted throughout colonial towns.

• **Skin flicks**, 1970s. The adjective "skin" suggests that stag movies were getting bolder, with actresses showing more skin. Skin flicks were shows in "skin houses," theaters that either specialized in pornographic movies or offered them late at night after the regular feature had been put back in the can.

• **Porn movies**, late 1960s. The term "skin flick" was replaced by "porn movie," which was shown in a "porn house." Linda Lovelace has been billed as the first true *porn star* for her performance in the 1972 porn classic *Deep Throat*, in which she played a woman with a clitoris in her throat. The movie was a breakout event for porn, receiving unusual attention in the mainstream press.

• **X-rated movies**, late 1960s. In 1922, the Motion Picture Producers and Distributors of America (MPPDA) chose attorney Will H. Hays to set up a rating system for movie decency. A former Republican National Committee chairman and postmaster general under Warren Harding, Hays developed a strict censorship code. But it was not strict enough for the U.S. Catholic church, which in the 1930s developed its own National Legion of Decency. Both groups went ballistic over Rhett Butler's language in the closing scene of the 1939 classic *Gone With the Wind*, "Frankly, my dear, I don't give a damn."

By the late 1960s, "damn" was the least of the motion picture industry's rating headaches. In 1968, the industry released a new rating system, giving us:

G, all ages permitted,

PG, parental guidance suggested,

R, restricted, persons under seventeen must be accompanied by a parent or guardian, and

X, no one under seventeen admitted.

An "adults only" movie house, 1962

Porn producers immediately began billing their films as "X-rated." When that lure wore thin, marquees promised "XX-rated" then "XXX-rated" entertainment.

At-Home Porn

During the 1980s, the advent of adult movies on videocassette and cable television shifted the consumption of porn from seedy movie theaters and backroom bookstores to the comfort of one's own living room—or bedroom. In 1995, Americans spent more than $150 million ordering adult movies on at-home pay-per-view TV.

Most of today's profits from porn are being generated by businesses not traditionally associated with the sex industry: mom-and-pop neighborhood video outlets, cable companies like Time Warner, and hotel chains like Marriott, Sheraton, Hyatt, and Holiday Inn, which earn millions of dollars each year by supplying X-rated films to their guests. In 1995, hotel guests spent $175 million to view porn in their rooms. Some couples check into hotels just to watch porn and perhaps to emulate their favorite stars. Hotels get a 20 percent cut of the profits.

Despite some of the toughest restrictions on sexually explicit materials of any Western industrialized nation, the United States is by far the world's leading producer of porn. It churns out 150 hard-core video titles *a week*, and young "actors" and "actresses" are entering the industry in record numbers. Porn "talent agencies" are commonplace in southern California, and porn "film critics" review the latest releases. Porn stars have fan clubs, autograph signings, and attend annual awards. Porn has gone legit.

Let's go back to the beginning of porn and prostitution.

THE FIRST PROSTITUTE; *GILGAMESH*, 2,000 B.C.E., BABYLON ◆

*G*ilgamesh is one of the great classics of Babylonian literature and one of the earliest recorded poems. Gilgamesh, hero of the epic, was a legendary Mesopotamian king, and the narrative poem about his exploits, completed about 2,000 B.C.E., contains an account of a great flood strikingly similar to the biblical flood. The epic also contains the first written account of prostitution.

At the time Gilgamesh is supposed to have lived, people in the Near East still worshiped sacred prostitutes. According to one story told in the epic, Gilgamesh was harassing a rival city by capturing their sons for his army and their daughters for sexual pleasures, including marriage. The oppressed people prayed to their god, who scooped up clay of the earth and created a "new man," a warrior named Enkidu, a fit rival to Gilgamesh.

Enkidu is described as an innocent, wild man, nearly invincible. Gilgamesh, fearful of defeat, decides to weaken his rival by tempting him with a temple prostitute: once the "newly created man" lost his sexual innocence through intercourse with a woman, he would be weak, human, and vulnerable. (The similarities with Adam and Eve's Fall in the Garden are striking.) Thus, a beautiful temple prostitute is sent to Enkidu, who's mesmerized by her:

> [She] untied her loin-cloth and opened her legs,
> and he took possession of her comeliness;
> She used not restraint by accepted his ardor,
> She put aside her robe and he lay upon her.
> She used on him, the savage, a woman's wiles,
> His passion responded to her.
> For six days and seven nights Enkidu approached
>   and coupled with the prostitute.

And there was harm from too much sex: it weakened and corrupted Enkidu. Sex also gave him "forbidden knowledge":

After he was sated with her charms,
He set his face toward his game.
But when the gazelles saw him, Enkidu, they ran;
The game of the steppe fled from his presence.
Enkidu tried to hasten [after them, but] his body
        was [as it were] bound.
His knees failed him who tried to run after his game.
Enkidu had become weak, his speed was not as before.
But he had intelligence, wide was his understanding.

After Gilgamesh defeats Enkidu in a trial of strength, the two men become best of friends. The legend, which contains the first exotic verse in Western literature, also contains several sexist themes that survive to this day: women are designed to ensnare men; sex with a woman weakens a man; the most desirable—and dangerous—woman is a beautiful young prostitute.

SACRED PROSTITUTION; EAST AND WEST; ANTIQUITY TO CHRISTIAN ERA ◆

*T*oday, even in countries where prostitution is legal, its practitioners are not considered sacred or holy. Yet such women once were personages of high station—priestesses who ran religions, not outraged them through scandal.

How did the woman of yore go from a sacred prostitute to a street whore?

Sex is not what it used to be. When prostitutes were sacred, brothels were housed in temples; sex was a sacrament, and intercourse was holy communion with the gods. Prostitutes were married to divinity (as nuns are now), and paid-for coitus was a pious act that put a man in the state of grace, not out of it. A prostitute's fees were turned over to a priest, not a pimp, and were used for the maintenance of the temple-brothel and to provide for her well-being.

Sacred prostitution was widespread and popular—and profitable, indulged in throughout the Middle East, Near East, and in Greece and Rome. Greek soldiers returning from battle would scale the scraggy bluffs outside of Corinth to reach the summit temple-brothel of Aphrodite. The beleaguered men, after months on the battlefield, would stay several days to be "rejuvenated," paying the sacred women in gold and gems, the spoils of war. It was incentive to do battle.

In many early religions, fertility rites and public sex acts were the equivalent of "sacraments."

The cynical (or envious) among us might be inclined to view all this as a flimsy ruse, a male rationalization for sexual license. And maybe it was, to a degree. But in ancient times religion was ineluctably entwined with every aspect of life; all actions had sacred underpinnings. Early states were theocracies.

Moreover, a major concern throughout the ancient world was fertility. It was an obsession. Today we are overpopulated, straining the earth's resources; machine power has usurped manpower. But when civilization began, communities were small and laborers few; extinction was only a low birthrate, or one plague, away. When we abort fetuses and pop pills to prevent conception it is hard to imagine a time when fecundity was an issue of survival of the species. Little wonder that all early societies were preoccupied with fertility rites, mother goddesses, and bacchanalia that paired teenage men and women by lottery. Religion not only encouraged sex, sex cults were religions.

Four thousand years ago, the ancients honored their harlots, as evinced in *Gilgamesh*. In the early second millennium B.C.E. of Hammurabi, women from the best families sought positions as temple prostitutes. In *Sex in History*, Reay Tannahill concludes that sacred prostitution "had its origin in fertility rituals" and that "the sacred prostitutes' earnings accounted for a substantial part of the temples' income." In other words, sex supported religion.

Three Kinds of Holy Whores

The authors of *Gilgamesh* classified sacred prostitutes into three groups:

- The **qadishtu** was a full-time temple harlot, always on call and available to any man who had the money.
- The **ishtaritu** was a servant of the chief goddess Ishtar. She copulated only with men of noble rank or with men with stellar military victories. Thus she was something like a high-paid call girl, out of the reach of the common man.
- The **harimtu**—the word is related to "harem"—was a semisecular prostitute who, once married, could no longer work at her profession. In modern terms, she'd be equivalent to a sexually liberated, promiscuous young woman, who, once married, became monogamous.

A girl's parents, usually around the time of her puberty, determined whether she'd become a sacred prostitute or a man's wife. Looks and figure played a major role in the decision.

PROSTITUTION IN THE OLD TESTAMENT ◆

The Old Testament records how the Canaanites and their neighboring tribes worshiped idols through sacred prostitution. For at least two thousand years, the people of Canaan engaged in sacred prostitution, which the first Semites in the region, the Amorites, found irresistible. Even the later Israelite conquerors were strongly attracted by the holy prostitute system of worship and, against their own leaders' vehement opposition, converted to the ancient sex cult.

Many of the Old Testament's references to prostitution indicate acceptance of the prostitute as a fact of life:

- Jephthah was the son of Gilead and a harlot. Although prevented from inheriting because his mother was not his father's legal wife, he was not taunted because of his mother's profession.
- Samson the Nazarite, who was dedicated to God while still a fetus, enjoyed the prostitutes at Gaza, as did many other holy men.

"It is significant to note," writes a contemporary biblical scholar, "that the Bible's protest against prostitution proscribed its practice not so much for its

THE CLAP ◆ *How did the genital mucus discharge, caused by gonococci bacteria, get the name "clap"? After all, venereal disease—named after Venus, Roman goddess of love—is nothing to applaud.*

The sixteenth-century word "gonorrhea" is from the Greek gonos, *meaning "seed," also the basis of our word "gonad." A discharge of pus from the penis is hard to overlook, though ancient peoples often confused the white mucus with semen itself. The Late Latin* gonorrhoea *meant "morbid loss of semen."*

"Clap," dating to 1587, is from the Old French clapoir, *meaning "a bubo" or swollen lymph node, especially in the groin. Physicians realized that a man with a continually dripping penis always had a palpable "bubos" in his groin. So, too, did people suffering from the "bubonic" plague—hence the name. Thus to have "the clap" meant you had swollen lymph nodes.*

Is gonorrhea mentioned in the Bible? All of Leviticus 15 is devoted to an abnormal discharge from male and female genitals. The condition was considered so contagious that an infected person was isolated. Any object he or she had touched was regarded as unclean and destroyed. Hebrew, Greek, and Latin versions of Scripture use words like "discharge" or "issue." Many scholars believe the disease was gonorrhea.

immorality as for its idolatry." When the Hebrew writers of the Bible condemned Israel for apostasy, they wrote of the nation "whoring" after other *gods* (Exodus 34:15; Leviticus 17:7, Judges 2:17). A sin far greater than prostitution was violating God's First Commandment to Moses: "I am the Lord thy God, thou shalt not have strange gods before me."

The truth is that prostitution persisted among the Hebrews and was occasionally pursued even in the Temple itself. Only the most stringent measures eventually abolished the cult of the sacred whore. Not surprisingly, the ancient Hebrew biblical word for a female cult "prostitute" (derived from the Babylonian), *k'dashah*, is related to the Hebrew words for "holiness" and "consecration."

The Israelites who embraced Yahweh and the concept of monotheism finally turned their backs on sexual fertility rites and sacred prostitution. The new laws, contained largely in Leviticus and Deuteronomy, stated that:

• A priest could no longer marry a whore because she would render him unclean and unfit for service (Leviticus 21:7, 21:14)

• The money that a prostitute was paid for her services could no longer be used to pay temple dues or to support the temple in any way (Deuteronomy 23:18).

• A priest's daughter could no longer become a sacred prostitute, and if she did sell sex for money she was to be burned to death (Leviticus 21:9).

• And where a parent could once choose the career of sacred prostitution for a daughter, a father could not "demean your daughter by making her a harlot" (Leviticus 19:29).

One of the most detailed descriptions of the wiles of the whore is found in the Book of Proverbs (7:9–27). A father tells his son about a young man he saw seduced by a prostitute:

> *In the twilight, in the evening, in the dark of night: Behold, there he met a woman with the attire of a harlot . . . So she caught him, and kissed him, and with an impudent face said to him . . .*
>
> *I have decked my bed with covering of tapestry, with carved works, with fine linen from Egypt. I have perfumed by bed with myrrh, aloes, and cinnamon. Come, let us take our fill of love until the morning; let us solace ourselves with love. For the good man is not at home, he is gone on a long journey . . .*
>
> *With her much fair speech she caused him to yield, with the flattering of her lips she forced him.*
>
> *He goes to her stairway as an ox goes to the slaughter, or as a fool to the correction of the stocks . . .*
>
> *Listen my children, attend to the words of my mouth. Let not your heart decline to her ways, go not astray in her paths. For she has cast down many wounded. Many strong men have been slain by her. Her house is the way to hell, going down to the chambers of death.*

THE DECLINE AND FALL OF THE SACRED HARLOT ✦

The practice of sacred prostitution crumbled slowly, and its fall is closely associated with a general change in attitude toward women, a downrating.

The Israelites of the Old Testament were not the only ones to strip the

---

WIVES AS WHORES ◆ *Sex in imperial Rome was wild—for men, that is. A married man could legally have sex with female slaves, prostitutes, divorcees, and widows but not with a virgin or a wife.*

Strict adultery laws forbade married women from any form of extra-marital sex. The crime of adultery itself was defined as sex with a married woman, not with a married man. If an adulterous wife was caught, the punishment was forfeiture of her property and exile.

Roman wives were very clever when it came to finding a loophole in the law. Many, from well-to-do families, registered as prostitutes. Ancient Roman law clearly stated that any women listed in the prostitute registry could not be punished for sex acts. The law had been written by men for their own pleasure, and to encourage as many women as possible to register as prostitutes. Many lustful wives took advantage of the letter of the law.

The Roman biographer and historian Suetonius (c. 69–c. 140 C.E.) officially complained about this legal technicality and insisted that something be done about it. "Married women from well-known families are registering as prostitutes," he wrote. "They are escaping punishment for their adulteries by renouncing the privileges of their rank in society."

---

professionalism and honor from prostitution. The Babylonians eventually turned prostitution into a onetime chore for every female. "Every woman who is a native of the country," wrote Greek historian Herodotus (c. 485–c. 425 B.C.E.), "must once in her life go and sit in the temple and there give herself to a strange man. She is not allowed to go home until a man has thrown a silver coin into her lap and taken her outside to lie with him."

A woman could not select her onetime mate: "She must go with the first man who throws her the money. When she has lain with him, her duty to the goddess [Ishtar] is discharged and she may go home."

This was token prostitution, at a pedestrian level, and it could be cruel. "Tall, handsome women quickly managed to get home," says Herodotus. "But the ugly ones stay a long time before they can fulfill the condition which the law demands, some of them, indeed, as much as three or four years":

Pathways are marked out in all directions among the women so that strangers can conveniently pass among them and make their choices. Once a woman has been seated, she may not return home until one of the strangers has tossed a coin in her lap and has had sexual intercourse with her outside the temple.

When he casts the coin, he must say; "I invite you in the name of the goddess." It doesn't matter how little money he gives because he won't be rejected, for that would be a sin, since the money belongs to the temple.

She follows the first man who tosses a coin and she never rejects anyone. Once she's finished having sex, she has fulfilled her vow to the goddess and can go home. Afterwards no gift, no matter how generous, will buy her.

Modern historians believe that the Babylonian custom of onetime prostitution described by Herodotus may have existed for several reasons: the ancient belief that intercourse with a virgin was dangerous and that the danger could be lessened through her defloration by a stranger; the ancient taboo against the shedding of the blood of the first night; physical preparation for marriage, such that the woman was ready to accept the sexual advances of her husband. Herodotus himself claimed that the custom of onetime prostitution was a religious act, a fertility offering by the woman, to a goddess, so that she would be granted a husband and many children.

Sacred prostitution was most strongly weakened by the compilers of the Old Testament. And the later rise of Christianity did it in entirely.

The biblical language that condemns prostitution is at times racy. The Book of Ezekiel uses harlotry as a synonym for the sins of Jerusalem. Damned women are pictured "lying in wait at every corner," they solicit a man by "capturing him with the eyelids" and hold him in their beds "until the morning." She "doted upon her paramours," men "whose members [penises] were like those of asses, and whose issue [ejaculate] was like that of horses," and the Lord assures that her "harlotry shall be uncovered" and that she will suffer in hatred.

One Old Testament writer reminds prostitutes that as they age their beauty fades and men forsake them. In the "song of the aged whore," an old prostitute can attract men's attention only with music:

SYPHILIS, THE FRENCH DISEASE ♦ *The name "syphilis" first appeared in the title of a 1530 Latin poem,* Syphilis sive Morbus Gallicus, *literally "Syphilis or the French Disease," by Italian physician and astronomer Girolamo Fracastoro. The hero of the tale is a shepherd named Sifilo, who in the poem becomes the first victim of the illness.*

In his introductory words, Fracastoro spoke of "a fierce and rare disease never before seen for centuries, which ravaged all of Europe and the flourishing cities of Asia and Libya, and invaded Italy in that unfortunate war whence from the Gauls it has its name."

Why Fracastoro chose the name for his shepherd—and hence the illness—has never been fully explained. He may have adopted it from the Greek legend of Sipylus, the name of a child slain by Apollo.

Even more mysterious than the name of the disease is its origins. The best modern conjecture is that the illness, caused by a spirochete bacterium, Treponema pallidum, *originated in Africa, as the AIDS virus probably did.*

Representation of syphilis, the "French disease," Morbus Gallicus, *as divine punishment.*

Take a harp and wander about the city,
O forgotten whore.
Produce sweet music and sing many songs
So that you will be remembered. (Isaiah 23:16)

In the New Testament, Saint Paul is one of the harshest critics of prostitutes. A man who has sex with a harlot, says Paul, becomes as impure as she is:

Do you not know that your bodies are the organs of Christ? Shall I take then the organs of Christ and make them a whore's organ? Never!

You know, do you not, that whoever joins himself to a whore becomes one body with her? For as it is written, "the two become one flesh" (1 Corinthians 6:15–16).

PROSTITUTION, THE LESSER OF TWO EVILS •

Two major Christian theologians took a curiously bizarre stand on prostitution. Both men condemned it as a vile practice, as they did any kind of sex outside of marriage. However, Saint Augustine and Saint Aquinas both argued that if prostitution were disallowed entirely, unmarried men and widowers would be driven to an even more sinful expression of lust: homosexuality. If a horny man without a wife could not pay to fornicate with a female prostitute, he'd resort in time to buggering other men.

Aquinas compared female prostitution to a stinking sewer beneath a splendid palace. If the sewer is closed off, then the palace itself will fill up with vile waste. The palace will be more uninhabitable than before. Thus, reasoned the saint, if female prostitution were eliminated, the world itself would be contaminated by male-on-male "sodomy."

Martin Luther

In the sixteenth century, Protestant reformer Martin Luther adopted a similar attitude. When another influential Protestant suggested that all "whores" in Germany be seared with a red-hot iron on the cheeks, forehead, and forearms, Luther took a gentler stand. He advised town officials to proceed with caution in closing brothels. For one thing, the total elimination of the evil of prostitution would dangerously drive up unemployment, said Luther, since thousands of women would no longer have a means of supporting themselves.

Major Christian saints have found a rationale to justify prostitution: it reduces incidences of rape and homosexuality.

(A single woman then had few legitimate employment opportunities.) And, too, men who frequented prostitutes, said Luther, would turn to the greater evils of homosexuality and, perhaps, beastiality.

Essentially, what these three male theologians were saying is that if a man can't screw a woman when he feels the urge to, God help young boys, ducks, and sheep.

And so, in time, the sacred prostitute was pushed out of the temple and onto the street. Communion with her no longer linked a man directly with divinity, though an ecstasy could still accompany the experience. She kept her money for herself, and churches made up the deficit by selling other things —like indulgences. She became a despised woman of low, disreputable standing, socially ostracized, though not entirely unpopular. In time she became a "professional," and in many countries her profession has become legal.

Though *sacred* prostitution has ended, the end of prostitution itself will probably never be recorded. The end is certainly not coming in an era when top politicians and major television ministers pay women for sexual favors. Indeed, it sometimes seems that it would be easier, and politically safer, if the prostitute were again sacred (respected), her profession holy (legitimate), her fees taxed, her health monitored, and her house of operation, if not a temple, then not a seedy motel either.

Fear of AIDS and the availability of pornography are two reasons for the decline in modern prostitution.

MODERN PROSTITUTION'S DECLINE; 1960S TO PRESENT ◆

For the first time in thousands of years, sex for money is on a precipitous decline. Fear of AIDS is one factor, the easy access of video porn another. But a greater reason is the development of simple contraceptives and the sexual revolution that began in the 1960s. Men no longer have to buy sex because so many attractive young women give it away for free. Free love, and the subsequent decline of the double standard, undermine prostitution.

In 1948, sex researcher Alfred Kinsey reported that 69 percent of the white males in his sample had been with prostitutes; 15 percent of those men visited prostitutes on a regular basis. Bachelors, divorcees, and widowers made up the largest portion of regulars, men without ready sexual access to a wife. Today the number of white males who visit prostitutes is under 10 percent.

"Kinsey's findings emphasize what in our opinion are the two most significant factors relating to the decline in prostitution," write Vern and Bonnie Bullough in *Women and Prostitution: A Social History,* "the development of effective contraception and the current sexual revolution, both of which have seriously undermined the double standard. Because of these changes, women, particularly some of the younger ones, have become more willing to participate freely in sexual activities, with the result that the de-

PHONE SEX ◆ *Each evening, between 9 P.M. and 1 A.M., an estimated quarter of a million Americans pick up the phone and dial a number for commercial phone sex. In the porn trade, these calls are referred to as "audiotext"—as opposed to dirty pictures and lewd written words.*

The average call by a man—or woman—lasts six to eight minutes. The average charge ranges from eighty-nine cents to four dollars a minute. Industry insiders claim that three-quarters of the callers are male lonely hearts seeking conversation with an attentive woman. For these men the sexual content of the call is of secondary importance.

Some callers get a taped message. But most connect with an "actress"— a scripted womn who may be a bank teller or housewife by day and is looking to pick up a little extra cash with night work. The easy access and anonymity of phone sex account for its great commercial success. In 1996, Americans spent between $750 million and $1 billion on telephone sex. AT&T, once known by the wholesome maternal name of Ma Bell, is one of the biggest carriers of phone sex. Ma has become a Madame.

To get around FCC obscenity laws, the dirtiest phone sex is routed through "actresses" in the Dominican Republic, Aruba, Africa, or Russia. International sex calls have become a lucrative business for foreign phone companies, who share in the profits. The complex routing system helps explain why the volume of long-distance calls to the tiny African island nation of São Tomé in 1995 jumped from 40,000 minutes to 13 million minutes. When you reach out and touch someone during phone sex, your reach just may embrace the globe.

mand for the services of professionals is diminishing. Though many of the early twentieth-century advocates of women's liberation hoped to raise men to what they regarded as the women's higher standards of celibacy, what has in fact happened is that neither women or men are putting quite so much emphasis on female chastity as was once the case."

CHAPTER 17

Heels and Squeals

STILETTOS TO FUCK ME PUMPS

*One day these boots are gonna
walk all over you.*

NANCY SINATRA: SONG LYRICS

STILETTO HEELS; ITALY, LATE NINETEENTH CENTURY ◆

A dominatrix, or fem dom, about to sadistically humiliate a male slave through a "power exchange"—the willing surrender of sexual control by a submissive to a dominant (D&S) or by a bottom to a top (T&B)—must be appropriately dressed for their intimate tête-à-tête (head to head)—or tête-bêche (head to foot; if that's their thing). She must wear a black leather mask (for the sexual turn-on of anonymity), crack a braided black whip (to inflict pain and encourage discipline), don a black silk bra (the color suggests all things taboo), squeeze into tight black spandex hot pants (that mimic dark skin), and step into black vinyl, stiletto-heeled boots, with which she will spike the naughty masochist groveling under her authoritative foot.

Fem doms before the late nineteenth century may have had black masks, whips, corsets, and tight pants, but they did not sport the advantage of stilettos. The high, thin, sharp, spiked footwear originated in Italy near the

Stiletto heels on a pair of "fem doms," 1930.

turn of the twentieth century, and was worn only by the highest-priced dominatrices.

Word Origins

The word "stiletto," dating from around 1611, is Italian for "small dagger," a short, slender knife. In the fashion trade, a stiletto was any sharp pointed instrument used for piercing holes for eyelets or embroidery.

In America, the first recorded use of the term "stiletto heel" was in 1953; designating a high thin heel narrower than a spike heel.

The Italian for "dagger," *stilo*, is from the Latin *stilus*, a slender, pointed etching instrument—a stylus—used to scratch the first written words onto clay and wax tablets in the figures of cuneiform and hieroglyphics. The stylus was humankind's first pencil, an instrument by which a teacher, a disciplinarian by trade, instilled fear and learning in a student. Fear and learning are just what a fem dom's stilettos are intended to instill in a male heels fetishist.

One high-priced Manhattan dominatrix, who charges in excess of $350 an hour and disciplines only male executives, explained what stilettos mean to her client:

> *The heels push my ass, real high, and make me taller. They give me an advantage over my client. I put them on and get a rush of power, knowing I could waste any man I choose to. I am not a violent woman, not really,*

but in stilettos I become real aggressive. High spiked heels bring out the tigress in me. I can shout, "Down on the floor, you turd! I said down. NOW, you worthless CEO."

MALE FOOT FETISHISM ◆

*B*rowsing through an adult video store in a tree-lined, suburban neighborhood of Long Island, I came across:

Foot Worship, Stiletto Sluts, High-Heeled Dominatrix, Dykes in Spikes, Eastern Foot Torture, Toe Fucks.

Among the videos, shoes and feet were conspicuously well represented, trailing in number only such understandably erotic body parts as breasts, legs, and behinds.

I could not find an equivalent section on the eroticism of men's shoes and feet—no tapes entitled *Studs in Construction Boots, Pretty Boys in Penny Loafers, Blond Surfers in Smelly Sneakers.* Apparently women are not sexually into men's shoes or feet.

Unlike women's shoes, you'll never find men's footwear advertised as offering "peep toes," "naked heels," or "bare insteps." Most women don't care about seeing men's feet bare; many think they are ugly.

Psychiatrists estimate that perhaps 10 percent of the world's men, a conservative estimate, are foot or shoe fetishists.

While researching foot fetishism, I came across a conversation between two women in a book:

"Men find bare feet in sandals a real turn-on. So much cleavage."
"Cleavage?"
"Cracks between your toes? Some men see a toe crack as an intimate body slit. In sandals, you're showing eight vaginas at once."
"God! What kind of shoes can I wear that won't attract fetishists?"
"Sneakers. Until they get smelly."

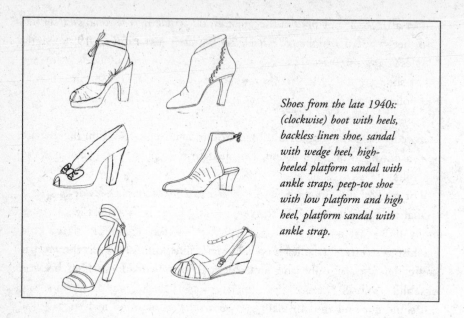

Shoes from the late 1940s: (clockwise) boot with heels, backless linen shoe, sandal with wedge heel, high-heeled platform sandal with ankle straps, peep-toe shoe with low platform and high heel, platform sandal with ankle strap.

SHOE = FOOT = AROUSAL: FETISH LOGIC ◆

*F*oot worship is a major male fetish, and high heels are *the* single article of female attire most commonly fetishized. Shoes with thin, steep heels—preferably with open toes—are especially hot, as are low-cut backs or, better-yet, no backs at all. "Sling-backs" reveal a woman's full naked heel.

In the nineteenth century, lacy whalebone corsets outranked shoes as men's favorite cultish sex object. (Back then, women's shoes did not look all that different from men's, so there was nothing to get excited about.) Today, when women no longer wear corsets—except dominatrices—female footwear ranks as men's favorite fetish article of clothing.

The erotic appeal of high heels has much to do with the way they shape the calf muscle, thrust out the rear end, and cause a woman—or transvestite—to walk with a delicate gait and decided wiggle. The Chinese once bound young girls' feet not only because Chinese men found small feet erotic, but also because a woman with stunted feet walked with a demurely stammering gait. When a woman's rear end wiggles, so does her bust. Men have always liked to see women wiggle, in one way or another.

"I don't know who invented the high heel," said Marilyn Monroe, who perfected the wiggle as an art form, "but all women owe him a lot."

For a fetishist, not only is the most erotic article in a woman's closet her high heels, but the higher the heel the hotter it gets him. In 1994, Marla Maples' male publicist was convicted of stealing scores of heels from her closet shortly before Ms. Maples became Mrs. Donald Trump. She allowed the police to set up a hidden camera, which caught the man in the act. Released from jail, he went back to stealing other women's pumps, stilettos, and wedgies. Sex fetishes, like all perversions, are deeply rooted in the psyche. Can a child molester be cured? Can a high heels thief? Such men may be rehabilitated, but the urge will always be there.

For men who like to be sexually dominated by women, high heels hold a special allure. "The idea of a woman wearing heels is to emphasize her naturally dominant and aggressive personality," wrote one male "slave" in a fetishist newsletter. "Leather is firm and hard like skin. A heel lifts the woman above the man, puts her on a pedestal. A man worshiping high heels is humbling himself before the superior sex. I feel grateful to kiss her shoes."

Psychiatrists say that all shoe fetishists are at heart masochists in search of an object to fixate upon.

Fetish Origin

For a true foot fetishist, any shoe—even a smelly old sneaker—can be a sexual turn-on. It's not the shoe itself that is the primary erotic object but the foot that once wore it. In fact, the foot itself is often a more important primary sex object than the woman who owns the foot and wore the shoe.

Many foot fetishists can recall erotic (or traumatic) encounters with feet in childhood: an adult's foot that playfully and pleasurably rubbed against a crotch; a parent's shoe that became a secretive, private plaything; being tickled (or tormented) while being held down and made submissive by an adult's foot. Yet not every male child who has such experiences develops a foot fetish.

What can be said with certainty is that fetishists are almost exclusively men, who can eroticize easily over body parts—even body adornments. Their biology has made them that way. From a reproductive standpoint, a male needs to get hard fast and stay that way; nature has constructed him so that he turns on quickly—in response to women, to parts of women, or to their clothing. A male executive seated at his desk, engrossed in balancing the company's books, can be sexually sidetracked by a shapely leg passing by, irrespective of whom it belongs to. A passing pair of high heels could turn him on. With virtually no conscious thought, the "pencil" between his legs can become as stiff and straight as the pencil in his hand. His hand might even change pencils.

RABBIT'S FOOT = PENIS = GOOD LUCK CHARM ◆

*W*hat male shoe fetishists don't realize is that the foot has been viewed for centuries as a phallic symbol—often a phallic substitute. The equation "foot = penis" was appreciated long before Freud made the connection.

The rabbit's foot became a good-luck amulet associated with male fertility some twenty-five hundred years ago. Celtic tribes living in western Europe worshiped the rabbit, envying the fecund animal for its large and frequent litters. They believed that a man who carried around a rabbit's foot—the symbolic equivalent of the animal's indefatigable penis—would father many children.

Thus, in a way, some foot fetishists can be said to have a penis envy complex. The large, bony, always-hard foot, itself a kicker and penetrator, is an impressive substitute for the smaller, shrinkable, less reliable penis.

It is only one step from the foot to the shoe: *penis = foot = shoe*.

A man obsessed with feet—repelled by a man's feet, turned on by a woman's—views the foot of the opposite sex as a magic charm, like a rabbit's foot. This reliable charm soothes his anxiety about the sex act and his sometimes unreliable erection. Performance anxiety is a male fear, and another reason why fetishism is almost always a male perversion.

A man can seek out an ideal foot on a women, kiss it, lick it, possess it, and worship it. In doing so, he grasps the two things he wants most in his sex life but lacks: a woman and a reliable penis. These two are embodied in one easily obtainable object: her hard shoe.

What is the preferred color of women's footwear among shoe fetishists?

Black, psychiatrists report.

What is a dominatrix's favorite footwear?

Black patent leather boots with piercingly pointed spikes. Psychiatrists have written volumes on the subject.

The Not-So-Great Gatsby

F. Scott Fitzgerald was quite candid about the fact that women's feet—and footwear—excited him, especially high heels. In a scene from his first novel, *This Side of Paradise* (1920), Fitzgerald portrays a man's feet as ugly, a symbol of evil and sexual immorality: "The feet were all wrong. It was like weakness in a good woman, or blood on satin."

But Fitzgerald loved women's feet and footwear. One biographer argues that Fitzgerald's obsession with feet, "which stick out stiffly and were strongly associated with sex," supports the rumor that the great novelist had a small penis. Fitzgerald's favorite color of women's footwear was, perhaps significantly, black.

FUCK ME PUMPS; 1940S •

*T*he naked female foot is a turn-on in part because men eroticize easily over female body parts. Frederick's of Hollywood has always promoted its open-toe and open-heel models as sexually suggestive because they reveal foot flesh and toe cleavage. Two highly popular models were named "Open 'n Inviting" and "Open to Suggestion."

The more flesh a woman exposes—anywhere on her body—the more a man's libido tells him "she's available." This is how the low-cut, backless, open-toe shoes popularized in the 1940s by Joan Crawford came to be called—by gay men, originally—"fuck me pumps." The wearer is revealing nearly her entire foot, and all her toe cleavage. What's more, the naked heel is raised up and inviting, like an arched female buttocks presented to a male. "Do it to me" is what the shoe says to many men.

Essentially the shoe is a sandal given the erotic lift of being mounted on a high wedge or heel. Thus it's both the nakedness of the foot and the presentation of the elevated heel that merited the shoe its nickname. The word "pump," of course, carries its own sexual overtones.

Pumps and Scuffs

Some two centuries ago the French popularized the "pump"—French *pompe*, "an ornament"—a low-cut shoe without straps or ties that was spruced up with bangles and bows.

The Germans also produced a pump. It was a loose slipper, plain or jeweled, with a low heel.

Some linguists maintain that "pump" is onomatopoeic for the "plump, plump" sound its heel made in flapping against a wood floor.

A later woman's bedroom slipper, the "scuff," was named for the scuffing sound it made in the bedroom and around the house.

BULL DYKES IN BOOTS ✦

*N*ot everyone is likely to accept the psychological equation in which a foot or shoe symbolically equals a penis. But, interestingly, lesbians, who have no penises but do have feet, have used this pre-Freudian equation time and again in literature and language:

• In many Portuguese-speaking countries, a "butch dyke" will flatteringly refer to herself as a *sapatão*, "big shoe."
• In Brazil, the most complimentary slang for a tough, masculine bull dyke is *coturno*, "army boot."
• The term for a feminine "lipstick lesbian" is *spatilha*, "slipper"—the small, delicate kind of footwear worn by ballerinas.

Thus many lesbians refer to themselves in terms of shoes and boots. Some psychiatrists maintain that this behavior is, plain and simple, a reflection of penis envy.

GAYS IN BOOTS ✦

*F*or most gay men, the penis is a primary sexual object. But gay men have built an entire subculture around boots (black boots in particular): cowboy boots, construction worker's boots, motorcycle boots, and riding boots—the last, a name highly suggestive in itself.

The homosexual counterpart of the heterosexual fetishist who is fixated on women's high heels is the gay "boot slave," subservient to his boot-wearing, boot-stomping master.

Among male fetishists, straight men prefer steep high heels; gay men like large sturdy boots. Straight men prefer *black* heels, gay men *black* boots. This is no idle comparison—the first elevated heels appeared on men's *black* boots. The first humans in black high heels were not women, or gay men, or drag queens but heterosexual men.

"BOOT"; ENGLAND, POST-SIXTH CENTURY ✦

*I*f the word "boot" is so sexually charged, where did it come from? Is a boot, from a linguistic perspective, symbolically a penis?

The word "boot" is from the Old English *bot*, meaning "advantage." To the Anglo-Saxons the word was akin to the comparative "better" and the

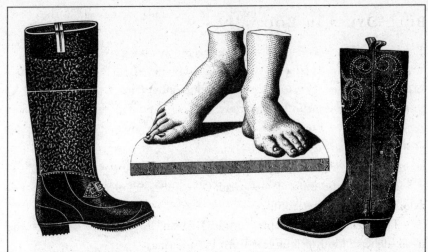

"Boot" is from the Old English bot, *meaning "advantage" or "the best" and carried sexual overtones.*

superlative "best." It is not hard to see how a man might apply words like "advantage," "better," "best" to his prize member. Linguists say this is exactly what happened. "Boot" became one of the many slang expressions for penis. Boots were big and highly prized—just like the male organ.

Many "boot" expressions have a sexual subtext:

• *"**You bet your boots**"* originated as a dare in which a man risked loosing his most valuable possession—his boots, and, symbolically, his penis.

• *"**He had a knife and a gun 'to boot.'**"* At the end of a sentence "to boot" conveys an advantage. Thus, since Anglo-Saxon times, a man with a boot (big penis) had an advantage. He was "better" than other men. He was the "best."

• ***Boot camp*** is a military training center. Because military men wear boots? In part. But also because rigorous training gives men the "advantage" of becoming the "best" soldiers, the meaning of the word "boot." Some recruits are of course "booted out" of boot camp. They don't "measure up."

• ***Bootees*** are shoes we put on babies' feet, an expression perhaps of our hope for their future. He or she will have all the advantages, will be the best.

• ***Booty*** is the valuable gain or prize of robbers or plunderers. The word shares an origin with "boot," the prize from plunder being seen as the "best" of what is stolen from a village or town.

• **Bootlick** is a colloquialism meaning to gain favor by fawning servility; to act as a slave. In the equation of boot = penis, to "bootlick" up to a superior male is to symbolically give him a "blow job."

• **Boots and saddle**, meaing any kind of mounted drill or formation, derives from the French calvary's bugle call to "mount" and prepare for "action", *boute-selle*.

• "**These Boots Are Made For Walkin'**," Nancy Sinatra's smash single of 1966, was a dominatrix's ballad, aggressive in its beat and lyrics. Frank Sinatra's daughter donned white patent leather boots as she threatened to "walk all over you." " 'Boots' is hard," Nancy said when asked about the song's sexual overtones, "but I'm as soft as they come."

• When we threaten to kick someone, we say, "**I'll boot you in the ass**." Symbolically we mean "put a prick up your ass" or "fuck you over." A foot/shoe fetishist may in fact be a masochist with fantasies of anal violation.

• To load a software program, you **boot the computer** or electronically "turn it on"—the phrase is doubly suggestive. A good computer, mindless slave that it is, responds instantly, obeying your every command.

When all of the evidence is looked at, a boot is in many ways a penis; the nickname fits like a hand in a glove. Centuries ago, a man with a big boot had an "advantage"; he had "the best" thing he could have. From the rabbit's foot to the Anglo-Saxon's boot, the penis comes in many disguises.

This poses an issue that therapists discuss: is a woman with a closet full of shoes, neatly arranged in rows, on racks—Imelda Marcos, say, or Marla Maples Trump—really collecting penises?

Many women, especially feminists, would find these speculations repellent. "If a cigar can be just a cigar," Gloria Steinem might snap, "then heels can be just heels. A boot, a boot." Masochistic men would find that put-down a turn-on.

CINDERELLA AND THE "GLASS SLIPPER" ◆

*S*ome shoe fetishists are fascinated by foot mutilation; the unknown creator of the "Cinderella" fairy tale certainly was. The original story is more than a thousand years old. In the sanitized version told today, cleaned up in the late seventeenth century by French storyteller Charles Perrault,

*French cavaliers in stylish
high-heeled shoes.*

Cinderella's stepsister tries on the lost slipper (originally made of "fur and silk") but it doesn't fit.

In the original version, the hefty, ugly stepsister hacks off her heels, then her toes, to fit into the slipper and win the prince's heart. The unsuspecting prince marries the mutilated girl and is later told by a bird that the foot in the shoe is not intact.

The fairy tale seems to be the fantasy of a true foot fetishist. Perrault eliminated the foot mutilation, making the butchery forever more impossible by describing the slipper as made of "glass." He did not choose glass by accident; the transparent material was chosen to display to people acquainted with the original bloody tale in oral tradition that foot mutilation need not take place.

HIGH HEELS: FRANCE, SIXTEENTH CENTURY ◆

To get to the origin of high heels, which first appeared in the 1590s, let's work our way through the centuries, starting with the open-toe, open-heel sandal.

Brown Unisex Sandals

The oldest shoe in existence, still in fairly good condition, is a sandal. It's constructed of woven papyrus and was discovered in an Egyptian tomb dating from 2000 B.C.E. Originally dark brown, it is now almost black.

Everyone wore dark brown sandals back then, if they wore shoes at all.

Because there was as yet no "right" or "left" sandal, there was no confusion over which shoe fit which foot. Since men and women wore the same kind of sandal, a unisex style and color, there probably were no male Egyptian sandal fetishists four thousand years ago.

Leather Moccasins

The first nonsandal shoes were leather wraparound moccasins, a favorite among Babylonian men and women around 1600 B.C.E. A high-quality moccasin might be laced around its rim with rawhide so it could be tightened to firmly fit the foot.

Moccasins came in only a few sizes—perhaps small, medium, and large —but in only one color: brown. There was no "right" or "left" moccasin; after wearing a pair for a while the shoes became right or left on their own. Psychiatrists say that when people wear unisex items, clothes fetishism is absent from a culture. We can assume then that Babylonian men did not get sexually excited over Babylonian women's moccasins.

Sexy Colored Shoes

The Greeks and Romans in the centuries prior to Christ's birth established shoe guilds, made footwear trendy, and introduced the first "right" and "left" shoes. Greeks bleached their sandals or moccasins white, or dyed them red, and they varied the thickness of the soles, and made laces and leg straps from hemp and esparto grass. All of this diversity and stylishness made shoes sexy items of dress.

Upper-class Roman women wore white or red shoes as everyday footwear. On special occasions—at the coliseum or theater—they'd changed to yellow or green shoes. A person could buy a shoe in, say, "small," "medium," or "large," but there were no scaled sizes yet. Wealthy people had shoes custom-made to their feet.

While a shoe is a simple article of clothing, the word itself is complex. In English, "shoe" evolved through seventeen spellings, with thirty-six variations for the plural, "shoes." The word is from the Anglo-Saxon verb *sceo*, "to cover."

Standard Shoe Sizes

In 1305, England's King Edward II decreed that for a standard of accuracy in certain trades, an "inch"—Latin *uncia*, "twelfth part"—be taken as the length of three dried barleycorns laid end to end; thirty-six barleycorns equaled a "foot."

British cobblers adopted the measure and began manufacturing footwear in standard sizes. Shoes came in various colors, styles, and sizes—but mostly for men; women's shoes were fairly plain and simple since they were hidden under the long dresses and gowns both popular and practical throughout the Middle Ages. As yet, no shoes had elevated heels, and when the daring new lifts would arrive—heels as much as three inches high—they would not be on a woman's shoe.

Frenchmen in High Heels

Frenchmen wore the first high heels and, by all accounts, liked the lift they gave. Perhaps they even liked the way the heels shaped their calves and pushed out their butts. Men in heels certainly did not complain about the stylish shoes being uncomfortable or hard to walk in. The early heels were only two inches high and squarish in cross section; a fashionable Frenchman wore them from sunrise to bedtime. High heels were all the rage in France at the close of the sixteenth century and shortly thereafter in England and Italy.

Italian Men in Platform Shoes

Italian men, somewhat shorter than British and French men, adored high heels and produced some of the highest lifts of the time. They introduced the platform shoe—which entertainers like Elton John in the 1970s would exaggerate to almost dangerous heights, with a unisex appeal. Italian men wore both high heels and platform shoes for daytime work and evening entertainment. If women were envious, no historian recorded it.

The Advantage of Heels

Men had turned to heels gradually and for a practical purpose.

The first elevated heels appeared on riding boots, so that a man's shoes locked into the stirrups. (Women rode sidesaddle.) There are many reports of men liking the added height that a heeled shoe gave them; the average male during the medieval period was several inches shorter than the man of today. Proper prenatal care and good nutrition throughout the growing years have added inches to humans' height—and years to longevity.

Heels had another advantage. With overcrowded cities and poor sanitation—no plumbing or flush toilets—people during the Middle Ages tossed

Women's decorative French high heels (left). Men were the first into heels but retained them only on their boots.

the waste from their tables and chamber pots into the street. This sludge and slime are what gave the word "gutter"—Latin *gutta*, a "drop" in the street —its figuratively foul meaning. The night's dinner, both scraps that went uneaten and everything that was digested and later voided, all ended in up in the gutter, a channel, or "drop," in the side of the street. Shoes with thick soles and high heels lifted the wearer at least a few inches above the stench and filth.

Women lifted their skirts a modest few inches so the fabric would not drag in the sludge.

WOMEN TAKE OVER HIGH HEELS; FRANCE, EIGHTEENTH CENTURY ◆

*M*en's monopoly of high heels lasted for less than a hundred years. France's Sun King, Louis XIV, had helped make high heels an escalating fad among men at court. During his reign (1643–1715), the longest in European history, France attained the zenith of its military power, and the French court reached an unprecedented level of culture and refinement. But none of Louis's towering achievements could compensate for his size. He was short and did not conceal his envy of tall men.

One day the monarch had his cobbler add extra inches to his two-inch high heels. The noblemen at court, in a rush to respectfully emulate the king,

RED FOR STRAIGHTS, LAVENDER FOR GAYS ♦ *Today the visual medium of television has made the white shirt and red necktie de rigueur for male politicians on the TV stump. Businessmen have also picked up the red necktie as a strong statement of male attire.*

Red, we say, is an aggressive male color—the color of blood, the facial flush of anger, the daring shade of a matador's cape.

Around 1900, red was the primary homosexual color. Homosexual men wore red neckties and carried red pocket handkerchiefs as a coded way to identify themselves in an era when no man was publicly "out." In 1909, the Chicago Vice Commission alerted police precincts that homosexuals throughout the city recognized each other by wearing red neckties. Arrest men in red ties. Sexologist Havelock Ellis studied homosexual men in New York City and Philadelphia and discovered the same color code of dress. "Perverts" wore white shirts with prominent red neckties; what he called "the badge of all their tribe."

In the 1970s, another color identified gay sexual preferences. A red hanky worn on a right-side pants pocket signified a "top," an "inserter," the active partner in intercourse. A man who wore a red hanky in his left pocket was signaling that he was a "bottom," a "receiver," the passive partner in coitus.

Today, with homosexuality out of the closet and gay enclaves in most big cities, gay men no longer need to color-code themselves by dress. Now it's a matter of pride. By the 1990s, lavender was the bold, defiant statement of homosexual identity. And pink triangles, used by the Nazis to stigmatize homosexual men, appeared on buttons and pins that expressed gay solidarity.

instructed their bootmakers to make their heels higher as well. This in turn forced Louis into even higher heels. Footwear historians have tracked this upward trend, which became such a fad that women got in on it. When heels lost their purely practical function, they became trendy affectations, fair game for both men and women. By the eighteenth century, women at the French court wore brocaded high-heeled shoes with elevations of up to four inches.

The Sexes Part Ways Over Heels

A strange thing happened. As women's heels grew higher and more decorative, studded with semiprecious stones, men's heels gradually came down and were divested of adornments such as buckles, buttons, and bows. Women came to view ornate high heels as the epitome of femininity. Men came to regard elevated heels as uncomfortable and unmanly.

Why?

Seldom do men and women equally embrace a fashion trend, and when they do the mutual enthusiasm lasts only briefly. The opposite sexes like being opposites in as many ways as possible. When French and Italian men began to be turned on to the female leg in decorative high heels, they did not like to see the same erotic footwear on the feet of men. All but a few men stopped wearing high heels, which went from being a man's standard footwear to one of his favorite sexual fetishes.

A historical split had occurred. By the end of the eighteenth century, women were in high heels to stay, and men had abandoned the style, going back to simple, flat shoes and low-heeled boots.

For decades, shoes with heels were called "French heels" or "Spanish heels" or took the name of the footwear designer; we'd say today "CK heels," or "DKNY heels."

In the 1920s, the term "high heels" passed from being merely a statement of height to connoting an enticing feminine fashion, and "high heels" became a sexually charged phrase.

In our culture, high heels came to be associated with sophisticated women, seductive screen goddesses, the working footwear of prostitutes, and an indispensable article of attire for transvestites. Who has ever seen a street hooker, a drag queen, or a male transvestite in flats? *High Heels* magazine's motto is "Flat is a dirty word."

CHAPTER 18

Dressed To Thrill

NYLONS TO CODPIECE

The thought of where stockings are headed
when they pass up a skirt fills me with envy.

MILTON BERLE

"NYLONS" TO MEN, "HOSE" TO WOMEN •

"Hose" is slang for "penis." It is also short for "hosiery."
You will never hear a man refer to women's stockings as "hose"
—the association is all wrong. To a man, a hose is that thing between his
legs, or what he uses to put out fires or douse the lawn. Filling up with fluid,
a hose swells from flaccid to firm then forcefully squirts out its discharge.
Men, when they refer to women's sheer leggings, prefer terms like "stockings," "fishnets," or "nylons."

Women have always liked the word "hose," and so have drag queens. For
women, the word carries a double meaning, one innocent, one sexual. The
tubular article of clothing running up her leg, under her skirt, and aiming
straight toward her vulva is a "hose."

Freud found women's stockings an ideal article for male fetishism. A woman's legs are, after all, a pathway to her genitals. As she rolls stockings up
her legs, she is directing the eye straight to her major sex organ. She is

pointing the way to the promised land. If, in addition, the stockings have seams running up the backs, the dark lines serve as This Way directionals. If the stockings attach to a garter belt, that decorative ring-around-the-thigh serves to frame the vagina.

Furthermore, *black* stockings on a white-skinned woman accentuate the crotch. They place the prized genitals on a black pedestal, white-lighted.

Nature uses the same effects. A bee is led to honey by directional markings on a flower's petal. The patterns are a landing strip, with taxiing instructions on how to dock at the honey pot.

Stockings on a woman tell a man where to pull in and pollinate.

MALE CASTRATION FEAR ◆

Freud loved to talk about stockings. To a male stocking fetishist, a woman's "hose" may be a substitute for her lack of a penis, which, as a very young boy, he thought all girls had. Every boy, after all, is surprised to learn that a girl does not have the organ, or "hose," he has—"nothing" is there. She's been castrated, is his early conclusion. It's possible he might one day be castrated, too. This is one way in which a stocking fetishism takes hold of a man. For Freud, the woman's "hose" becomes a phallus substitute, with which he fits her in order to assuage his own fear of castration:

> The fetish is a substitute for the woman's [the mother's] penis that the little boy once believed in and . . . does not want to give up . . . For if a woman had been castrated, then his own possession of a penis was in danger.

A stocking, or "hose," fetish represents an unconscious "compromise," said Freud, between the "unwelcome perception" that the woman/mother has no penis, and the wish and earlier belief that she does. Deep in his mind, the true fetishist reassures himself: "Yes, a woman *has* a penis, it just looks different from mine. Something has taken its place."

All men are fetishists to some degree, but only a small percentage become pathological. And, too, any object can become a phallic substitute; fur and hair, as we've seen, are two of the most obvious ones, since they have a straightforward associated with the crotch. Men can get sexually attached to a wide variety of nonsexual objects. A plethora of categories exist:

- **Hyphephilia**—arousal by female hair, animal fur, or any kind of fabric, usually delicate or skinlike.
- **Mysophilia**—arousal by smelling or chewing on soiled or sweaty female apparel.
- **Olfactophilia**—arousal by the odors of parts of the body, especially the genitals or anus.
- **Transvestophilia**—arousal from wearing female clothing, especially undergarments; largely a heterosexual condition.

Richard Krafft-Ebing, in *Psychopathia Sexualis* (1886), justified male fetishism by way of an analogy: "The adoration of separate body parts—or even articles of clothing—on the ground of sexual urges, frequently reminds us of the glorification of relics or sanctified objects in religious cults." As observed earlier, the word "fetish" is from the fifteenth-century Portuguese *feitiço*, a saint's relic, rosary, or any religious article.

If fetishism functions, as many psychiatrists believe it does, as a defense against castration fears, this would support Kinsey's conclusion—and that of many other sex researchers—that "fetishism is an almost exclusively male phenomenon."

Freud went further. He suggested that a boy's early "fear of castration caused by the sight of the female genitals"—nothing's there!—leads some boys to grow up to be fetishists. Other boys, more fearful, become homosexuals and have nothing to do sexually with penis-less, penis-hungry women. The brave majority of boys attempt to repeatedly conquer their fear by putting their own penis into the crotch of a woman. By providing her with the organ she's lost, they calm the dread of one day losing their own.

PANTIES AND PANTY HOSE •

*P*anties, by concealing a woman's penis-less crotch, also assuage castration fear and thus are a favorite fetish object—so many psychiatrists say.

With more certainty, linguists have identified these word origins:

- **Panty hose**—the word dates to 1963. The one-piece female undergarment, consisting of hosiery with a panty-style top, is a sexually charged item. For fetishists, panty hose comprises two parts: "panties" (the female part) coupled with "hose" (the male part). Linguistically the word is a marriage of

Men wore the first panty hose at a time when women's legs were still hidden under floor-length gowns.

"panty" + "hose," or "hers" + "his." A similar skintight combination of panties with leggings was first worn in the eleventh century *by men.*

• *Panty raid*—the collegiate term originated in the early 1950s to describe a mass male raid on a female dormitory to obtain panties, or any ladies lingerie, as trophies.

The fad is thought to have started in late March 1952, the beginning of spring, at the University of Michigan (some say the University of Missouri) with a male shout of "To the girls' dorm!" The harmlessness of the spirited high jinks was evidenced in the responses. More often than not, gleeful and squealing, girls complicitously tossed down their panties, stockings, or bras.

By May of that year, girls were shouting up to men's dormitory windows, demanding jockstraps, jockey briefs, and boxer shorts. This kind of behavior today could probably get a student expelled on grounds of sexual harassment.

• *Pantywaist* is a 1930s term for a male homosexual or "sissy." It was a stereotypical allusion to his narrow waist and overall female-like slenderness.

• *Panty*—first recorded in 1908 (also as "pantie"), is the diminutive of, or female form of, "pants" (or "pant"). It was first defined as a "woman's or child's undergarment covering the lower trunk and made with closed crotch."

• *Pants*—short for *pantaloons*, dates from about 1840. In Italian, *Pantalone* was a fictional character in the commedia dell'arte, a skinny old dotard who wears spectacles, slippers, and a tight-fitting combination of trousers and stockings, which were called, around 1590, "pantaloons."

"Sex Appeal" Theory of Fashion ◆

Fashions change—and quickly today. In the twentieth century, change has accelerated from decade to decade, then year to year, now season to season.

Why do we change styles so quickly? Is it so manufacturers can sell more goods for more gain? Certainly that is a major reason.

But those who study the psychological effects of styles say there's a sexual reason as well. Although Freud's work on fetishism is highly regarded, it's not the last word, especially since women have entered the fields of psychiatry and fashion design. The most popular explanation for the link between fashion and eroticism—and rapid changes in styles—is the "sex appeal" theory, also known as the theory of "shifting erogenous zones."

Proponents of the theory argue that the primary purpose of *all* women's fashion is the desire to continually reattract the opposite sex. The driving force behind seasonal changes in styles is to arouse men sated by last season's "look" to turn on to a new "look." In today's sexually liberated and sex-saturated times, fashion is driven by the "seduction principle." With so much sexual imagery in the media, men get sated quickly, and women must work hard to reseduce them with styles that continually shift the erogenous zone —from breasts to bellies to backs to legs to hair to lips.

Men, for their part, positively yearn to be reseduced, over and over again.

All of this seduction, says the theory, is to fulfill the biological imperative to continue the species, even if the sexes thwart conception at every chance they get.

Show This, *Hide* That

According to the sex appeal theory, women's styles—and, within the last decade, men's, too—attract the opposite sex by the titillating exposure, or concealment, of various erotic zones. Female breasts/male pecs. Female derriere/male buns. Female arms/male biceps. Svelte female legs/muscular male thighs. Long, luxurious hair on both sexes/short hair or shaved heads on both sexes. Exposed belly button on both sexes/ring-pierced belly buttons on guys and gals. Any zone will do.

The essential element is that fashion keeps shifting emphasis from one zone to another. Cover this, expose that. Next season expose that, cover this. Once a fashion trend has evolved to the point that a body zone is overexposed—that we've become sexually jaded to it—fashion must shift gears and emphasize some previous zone.

Which theory is correct? Freud's fetishism theory? The capitalist imperative that the faster a style becomes "dated," the faster people rush out to purchase new clothes? The modern sex appeal theory? The answer is probably a combination of all these.

SOCKS FOR WOMEN, HOSE FOR MEN: EUROPE, FOURTH CENTURY B.C.E. ◆

*H*ave you ever wondered how certain articles of clothing get assigned to the male or female sex? Why are certain clothes gender-specific? The whole concept of cross-dressing, or drag, is based on such simple gender assignments.

Today, men wear calf-high socks, and women wear thigh-high hose or stockings, but that was not always the case. The three words—sock, hose, and stocking—were originally not identified with the items we associate them with today. The articles of clothing did, however, have distinct gender associations. One sex dared not wear the garments of the other.

Sock

The original sock, or *soccus,* was a soft, leather slipper that covered mainly the toes and heel. It was worn by Roman women—and by effeminate men or men who wished to cross-dress. Its delicacy made it distinctly feminine. In the theater, a mime was guaranteed a laugh if he simply sashayed across the stage in ladies' "socks."

The *soccus* slipper was the forerunner both of our word "sock" and of a man's modern midcalf sock.

How did men come to wear socks?

From Rome, the soft leather *soccus* traveled to the British Isles, where the Anglo-Saxons shortened its name to *soc.* Rugged Anglo-Saxon men adopted the soft *soc* as their own form of footwear but wore it *inside* their coarse boots. On long military maneuvers, for which the Anglo-Saxons were famous, a *soc* protected their feet from abrasion. Thus, a lady's shoe became a man's sock. By changing its function—from outside footwear to inside footwear, from visually apparent to hidden—the *soc* crossed clothing's gender barrier. Once inside a boot, the *soc* was on its way up the ankle to become the modern sock.

Pants wrapped to tightly fit the calf were the first "stockings."

The Roman *soccus* also traveled to Germany, where it was also worn inside a boot. Its spelling was abbreviated to *socc*, which until the nineteenth century meant both the cloth footwear *and* a lightweight shoe.

HOSE TO HOSIERY; ROME TO RENAISSANCE ENGLAND ✦

Today it is women who wear tight leggings or hosiery, but men started the fashion.

In ancient times, men in warm Mediterranean countries wore wraparound skirts and had no need for the leg protection of pants. In the colder climates of northern Europe, though, Germanic tribes wore loose-fitting trousers reaching from the waist to the ankle, called *heuse*. For additional warmth, the trouser fabric was crisscrossed with rope from ankle to knee to keep out drafts. Pants, in a sense, were crudely molded into hose.

This style of wrapping pants to the leg was not unique to northern Europeans. When Julius Caesar led his Roman legions in the conquest of Gaul in the first century B.C.E., his soldiers' legs were protected from cold weather and the thorns and briers of northwestern forests by *hosa*—wrapped leg coverings of cloth or leather worn beneath the short military tunic.

About six centuries later, in England, the word *hosa* had become "hose." Interestingly, the Indo-European base for "hose" means "to hide", "to conceal"—as leg wrappings hid legs. It is through this meaning of tubular concealment that "hose" became the name for a water-carrying "pipe," slang for "penis," and later the name for the watering implement.

When "hose" became slang in England for "penis," the British renamed leg coverings "hosiery." Hosiery, then, is the polite form of the word "hose."

In the seventeenth century, when the condom—made then of waxed linen or animal gut and tied to the penis at the base—was introduced in England, the penile covering was called a "hose." At night, a man might slip his legs into one kind of hose and his penis into another. A woman rolls on her hose the way a man rolls on a condom.

PRIESTS IN WHITE STOCKINGS; ROME, LATE FOURTH CENTURY ◆

*L*ogically, it might seem that the Roman leg hose (*hosa*), which ran from the ankle to the upper thigh but did not cover the foot, would eventually be stitched to the soft Roman slipper (*soccus*) to make an entirely new item of clothing, a stocking. But this is not what happened.

The word "stocking" itself does not appear in the vocabulary of dress until the sixteenth century, though the garment had appeared centuries earlier. The forerunners of sexy modern stockings were *udones* (singular, *udo*), a favorite foot-and-leg garment of the early church fathers of Christianity.

By 100 C.E., Roman men were wearing a cloth foot sock called an *udo*. The earliest mention of the garment is found in the works of the Spanish-born Roman poet and epigrammatist Martial, who wrote that in *udones*, the "feet will be able to take refuge in cloth made of goat's hair."

At the time, the *udo* fitted over the foot and shinbone. Within a hundred years, Roman tailors had extended it to just over the knee, to be worn inside boots. Men who wore it without boots were considered effeminate, and as these kneelength stockings crept farther up to eventually cover the thigh, the stigma of effeminacy for men who wore the new styles increased.

History does not record when and why the opprobrium of effeminacy attached to men wearing stockings disappeared. But the taboo went slowly away, and Catholic clergymen seem to have been the trendsetters. In the fourth century, the church adopted above-the-knee stockings of white linen as part of a priest's liturgical vestments. With priests in stockings, other men found them safe to wear. A century later, church mosaics display full-length stockings—to the upper thigh—as the vogue among the clergy. The male laity soon copied the fashion.

Stockings had arrived and priests and noblemen were wearing them. But not yet women.

FRENCHMEN IN PANTY HOSE; ELEVENTH CENTURY ◆

The popularity of formfitting stockings among men grew in the eleventh century. Weaves were getting tighter and more "elastic," and the new stretch legwear—which now also covered the crotch and buttocks and extended up to the waist—was known as "skin-tights." They were panty hose, essentially, and were worn without jockstrap support. All of a man's assets, front and back, were on display.

When William the Conqueror crossed the English Channel in 1066 and became the Norman king of England, he and his men, in skin-tights, introduced the sexy style to the British Isles. And indeed the style was sexy. His son, William Rufus, wore French panty hose of such sheer, translucent fabric, clinging tightness, and exorbitant cost that they were immortalized in a poem. A muscular, well-proportioned nobleman presented in skin-tights at court could elicit a stir of whispers among the ladies.

Men's tights got even tighter and sexier as the centuries passed. Experimental blends of wool and cotton produced tights that were scandalously revealing and advertised with a voguish new word: "elastic"—from the Modern Latin *elasticus*, meaning "springlike."

By the fourteenth century, men's skin-tights, or panty hose, could be purchased in white, brown, or black. The garments were often suggestively tight, nearly transparent, and still worn with no jock undersupport. The Christian church condemned the male fashion of the day as immodest. Nu-

William the Conqueror (center), in panty hose— detail from the Bayeux Tapestry, eleventh century.

Early warriors with wrapped calf leggings (right). Young Venetian man, member of "the Hose Gang." They wore long, tight bicolored stockings with short jackets and plumed hats.

merous paintings of the period depict proud men in stretch panty hose parading like peacocks.

ITALIAN TEENS WITH SHAVED HEADS IN BICOLORED TIGHTS; FOURTEENTH CENTURY ◆

A group of rebellious young Venetian men made skintight panty hose ever more scandalous in the fourteenth century, splitting teenagers and parents into opposing camps over dressing up.

The young men called themselves the *Compagnia della Calza*, the Hose Gang. They worn torso-hugging waist-jackets, pheasant-plumed hats, and elastic tights with each leg a different color; the right leg might be white, the left leg black. The colors called attention to their crotches and, from the rear, erotically mimicked nature's own crack. They also shaved off *half* their hair, giving their heads a similar two-tone effect. These Italian men were among history's first rebellious punks.

In their teens and twenties, they staged public entertainments, masquerades, and song concerts, and their dandyish, sexy outfits were copied by youths throughout Italy. Geoffrey Chaucer attacked and belittled the attire in *The Canterbury Tales*, and one fashion chronicler of the period complained:

Young men are in the habit of shaving half their heads, and wearing a close-fitting cap. Surely their most offensive attire is their ridiculous hose. Decent people find the tight-fitting hose to be positively immodest.

To spoof the outlandish fashion, an Italian playwright devised the stage buffoon known as a "harlequin"—from the Italian *arlecchino*, meaning "a demon." Over the next two centuries, harlequins appeared in comedies and pantomimes with shaved heads, masked faces, variegated tights, and carrying wooden swords.

Men's skintight, multicolored panty hose—which proudly showed "a basket" —seem to have been the first rebellious fashion statement made by teenagers.

Tight male panty hose were about to evolve into a penile fashion statement that would be carried to ridiculous lengths—and that modern designers, to no avail, have occasionally tried to bring back: the codpiece.

MEN STUFFING THEIR CROTCHES: CODPIECE; FIFTEENTH AND SIXTEENTH CENTURIES ◆

"Cod" is from the Middle English *codd*, meaning "a cushion." The word is also slang for a man's scrotum and testes, an allusion to the way his organs bulge noticeably in tight pants.

Panty hose did not have pockets. Where did a fashionable man in the Late Middle Ages carry his coins, keys, cosmetics (powder and perfume), and other small personal effects?

Fashionable young Italian men in the fifteenth century with belt purses, a male accessory that returned to vogue in the 1990s.

Engraving of a man wearing an exaggerated codpiece.

In his codpiece. The penile pouch began as a practical crotch pocket. It allowed a man's hips and buttocks in skin-tights to remain streamlined and naturally sexy, and added size—a bulge—exactly where he wanted to boast of it most.

The codpiece, which was worn for less than two hundred years, was one of the strangest, most obviously erotic styles ever devised. Codpieces went out of fashion only after they'd grown to such outlandish frontal protrusions—extending over four inches—that they were as cumbersome as they were comical. In terms of illusion, the codpiece did for a man's penis what woman's falsies—or implants—would do for breasts.

How exactly did the codpiece originate?

"Showing a Basket"

In the early 1500s, noblemen started asking their tailors to make a penile flap, or *fly*, in the front of their skin-tights. This way a man did not have to pull down his panty hose, and stretch out the waistband, every time he needed to urinate. Men did not wear underpants beneath their skin-tights, since they wanted nothing to mask the natural contours of their bodies. But the fly often opened on its own, either when a man sat down or because the fabric eventually lost its elasticity. Penises popped out.

For the sake of modesty, men began to stuff cloth inside their crotch flaps. The first men to do this must have liked the attention it got them because one cloth led to two and then three, and all men soon had "baskets"—a curious word used by gay men for a penile bulge through one's pants.

With no pockets in their skin-tights and the only opening the fly in the front, men turned the codpiece into a practical pocket, or basket. A man would wrap his coins, keys, and personal effects in a piece of cloth, an impromptu purse, and stuff the pouch into his crotch flap. Soon men were asking their tailors to design into their panty hose a permanent frontal pouch, or "cushion" (*codd*), which served as a convenient carrying *basket*. A practical design can became an outlandish fashion affectation, and that is what happened to the codpiece. By the time the style was abandoned, in the late 1600s, men's waistcoats and pants had pockets.

Performance Fear

I asked several psychiatrists who study clothing fetishism if they thought the codpiece would ever make a return. Designers have attempted to bring it back; men have rejected it. I got a unanimous no, and the reasoning couldn't have been simpler.

As a sexually liberated society, we've come to have high expectations about pleasure, arousal, sexual satisfaction, and male performance. Women have come to expect more from men sexually and talk openly about penile size and its relation to erotic aesthetics and orgasm. Hard-core videos allow every woman to compare her husband's erection to that of superstars. A male penile fashion that promises a woman more than a man can deliver is bound to disappoint. The average man, with an average-size penis, does not want to risk that—performance anxiety is already too common a complaint. Wearing a codpiece would only aggravate it.

Gay men have abandoned stuffing their crotches, or "showing a basket," a practice not that uncommon a few decades ago. While there are many social and psychological reasons for this, one appears to be the possibility of disappointment. Men and women, straight and gay, are simply too savvy today to fall for a transparent ruse or tolerate one foisted on them.

WOMEN IN STOCKINGS AND GARTERS; PRE-SIXTEENTH CENTURY ◆

The word "stocking" does not appear in the vocabulary of dress until the sixteenth century, and then it is applied to *women's* stockings. The word derived from the Old English *stocc*, meaning, at various times, "stick," "stub," and "leg." A stocking, then, was a leg covering, specifically a woman's leg covering.

A fourteenth-century British illustration of an attendant handing a stocking to her mistress. It is the first pictorial evidence of a woman wearing stockings.

For centuries, men had been wearing leg coverings called hose and skin-tights. Men had also held up their hose with a "garter"—Old French *gartier*, literally "shank" of the leg. Certain men's garter societies specified the color of the garters that their members had to wear. In England, the highest civil and military honor during the Late Middle Ages was membership in the Most Noble Order of the Garter.

Had women not been wearing hose and garters all of these centuries?

Historians really don't know. They believe women may have worn stockings for warmth as early as 600 C.E. and garters at some point thereafter. But because women's long gowns concealed their legs, there is scant evidence in paintings and illustrated manuscripts that, as one eighteenth-century writer expressed it, "women had legs."

Among the earliest pictorial evidence of a woman in stockings is an illustrated 1306 British manuscript. It depicts a lady in her boudoir, seated at the edge of the bed, with a servant handing her one of a pair of stockings. The other stocking is already on her leg.

One of the earliest literary references, in Chaucer's *Canterbury Tales*, comments that the Wife of Bath wore stockings "of fine skarlet redde."

References to women's stockings are extremely rare up until the sixteenth century. Female legs, though undoubtedly much admired in private, were

Queen Elizabeth I, who favored silk stockings; an eighteenth-century loom for knitting stockings.

never to be mentioned in public. During these centuries, Christianity was a major force in the lives of many people, and women were portrayed as virgins or mothers, never as sex symbols; bared female legs were scandalous.

In the sixteenth century, a British gift of silk stockings for the queen of Spain was presented with full protocol to the Spanish ambassador, who, drawing himself haughtily erect, proclaimed, "Take back thy stockings. And know, foolish sir, that the Queen of Spain hath no legs."

EROTIC SILK STOCKINGS AND GARTER GAMES; ELIZABETHAN ENGLAND ◆

In Queen Elizabeth's England, women's stockings fully entered history, and with highly erotic overtones. Due largely to Elizabeth's love of silk stockings, women at court began to wear them and to coquettishly flash a glimpse of "silk legs" at men. A popular game at court was prick the garter, in which a man tried to snap a woman's garter belt. The phrase was loaded with double meaning, since the verb "prick" meant "to snap" and was also slang for "penis."

Stockings are described in extant texts as "scarlet crimson" and "purple" and as "beautified with exquisite embroideries and rare incisions of the cutters art." In 1561, early in her rein, Elizabeth was presented with her first pair

"THING" = SEX ORGAN ♦ *The first recorded use of the word "thing" as a euphemism for "cunt" and "cock" appears in Chaucer. To-day a mother might say to a child, "Don't touch your thing," or a child might say, "I hurt my thing." This use of the word is at least six hundred years old.*

Chaucer's garrulous and racy Wife of Bath explains that the different odors of male and female genitals is how the sexes tell each other apart—by sniffing their "thynges":

> *. . . our bothe thynges smale*
> *Were eek to knowe a female from a male,*
> *And for noon oother cause . . .*

of knitted silk stockings, which converted her to silk for the remainder of her life: "I like silke stockings so well because they are pleasant, fine and delicate and henceforth I will wear no more cloath stockings."

It was also during Elizabeth's reign that William Lee, in 1589, invented the "loome" for machine-knitting stockings. Lee wrote that for the first time stockings were "knit on a machine, from a single thread, in a series of connected loops." Lee's stocking loom, coupled with Elizabeth's plea—"That this fashion of mine bring up a new trade in which many of my people may be employed"—launched the hosiery industry.

Samuel Johnson, who admitted that the mere thought of stockings and garters was enough to confound a day's writing, said to an actor friend, "I'll come no more behind your scenes, David, for the white silk stockings of your actresses excite my amorous propensities."

"THE DUCHESS OF BLUSH" GARTER; ENGLAND, 1791 ♦

*O*nce women began wearing stocking and garters, and teasing men with them, the items become highly erotic. Many customs and expressions developed around a lady's stockings and garters:

• Men collected the silk stocking and lace garters of their mistresses and showed the trophies to other men.

• The phrase "casting her garter" meant a girl had high hopes of "hooking" a husband.

• A bride, on her wedding night, let her husband remove her white (for purity) garter as a symbol of the deflowering that was to follow. For shy women, the actual sex act may not have occurred for days or weeks. The garter kept the husband hoping.

• The literature of the period is full of bawdy puns and jokes about garters. Fanny Hill, the lusty heroine of John Cleland's *Memoirs of a Woman of Pleasure* (1749), probably the most famous erotic novel ever written, removes her garter in front of a man, saying, in effect, the barrier to pleasure is gone. Garters in Cleland's day were called "circlets of honor." Once a man got past the garter, he knew conquest lay before him.

• The most popular joke of Cleland's day: *"Why's a garter belt called the giggle line? Once you're there, you're laughing."*

• Women had teasing phrases embroidered on their garters: "My heart is fixt, I cannot range," reads a garter from 1717. Of course any man who got far enough up a leg to read a woman's garter knew the phrase was a come-on. "No Search" reads a garter from 1737. One woman's garter boldly read "I love too much to change."

• A racy rhyme from the era:

Why blush, dear girl, pray tell me why?
You need not, I can prove it.
For tho' your garter met my eye,
My thoughts were far above it.

In the 1780s, Martin Van Butchell, a dentist in London, England, applied for a patent for "spring bands, or fastenings, for various purposes." One purpose of the small, coiled spring of brass wire was to secure false teeth in the mouth. Another was to implant the tiny spring into the padded lining of a garter, giving it real elastic tension.

"The Duchess of Blush" garter, in bright red, was one of the dentist's best-sellers of the 1790s. He concocted the name when he learned that Princess Frederica of Prussia, who married the Duke of York, second son of George III, in 1791, had worn one of his spring garters during the wedding.

NYLONS; UNITED STATES, MAY 15, 1940 ✦

*I*n May 1937, a fashion critic wrote: "Legs, though no longer as wildly exciting as in the Naughty Nineties, still have the power to charm." Silk stockings had become commonplace and thus lost some of their erotic luster. But silk was about to be replaced by a new, synthetic fiber that would again make legs naughty, and nicer than ever. Nylon, a long-chain polymer spun into yarn, would become the hot, trendy new name for stockings. Nylon would soon become one of the most important innovations in the history of underwear.

How did the name "nylon" originate?

Despite popular legend, it is not true that the word emerged as a compromise between rival research chemists working on the new material in New York and London: NY + LON. Developers of the fiber, du Pont chemists, working in Wilmington, Delaware, coined the term from the names of two earlier synthetic fibers, vinyl and rayon: (vi)nyl + (ray)on.

A polyamide plastic derived from carbon, oxygen, and hydrogen, nylon was the result of fundamental research begun at du Pont by Wallace H. Carothers and his staff in 1928. The aim of the research was not to create a new synthetic clothing fiber—certainly not nylon stockings—but merely to study the process of polymerization: how very small molecules can be made to link together to form very large ones. Carothers discovered that starting with a treaclelike mass of polymers, he could spin out a fiber of extreme tensile strength, far stronger that silk. Carothers died in 1937, a year before du Pont announced the discovery of nylon and three years before women could purchase the first "nylons."

Nationwide "Nylon Day"

Because of the public relations fanfare surrounding the debut of nylon stockings—"impossible to snag" . . . "no runs ever" . . . "a single pair will last a lady a lifetime"—there is no uncertainty about their origin. Those hyped claims terrified the hosiery industry, which envisioned a quick, onetime windfall followed by virtual bankruptcy. Fortunately for the industry, one pair of nylons did not last a woman a lifetime.

The story begins on October 27, 1938, when du Pont announced the development of a "miracle fiber, "passing in strength and elasticity any previously known textile fibers." Nylons were displayed at the 1939 World's

Fair in New York, and women who had tested the stockings gave testimonials: "unbelievable hours of performance," "never a run," "I can work on my feet all day." American women couldn't wait to roll on their first—and presumably only—pair.

Du Pont had shipped selected hosiery manufacturers spools of nylon yarn, which they agreed to knit according to company specifications. The operation was top secret. The mills, in turn, shipped a certain number of nylons to select stores across the country, on the promise that none be sold before "Nylon Day"—May 15, 1940.

The hysteria that had been mounting across the country erupted early that morning. Newspapers later reported that no consumer item in history ever caused such nationwide pandemonium. Women queued up hours before stores opened. Hosiery departments were stampeded for their limited stock of nylons. In many stores, near riots broke out. By the close of that year, thirty-six million pairs of nylons had been sold, and that number could have been much higher had more stockings been available. Even du Pont had underestimated their popularity.

SEXY BLACK STOCKING SEAMS ◆

*I*n a remarkably short time, silk stockings were virtually obsolete, and nylon stockings became simply "nylons."

No one in the industry foresaw the start of World War II, with the proprietary need for nylon in parachutes, ropes, and tents. Consequently, during the war years, nylons were in short supply, a prized commodity sold on the black market. Women who couldn't afford them colored their legs dark beige with "leg paint" and drew a fake "seam" up the back with an eyebrow pencil.

Du Pont chemists had envisioned seamless nylons, but given the looms of the day, the stockings were easier and cheaper to produce in sheets of nylon that were then folded over and stitched with black thread. Black seams, however, turned out to be a sexy extra on stockings. Women loved the long, black lines running up their legs and under their skirts—and so did men. Women also loved to play at "straightening their seams," which bent them into a position that drew attention to their legs and rear end. For men, the black lines were directional arrows for the place they wanted most to go to.

During World War II, when nylon stockings were in short supply, many women drew black seams up the back of their bare legs.

NYLON ENVY ♦

*I*n England, nylons were exceptionally rare. Because of the war effort, nylons had not gone on sale overseas. Every yard of nylon thread that du Pont sold to British nylon spinners went into jungle tents, glider towropes, and tarpaulins. The trickle of nylon stockings that found their way into England came from traveling U.S. businessmen and, mainly, from American GIs.

The sheer-clad legs of the lucky few British women in nylons were the bitter envy of their less fortunate sisters. An American GI in London with a pair of nylons from home was in an enviable bargaining position with a lady, as seen in this British rhyme of the day:

Have you got a fag, boy, have you got a flame?
Have you got some chewing-gum?
Like to know my name?

Have you got a fag, boy, have you got a match?
Have you got some chocolate?
I might lift the latch.

Have you got a fag, boy, have you got a light?
Have you got some nylons?
I'll be yours tonight.

For about twenty years, stockings came only in medium brown and fawn, had seams up the back, and were held up either by girdle snaps or garter belts. But in the 1960s, when dresses began to get shorter and shorter, ultimately rising high above the knee, a woman's nylons were on display as never before. Change was necessary.

First, nylons were manufactured in outfit-coordinating colors. Then, to make wearing a short skirt decent, stockings were weaved over the hips to create modern panty hose—the sheer, revealing attire that men had worn centuries ago and that became a standard among acrobats and ballet dancers. Women's panty hose were not a new invention in the 1960s but an old garment that the miniskirt fashion put to new use. One early ad teased, "Jane isn't wearing panties. She's wearing something much better—Hug-Me-Tights."

Fetish Fashions

As nylons had made silk stockings obsolete in the 1940s, panty hose virtually destroyed the nylons market thirty years later. The classic item with the seam up the back lasted only about three decades. By 1971, sales of classic nylons had dropped to a mere 5 percent of the market. Women's magazines routinely ran tips telling housewives what they could do with their old nylons:

- Use your nylons to strain jam or soup
- To cover your hair rollers while sleeping at night
- Weave old nylons into rag rugs
- Use them to stuff teddy bears and rag dolls
- They're great for drying tulip bulbs in potting sheds
- Stuff old nylons with paper and stretch them at the base of a door as a draft-stopper
- Punch small holes in your old nylons and pack them full of birdseed; they make great outdoor feeders.

The girdle and garter had also become dead fashions—except, of course, among fetishists, for whom, along with classic nylons, they remain prized. Thus, items that once were a woman's standard attire exist today almost exclusively as erotic S&M and B&D essentials. In that sense, the tightly laced dominatrix, in her corset of punishing stays, her severe bodice booster, her black-seamed nylon stockings, and her thigh-high garter belts can be viewed as a mannequin in an underwear museum, displaying common women's fashion from decades past. Fashion styles may be transitory, but some male fantasies are forever.

CHASTITY BELTS; ANTIQUITY TO PRESENT ◆

*N*othing speaks worse of a husband's lack of trust in his wife—or of his own paranoia—than the chastity belt, also known as the "girdle of purity." The lockable device, which for centuries came in two strategic designs, fitted around a woman's genital zone. It reached peak popularity during medieval times, when crusaders and other peripatetic knights were away from their wives for months at a time.

The belts existed in quantity at one time, the handiwork of blacksmiths. Many can be observed today, mounted on mannequins or suspended by wires at museums such as the Cluny in Paris.

Believe it or not, more chastity belts are manufactured and sold today than at any time in the past—but their purpose has changed. The original belt was intended to ensure a wife's fidelity or guard a virgin's chastity. Nineteenth-century belts were worn to prevent a young girl from masturbating. Today's models, which can be purchased through sex catalogs and novelty shops, are really sex toys, no longer intended to ensure chastity but to invite a dogged lover's violation. Psychologically, any device that temporarily thwarts sexual pleasure and must be painstakingly removed prolongs foreplay and heightens arousal.

Let's start with the early models.

Partial Pudenda: Preventing Vaginal Entry

During the Middle Ages, a husband about to embark on a journey could lock his wife into a "partial pudenda" whose metal plate covered only the region of the vulva. The pudenda—Latin *pudere*, "to be ashamed" and the origin of our word "prudishness"—contained a narrow vertical slit through which the wife could urinate, though with no special accuracy. The aperture was usually fitted with outwardly pointing metal teeth, often spring-loaded, to discourage a suitor's exploration with so much as a finger.

Full Pudenda: Preventing Vaginal and Anal Entry

A traveling husband who suspected his wife might indulge in exotic pleasures could resort to a "full pudenda," which covered both the anterior and pos-

---

BUSINESSWOMEN IN PINSTRIPED SUITS ◆ *In the late 1970s, it became fashionable for businesswomen to don neckties and three-piece pinstripe suits. The look was supposed to be aggressive and competitive; some women even adopted a man's fedora hat. Executive women entering the corporate world attempted to look like their male counterparts.*

Designers pushed the "imitation man look." Runway models paraded in suits and ties, demonstrating how "women in industry" should dress to become a success. The fashion, at its extreme, was short-lived

John T. Molloy researched the "imitation man look" and analyzed it in The Women's Dress for Success Book *(1977):*

"My research indicates that a three-piece pinstriped suit not only does not add to a woman's authority, it destroys it. It makes her look like an 'imitation man,' and that look always fails.

"The 'imitation man look' does not refer to looking tough or masculine. The effect is more like that of a small boy who dressed up in his father's clothing. He looks cute, not authoritative . . .

"The same thing applies to women. When a woman wears certain clothes with male colors or patterns, her femaleness is accentuated. She frequently looks more *diminutive. And this reduces her authority.*

"My testing shows that some men find the 'imitation man' look sexy. Other men are completely turned off by it. In either case a woman's authority is diminished.

"This is a prime example of why research is necessary. Obviously those fashion designers who turn out 'imitation man' clothes and call them career apparel are advancing only their own careers."

---

terior regions. In addition to the small urination slit, the full pudenda had a larger rear aperture that allowed for defecation but the rear orifice could not be too large, since it had to prevent anal intercourse. The rear slit also had a set of metal teeth to discourage intercourse.

With a full pudenda, maintaining bodily cleanliness was even more difficult—which, in itself, could serve as a deterrent to some would-be suitors. Physicians of the period claimed that a woman could wear a full or

Simple front-back chastity belt (left). Wife in a chastity belt steals the key from her husband to give to her lover (center). Front, or vaginal, belt.

partial chastity belt for months at a time without ill effects, so long as she bathed frequently.

FIRST CHASTITY BELT; OLD TESTAMENT TIMES ◆

*I*n various forms, mechanically imposed chastity has been forced on women since ancient times.

Homer's *Odyssey* describes how Aphrodite betrays her husband, Hephaistus, and to prevent further infidelities he forges a "girdle" for her privates. The Greeks, though, never adopted the device. It is thought that twelfth-century crusaders learned about chastity belts during their travels in the East, where they also encountered the practice of female infibulation, in which the lips of the vagina are temporarily fastened closed with rings or wires. Virgins were infibulated from the age of puberty until the day they married; it was the husband who finally removed the obstructing rings or wires.

Some scholars claim that the Bible records the existence of a chastity belt in the Old Testament. It does so in connection with the building of the Tabernacle during the Israelites' wandering through the desert from Egypt to the Holy Land. Moses requested that the people donate possessions to raise funds for the construction of the Tent of Meeting, and women brought forth bracelets, earrings, signet rings, "all jewels of gold." Among the objects is a *koomaz*—today the word is translated to mean "plate." Rabbi Rashi, the renowned eleventh-century French biblical scholar, claimed that the word originally described "a golden vessel fixed on a woman's private part." In support of this interpretation he offered quotations from the Talmud, the compendium of Jewish law and commentary, in which the authors assert that *koomaz* is an abbreviation of the phrase (in Hebrew) "here is the place of shamed deeds."

FLORENTINE GIRDLE; ITALY, EARLY RENAISSANCE ◆

*T*he use of chastity belts did not flourish until the twelfth century. The first models were produced in Italy and were called Florentine girdles. As they were adopted throughout Europe during the Holy Crusades, the contraptions acquired such names as "girdle of Venus," "drawers of iron," and "padlock of purity." It is under this last title that French writer and philosopher Voltaire (1694–1778) penned a poem of frustration to his mistress:

LE CADENAS—"PADLOCK OF PURITY"

I triumphed; Love was master
And I was nearing these too brief instants
Of my happiness, and yours perhaps
But a tyrant wants to trouble our good time
He is your husband: a prison keeper of sex
He has locked the free sanctuary
Of your charms; and abusing our desires
Retains the key to the sojourn of pleasures.

Oldest Model in Existence

The earliest extant description of a Florentine girdle is found in a German manuscript, *Bellifortis* (1405), which tells a husband about to go off on military maneuvers what kind of girdling device he needs to ensure his wife's fidelity.

The oldest model still in existence once belonged to the infamous Italian despot Novello Carrara, who in 1388 upon his father's abdication as ruler of Padua, became Francesco the Younger. Novello preferred a full pudenda for his wife to wear in his absence. For her comfort, he padded the interior of the metal girdle with soft leather. Her frontal chastity was fortified by thirty-six metal porcupinelike spikes, while the small anal orifice discouraged entry with fifteen razor-sharp teeth. When at home, the sexually adventurous Novello liked to hazard intercourse by attempting to violate his wife *through* the girdle. In this sense, it also served as a sex toy.

Imprisoned following a political battle between Padua and Venice, Novello was strangled by his Venetian captors in 1406. His wife's pudenda remains in perfect condition, prominently displayed among medieval armory in the Doge's Palace.

Corpse in a Girdle

A chastity belt from the same period as Novello's was discovered in 1889 in Italy, during an exhumation of corpses from a churchyard. The woman had been buried in her locked belt, which protected her vagina and anus, and which four hundred years later encircled her fleshless skeleton. It is possible that the woman died while wearing the belt in her husband's absence, and the family, without the key, had no choice but to bury her in the girdle. It's also possible that the women was a lifelong virgin and was buried in her belt as a statement of that fact. Perhaps she'd thrown away the key.

To us, today, a chastity belt is a bizarre, cruel, sexist invention, but a husband's insistence that a wife wear a pudenda in his absence was not considered harsh treatment centuries ago. A woman's body was then the exclusive property of her mate, who could do with it what he wished. In a perverse way, locking a wife in a chastity belt was a compliment: it showed that a husband cared. The devices were still being advertised in the late nineteenth century, but to prevent young girls from masturbating.

According to historian Reay Tannahil in *Sex in History*, female chastity belts to prevent masturbation were still being sold through surgical instrument catalogs into the 1930s. They fitted from a girl's crotch up to her navel, and the metal exterior was padded on the inside with rubber for comfort.

CHASTITY BELT LORE •

*T*here are many anecdotes, both horrible and humorous, associated with chastity belts.

• **The Blacksmith's Deception**. A knight, about to embark on a crusade, commissioned a village blacksmith to forge a full pudenda for his attractive

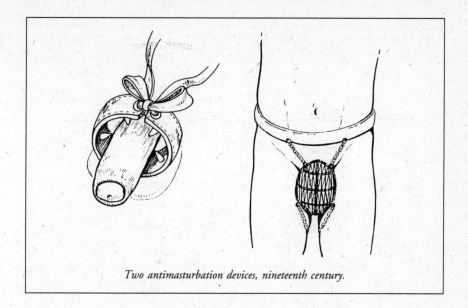

Two antimasturbation devices, nineteenth century.

young wife. The blacksmith, who had long admired the woman, made an extra key and kept it for himself. The blacksmith and the wife played while the husband was away for more than a year. She got pregnant, bore the blacksmith's son, and gave the baby away.

• **Pregnant in a Chastity Belt.** A faithful wife, locked into a chastity belt, discovered that she was pregnant with her husband's child some months after he'd locked her in and left on a crusade. He had the only key. Her pregnancy progressed, and eventually the village blacksmith had to be called in to saw off the pudenda.

• **Saint Rose of Lima.** Today she's called the founder of the "School of Aggressive Chastity." Baptized Isabel de Flores y del Oliva in Lima in 1586, Rose became the first person in the Americas to be canonized by the Catholic church, though her holy status has since been questioned.

Rose supported her aged and indigent parents by selling flowers and handmade embroidery. Extraordinarily devout, at an early age she underwent an agonizing surgical procedure (its nature is unknown) that awoke in her an appetite for suffering. Her self-inflicted tortures, which the church has since come to view as pathological rather than pious, are chilling: to deface her beauty, and thus preserve her virtue, she cut her cheeks and rubbed pepper into the wounds.

At age twenty, Rose shunned a marriage proposal to become a Dominican nun. She donned a chastity belt and threw away the key. Her self-inflicted

MALE CHASTITY BELT ◆ *During the Victorian era, a male version of the chastity belt was introduced in England; more accurately, it was a form of male infibulation. An adolescent boy's foreskin was pulled down over the top of the penis, gathered together, and four holes were punched around the skin, then laced through with two opposing lock-and-key rings. The glans, or penile head, was thus locked away. The device not only prevented the boy from masturbating, but the pain of getting an erection discourage him from entertaining sexual fantasies.*

In a variation on the rings, in the 1820s, a professor of surgery at the University of Halle, Karl August Weinhold, infibulated the foreskin with tight loops of wire, topped off with sealing wax. A parent could periodically check to see if a son had broken the seal to play with himself. "Self-pollution" was then among the most dangerous of vices, physically and spiritually; it was believed to destroy one's health as thoroughly as it damned one's soul. Weinhold suggested that all indigent bachelors between the ages of fourteen and thirty, who had dim prospects of marriage, be rounded up and infibulated with a wire that was then soldered closed for life.

The grotesque plan was never carried out—at least not on indigents in the general public. But in hospitals and mental institutions throughout England chronic masturbators (those caught) were routinely infibulated. A colleague of Weinhold instituted the procedure at one asylum and reported in 1876, "The sensation among the patients was extraordinary,. I was struck by the conscience stricken way in which they submitted to the operation on their penises. The technique is thoroughly successful. I mean to try it on a large scale, and go on wiring all masturbators."

penances became increasingly cruel. With a perverse pleasure, she scourged herself daily, continually chewing bitter herbs, submerged her hands in caustic lime, and fasted until she was skeletal. Throughout all of this, she wore a hair shirt and a silver circlet studded on the inside with thorns. Whenever she had to walk more than a few feet, she dragged a heavy wooden cross over her shoulder.

St. Rose's feast day is August 30, and her sanctuary in Lima is a place of annual pilgrimage. Its greatest treasure, pictured on postcards and photo-

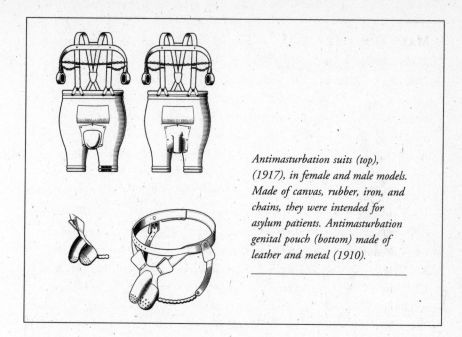

*Antimasturbation suits (top),
(1917), in female and male models.
Made of canvas, rubber, iron, and
chains, they were intended for
asylum patients. Antimasturbation
genital pouch (bottom) made of
leather and metal (1910).*

graphed by devout visitors, is the deep well into which the young Rose threw
the key to her chastity belt.

• ***Saint Mariana of the Iron Girdle.*** Saint Mariana de Jesús Paredes y
Flores, the seventeenth-century "Lily of Ecuador," also donned an iron girdle
and threw away the key. There are additional similarities between the two
young women, as Frances Parkinson Keyes makes clear in her dual biography,
The Rose and The Lily (1961). At age eight, Mariana was already punishing
herself by wearing crowns and belts of thorns. At puberty, swearing lifelong
virginity, she strapped herself into a chastity belt of her own design, made
more intimidating by its rows of thistle spikes and vine thorns.

For the duration of her reclusive life, Mariana ate only one slice of
bread a day, slept for no more than three hours a night, and kept as her
sole companion an effigy in a coffin as a continual reminder of death.
Every Friday, the day of Christ's crucifixion, she would remove the effigy,
climb into the coffin, fold her arms across her chest, and sleep her three
hours there. She died a virgin and was canonized in 1950. Her feast day is
May 26.

While many of the hundreds of chastity belt stories are probably apocry-
phal, together they depict an era in which women were often belted into

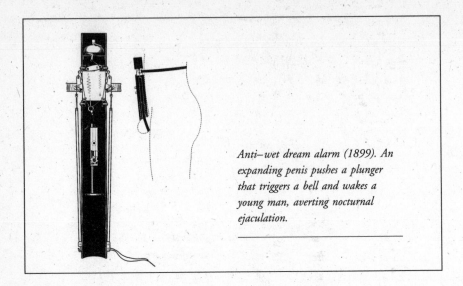

Anti–wet dream alarm (1899). An expanding penis pushes a plunger that triggers a bell and wakes a young man, averting nocturnal ejaculation.

girdles to keep admirers away. Among pudenda lore it is not always easy to separate fact from ribald fiction, or a true chastity belt from a hoax. Indeed, in the 1950s, the Cluny Museum stopped displaying all but one of its belts, under the suspicion that the artifacts were latter-day blacksmiths' jokes.

MODERN SEX TOYS ✦

*M*ale infibulation rings and female chastity belts no longer exist as serious items. Now they are sold as sexual playthings—and are more in demand than ever. Their original purpose of preventing pleasure has been perverted to that of heightening it.

The modern equivalent of the male infibulation ring, which is available through sex catalogs and novelty shops, is a small brass spike, or stainless steel ring, that fits through a man's pierced foreskin, as an earring loops through a pierced ear. Clamps, or a screw mechanism, allow the device to be removed. Basically, a spiked penis, locked away, is saying to its wearer's partner you must work to undress and free me before you can use me.

There are variations on the spike or ring. The Pleasure Chest, a New York–based chain of erotic appliance stores, markets a metal tube that slips over the penis and is fastened around the testes with a chain and combination lock. The incentive is to find the right combination to win the prize.

The modern female chastity belt is made of leather or vinyl, usually black, and is a welter of intricate laces, front and back. The sexual thrill comes from temporarily impeding the inevitable act as the aroused lover struggles to unlace the locked-away object of his affection. The device is not much different from the kind of elaborate gift wrappings and bows used on presents to elevate the receiver's expectations. Psychologically, any device that temporarily thwarts pleasure and must be removed to achieve ultimate satisfaction, prolongs excitement and heightens arousal. A wrapped gift is always more enjoyable than an unwrapped one.

CHAPTER 19

Life's a Drag

RuPaul to Dennis Rodman

*You're born naked
and the rest is drag.*

RUPAUL

"DRAG"; ENGLAND, 1850S ◆

A "drag" is a man or woman in the clothes of the opposite sex. People do this for any number of reasons. If a gay man makes a habit of going in drag, and donning fancy dress, he's a "drag queen." Dennis Rodman is a drag; RuPaul is a drag queen.

How did this usage of "drag" originate?

The everyday word "drag," meaning to "pull something slowly and heavily along," and thus to leave "a trail on the ground," dates to about the fourteenth century and derives from the Middle English *draggen*. A host of terms employ this definition:

• *drag race*, dating to 1949, is an acceleration contest between vehicles whose tires leave a "trail" on the road.

• *drag strip*, from 1952, is the site of a drag race; a "trail" of tire marks on the ground bears witness to that.

Cross-dresser Hannah Snell, in military dress and, later, onstage exploiting the discovery of her sex. Illustrations from a Dutch biography (1750), The Female Soldier.

• *drag hunt*, eighteenth century, is an animal hunt in which a scent or bait has been dragged along a "trail" that determines the route of the chase.

• *drag dance*, 1930s, was a dance in which a man supported and dragged a woman's "trailing" body through a variety of steps.

• *drag bunt*, 1949, is made by a left-handed batter by "trailing" the bat while already moving toward first base.

Two explanations have been offered for the cross-dressing meaning of "drag." Both involve "pulling something slowly and heavily" and leaving a "trail."

Ancient Origin

Some linguists have suggested an ancient origin of the term "drag." When the Romans castrated a man to make a eunuch, they "drew out" his testicles, leaving a trail of blood. Some castrated men, deprived of much of their testosterone, blossomed embarrassingly into voluptuous women. To minimize social scorn and cruel jokes, many castrated men masqueraded in women's clothes. Such a man was called a *traho*, or "drag"—he'd had his testicles "dragged out."

Modern Origin

A more recent origin of the word dates to the 1850s. In British theater, "a drag" was a fancy, floor-length petticoat worn by a male actor playing a female role. Cross-dressing has a long comedic history in British theater. The petticoat "dragged" as the actor crossed the stage, and he derived many laughs from the effeminate way in which he whipped the trailing end around when he turned. Thus an actor playing a cross-dressing part was named after his petticoat, "a drag."

"TO CAMP IT UP" ◆

*T*o get laughs, the transvestite actor in a petticoat "camped it up"— he flaunted his effeminate behavior, engaging in exaggerated "feminine" mannerisms. Lexicographer Stuart Berg Flexner traces the origin of "camp" to the Italian *campeggiare*, meaning "to stand out" as different from the rest. Any one who "camps," in or out of drag, certainly is easily spotted.

This usage of camp is not to be confused with the kind of "camping" engaged in by boy scouts and militia groups. Their "camp" more directly derives from the Latin *campus*, meaning "a field, a large plot of ground"— the origin of the word "campus," dating to 1774, meaning a university's grounds.

"Camp" also came to mean any self-conscious flaunting, any ostentatious display of behavior or bad taste. Susan Sontag's 1964 article "Notes on Camp" in the *Partisan Review* extended the meaning to include any vulgarity one adopts as a style in art, architecture, or life.

Sex researcher C. A. Tripp, in *The Homosexual Matrix* (1975), gives a more recent origin for gay "camp": a cluster of people, as in an army camp, a nudist camp, a summer camp, or a political camp. Tripp claims that in New York in the 1930s, young gay males in the theater lived together in groups to save on rent. "These groups were called camps," says Tripp. "Later, by association, the kind of behavior often seen there—highly animated reactions involving an overemotional stacking of emphasis—came itself to be called camp."

CROSS-DRESSING; ANTIQUITY TO PRESENT ◆

*C*ross-dressing is a simple term for a complex set of phenomena. It ranges from simply wearing one or two items of opposite-gender clothing, as a panties-and-bra male fetishist might do, to the elaborate full-scale burlesque of drag queens.

Carl Jung argued that the urge to cross-dress is, to some degree, in everyone. Jung felt that a man or woman was incomplete and unconsciously sought to identify with the opposite sex to achieve completeness. The belief is the basis of a famous Greek myth that gave us the word

> **Hermaphrodite.** Hermaphroditus was the son of the Greek god Hermes and the goddess Aphrodite. As a lad of fifteen, he fell in love with a beautiful nymph, who begged the gods to unite them as one being, endowed with both sex organs. Her wish was granted, and we gained the word "hermaphrodite" = *Hermes* + *Aphrodite*.

Young children, if not scolded for it, get a kick out of wearing gender-bending clothing, and a favorite Halloween custom has always been opposite-sex drag. "Senator Edward M. Kennedy donned a blond wig, falsies and a miniskirt, playing 'Fawn Hall' to nephew Joseph P. Kennedy's 'Colonel Oliver North' at an annual off-the-record staff Christmas party," reported the *Boston Globe* in 1987.

Cross-dressing allows us to express a different facet of our persona—part of Jung's argument. In the 1982 movie *Tootsie*, Dustin Hoffman's female character, Dorothy Michaels, is much more sensitive, perceptive, and understanding than Michael Dorsey, the out-of-work actor who in desperation assumes the role of Dorothy. Hoffman claimed the role allowed him to explore his "feminine side" and learn a lot about his personality.

SOLDIERS IN DRAG •

*C*ross-dressing is as old as recorded history. Male soldiers have disguised themselves as women to lure unsuspecting opponents. Josephus, the first-century historian, recorded instances of military drag as part of the strategy of a band of guerrillas led by John of Gischala. In his *History of the Jewish War*, he wrote of how effective they were:

> *They decorated their hair, and put on women's garments, and made up their faces with many ointments. They appeared very comely, and had much paint around their eyes. They imitated not only the adornments of women, but also the mannerisms of lustful women.*
>
> *While their faces looked like the faces of women, they killed with manly right hands. Their gait was effeminate, but when they attacked they became warriors, drawing their swords from under their finely dyed cloaks. They killed everyone they came upon.*

*Ann Mills (left), a female English sailor of the eighteenth century. Cross-dresser
"Mother Ross" (right) fought around 1700 as an English soldier.*

This kind of military drag gives new meaning to "don't ask, don't tell."

Women living in a male-dominated world have masqueraded as men in order to gain political and material advantages. French writer George Sand, born Amandine-Aurore-Lucile Dupin, 1804–1876), who pioneered the social novel, was a cross-dresser. She said she found women's clothes of her day too restrictive and also wanted to drink and smoke and fit in to the company of literary men.

JOAN OF ARC, 1412–1431 ◆

*H*istorically, Joan of Arc is the most famous female cross-dresser. With close-cropped hair, dressed in men's armor, the French heroine helped defeat the English at Orléans in 1429. Contrary to popular opinion, Saint Joan was "martyred" by the Catholic church not for her refusal to renounce her "voices" of heavenly angels and saints, but because of the abomination of male drag. No less than five charges against Joan detailed her transvestitism as a sin of "unwomanliness" and "immodesty."

The priests of the Inquisition charged that "voices" had ordered "this woman in the name of God, to take and wear a man's clothes; and she had worn them and still wears them stubbornly obeying the said command, to

*Joan of Arc's primary offense in
the eyes of the church was her
cross-dressing as a man.*

such an extent that this woman had declared she would rather die than
relinquish these clothes."

Joan pleaded: "The dress is a small, nay the least, thing."

Throughout her trial, Joan identified herself as a woman in men's clothes,
insisting that she had never tried to pass herself off as a man. Her defenders
went further. They argued that Joan's miraculous victory at Orléans was a
sign from God that the biblical injunction against cross-dressing was no
longer valid. The Lord, they said, had made this cross-dresser a sign of divine
revelation. Joan was burned at the stake for "witchcraft" on May 30, 1431.

Twenty-five years later, the church that had condemned her concluded
that she was a holy woman and had indeed heard heavenly voices. The
reevaluation was political, not spiritual. By exonerating Joan, the church removed the shadow that had hung over the French dauphin's holy consecration as king at Joan's behest; and, too, a growing mass of Catholics had
begun to view Joan's death as martyrdom.

Her cross-dressing, however, remained an obstacle to her sainthood. Finally, in 1909, the Vatican officially declared Joan "blessed," and in 1920
Pope Benedict XV canonized her, though he'd not intended her to become
the patron saint of lesbians, which for many she's become.

The church did not accept her defender's argument that the Bible had it
wrong about cross-dressing.

Illustration from The Female Warrior *(late seventeenth century), which related how a woman in man's attire obtained an ensign's rank.*

CROSS-DRESSING—A BIBLICAL SIN? ◆

*T*he biblical injunction against cross-dressing is found in Deuteronomy (22:5). This fifth book of the Old Testament is largely a reiteration of the laws and regulations communicated to the Israelites at Sinai:

> *The woman shall not wear that which pertains to a man, neither shall a man put on a woman's garment; for all that do so are abomination unto the Lord thy God.*

Many biblical scholars argue that this prohibition is not about the sin of cross-dressing but a condemnation of pagan forms of worship in which cult priests, variously addressing gods and goddesses, cross-dressed. In many religions that predate Judaism, male priests donned female attired to invoke fertility goddesses, while female priestesses dressed as men to communicate with male gods of thunder, lightning, and crop production. Moses, the "traditional author" of Deuteronomy, wished to stamp out all traces of pagan worship. By prohibiting cross-dressing, he further solidified his faith of monotheism.

Into modern times, cross-dressing has played a sacred or special role in many parts of the world:

Shaman—Cross-Dressing for Power

Among the nomadic Turco-Mongol tribes of Siberia, men who don women's clothing are regarded as holy shamans. By cross-dressing they become powerful creatures, "witch doctors," who have control over supernatural forces. A shaman cross-dresser is highly regarded as a healer who stands between humans and the spirit world.

Shamans in female clothing can also be found in such widely separated places as Malaya, the Celebes Islands, Patagonia, and the Aleutian Islands. Female dress on a shaman does not imply effeminacy or homosexuality; the man may have a wife, children, and several mistresses.

Berdache—Cross-Dressing by Conscience

Among North American Indians, especially those with a warrior ethic such as the Sioux and the Crow, the *berdache* is a cross-dresser who is not a shaman. Typically, a teenage boy makes a pilgrimage into the desert to receive a vision from the gods as to what his role in life shall be. Some boys receive visions that they are meant not to be warriors but cross-dressers. The boy dons women's clothes, performs women's work, serves as a communal baby-sitter, and is accepted by the tribe.

Some social scientists have suggested that a boy becomes a *berdache* because he fears the rigorous, bloody life of a warrior—out of cowardice, that is. Or maybe he is a conscientious objector at heart. In some tribal cultures, male cross-dressers go to war but can only carry provisions, not weapons. Whatever the reason for becoming a *berdache*, the choice carries no shame or opprobrium. However, his decision to cross-dress is irrevocable: a *berdache* dresses as a woman for life.

Mahu—God-ordained Cross-Dresser

In Tahiti, a man who dresses as a woman is a *mahu*. Each Tahitian village is allowed only one cross-dresser. God created the revered position, and when it becomes vacant, there are many potential candidates to fill it, since parents encourage boys from an early age to practice cross-dressing, effeminacy, and mastering household chores.

The village *mahu* most be skilled in cooking, quilt-making, baby-sitting, and braiding palm leaves into thatch for rooftops. Tahitians define a *mahu* as a man "who does women's work." He may also act as the village's only homosexual, playing a passive role in intercourse with Tahitian men.

Sexually available women are not hard to find in Tahiti; and a single *mahu*'s domestic skills are not necessary for the functioning of a village. Why, then, does the cross-gender role exist in Tahitian culture? After all, in terms of dress, what separates a *mahu* from other men is basically a grass skirt.

Robert I. Levy, in *Tahitians: Mind and Experience in the Society Islands* (1973), argues that the *mahu* serves as a symbolic gender marker. Tahitian men and women are not all that different physically: both sexes have smooth hairless skin and long dark hair. Thus, says Levy, Tahitian men do not have a strongly defined masculine self-image. But, through comparison with an effeminate, skirted, sexually passive *mahu*, they can assure themselves of their own male identities. The unconscious logic is, since I am not an effeminate *mahu*, I must be a macho man. In the West, a similar logic underscores the gay bashing by certain gender-weak males: if I beat up a fag, I must be straight.

CALLING A MALE "SHE" ◆

*D*uring the Middle Ages, cross-dressing was often associated with heresy and witchcraft but, significantly, not with homosexuality. In fact, cross-dressing was not regarded as a sign of lesbianism or male homosexuality until the eighteenth century and then, for men, it become associated with innate effeminate behavior. Transvestite stage entertainment was a legitimate centuries-old phenomenon, involving straight, and undoubtedly gay, performers. But the blatant drag queen, openly "out" and outrageous, is a relatively recent spectacle.

Cross-cultural studies of homosexuality—from Brazil to the United States, from Peru to the Philippines—show that gay men and women, worldwide, linguistically "cross-dress." Jokingly, they assume pronouns of the opposite gender, something unheard of among heterosexuals. A gay man may refer to a male companion as "she," while a lesbian might call her lover "he," or "my boyfriend." Linguistic cross-dressing appears to be ancient: evidence of pronoun reversal is found in ancient Greek and Roman comedies and graffiti. Calling a "he" a "she" always got a laugh.

TODAY'S MEN IN DRAG ◆

*T*oday cross-dressing has become a vogue. RuPaul, the best-known cross-dresser of the day, enjoyed not only a strong-selling 1995 autobiography, *Letting It All Hang Out*, but also a hot cable television interview show. The gay drag queen has "crossed over" to straight-audience appeal. Heterosexual radio personality Howard Stern, self-proclaimed "king of all media," has donned drag so regularly he almost qualifies as a full-fledged "drag queen."

New York Mayor Rudolph W. Giuliani appeared at a 1997 reporters' high-jinks dinner in high heels, frilly pink gown, and a platinum-blond wing. He called himself "Rudy/Rudia" and arrived on the arm of *Victor/Victoria* star Julie Andrews, who was dressed as a man. As "Rudia," a "transvestite nightclub chanteuse," the mayor sang a breathy version of "Happy Birthday, Mr. President," à la Marilyn Monroe, and waved daintily at the crowd of thunderstruck spectators.

For the record: Rudolph Giuliani was not the first New York mayor to don drag: in 1984, Mayor Edward I. Koch wore a long gold lamé bodysuit to the same press function, with a mechanical pigeon on his head.

Cross-dressing is a staple of today's music videos. And Chicago Bulls basketball star Dennis Rodman arrived at a book signing in 1996 dressed in white tulle and silk bridal attire. The six-foot-eight, 210-pound forward tossed back his veil, exposed a blond wig, and, with a white-gloved hand, signed copies of his autobiography, *Bad As I Wanna Be*.

A Transsexual at the Super Bowl

A measure of how mainstream cross-dressing has become was given at the 1997 Super Bowl, arguably the year's most heterosexual TV event. Family-oriented Holiday Inn Worldwide ran a television commercial featuring a "man" dressed as a woman. The ad showed an attractive female drawing admiring male glances at a class reunion. She turns out to be a class alumnus who had had a sex-change operation. Technically, she was no longer a cross-dresser, but the ad itself was daring and featured a real-life transsexual. The hotel chain, which itself was undergoing a dramatic $1 billion renovation program, created the ad to emphasize its own "change." In a consumer sampling poll, Holiday Inn found that the vast majority of people liked the ad and in no way found it offensive. You've come a long way, lady, sir.

Dutch cross-dresser Geertruid ter Brugge served as a dragoon in the Dutch army—print, c. 1700.

WHO CROSS-DRESSES—AND WHY •

*T*here are several types of serious, lifelong cross-dressers, or "transvestites"—from the Latin *transvestire* = *trans,* "across" + *vestire,* "to dress."

Though the practice is ancient, the word "transvestite" was coined in 1910, by Magnus Hirschfeld, a contemporary of Freud, and did not enter American dictionaries until around 1922.

Four types of cross-dresser:

• **Married Man.** Most cross-dressers by far are married men. They live an openly heterosexual life but enjoy a private fantasy life in which they secretly wear women's clothing—often their wives', since it is readily available. Some of these men are merely aroused by wearing female attire. Others may be latently homosexual and marry for outward respectability.

• **Drag Queen.** Only a small percentage of gay men, almost always effeminate, make cross-dressing a lifetime habit. They are, in the vernacular, "drag queens," a term first recorded around 1941. RuPaul is the most famous modern example.

• **Bull Dyke.** A somewhat larger number of lesbians (actual estimates for all gender types vary widely) routinely wear men's clothing.

• **Transsexual.** The transsexual cross-dresses because he or she feels trapped in a body of the "wrong" sex. The brain of a transsexual male tells him he is really a woman, while his genitals and body hair remind him to the contrary. A transsexual woman experiences analogous confusion. It is this type of cross-dresser who often submits to sex-reassignment surgery to acquire genitals in harmony with the mind.

The factors that produce cross-dressers are complex and not thoroughly understood, yet research has produced some general outlines. In *Cross Dressing, Sex, and Gender* (1993), Vern and Bonnie Bullough, who've written extensively about gender roles, summarize two decades of studies:

Male Cross-Dressers

Both married men and effeminate gay men who cross-dress as a lifestyle may go through similar stages. (The transsexual seems to be a special case.) One important part of the evolution may involve the child's first episode of cross-dressing and masturbation. Here, in summary, is a possible course of development of male transvestism:

STEP 1. Genetics, hormones, and neural brain patterns produce a boy who is less active and aggressive than his peers.

STEP 2. Family and social factors influence the child. His family may place a high premium on respectability and conformity, and stigmatize homosexuality. They may be highly homophobic. Various social forces reinforce these beliefs in the boy's mind.

STEP 3. As a child or adolescent, he stumbles onto the joy of cross-dressing *and* masturbation. Orgasm serves as a reinforcement to cross-dress again and again. Because his activity remains clandestine, he is spared punishment and any loss of respectability.

STEP 4. If he is to be an ostensibly heterosexual cross-dresser, he marries a woman. Marriage affords him respectability. Thoughts of his same-sex orientation are suppressed. A man who accepts his homosexual urges may go on to live an openly gay life as a transvestite.

STEP 5. His partner either supports his cross-dressing or grudgingly accepts it—or leaves him. If the partner leaves, his cross-dressing activities accelerate. A supportive partner also helps the activity to increase. A grudging partner may hamper the activity, but the relationship is probably not pleasant or lasting.

STEP 6. If he discovers transvestite clubs or publications, his cross-dressing activities are shaped by the norms of the group. His cross-dressing escalates, he adopts a feminine name, and going out in female dress in public—and passing for a woman—become a valued goal.

Female Cross-Dressers.

Most of the research to date has been done on male cross-dressing, and little is really understood about female transvestitism. That said, the events that lead to becoming a lifelong male cross-dresser are determined from available research on such women and from extrapolation of male transvestite data:

STEP 1. Genetics, hormones, and neural brain patterns produce a girl who is more active and aggressive than her peers.

STEP 2. Family and social factors influence her development. She may readily find playmates who support her rough-and-tumble play and find little or no support for traditional feminine attributes.

STEP 3. At adolescence or young adulthood she realizes that her erotic attachments have a same-sex orientation. Missing here, apparently, is the link between cross-dressing and orgasm, which is found in the development of male cross-dressers.

STEP 4. She finds a mate and lives a lesbian lifestyle which, for her, includes regular male cross-dressing. She may adopt a traditional male work-role and full-scale male lifestyle. Female cross-dressers often claim that they find male clothes more comfortable and practical.

CHAPTER 20

John Wayne Bobbitt

EUNUCH TO CASTRATO

Doc, can you sew it back on?

JOHN WAYNE BOBBITT

JOHN WAYNE AND LORENA BOBBITT; MANASSAS, VIRGINIA, 1993 ◆

The most famous modern case of penile amputation in America involved John Wayne Bobbitt and his wife, Lorena. She would later claim in court that her act of desperation was the result of years of psychological abuse by her ex-marine husband.

Early one morning in 1993, after John had passed out from too much alcohol, Lorena severed his penis with a kitchen knife. Driving her getaway car from their Virginia apartment, she tossed the bloodied organ out the window, into a field.

Urologist James Sehn was at the hospital when John Bobbitt was wheeled in.

"My wife cut me," said the ex-marine, his voice amazingly calm.

Sehn pulled back the sheet. Nothing was there except a clot of blood at the body wall.

"Doc, can you sew it back on?" Bobbitt asked.

"We don't have the penis," Sehn said. He explained that the local police were searching along the roadside for the organ, but if it didn't turn up—and in good condition—not much could be done.

Sehn recalled telling John Bobbitt, "If we're not able to find the missing part, we're going to have to close over the stump. You'll have to sit down to urinate, and, I'm afraid, you'll never again have sex as you've known it."

"Do your best, Doc," said Bobbitt, giving Sehn a high five. Then an anesthesiologist put him under.

Amazingly, the penis was found—and in excellent condition, considering what it had been through.

"I felt sick to my stomach when I saw it," said Sehn. Several police officers at the Manassas hospital had clutched their own crotches when the severed organ was carried in. Sehn, assisted by plastic surgeon David Berman, began the painstaking procedure of reattaching tiny blood vessels and nerves that have the thickness of a hair.

Since the 1970s, there had been about ten cases of penile reattachments in the United States. Neither Sehn nor Berman had done such an operation before. They had a general idea of what they had to do, but doing it was a challenge.

"I knew the anatomy real well," said urologist Sehn. "That was my end of it. Dr. Berman had reattached some severed fingers."

The doctors had to worry about the deep dorsal vein. Blood flows into the penis through multiple channels, but it exits only through that one tiny tube. Unless the blood could get out of the penis after Bobbitt had an erection, circulation would stop, the bloated organ would turn blue, and the reattached organ would die a slow death.

The surgery took several hours. When the doctors finally released the tourniquet around the penile shaft, the head of the penis turned a rosy pink. Using a Doppler probe, they listened to blood flow and were satisfied that the dorsal vein was working properly.

"Great news," Sehn said to Bobbitt when he woke up. "The police found your penis, and we were able to sew it back on."

Bobbitt smiled and gave him a grateful high five.

A week later, John Wayne Bobbitt walked out of the hospital. A year later, he starred in a hard-core porn video, in which he had intercourse with three shapely actresses. The penis worked perfectly, its appearance marred only by a darkish ring around the shaft, a shadow from sutures and scar tissue.

Bobbitt went on the road, touring adult clubs promoting his film. In 1996, he canceled an appearance in a Stockton, California, porn store, citing his new status as a minister. He had been ordained a reverend the week before by the Universal Life Church of Las Vegas. He had, one might say, been born yet again.

"Bob It"; 1675 •

The Bobbitt case got a lot of media attention. "*Bob it*" was a 1920s expression for cutting anything short. Flappers wore bobbed hair.

In fact, "bob," meaning to "cut short," dates to 1675. Horses' tails were cropped or bobbed. Bobby socks, dating to 1943, are short socks reaching just above the ankle. A bobcat was so named in 1888 because of its stubby tail. Lorena Bobbitt bobbed her husband's tail.

In *Eve's Revenge* (1994), a compendium of feminists barbs, Tama Starr collected female reactions to the Bobbitt incident:

• "There are women who say he got what he deserved for being an insensitive lover alone." Amy Pagnozzi, *New York Daily News*, November 6, 1993.

• "Every woman I've talked to about this says, 'Way to go!' " Lynne Nelson, *The New York Times*, November 10, 1993.

• "There are a lot of women who . . . wish they'd had a chance to get their own revenge. So I certainly think that explains the number of women who have said, 'Yeah, well, he got what he deserved.' " Kim Gandy, executive vice president of NOW, Associated Press report, 1993.

Upon her arrest on June 23, 1993, Lorena Bobbitt made a statement to police:

"He always had orgasm, and he doesn't wait for me to have orgasm. He's selfish. I don't think it's fair, so I pulled back the sheets and then I did it."

100 SEVERED PENISES ♦ *A severed penis is almost always the result of self-mutilation by a psychotic or of accidental trauma. Mutilations by wives, as in the Bobbitt case, are extremely rare. However, the medical literature does include one curious outbreak of penile amputations by wives.*

It occurred in Thailand between 1973 and 1980. Thai wives took to punishing their adulterous husbands by getting them drunk and then, while they slept in a stupor, cutting off their disloyal instruments. An article by a group of Thai surgeons, "Surgical Management of an Epidemic of Penile Amputations in Siam," published in the American Journal of Surgery in 1983, reported that there had been at least one hundred cases of wifely retaliation. Graphic press accounts, including interviews with women who unashamedly endorsed their method of revenge, sustained the epidemic.

Many of the severed penises could not be surgically reattached because they could not be found. The traditional Thai home rests high up on pilings, with the family's pigs, chickens, and ducks living underneath. Most wives tossed their husbands' penises out the window and into the barnyard, where the organs were eaten, either swallowed whole by pigs or pecked apart by hens. During the seven-year wave of amputations, Thai men developed a common saying: "I better get home or the pigs will have something to eat."

Several salvaged organs were reattached, but the microsurgical methods of the 1970s left them numb and unfunctional. Since then, reattachment surgery has made great strides.

EUNUCH; ALL CULTURES, ANTIQUITY ♦

*W*hy cut off a man's balls or penis? The reasons are as numerous as the benefits. A man without balls is uniquely qualified for many purposes; without his penis, he's qualified for even more.

The word "eunuch" is from the Greek *eunouchos* and Latin *eunuchus*, meaning "keeper of the bedchamber," an allusion to one of a eunuch's many functions.

Men have been cutting off other men's balls since antiquity and for a number of reasons:

- **Prisoners of War.** Conquerors testically castrated the vanquished as a means of subduing them; without testosterone, aggressive tendencies wane. Ball-less men make better slaves. This punishment was carried to humiliating extremes among American Indians, where it was the women of the winning tribe who amputated the testicles of the defeated.

- **Salvation of the Soul.** In certain Christian sects men castrated themselves—testes *and* penis—to quench temptation and avert sin. Saint Matthew addresses such zealots who "have made themselves eunuchs for the kingdom of heaven's sake (19:12)." Biblical scholars believe that at one time the passage went so far as to recommend castration as a means of spiritual salvation but was later toned down to its present wording: "He that is able to receive it [castration], let him receive it"—certainly no condemnation of the operation.

- **Revenge.** In the Orient, a vengeful husband could demand in court the testicular castration of his wife's lover—and get it. Or a slothful Chinese might remove his own testes to obtain a pension and dispensation from work at a time when the government sought to limit population growth.

- **Male Opera Sopranos.** In post-Renaissance Italy, impresarios testicularly castrated choirboys so that youths as adults could sing as full-bodied sopranos in the best cathedrals of Europe. The Catholic church officially discouraged the operation, but the Vatican's interest in emasculated men for its own choir kept the *castrati* bel-cantoing into the twentieth century. The last castrato, Alessandro Moreschi, died in 1922, leaving behind the only recordings of that unique, unnatural voice: high and flexible like a female's, robust and powerful like a male's.

- **Toy Boys.** In imperial Rome, some of the handsomest men were testicularly castrated against their will to become the toy boys of wealthy matrons who could copulate at whim without worry of pregnancy.

By making the fateful incision a little higher, the penis was removed to produce a eunuch, who, because he could not copulate at all, was in great demand in all spheres of society. Roman eunuchs served as "safe" cooks and bedchamber servants in stately homes, as transvestite "wives" of buggering bisexual Roman emperors, and as close and constant companions of prominent church fathers, including many cardinals and several popes.

- **Guardians of Harems.** In the East, eunuchs served as the hands-off protectors of sultans' harems.

- **Punishment.** During the reign of England's Henry II (1154–1189), castration was reserved for refractory priests who refused to side with the king against his counsel-turned-critic, Thomas Becket. Scottish philosopher David Hume, in his *History of England*, recounts how the king "ordered a group of them [priests] to be castrated, and caused all their testicles to be brought to him on a platter." The empiricist philosopher viewed the loss as insignificant: "Of the pain and danger they, the monks, might justly complain, yet since they had vowed chastity, he deprived them of a superfluous treasure."

• *Fate of Rapist.* Throughout history, castration was used on rapists. For first offenders, the ancient Romans crushed a man's gonads between stones; for a second offense, they were cut off.

The ancient Greeks also used castration to punish rapists. The offender was called a *spados*, meaning "to draw out" or "drag," a description of how the testes were removed from the scrotum. Despised in Greek society and denied employment, such men, who had had their testes "dragged," often masqueraded as women—one suspected origin of the slang expression "drag" for a man in woman's attire.

Some punishments were more gruesome than others. In the fifth century B.C.E., Greek historian Herodotus tells of a unique treatment of a rapist devised by the nomadic Samaritans. A sturdy rope would be drawn tightly around the man's genitals, then he would be hanged from a tree, one hand bound behind his back, a sharp knife placed in his other hand. If he chose, he could cut himself free by self-castration.

• *Teachers of Children.* The Greeks, unlike other cultures, used castration only to punish rapists. They did not castrate prisoners to subdue or humiliate them, and they never produced a class of haremlike eunuchs, so high was the esteem in which the Greeks held manhood. The eunuchs who lived in Greek territories were attributed to the work of the Phoenicians. They were brought to Greece by the aristocracy as "safe" instructors for their male and female children.

• *In France.* Castration as punishment for rapists was finally abolished in France by Napoleon. Instead, the emperor instituted a scale of fines for all sex offenses: thirty-five francs for a man guilty of lifting a woman's skirt to the knee; seventy francs if he lifted it to the thigh; two hundred francs if he "had his way with her"—that is, raped her.

• *In the United States.* In 1975, two California criminals convicted of child molestation, Paul de la Haye and Joseph Kenner, requested they be castrated instead of risking a likely life sentence. The judge agreed. Arrangements were made to have the men hospitalized, anesthetized, and surgically castrated. But the operations were canceled when the urologist scheduled to perform the surgery was advised by his colleagues at San Diego's University Hospital that he was risking a lawsuit for assault and battery that probably would not be covered by his malpractice insurance. When the county urological society offered the same opinion, the surgeon backed out. The two men were sent to prison, genitalia intact.

In 1996, another child molester in the United States asked to be testicularly castrated upon release from prison. He told the probation board that he most likely would molest other children, since the urge was beyond his control. But the man was denied his wish. Castration after puberty, especially decades later, can diminish spontaneous sexual fantasies, but it only slightly dampens the libido. The adrenal glands continue to produce male sex hormones.

• *In California.* Governor Pete Wilson, in September 1996, signed into law a measure making California the first state to require chemical castration of repeated child molesters. Under the measure, those convicted of committing a second crime against a child under thirteen years of age must receive weekly injections of Depo-Provera, which curbs sexual desire. Offenders who don't want weekly injections can choose to be surgically castrated instead.

The chemical procedure is already in use in Europe. The rate for repeat-sex offenders dropped from 100 percent without chemical castration to just 2 percent with the weekly injections.

ORIGIN OF CASTRATION; EUROPE AND ASIA ♦

𝒞astration is ancient, first performed on animals after an astute, accidental observation.

About ten thousand years ago, early man began domesticating animals for their meat, milk, and hides and then employing them as draft animals to supplement human muscle power. More than once, it was observed that a diseased bull or buffalo that had amputated its testes on a jagged tree stump recovered to become a more docile, tamable animal.

Soon man was wielding a knife to do what the tree stump had done—to beasts of burden and to captured warriors from neighboring tribes. He turned rowdy roosters into fat capons (Latin *capo*, "to cut") for eating, wild horses

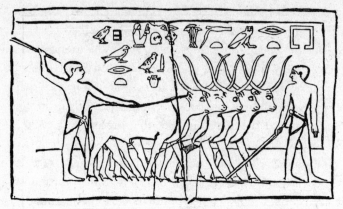

Astute observation: a castrated bull was a better worker.

into gentle geldings (Middle English *geldr*, "barren") for riding, oxen (German *Oshs*, "bull") into dutiful beasts of burden, and captured men into humiliated eunuchs.

By 2000 B.C.E., castration was a favorite agricultural practice, as well as a military sport of the Egyptians, Assyrians, Ethiopians, and Israelites. Genitalia of prisoners became trophies of war, with a peck of penises more impressive than a tally of testes. Many ancient monuments and stone reliefs depict conquerors brandishing the genitalia of their enemies. The inventory of trophies taken by Egyptian troops that invaded Libya in the thirteenth century B.C.E. lists a total of 13,320 penises, six belonging to generals—not that they are recognizable as such.

A stone relief in the ancient city of Thebes (modern Luxor and Karnak), showing a band of victorious Egyptian men scooping their trophies into a great pile, bears the inscription:

Prisoners brought before the king, 1000. Phalli collected, 3000.

In 597 B.C.E., Nebuchadnezzar, king of Babylon, conquered Jerusalem. He destroyed its great temple and cut from thousands of Jewish male prisoners every inch that the circumcision had left behind.

The practice of one man taking another man's privates home as proof of victory was so common in ancient times that it is described in the Bible. David (1 Samuel 18:27), to prove he is worthy of becoming Saul's son-in-law, goes off and returns with two hundred foreskins from conquered Philistines who were not merely circumcised but fully castrated.

Emperors Augustus (right) and Tiberius favored testicular eunuchs as sex toys.

EUNUCHS FOR PLEASURE; ROME, PRE-CHRISTIAN ERA •

A Roman eunuch, lacking testes and penis, was fittingly called a *voluptas*—Latin for "pleasure" and the origin of our word "voluptuous"—for the soft, rounded, feminine distribution of his body fat. Eunuchs became the main attraction in the orgies staged by the emperors Octavius (27 B.C.E.–14 C.E.), Tiberius (14–37), and Caligula (37–41).

Octavius, as Augustus Caesar, made no secret of his fondness for castrated men. His sexual indulgences with them, in which he was the active partner and they were the passive pawns, led to his being referred to as effeminate and emasculated himself. Once, when he was attending a play, an actor spoke a line about a favorite fey eunuch beating a tambourine—*"Videsne ut cinaedus orbem digito temperet?"* ("Do you see how this buttboy's finger beats the orb?")—and the knowledgeable audience immediately glanced toward the royal box and burst into wild applause, to which Octavius bowed.

Daisy Chain

Tiberius, even more licentious, introduced at his orgies the gonadless *spado*, a eunuch who retained a functional penis. These pleasure slaves, under Tiberius' orders, engaged in the notorious *spintria*, or "daisy chain," which Suetonius, the second-century biographer, defined as "men joined front to back in sexual union." The human sex chains had up to twenty or more links, and Tiberius could often be found at the center. The whole point of the game was to see how many men in a row could anally copulate; maintaining one's own rhythm was the trick.

Caligula, among the most debauched of the Caesars, enjoyed public copulation with a favorite eunuch priest. The emperor was eventually slain by Chaerea, his military guard and frequent bed partner, for having embarrassed Chaerea in front of his peers. Chaerea, by all accounts, was not a eunuch.

A Lady's Man

In Roman times, it was the testicular eunuchs (and not the nobility who made liberal use of them) who were blamed for the decline in morals. One reason offered was obvious: with ball-less men, Roman noblewomen could engage in sex willy-nilly without fear of pregnancy. Martial, the first-century Roman epigrammatist, wrote, "The Roman woman wants the flower of marriage and not the fruit." His contemporary, the satirical poet Juvenal, explained that, "Some women always delight in soft eunuchs and tender kisses, and in the absence of a beard, and the fact that the use of abortives is unnecessary."

As latex condoms and the pill in modern times have sexually liberated women, two thousand years ago their equivalent was the penis-intact ball-less *spado*. Sex with him was always fun and never dangerous. These safe, copulating men became an essential part of a lady's retinue, accompanying their mistresses to the opulent Roman baths, lounging with them on their silk-draped litters, and pleasuring them on command. In imperial Rome the affluence of a woman was measured by the number of *spadones* in attendance.

A Man's Man

Eunuchs were even more popular among Roman men. Lucian, the second-century Greek satirist, writing about the "Greek vice" (homosexuality), argued that eunuchs corrupted Roman morals because of their temptingly androgynous appearance to heterosexual men in high places. Looking both male (*andros*) and female (*gynos*), they provided an easy rationalization for borderline bisexuals to cross the border. Being plump, soft, smooth-skinned, and hairless, says Lucian, "with breasts even firmer than a woman's," eunuchs tempted everyone from emperors to generals.

The most flagrant emperor to flaunt his exploits with *spadones* was Nero, who ruled from 54 to 68 C.E. He is said to have indulged in orgies of up to sixty eunuchs at a time. His favorite, Sporus, dressed as a woman, he married

> **HOW TO CASTRATE** ◆ *The ancient method of fully castrating a boy or adult male—removing testes and penis—was no different from that practiced in the Middle East into this century.*
>
> *To obtain a eunuch for a harem or to permanently punish a rapist, the individual was strapped, arms and legs, to a table. A thin cord was knotted tightly around his genitals, and, with a sharp razor, the organs were amputated. The wound was cauterized by the application of a searingly hot poker or molten tar. The mutilated youngster or adult was deprived of water for several days to prevent urination, which could infect the healing region.*
>
> *Then he was forced to drink enormous amounts of water, until the pressure in his bladder literally pushed the urine through layers and layers of scar tissue—providing him with an orifice.*
>
> *Not that many survived; the morality rate was about eight in ten. If he was one of the lucky ones, he began his new job as a docile, sexually nonthreatening slave. This operation was still being performed at the turn of the century on boys seven to ten years old.*

in public with much pomp. Nero claimed that he took Sporus as a bride because the castrated youth bore a resemblance (which not everyone saw) to his deceased pregnant wife Poppaea—whom, as legend has it, he murdered with a kick to her womb. Nero was, as Juvenal observed, not afraid to appear on the street "with this castrated spouse whom he publicly caressed."

SEX AND THE FALL OF ROME; THIRD TO FIFTH CENTURIES ◆

*E*unuchs became the easy scapegoats for a general decline in Roman morals.

While it is true that emasculated men were used by nobles of both sexes, it is equally true that eunuchs were the ones truly being *used*—by adults, who could judge right from wrong and who demanded that handsome young men be surgically castrated for purposes of pleasure.

The penchant for sex with eunuchs was responsible, claimed Livy, in his monumental first-century history of Rome, for the tidal wave of "pederasty" that swept across the empire, into every class, corrupting and weakening society—a total loss of morals.

Today we think of pederasty exclusively as sex between a man and a young boy. The word's roots literally mean that: *paid*, "boy" + *erastis*, "lover." But the coupling Livy referred to included the adult eunuch who in his androgyny was boylike and who, if testicularly castrated before puberty, underwent arrested penile development, leaving him even more like a boy.

Historians agree that the period of Roman licentiousness and the popularity of eunuchs strongly coincided. In Rome, an entire street, the Via de Toscani, the red-light district, became the province of prostitutes, perverts, eunuchs, and their assorted clients. By slur the sellers were "the suffering," but they were undeniably popular, especially the emasculated men who had been forcibly castrated as boys or who, on their own, chose to have it done by the street's *tonsores*, or "barbers."

By the beginning of the reign of Caracalla in 211 C.E., Rome had so many *voluptates* and *spadones*, as young as seven years old, that they could be bought for a "talent," a single silver coin. Age seven was the lower limit only because the emperor Domitian, around 84 C.E., had ordered that no boy should be prostituted or emasculated prior to his seventh birthday.

When did the abuses end?

In a sense they didn't. The empire fell first.

CHRISTIANITY AND CASTRATION ♦

The Christian emperor Constantine I made a dent in the number of eunuchs when he ordered capital punishment for castrators early in the fourth century. Later that century, the firebrand Saint Jerome railed against patrician matrons who surrendered to libidinous pleasures because with eunuchs they couldn't become pregnant. When Constantine moved his court east to Byzantium, many of Rome's emasculated men were relegated to monasteries, which is perhaps a perverse place to send sex slaves. One monastery, called Topos, in the Taurus Mountains of Turkey, was reserved exclusively for *voluptates* and *spadones*.

Constantine I embraced Christianity and made it the state religion. But his sons and their successors embraced concupiscence, and eunuchs returned as a centerpiece of the Roman court. When Constantine died in 337, his three sons divided the empire among themselves. Constantine II granted high office to the eunuch Eusebis, who proceeded to fill the palace and its many administrative positions with co-castrates.

Astonishingly, castration became a prerequisite for choice civil service jobs. For eunuchs, without their own families, could and did devote full loyalties to the emperor. "Even the noblest parents," wrote a later historian, "were not above mutilating their sons to help their advancement, nor was there any disgrace in it."

Eunuchs wielded such power and influence that eighteenth-century English historian Edward Gibbon, in *History of the Decline and Fall of the Roman Empire*, summed up the decades after Constantine the Great's rule: "They multiplied in the palaces of his [Constantine's] degenerate sons, and insensibly acquired the knowledge, and at length the direction of the secret councils."

In a sweeping and questionable generalization, Gibbon concluded, that "if we examine the general history of Persia, India, and China, we shall find that the power of the eunuch has uniformly marked the decline and fall of every dynasty."

Gibbon maintained that eunuchs were mentally inferior to "whole men" and consequently mishandled matters of government. Dynasties thus fell more from incompetence than sexual degeneracy. But the case for diminished mental capability is unsupported by modern science. On the other hand, if hedonism played a part in the fall of the Roman empire (one popular argument), eunuchs, at court and in the red-light district, were perhaps minor players, if not pawns, in the larger game of moral corruption that weakened the weave of Roman society.

THE PERSIAN BOY ◆

One of novelist Mary Renault's most popular historical romances is *The Persian Boy* (1972), a fact-based story of the romance between Alexander the Great and a Persian eunuch named Bagoas. Alexander (356–323 B.C.E.), king of Macedonia and the military conqueror who helped spread Greek culture from Asia Minor and Egypt to India, became enraptured with the beautiful androgynous youth and took him along on his military crusades. After Alexander's death, Bagoas, who had been fully castrated (penis and testes) as a boy, went on to become an influential politician and a military leader himself.

Eunuchs in Persia could rise to high positions in government. Bagoas first

Abduction into a seraglio was a beauty's fate. Harem eunuchs survived into the twentieth century.

became the confidential minister of Artaxerxes III, king of Persia's Achaemenid empire. Then, as commander in chief of the Persian forces that conquered Egypt in 343 B.C.E., Bagoas became the real master of the Achaemenids. The king did nothing without his eunuch's advice. Everyone at court suspected that Bagoas' real influence over the king was in the sack.

In the end, so to speak, Bagoas gave a bad name to eunuchs in high places. He murdered the aged king, then poisoned all of the king's sons except Arses, whom he placed on the throne as coruler with Darius III. Two years later, he poisoned Arses for attempting to have a mind of his own. And when Darius, then sole king, attempted to assert his independence, Bagoas laced the royal wine with poison. Amid such machinations it was not hard to be suspicious—and Darius was. He forced his chief eunuch to drink the libation, proving the suspicion and putting an end to the tyranny. So much for conventional wisdom that eunuchs are passive, docile, and nonaggressive.

HAREM EUNUCHS; BYZANTINE EMPIRE ◆

*I*t is ironic that Byzantium, which under Constantine the Great was to have no eunuchs, became in time the world's leading center of castration.

In the seventh century, the caliph Muawiyah, founder of the Umayyad dynasty, initiated the practice of using eunuchs to guard harems. Earlier sultans, who were little more than nomadic chieftains, were unacquainted with the concepts of harems and eunuchs.

The word "harem" in Arabic means "prohibited" or "illegal." It also stood for that part of the Muslim household, the seraglio, in which scores of wives and concubines lived. No cock-and-balls servant could be entrusted to look after them; the job fell to "guardians of the bedchamber"—full eunuchs, missing testes and penises.

During this so-called seraglio period of the Byzantine Empire, a corps of well over a thousand castrates protected the royal harem. The emasculated men also ran the academy that trained "whole" men for government service, and they headed the branch that decided which boys, from which families, would be *honored* with emasculation, which came with its own economic and social benefits.

The word "seraglio" is from the Italian (*serraglio*) from *serrare*, "to lock up." At first it applied only to the off-limits part of the palace that held the concubine—Latin *concumbere*, "to lie down with"—but, in time, came to be the name for the entire palace. The whole place was "padlocked."

Islamic historians claim that the practice of having eunuchs guard women was unknown among the Ottoman Turks until they took over the Byzantine Empire in 1453.

Linguistically, the setup was that *eunuchs* protected *harems of concubines* in the *seraglio*. A world of padlocks and prohibitions, unlimited sex for the privileged few, all watched over by ball-less and prick-less men. No wonder that one of the promised rewards for Muslim men in Islamic heaven is a countless number of beautiful maidens.

THE LAST EUNUCH; CHINA, 1996 ◆

*P*alace eunuchs, as civil servants or guardians of concubines, were a reality in China until December 17, 1996, when eunuch Sun Yaoting died just short of his ninety-fourth birthday. Like the thousands who preceded him through Chinese history, Mr. Sun had been emasculated as a boy. The crude and risky operation was arranged by his family, who were looking for a way out of poverty and into the private realm of China's highest rulers.

Using only hot chili sauce as a local anesthetic, the doctor performed the operation in one fateful swoop, using a small, curved knife. Only months after Mr. Sun's family forced him through the ordeal in 1911, the Manchu dynasty, which had ruled China since the mid-1600s, was overthrown, bringing an end to the castration system.

A eunuch traditionally preserved his genitals in a jar, to ensure that they would be buried with him, in the belief he'd be reincarnated as a "full" man. Mr. Sun was not so fortunate. During the Cultural Revolution, a decade of intense political and social upheaval that began in 1966, his family opened the jar, removed the proverbial family jewels, and disposed of them. They were afraid of being punished by marauding Red Guards if such a symbol of China's feudal past were discovered. Before his death, Mr. Sun joked that he would probably be reincarnated as a neutered cat or dog.

In the 1930s, an American journalist in Peking, Vincent Starrett, interviewed and photographed thirty-three palace eunuchs ranging in age from sixty to eighty. The emasculated elders were "thin, hairless, fat-lipped and bejowled . . . with shrill voices and hair which hangs down to their necks." Relieved now of servile duties, they were "fellows of a certain spirit . . . one still wearing the velvet pants of the days of former splendor, whereas most of the others were dressed in coolie cloth."

TRANSSEXUAL SURGERY: CHRISTINE JORGENSEN; DENMARK, 1950S •

*I*n 1950, an American ex-GI named George approached Copenhagen surgeon Christian Hamburger, complaining of severe depression and a nagging conviction that his mind was that of a woman. He could not continue life as a man, he said. Nature had mistakenly given him a male body. He'd been secretly dressing as a woman for some time; he'd self-administered estrogen injections; and he'd shaved his pubic hair into a woman's triangular shape. The remaining "detestable" problem was his penis and testes. Could the doctor remove them—and replace them with a vagina?

After conducting a thorough physical and psychiatric evaluation, Hamburger treated him with large additional doses of female hormones. George's body developed a decidedly feminine contour, and his voice, behavior, and gait became markedly feminine. His sparse beard was removed by electrolysis.

The patient, who later took the name Christine Jorgensen, was then testically castrated under provisions of the Danish Sterilization and Castration Act of 1935, which allowed castration for patients whose sexuality made them likely to commit crimes or suicide. The surgical removal of the testes alone

---

PATRON SAINT OF EUNUCHS ◆ *In an abandoned garden overgrown with weeds, American journalist Vincent Starrett walked among the tombstones of more than seventeen hundred eunuchs from past dynasties. Most prominent was the grave of Kang Ping Tieh, patron saint of Chinese eunuchs and known as the Iron Duke.*

Five centuries earlier, Kang, with his genitalia intact, was a general to Emperor Yung Lo. As the story goes, one day the emperor went hunting and left Kang to oversee Peking's Forbidden City, whose most forbidden inhabitants ("forbidden" to anyone but the emperor) were the collection of imperial concubines. The honor was great, as was the temptation; previous generals had been executed for allegations of sexual dalliances in the emperor's absence.

Kang, despite his intended chastity, was certain that palace rivals who wanted him out of the way would level similar charges against him. He developed a plan. The night before the emperor's departure, Kang gripped his own genitalia in his hand and with a sharp knife amputated everything. He hid the severed organs deep in the emperor's saddlebag and, a little light-headed from loss of blood, assumed his duties as guardian of the Forbidden City.

No sooner had the emperor returned than Kang was called to account for how he had spent his nights. To the charge that he had frolicked among the seventy-three royal ladies, Kang ordered, "Bring in the emperor's saddle." He requested that the emperor himself reach into a remote pocket of the bag.

The extracted organs, black, pungent, and shriveled, were recognizable nonetheless for what they once had been. The emperor, overwhelmed by the selfless gesture, promoted the general to chief eunuch, lavished him with gifts, and proclaimed him holy.

---

is an orchiectomy, from the Greek *orchis,* "testicle"—also the origin of the flowering "orchid," because of the plant's bulbous root.

In 1952, Christine Jorgensen asked if his "detested male sex organ" could be removed, and Dr. Hamburger amputated the penis. No attempt was made to construct a vagina. Hamburger and his colleagues reported the case the next year in the *Journal of the American Medical Association,* pointing out that they had discovered a similar case in 1943 in Germany.

Actually, there were several earlier cases of "transsexual" surgery.

Lili Elbe

The best-known case of early transsexual surgery was that of Lili Elbe, described in *Man Into Woman* (1933) by Niels Hoyer. Lili had started life as the well-known Danish painter Einar Wegener, who'd become convinced that a female twin entity shared his body. He visited several doctors, wondering what could be done about the unwanted twin. Some told him he was a latent homosexual, suggesting that if he would admit to it he might be happier. Others treated his penis and testes with X rays, presumably to drive out the female entity. Other doctors told him he had a set of rudimentary female organs lurking inside his body. Today doctors would probably say his "feminized" brain, a fetal developmental error, was telling him he was a woman.

Wegener eventually went to Berlin, where he found a surgeon who removed his penis and testicles, then implanted ovarian tissue from a healthy twenty-six-year-old woman into his abdomen. Einar Wegener obtained a new passport in the name of Lili Elbe, and the king of Denmark declared her earlier marriage null and void. Lili later returned to Berlin to have a vagina constructed so that she could marry a French male painter and engage in normal intercourse. Unfortunately, she died in Berlin in 1931, during her postoperative recovery, though "recovery" seems hardly the right word.

But it was the case of Christine Jorgensen that grabbed media headlines in 1952. She became world-famous, sold her story to the Hearst newspapers, penned an autobiography, and went on the lecture circuit. Within months of the surgery, the Danish medical team had received more than five hundred letters from people pleading for the same operation: men who felt they were women trapped in a male body, and a lesser number of women who felt they were men trapped in a female body.

"Transsexual"; 1950s ◆

*D*r. Hamburger, in his journal article, had referred to Christine Jorgensen's condition as "genuine transvestitism." The adjective "genuine" was to distinguish the ex-GI's fundamental belief that he *was* a woman from the behavior of male cross-dressers who readily accept their maleness—even delight in it—but occasionally dress in women's clothes: "behavioral" transvestites. The word "transvestite," as we've seen, dates to about 1922.

By the 1950s, doctors were performing "sex reassignment surgery" and calling the underlying condition "transsexualism." *Merriam-Webster's Collegiate Dictionary* dates the word to 1957, but it appears to have been bandied about earlier.

In a paper read before the Society for the Scientific Study of Sex in 1963, Dr. Harry Benjamin claimed he had been using "transsexualism" in his lectures for the past ten years. Benjamin attributed the first use of the term to Dr. David O. Cauldwell, who had written a 1949 article for *Sexology* describing a case of "psychopathia transsexualis" in which a young girl felt she was really a man.

Public awareness of how transsexualism differs from transvestism was heightened in 1972 with the sex reassignment surgery of British journalist James Humphrey Morris, who took the name Jan. As a man, he had covered Sir Edmund Hillary's successful climb of Mount Everest. In a best-selling autobiography, Jan explained her fundamental conviction that she had always been a woman trapped in a man's body, and that her wife and four children had supported her decision to undergo sex reassignment surgery.

In 1980, transsexualism was recognized as a genuine illness in the third edition of the *Diagnostic and Statistical Manual of Mental Disorders*. In a person who has reached puberty, the condition is characterized by two major criteria:

• Persistent discomfort and sense of inappropriateness about one's assigned sex.
• Persistent preoccupation for at least two years with getting rid of one's primary and secondary sex characteristics and acquiring the sex characteristics of the other sex.

LUCIANO PAVAROTTI, SOPRANO? ◆

*W*e are accustomed to the phenomenon of sexually androgynous singing superstars, genetic men who go out of their way to confound their masculinity: David Bowie, the artist formally known as The Artist Formerly Known As Prince, Boy George, Michael Jackson. On the other side, there's k. d. Lang. The list gets longer every year; androgyny has its own box-office appeal. But the phenomenon itself is centuries old.

The concept of a singing superstar, besieged by crazed fans who beg for autographs and toss undergarments onto the stage, goes back to the days when choirboys were castrated so that their youthful soprano and contralto voices would not deepen. The concept may seem barbaric today, but for a time it was shockingly commonplace.

Its homeland was Italy. At the fad's peak, around 1750, more than two thousand Italian sons annually lost their balls for the sake of the musical arts. To put the phenomenon in modern perspective: if Luciano Pavarotti had been born two centuries ago, he'd have probably had his balls cut off by age nine. Instead of being the world's greatest tenor, he'd have been the world's greatest soprano—and the largest. Physical size, as we'll see, was a salient feature of the castrati.

Two historical events paved the way: Christianity and opera. The former forbade women to sing in church; the latter needed strong, high-pitched voices. The solution was obvious. A poor family with a prepubescent son in possession of a lovely soprano voice turned him over to a castrator in hopes that their adult superstar could one day support them in their dotage.

Though thousands of boys became castrati, only a few dozen achieved superstardom. The odds against making it to the top of any profession haven't changed: spectacular success has always been a long shot.

• Castrato—Italian for a castrated young male whose adult voice is that of a soprano—*sopra*, Italian for "above"—the highest human singing voice, usually ranging two octaves or more above middle C. The word "castrato" is from the Latin *castrare*, "to castrate," and was first recorded in English in 1763.

The Mechanics

At puberty a male's vocal cords thicken in response to large spurts of testosterone from the gonads, and the voice deepens. By analogy, imagine moving your fingers across the neck of a guitar from the thinnest strings, which produce the highest-pitched sounds, to the thickest strings, which produce the lowest bass notes. Remove the gonads early enough, say between the ages of seven and ten, and the boy's lovely high soprano never deepens to become a baritone or bass.

But—and this is crucial—the boy still grows to manly proportions. His lung capacity expands, his diaphragm muscles strengthen, and his thin, clarion soprano blossoms into a large, booming soprano, one that no woman ever produced—or could.

*Alessandro Moreschi,
the last castrato.*

It is an unnatural voice, and one we will never hear firsthand. However, the practice of castrating young choirboys to keep their vocal cords thin ended only late in the nineteenth century—so late, in fact, that one castrato, the Vatican's own Alessandro Moreschi, director of papal music, was able to make gramophone recordings.

THE LAST CASTRATO: ALESSANDRO MORESCHI (1858–1922), DIRECTOR OF PAPAL MUSIC ◆

For centuries, the Catholic church in Rome was a major employer of castrated sopranos, employing them in the Vatican Chapel choir into the twentieth century. Until his death in 1922, Alessandro Moreschi, a plump, smooth-skinned soprano, was the director of papal music and of the Sistine choir.

The church claimed that Moreschi, and its other male sopranos who lived into the twentieth century, actually had balls but just possessed unusually high male voices—they were *falsetti,* singing in an unnaturally "false" vocal style. But when Moreschi died, the Vatican refused to have his body autopsied, which would have proved he was indeed a castrato.

A castrato retains his penis.

Ball-less Singer on Compact Disc

To the church's dismay, Moreschi had made twelve cylinder recordings in 1902 and 1904, at the request of Thomas Edison, inventor of the gramophone.

Edison had aggressively gone after the rarest singer of the day, determined to record the last castrato voice. On the cylinders Moreschi was listed as "*Soprano della Cappella Sistina*," and the accompanying text made it clear that he was a castrato. One line of copy in particular stood out: *Evviva il cotello,* "Long live the knife," the enthusiastic cheer of fans throughout the castrato's era.

The recordings, of arias and church songs, were transferred to a compact disc in the early 1990s. In a high, reedy, emotional voice—"a sob in every note" read the liner notes (one is left to wonder what Moreschi is sobbing for)—the world's last castrato sings such standards as "Ave Maria."

The CD also contains the voice of Moreschi's employer, Pope Leo XIII, pontiff from 1878 to 1903. The Pope's lavish comments on Moreschi's singing, recorded by Edison's company in Rome five months before the pontiff's death, are the oldest vocal recording of a pope. It is odd that it is an expression of exuberant praise for the singing of a ball-less man—to his credit, Pope Leo condemned the practice of castrating boys to turn them into sopranos.

GLOWING REVIEWS ◆

*A*round 1900, Italian author Enrico Panzacchi listened to Moreschi and several other castrati in the Vatican choir. In his long career he'd heard many great singers, but still he was mightily impressed:

> *What singing! Imagine a voice that combines the sweetness of the flute, and the animated suavity of the human larynx—a voice that leaps and leaps, lightly and spontaneously, like a lark that flies through the air and is intoxicated with its own flight; and when it seem that the voice has reached the loftiest peaks of altitude, it starts off again, leaping and leaping still with equal lightness and equal spontaneity, without the slightest sign of forcing or the faintest indication of artifice or effort; in a word, a voice that gives the immediate idea of sentiment transmuted into sound, and of the ascension of a soul into the infinite on the wings of that sentiment. What more can I say?*

In 1995, Sony Pictures Classics released *Farinelli*, about one of the greatest castrati of all time. The real Farinelli (1705–1782) was a tall, handsome superstar who had money, talent, fame, and more adoring female fans than he could possibly bed, though he tried to accommodate as many as possible.

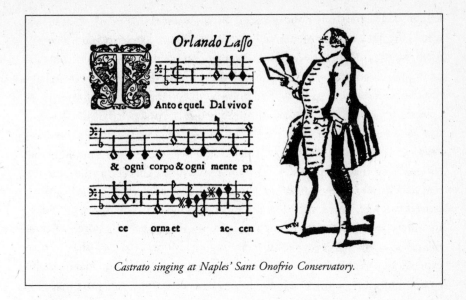

Castrato singing at Naples' Sant Onofrio Conservatory.

Loss of his testes had done little to diminish his sex drive; and because he couldn't get a lover pregnant, he was in great demand. Husbands boasted of their wives' "safe" trysts with Europe's greatest vocal star.

To give Farinelli, played by Stefano Dionisi, the "voice of an angel," sound technicians used a trick. All the operatic songs were recorded separately by a well-known tenor *and* a soprano. The technicians then digitized the two tracks, seamlessly blending male and female voices into a single sound that is truly otherworldly.

When did male children begin to be castrated specifically for the beauty of their voices?

BIRTH OF THE CASTRATO; ROME, THIRD CENTURY ◆

The first historical reference to a castrato appears in the eighty-volume *Romaika*, by the third-century Roman statesman Dio Cassius. His immense history of the empire, which beings with the landing of Aeneas in Italy and ends in the reign of Alexander Severus (222–235), seems to place the origin of the practice during the time of Emperor Septimius Severus (193–211). Dio Cassius says little of testicular castration in the service of singing, but in the decades straddling the year 200, castration of children had reached faddish proportions.

The first singing castrato was probably castrated by accident—that is, a boy with a lovely soprano had his testes removed for one of the many medical reasons that physicians recommended castration: hernia, epilepsy, and forms of mental illness. The boy survived the surgery and, amazingly, retained his soprano, which got more powerful but no deeper. This discovery appears to have occurred around the year 200. We know with certainty that the flowering of Christianity created the musical milieu in which the practice flourished.

Saint Paul unintentionally paved the way for singing castrati. As the evangelist who brought Christianity to the Gentiles in the first century, he wrote emphatically that women were forbidden to sing in church, an interdiction that ended only in the seventeenth century. A composer who scored a piece requiring a high voice had two options: a prepubescent boy or a man straining in a "falsetto" (Italian *falso,* "false"), a voice forced into a register higher than that of the natural voice.

Each had its drawbacks. A boy could be mischievous, unable to maintain concentration throughout a long church service, and just when he mastered the soprano repertoire his voice could deepen. The falsetto, on the other hand, possessed a peculiar, colorless, and harshly unpleasant vocal quality as well as a range more limited than a soprano's. For many years, these less than ideal vocalists constituted church choirs until someone discovered the castrato—and the church had a third option.

For the next seventeen hundred years, church fathers would openly deplore castration of boy sopranos but eagerly accept the singers into cathedrals and the Vatican chapel. Cardinals collected castrati for their private choirs and boasted of their acquisitions. Though poor families castrated singing sons for a fee paid by a bishop or cardinal, the standard explanation offered by church fathers was that the unfortunate lad had accidentally been emasculated by a charging boar. "The pig did it" excuse fooled no one, but it kept the practice thriving for centuries.

It would be misleading to blame the castrati phenomenon solely on the church's need for sopranos. The practice would reach its peak centuries later, due to two other vocal events: the development in the fifteenth century of an *a cappella* singing style that required a wider range of voices and a greater degree of virtuosity than a boy or a falsetto could muster, and, more significantly, the creation of opera at the end of the next century.

FIRST ANDROGYNOUS SUPERSTARS; ITALY, EARLY SEVENTEENTH CENTURY •

*T*he first androgynous singing superstars debuted in Italy. They were ball-less Italian men, and the phenomenon was enthusiastically championed by Pope Clement VIII. The pontiff, who reigned from 1592 to 1605, had a penchant for male sopranos.

Our word "opera" represents a form of theater comprising a dramatic text or libretto ("little book") combined with singing and instrumental accompaniment. Though previous works had combined poetic drama and music, thus prefiguring operatic development, the first true opera, composed by Jacopo Peri, was presented in Florence in 1597, five years into Pope Clement's reign.

Peri's *Dafne* did not feature castrati, but two years later, and two hundred miles away, two of the first male sopranos dazzled audiences in Rome. Those castrati, who as boys had supposedly been gored by pigs, were Pietro Paolo Folignato and Girolamo Rosini.

That year, Pope Clement heard each man sing at the Vatican and was impressed with the "sweetness and flexibility" of their voices. Vatican records show that the pope, a lawyer turned priest who sharpened the severity of the Inquisition, immediately preferred the castrato voice to the "shrill and acidulous tone of the soprano falsettists" who were then singing in the Vatican chapel.

Vatican Choir

Pope Clement wanted androgynous sopranos in his own choir. Peasant families throughout Italy heard of his wish and moved swiftly to offer up their sons.

Clement was a popular and influential pope. Although as a cardinal he had been charged with nepotism—for making three favorite nephews cardinals, one at the age of fourteen—as pope he won wide support for his strict orthodoxy, and especially for banning all books written by Jews—except, of course, the Bible.

Once the highest authority in Christendom more or less sanctioned castrated androgynous men as singers, the phenomenon became the vogue of Italy. Singing male falsettos suddenly found themselves out of work. Twenty-five years after the pontiff heard his first two castrati, *every* adult male in the Vatican choir was a ball-less soprano, as were most of the singers in cathedrals throughout Italy. That is rapid progress, considering it takes several years for a castrated nine-year-old to mature into an adult soprano. Clement's favorable review had clearly set knives flailing throughout the countryside.

In 1599, Pope Clement VIII launched the castrati phenomenon with his praise for the voice's "sweetness and flexibility."

Meanwhile, opera's popularity was spreading throughout Europe. Composers, following the Italian lead, were writing for higher and higher voices. For the first time in history a kind of international star-system arose. These stars were called *divi*—Latin, "male gods." Fleshy, beardless, ball-less, smooth-skinned, and androgynous, they were discussed, compared, and worshiped in fashionable drawing rooms from Portugal to Russia.

The story of the castrati is seldom told and virtually unknown by the general public, and opera aficionados regard it largely as a freakish sideshow. Anne Rice, in her 1982 erotic novel *A Cry to Heaven*, details what sex symbols castrati were in their day: adored by women and envied by men for their ability to give sexual pleasure without risk of pregnancy.

It has been convincingly argued that the Italian castrati were not only music's first real superstars but also entertainment's first real sex symbols. With their rapturous voices and safe sex appeal, they drove audiences wild. Their exploits on stage and off generated in the media of the day what we'd call tabloid titillation and scandals.

FIRST SUPERSTAR: BALDASSARE FERRI—1610–1680 ◆

*H*e had the girth and heft and double chins of Luciano Pavarotti, and the voice of Pavarotti *and* Joan Sutherland combined. His name was Baldassare Ferri, and he was the first superstar castrato.

Born in Perugia, Ferri displayed an extraordinary natural voice—clear, strong, and focused—from the time he started singing at age six. A tall, handsome youth, he became a church soprano in the local choir, where his voice caught the attention of the wealthy, opera-loving Cardinal Crescenzio. Smitten by both Ferri and his voice, the cardinal convinced the boy's parents that their son had a future on the operatic stage if only they'd consent to having him castrated.

Cardinal Crescenzio knew all about these matters. He'd advised other parents on the preservation of their sons' youthful voices. One day, at age ten, Ferri was given several shots of liquor, which made him light-headed, then he was stripped naked and immersed in a steaming hot bath. The heat numbed his nerve endings and allowed his scrotum to soften and expand. Underwater, his testes were tied off with a cord, then the boy was pulled out of the bath, quickly strapped to a table, and a professional castrator, who was also a barber, cut incisions in opposite sides of the sack and removed the boy's balls—A vasectomy of sorts.

When he healed, Ferri moved in with Crescenzio and lived lavishly on the cardinal's estate. The priest paid for singing lessons as the boy grew into a large, handsome young man. At age fifteen, Ferri made his operatic debut in Perugia, to extraordinary acclaim. He was literally an overnight sensation. Women found his androgynous handsomeness irresistible, and he was feted in every city in which he sang.

On his way to Florence to appear in an opera of Monteverdi, the young Ferri, already an easily recognized celebrity, was met three miles from the city gates by an adoring coterie of the town's most eminent men and women, who escorted him to his lodgings.

The world had never heard a voice like Ferri's, and word of mouth spread rapidly. Virtually every European and Asian monarch begged the singer to give a royal performance. He sang for King Sigismund III of Poland, and Queen Christian of Sweden invited Ferri to Stockholm, even though her country and Poland were at war. He consented, and a cease-fire was declared so that the singer could travel safely between the lines of the opposing armies, escorted by troops from both sides. He arrived safely in Stockholm, the war resumed, and Ferri sang nightly for two weeks for the queen. A superstar had temporarily stopped a war.

At age forty-five, Ferri performed at the court of Vienna, where he was persuaded to stay for twenty years, amassing a fortune in fees and gifts. He died in 1680, age sixty-nine, worth the equivalent today of three million dollars, which he left to charity.

What did Ferri—or any good castrato—sound like?

A critic in Ferri's time wrote:

Their timbre is as clear and piercing as that of choirboys and much more powerful. They appear to sing an octave above the natural voice of women. Their voices are brilliant, light, full of sparkle, very loud, and astound with a very wide range.

ANDROGYNY FAD; ITALY, 1650 TO 1850 ◆

*A*t the height of the castrati fad, around 1750, as many as two thousand young Italian boys were castrated every year. The slightest vocal aptitude could lead to genital mutilation; 70 percent of all Italian male singers were supposedly without balls. Audiences couldn't get enough of the talented androgynes. Hundreds of indigent parents sold their gifted sons to church cardinals, singing teachers, and music schools. In time the Vatican choir came to employ only castrati.

The operation became standardized, even humane. In the early days, too many promising choirboys had been lost to bungled surgery. Opium was now used to sedate a boy, and his balls were not removed; instead his sperm-carrying ducts were severed as in a modern vasectomy. The small, prepubescent testes would quickly shrivel and vanish.

The gender-bending aspect of the phenomenon titillated many people more than their love for opera. Spectators crowded into theaters eager to see firsthand these semimale curiosities. The vast majority of castrati were heterosexual, and most had no trouble getting and maintaining erections.

The castrati fad persisted for two hundred years. Though thousands of boys lost their gonads, most never acquired the compensating fame and wealth of a superstar for there was no way to forecast which youthful voice would mature into a spectacular instrument. The most talented boys ended up in Naples, the training center for castrati. The most famous of the city's four conservatories, Sant Onofrio a Capuana, began the practice of dressing student castrati in black cassocks, like priests.

By 1750, so many boys were being castrated—or butchered and killed by poor surgery—that the Italian government and the Catholic church were forced by public opinion to take a stand. Both officially condemned the butchery. The government made castration illegal—then turned its back to practitioners, since castrati were good business. A physician caught castrating a youth had only to claim that the boy's testes were diseased; he was saving the child's life.

The church made castration punishable by excommunication, but popes and cardinals welcomed the most talented mutilates into their choirs. The church eventually became *the* principle full-time employer of castrati, and it made most of their lives sheer hell. Failed singers, whose careers never took off, and who wanted to settle down with a wife, were forbidden to marry since they couldn't procreate—matrimony's primary purpose. Nor would the Vatican accept mutilated men into the priesthood—only into its choir.

A French travel writer journeying through Italy wrote, "The operation is against the law in all of these places, as well as against nature. And all Italians are so much ashamed of it, that in every province they transfer it to some other." The castration capital of the country was Bologna, known today for its cuisine.

In Italy, the center of opera, women were banned from the stage until the late eighteenth century and all female parts were taken by male sopranos or occasionally by women *en travesti,* though their popularity never equaled that of the castrati.

SWAN SONG; GIOACCHINO ROSSINI, 1850S ◆

*W*hat put an end to the phenomenon of the androgynous singers? Not the illegality of the operation, or the church's ostensible opposition to testicular mutilation. The castrati brought about their own downfall through the abuse of the power they came to wield over composers. Composers simply stopped writing for their voice. It was a case of a clash of titan egos. Testy divi against testy composers.

At their pinnacle in the eighteenth century, superstars could make or break a new opera, either by appearing in—or refusing to—its debut. The vain stars demanded that composers alter their scores to include flashy, audience-pleasing arias and reembellish songs from one performance to another to suit their whims. By the beginning of the nineteenth century, composers had had it with all the tampering and temperamental demands—and perhaps were jealous of singers who had come to outshine the songs.

Italian composer Gioacchino Rossini (1792–1868) turned the tide. In 1813 he composed *Aureliano in Palmira* for Giovanni Battista Velluti, the greatest castrato of the day. Though the florid work was already tailored to show off its star, Velluti, charged Rossini, vulgarized the music with endlessly tasteless vocal pyrotechnics—which sent the audience into a frenzy of applause. Rossini, also popular with audiences, never again allowed a male soprano to depart from his written notes. Velluti threw a public tantrum and threatened never to sing another Rossini score—though he did, for he was unable to resist the composer's music.

The castrati era was brought to an end by Wagner (left), Verdi (center), and the rise of female stars like soprano Jenny Lind, the "Swedish Nightingale."

Rossini's contemporary, Giacomo Meyerbeer (1791–1864), the last composer to write for the male soprano voice, also took a firm stand on singers adhering to the written score. He composed *Il Crociato in Egitto* (1824) for Velluti but kept the castrato reined.

As Wagner and Verdi achieved fame, they, even more than other composers, refused to tolerate musical tampering. Wagner was impressed with the force of the castrato voice and contemplated enticing one singer from Rome to sing the role of Klingsor in *Parsifal*—even willing to transpose the role for him. But he eventually abandoned the idea.

Also, female sopranos had gained greatly in popularity, making male sopranos look more like freaks. A new generation came to view the male mutilated for the sake of art as a pathetic figure to be pitied, not praised. Thus after two centuries of adoration, the castrati became an endangered species and moved toward extinction.

LAST GREAT CASTRATO: GIOVANNI BATTISTA VELLUTI; (1781–1861) ◆

hen the French invaded Italy in 1796, Velluti was a boy of fifteen, already in possession of a glorious and celebrated voice. Napoleon heard the young Velluti sing and exclaimed, unwittingly, "One must be only half a man to sing like that!" The general was, of course, right. But Velluti lost his testes in a circumstance that today would result in a monumental malpractice suit.

Velluti's proud father predicted that his son would grow up to be a military hero. Though the boy's mother had had her heart set on a girl, shortly after the birth she confided to a friend, "You ask whether I would have been happier at the birth of a girl baby. Oh, yes! But in that case. how could my husband have made her the valiant captain of whom he dreams?"

The family name, Velluti, is from *velluto*, Italian for "velvet." The mother's letter concluded, "Just think that the other day, while admiring him, his father exclaimed, 'This will be the first iron velvet!'"—meaning the first military member in the family. How did a boy who was to embody his father's most manly aspirations end up a eunuch?

Around age eight, young Giovanni came down with a cough and high, persistent fever. The exact ailment is unknown, but his health was entrusted to a local physician, who, to better attend to the youth, had him moved into his own home. At the time, castration was regarded as a cure for hernia, mumps, and a grab bag of complaints. The Vellutis allowed the doctor to treat their son at his own best discretion.

Days later, the lad was carried home on a stretcher, his groin bandaged. The fever was gone, and so were his gonads. The shattered father made the best of a deplorable situation and started the boy, who had already displayed a natural voice, on musical training.

The Castrato and the Pope
As a teenage castrato making his debut, Velluti greatly impressed Cardinal Chiaramonti, soon to become Pope Pius VII (1800–1823)—the pope who would excommunicate Napoleon. The cardinal and the castrato became great friends; each genuinely enjoyed the other's company. The older man's praises and financial support propelled the boy's career, and in 1801 Velluti made his operatic debut, the same year his sponsor was invested at Rome.

The pope and the eunuch remained friends and probably nothing more. By all accounts, Pius was chaste, befitting his chosen name. Velluti was anything but; he sexually carried on like many a modern star. Thoroughly heterosexual, he specialized in seducing his female fans, and his escapades were publicized throughout Italy.

The tall, handsome, spermless androgyne traveled through France, Italy, Germany, and Russia, becoming the lover of countless women, including an Italian baroness and a grand duchess, a relative of the czar. Many husbands, ignorant of the fact that the ball-less singer possessed an intact, functioning penis, never suspected their wives were having sexual affairs, just worshipful infatuations.

In 1849, Velluti had been retired for twenty years and living in Venice when

CONTRACEPTIVE FAILURE RATES ◆ *The following birth control methods show failure rates in one year of average use, based on women of reproductive ages, fifteen to forty-four. Failure rates with perfect use of these methods are lower, but couples rarely use methods perfectly.*

Method	Unintended pregnancy rate
No contraceptive	85
Spermicides	30
Withdrawal	24
Periodic abstinence	19
Cervical cap	18
Diaphragm	18
Condom	16
Pill	6
IUD	4
Tubal ligation	0.5
Depo-Provera	0.4
Vasectomy	0.2
Norplant	0.05
Testicular castration	0.00

Austrian troops besieged the city. On his way to visit a local doctor for melancholia, the singer was arrested and imprisoned. In his cell, Velluti occupied himself singing an aria, which happened to be a favorite of the arresting officer, an opera lover. The officer boasted to the singer that his father had heard the great Velluti perform that piece, to which the modest singer announced, "I am the great one." In the morning the prisoner was given a military escort back to his villa.

Velluti lived his remaining twelve years as such a recluse that his death came as a shock to the public, who had thought he was long dead. Several Italian newspapers reported that Velluti was the last of the castrati.

He was the last of the great stage castrati but not the end of the breed. As we've seen, castrati continued to sing in the Vatican choir into the twentieth century.

References and Comments

*T*hroughout this book I've cited references I've found helpful, quoted from, and leaned upon. This section makes more extensive comments on certain sources I found of particular interest. I do this for readers who might wish to pursue in more depth some of the subjects I've written about.

ON LOVE, KISSING, AND COURTING:

Diane Ackerman, *A Natural History of Love* (New York: Random House, 1994). Starting with love as depicted in ancient Egypt, Ackerman, in wonderfully sensuous prose, traces the ways men and women have wooed each other through Greece, Rome, the Middle Ages, and into modern times. She looks at such love molecules as the "cuddle chemical" and the "infatuation chemical." Highly recommended.

William Cane, *The Art of Kissing* (New York: St. Martin's, 1991). Though skimpy on hard facts about lip-puckering styles throughout the world, it is rich in anecdotal experiences, quotations, and techniques. Fun to browse.

John D'Emilio and Estelle B. Freedman, *Intimate Matters: A History of Sexuality in America* (New York: Harper & Row, 1988). The course of sexuality in America, due to the Puritans, is distinctly different from that in Europe, due to the "bisexual" Greeks and hot-blooded Romans. Starting with the era of settlement, the authors trace the evolution of sexual attitudes to our present-day "sexualized society." Highly recommended.

Helen E. Fisher, *Anatomy of Love* (New York: Norton, 1992). Subtitled "The mysteries of mating, marriage, and why we stray," Fisher's fascinating book provides surprising new sociobiological explanations of the roots of sex, love, courtship, and marriage.

Morton M. Hunt, *The Natural History of Love* (New York: Knopf: 1959). Beginning with the Greek "invention of love," Hunt covers ancient straight and gay romance, the evolution of marriage, the seething sexuality of the Puritans (whom he rightly calls the "Impuritans"), and other aspects of love up through the second sexual revolution. Hunt and Ackerman cover essentially the same terrain, but each book is uniquely informative.

George Ryley Scott, *Curious Customs of Sex and Marriage* (London: Torch-stream, 1953). The ceremony of marriage is central to every culture, and Scott covers most of the superstitions and strange rites that brides and grooms have engaged in.

ON WORD AND PHRASE ORIGINS:

As stated in the Introduction, the *Oxford English Dictionary* and *Merriam-Webster's Collegiate Dictionary* are my primary sources for the dates when words entered English. Other books were helpful in other regards:

Reinhold Aman, editor, *Talking Dirty* (London: Robson, 1993). This collection of essays considers the origins of abusive language, insults, and wicked jokes. Chapter titles give a glimpse of the book's approach: "The Poetry of Porking," "Tradename of American Condoms," "Offensive Language via Computer."

Ariel C. Arango, *Dirty Words: Psychoanalytic Insights* (Northvale, N.J.: Aronson, 1898). Extending Freud's study, Arango traces the psychic origins of dirty words to early infancy and childhood, examining their place and value in life— yes, value. After all, on many occasions dirty words are indispensable. No polite word will do.

Norrie Epstein, *The Friendly Shakespeare* (New York: Viking, 1992). Many books (including most of the others listed here) deal with the use of racy words in Shakespeare. Epstein's, though, is sheer fun to read, and a thoroughly painless guide to the Bard.

Stuart Berg Flexner, *I Hear America Talking* (1976) and *Listening to America* (1982) (New York: Simon and Schuster). The stories of thousands of words and phrases that are distinctly American. Both books are a delight to browse and a wonderful source of "origin" information.

Jonathan Ned Katz, *The Invention of Heterosexuality* (New York: Penguin, 1995). This book breaks new ground in the study of words and concepts dealing with hetero- and homosexuality. It quite effectively pulls the rug out from under prevailing assumptions on what is, and was, "normal" and "abnormal." Eye-opening reading for the open-minded and essential reading for everyone else.

Hugh Rawson, *Wicked Words* (New York: Crown, 1989). An entertaining treasury of curses and formerly unprintable terms, from Anglo-Saxon times to the present. To my knowledge, this is the best book on the origins of dirty words. Highly recommended.

Jesse Sheidlower, editor, *The F Word* (New York: Random House, 1995). Everything you always wanted to know about "fuck" and were afraid to ask. Never has the F-word appeared so many times on a book's every page.

ON HOMO-, BI-, AND TRANS- SEXUALITIES:

Vern L. Bullough and Bonnie Bullough, *Cross Dressing, Sex, and Gender* (Philadelphia: University of Pennsylvania Press, 1993). A more scholarly approach than Garber (see below) but no less fascinating. Cross-dressing, the authors claim, has implications for understanding the changing relationships between the sexes in our time. Highly recommended.

Susan Cavin, *Lesbian Origins* (San Francisco: ISM Press, 1985). Cavin attempts to look "without heterosexual bias" (as she states) at the origins of human sociosexual systems, and she develops a creative approach to lesbian feminist theory. Do lesbians have better orgasms than straight women? Read Cavin for the answer to this and other straight-gay women's issues.

Julia Epstein and Kristina Straub, editors, *Body Guards: The Cultural Politics of Gender Ambiguity* (New York: Routledge, 1991). Why are more and more men—and women, too—going in drag? Dennis Rodman, RuPaul, Howard Stern. This scholarly collection of essays investigates the rigid "gender boundaries" of sex and why some people feel a need to break out of the old molds.

Marjorie Garber, *Vested Interests: Cross-dressing and Cultural Anxiety* (New York: Routledge, 1991). This groundbreaking book explores the nature and significance of cross-dressing and our recurring fascination with it—especially today. Women have always cross-dressed—men's clothes are sturdy and practical for outdoor and indoor work. Women's sheer, frilly, pastel frocks are decorative—men wear them not for *practical* purposes but only comedic, psychological, or sexual ones. Garber's book is essential for anyone interested in the history and psychology of cross-dressing.

Dell Richards, *Lesbian Lists* (Boston: Alyson, 1990). From Amazonian queens and bull dyke warriors to butch feminists, Richards presents a snappy, in-brief look at lesbian culture, history, and personalities, often in tongue-in-cheek prose. Who was and who wasn't? Gay men and women may be familiar with some of Richards' lesbian lists, but straights may be in for many surprises.

Leigh W. Rutledge, *The Gay Book of Lists* (Boston: Alyson, 1987). Hundreds of fascinating lists of gay historical figures, politicians, popes, and hung men—gay athletes, gay actors, gay fathers, gays on network TV. Fun to browse if you're gay, and even more fun if you're straight. *The New Gay Book of Lists* (1996) is an update, including the latest "outings" and sexual revelations of the rich, famous, and infamous. Rutledge has cornered the market on "gay list" books.

C. A. Tripp, *The Homosexual Matrix* (New York: McGraw-Hill, 1975). A remarkably persuasive attempt to destroy the many myths that have surrounded homosexuality, the book is still groundbreaking but holds up less well now that scientists are pursuing the biological roots of sexual orientation.

ON KINKY SEX:

Gloria G. Brame, William D. Brame, and John Jacobs, *Different Loving: The World of Sexual Dominance and Submission* (New York: Villard, 1996). Reproductive relevance has long been the standard of sexual normalcy, but some people have always been kinky and pushed the sexual envelope. The premise of this far-reaching book is "sex for pleasure" where, for some people, pleasure involves pain, humiliation, and games. If you want to know all about sexual spanking, whipping, bondage, water sports, golden showers (urination), enemas, and the like, this book's for you. It comes with a humorous disclaimer: "Readers should not attempt any of the activities described in these pages." More to the point, readers should not be *forced* to try any of those activities, unless they're willing sex slaves. Highly recommended to the sexually curious. Perhaps the definitive guide to sex on the wild side. A primer on lovemaking and leather. Under many state laws, most of the sex practices in this book are criminal.

Ray B. Browne, compiler, *Objects of Special Devotion: Fetishism in Popular Culture* (Bowling Green, Ohio: Bowling Green University Popular Press, 1981). How much does fetishism influence consumerism? (More than you think.) What is the *National Enquirer*'s real appeal? (The untold fetish story.) How much fetishism is involved in fraternity hazing? In aggressive male contact sports like football and wrestling? (All those sweaty, panting men groping each other.) Good-luck fetish charms and why you wear the jewelry you do. According to these academics, the subtext of sex is everywhere and influences much of what we do.

Harriett Gilbert, editor, *Fetishes, Florentine Girdles, and Other Explorations Into the Sexual Imagination* (New York: HarperCollins, 1993). The 350 entries, by feminist writers with diverse views, tackle sex practices and customs throughout the world. Great browsing.

Valerie Steele, *Fetish: Fashion, Sex and Power* (New York: Oxford University Press, 1996). Kinky boots, corsets, underwear, body piercing—this book is a fetishist's dream. Steele explains how over the last three decades sexual fetishism has been increasingly assimilated into popular culture: Madonna's bustier, Michelle Pfeiffer's Cat Woman. Marshaling a dazzling array of evidence from pornography, psychology, and history, as well as interviews with individuals into sexual fetishism, Steele illuminates the relationship between one's street appearance, self-identity, and personal sexuality. Highly recommended.

Cathy Winks and Anne Semans, *The New Good Vibrations Guide to Sex* (Pittsburgh: Cleis Press, 1997). Kinky tips and hot techniques from the folks who run America's favorite sex toy store, Good Vibrations, a San Francisco institution since 1977. If you want to know what really goes on in America's bedrooms—the amazing number of people who purchase sex toys and how they rave about them—this book is the place to begin. Erotic massage, edible lubricants, specialized vibrators, the trendiest dildos, hottest fantasies, latest latex accessories, risk management and safe sex techniques, phone sex, computer sex, virtual sex, and just plain old good sex—it's all here. The book contains a "shopping guide" to the best sex-toy stores and mail-order catalogs.

ON WOMEN:

Rosemary Agonito, *History of Ideas on Women: A Source Book* (New York: Putnam, 1977). Agonito brings together the primary sources of Western civilization's attitudes toward women. From Genesis and Plato, to Rousseau and Hegel, to Engels and Freud, the writings of men have shaped our concept of women's beauty, brains, legal rights, virtues, vices, and bedroom behaviors. Agonito's commentary is insightful and well balanced. If you want to know what history's most famous men have thought of women—in their own words—this book is an excellent starting point. Highly recommended.

Vern L. Bullough and Bonnie Bullough, *Women and Prostitution: A Social History* (Buffalo, N.Y.: Prometheus Press, 1987). This comprehensive and fascinating treatment of the world's oldest profession explores such cultural subjects as: women as property, religion and promiscuity, sex and social class. When did prostitution begin? How was it regarded by past societies? When did the double standard between the sexes originate? How has it changed?

Susan Haskins, *Mary Magdalen: Myth and Metaphor* (New York: Harcourt Brace, 1993). Certainly the most fascinating, in-depth study. Who was Mary Magdalen? How did Christ view her? Haskins' thesis is that early Christianity turned her into a repentant whore when in fact she was Christ's first evangelist.

ON SEX IN GENERAL:

Dorothy Baldwin, *Understanding Male Sexual Health* (New York: Hippocrene Books, 1991). Devoted to men and their sex organs: how the penis and testes work, why they sometimes fail, and how to keep them in good health. I like the concise way Baldwin lays out her chapters: The Penis, Erections, The Testicles, Orgasm, etc. She is equally well focused and concise in presenting facts in an interesting, uncluttered manner. Highly recommended.

Kate and Douglas Botting, *Sex Appeal: The Art and Science of Sexual Attraction* (New York: St. Martin's, 1995). This father-and-daughter team (an unorthodox pairing for a sex book) have written a delightful, fact-filled book. They reveal what sex appeal is, who's got it, and how to make it work for you—assuming you've got it. Why should a woman who wants to attract a man never walk with a stride longer than three to five inches? What role do nose breadth, middle-finger length, and earlobe length play in the mating game? What is the evolutionary significance behind the popularity of blond hair in women? These are the kinds of questions this father and daughter tackle. Highly recommended.

Vern L. Bullough and Bonnie Bullough, *Sexual Attitudes: Myths and Realities* (New York: Prometheus Books, 1995). An excellent exploration of how social, moral, and religious attitudes have changed, from being founded on myths to relying on the latest scientific evidence. The authors argue that new knowledge about sex need not undermine morality, even though it challenges entrenched, often unfounded, assumptions about our sexual behavior. Excellent on such topics as pornography and obscenity, homosexuality, prostitution, and the sexual labeling of people. Highly recommended.

Alexandra Parsons, *Facts and Phalluses* (New York: St. Martin's, 1990). A compendium of amazing and bizarre facts that are not always science but fun to browse.

June M. Reinisch, with Ruth Beasley, *The Kinsey Institute New Report on Sex* (New York: St. Martin's, 1990). The original studies by Dr. Alfred Kinsey are the most quoted in the history of sex research. This new book supplements Kinsey's work with modern national surveys and the latest clinical information. An excellent reference book.

Kit Schwartz, *The Male Member* (1985) and *The Female Member* (1988) (New York: St. Martin's). These amusing facts and fables about the sex organs are a lightweight delight, and these books will give you more terms for them than all other books combined.

Robert A. Wallace, *How They Do It* (New York: Morrow, 1980). This hard-to-find book comes highly recommended. In short, amusing chapters Wallace details the sexual coupling of forty-six species: pigs, bats, sharks, bees, snails, kangaroos, wasps, ticks, horses, etc. Some courtships are savage, some whirlwind, some gentle, some lifelong, but all are fascinating. This little-known book could have a wide audience if only more people were aware of it. I love animals and raise many types of indoor birds and outdoor fowl. *Sexy Origins and Intimate Things* is dedicated to my three favorite pussies—one of whom, Boogie, insists on sitting on my lap as I write. I call her my Mews. Wallace's book is a favorite of mine.